Pensions, Labor, and Individual Choice
Edited by
David A. Wise

In recent years a decline in the labor force participation of older workers has combined with rapid current and projected increases in the number of older Americans, producing major policy debates over looming "crises" in social security and, to a lesser extent, in the private pension system. That private system is playing an increasing role in the support of retired workers and promises to be the subject of increasing scrutiny by economists and policymakers alike. The private pension system, however, must be viewed not only as a source of income support but as a major component of the long-term arrangement between a firm and its workers. It is this broader role, until now largely unexplored, that the contributors to *Pensions, Labor, and Individual Choice* emphasize.

The papers in this volume, developed from material presented at a recent National Bureau of Economic Research conference, address several aspects of the relation between varieties of labor coverage and participation in the labor force. A number of the contributors address the hotly contested topic of the effect of pensions on retirement, taking into account for the first time the complex features of benefit formulas. The authors assess the incentives offered by pension provisions and take into account other factors influencing retirement, such as health status, that have been ignored in previous studies. What emerges from these studies is strong evidence that individual decisions about when to retire are indeed directly influenced by pension options. The scope of this volume goes well beyond the retirement decision, examining such issues as the effect of pension plans, which typically place a premium on years of service or age at the time of leaving one's job, on the mobility of younger workers. In addition, the contributors address the insurance aspects of pension plans, which cannot be duplicated by private savings arrangements.

Both academically rigorous and highly relevant to policymaking, *Pensions, Labor, and Individual Choice* will be valuable to government officials, academics, and members of the business and labor communities.

(Continued on back f

Pensions, Labor, and Individual Choice

A National Bureau
of Economic Research
Project Report

Pensions, Labor, and Individual Choice

Edited by   David A. Wise

The University of Chicago Press

Chicago and London

David A. Wise is John F. Stambaugh Professor of Political Economy, John F. Kennedy School of Government, Harvard University, and research associate, National Bureau of Economic Research.

The University of Chicago Press, Chicago 60637
The University of Chicago Press, Ltd., London

Library of Congress Cataloging in Publication Data
Main entry under title:

Pensions, labor, and individual choice.

(National Bureau of Economic Research project
report)
  Bibliography: p.
  Includes index.
  1. Pensions—United States—Addresses, essays,
lectures.   2. Pension trusts—United States—Addresses,
essays, lectures.   I. Wise, David A.   II. Series.
HD7125.P393   1985   331.25′2′0973   85-1118
ISBN 0-226-90293-5

Relation of the Directors to the
Work and Publications of the
National Bureau of Economic Research

1. The object of the National Bureau of Economic Research is to ascertain and to present to the public important economic facts and their interpretation in a scientific and impartial manner. The Board of Directors is charged with the responsibility of ensuring that the work of the National Bureau is carried on in strict conformity with this object.

2. The President of the National Bureau shall submit to the Board of Directors, or to its Executive Committee, for their formal adoption all specific proposals for research to be instituted.

3. No research report shall be published by the National Bureau until the President has sent each member of the Board a notice that a manuscript is recommended for publication and that in the President's opinion it is suitable for publication in accordance with the principles of the National Bureau. Such notification will include an abstract or summary of the manuscript's content and a response form for use by those Directors who desire a copy of the manuscript for review. Each manuscript shall contain a summary drawing attention to the nature and treatment of the problem studied, the character of the data and their utilization in the report, and the main conclusions reached.

4. For each manuscript so submitted, a special committee of the Directors (including Directors Emeriti) shall be appointed by majority agreement of the President and Vice Presidents (or by the Executive Committee in case of inability to decide on the part of the President and Vice Presidents), consisting of three Directors selected as nearly as may be one from each general division of the Board. The names of the special manuscript committee shall be stated to each Director when notice of the proposed publication is submitted to him. It shall be the duty of each member of the special manuscript committee to read the manuscript. If each member of the manuscript committee signifies his approval within thirty days of the transmittal of the manuscript, the report may be published. If at the end of that period any member of the manuscript committee withholds his approval, the President shall then notify each member of the Board, requesting approval or disapproval of publication, and thirty days additional shall be granted for this purpose. The manuscript shall then not be published unless at least a majority of the entire Board who shall have voted on the proposal within the time fixed for the receipt of votes shall have approved.

5. No manuscript may be published, though approved by each member of the special manuscript committee, until forty-five days have elapsed from the transmittal of the report in manuscript form. The interval is allowed for the receipt of any memorandum of dissent or reservation, together with a brief statement of his reasons, that any member may wish to express; and such memorandum of dissent or reservation shall be published with the manuscript if he so desires. Publication does not, however, imply that each member of the Board has read the manuscript, or that either members of the Board in general or the special committee have passed on its validity in every detail.

6. Publications of the National Bureau issued for informational purposes concerning the work of the Bureau and its staff, or issued to inform the public of activities of Bureau staff, and volumes issued as a result of various conferences involving the National Bureau shall contain a specific disclaimer noting that such publication has not passed through the normal review procedures required in this resolution. The Executive Committee of the Board is charged with review of all such publications from time to time to ensure that they do not take on the character of formal research reports of the National Bureau, requiring formal Board approval.

7. Unless otherwise determined by the Board or exempted by the terms of paragraph 6, a copy of this resolution shall be printed in each National Bureau publication.

(Resolution adopted October 25, 1926, as revised through September 30, 1974)

Contents

Acknowledgments

This volume consists of papers presented at a conference held at the Dorado Beach Hotel, Puerto Rico, 23–26 March 1983, and is part of the National Bureau of Economic Research ongoing project on the Economics of the United States Pension System, which has been generously supported by the following organizations: American Telephone and Telegraph Company, the Boeing Company, E. I. du Pont de Nemours & Company, Exxon Corporation, Ford Motor Company, International Business Machines Corporation, the Lilly Endowment, the Procter & Gamble Fund, and the Sarah Scaife Foundation. I am grateful to Anna Uhlig for assistance in shepherding the volume through the editorial process.

Any opinions expressed in this volume are those of the respective authors and do not necessarily reflect the views of the National Bureau of Economic Research or any of the sponsoring organizations.

1   Overview

David A. Wise

During the past two decades the labor market participation of older workers has fallen dramatically. During this same period private pension coverage has been rapidly extended and social security benefits have been increased. While the observation that these two trends occurred over the same period of time does not mean that one caused the other, it does highlight the possibility that the two may be related. Motivated in part by these trends, the National Bureau of Economic Research has undertaken a study of the labor market aspects of pension plans as part of a larger project on pensions in the American economy. For the past two years, economists at several universities have been engaged in analyzing the nature of private pension plans and their potential incentive effects in the labor market. This volume represents the results of their work.

This overview is intended to introduce the reader to the subject, to motivate the work that follows, and to provide a distillation of the major findings of the volume. Trends in pension coverage and concomitant trends in labor force participation of older workers are discussed first. This serves as a background for our work and helps to motivate the issues that are addressed in the volume. Then the characteristics of the common defined benefit pension plans are described, emphasizing those attributes that are likely to affect labor force behavior. The intent is to demonstrate the order of magnitude of the potential incentive effects of these plans without attempting to present empirical estimates of the impacts, but suggesting that the response of workers to pension plan characteristics could be substantial. To introduce the reader to the subject, the discussion and illustrations in this section also emphasize the possible relationship be-

David A. Wise is John F. Stambaugh Professor of Political Economy, John F. Kennedy School of Government, Harvard University, and research associate, National Bureau of Economic Research.

1

tween pensions and retirement, while the volume papers cover a much wider range of empirical and theoretical issues. The next two sections review the broad range of the volume's empirical findings and theoretical conclusions regarding the impact of pension plans on the labor force, using the first section as background.

1.1   Trends in Pension Coverage and in Labor Force Participation

The rapid growth in pension coverage over the past three decades is documented in figure 1.1. (The material in this section is taken largely from Ellwood, in this volume.) Approximately 50% of the work force now has some form of pension coverage. Perhaps more significant, the rapid increase in pension coverage has been accompanied by a striking increase in the number of retired persons who collect some pension income, as documented in figure 1.2 (Ellwood, in this vol.). Pension coverage in the government sector is now nearly complete, but a large portion of the private sector still remains uncovered after rapid growth and coverage during the 1950s and somewhat slower growth and coverage thereafter (Ellwood, in this vol.).

With large portions of the private sector still uncovered, who is covered and who is not? What are the correlates of private sector coverage? First, there is a striking relationship between private pension coverage and union status. Nearly 80% of all union members report that they are cov-

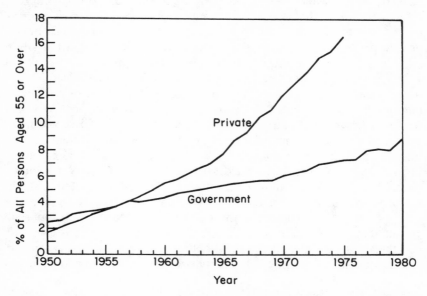

Fig. 1.1   Private and government pension coverage as a percentage of the civilian labor force (Ellwood, in this vol.).

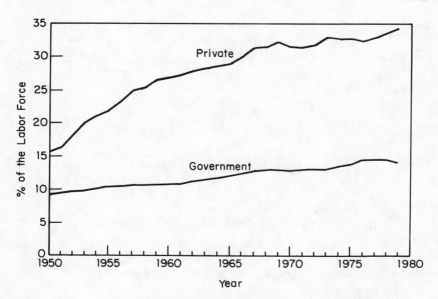

Fig. 1.2   Pension benefit recipients as a percentage of the civilian
population 55+ (Source: Kotlikoff and Smith, 1983).

ered by a pension plan, while only about one-third of all nonunion workers report such coverage. The relationship between pension coverage and
union status is evident in all major industrial categories. Pension coverage
is also much more common in large firms than in small ones. And in establishments in all size groups, coverage of union members is more common
than coverage of those not in unions (Ellwood, in this vol.). In short, the
descriptive evidence suggests that union status and firm size are perhaps
the two most prominent determinants of pension coverage.

In addition, the older, the more educated, and the wealthier are more
likely to be covered by a pension plan. Nonwhite workers, on the other
hand, seem just as likely to be covered as whites. A pattern emerges: workers who gain lesser rewards in the labor market typically are less likely to
have pension plans. Thus it appears that pensions do little to counterbalance differences among groups in wage earnings (Ellwood, in this vol.). In
summary, pension coverage appears to go hand in hand with union representation, large establishment size, and other economic compensation in
the labor market.

While pension coverage was increasing, there was at the same time a
striking decline in the labor force participation rate of older workers. For
example, between 1960 and 1980, the labor force participation rate for
men aged 55–65 fell from 87% to 72%. For those over 65, the rate fell
from 35% to below 20% (Ellwood, in this vol.). More detailed evidence
for the 1970s is shown in table 1.1. In particular, labor force participation

Table 1.1   **Labor Force Participation Rates of Men 60 and Older, 1969–79**

Year	60 to 64	65 +
1969	75.8	27.4
1971	74.0	26.3
1973	68.9	23.4
1975	65.4	21.9
1977	62.6	19.9
1979	61.1	20.3

Source: Selected issues of *Employment and Earnings,* table A–4.

fell from close to 76% in 1969 to 61% in 1979. Over the same period the rates for men 65 and older fell from 27% to 20% (Hausman and Wise, in this vol.).

1.2   The Structure of Pension Plans and Their Potential Incentive Effects

Having in mind the increase in pension coverage in recent decades and the substantial decline in labor force participation, it is informative to examine the provisions of pensions that might influence labor market behavior. The goal here is not actually to estimate the impact that pensions have on the labor market but rather to give a rough idea of the magnitudes of the incentives created by pensions and to point to the impact that various pension provisions have on these incentives. (The material in this section is taken largely from Kotlikoff and Wise, in this volume.)

Three-quarters of all persons and nearly 85% of all union members participating in private pension plans are enrolled in defined benefit plans where benefits are determined according to a specified formula. The remainder are enrolled in plans where benefits are directly related to contributions made on behalf of (and by) the employee and to the performance of the plan's investment portfolio. Virtually all government pensions are defined benefit plans. Because most workers are covered by defined benefit plans and because these plans are likely to have the most important effects on labor market incentives, the following remarks are confined to this type of plan.

Defined benefit formulas often are quite complex. Benefits are typically determined by years of service times wages in the last years of employment times a percentage figure (typically 1%–2%). In addition, plans typically have vesting provisions and many are integrated with social security. Early retirement provisions also are an important aspect of most plans. Because of the many plan variations and the complex details of the formulas, it is easiest to understand the potential incentive effects of the plans by considering pension accrual rates implied by a typical plan (Kot-likoff and Wise, in this vol.).

Consider first a worker who at age 30 begins participating in a defined benefit plan with the following characteristics: the plan calculates normal retirement benefits as 1% of average earnings over the last five years of service times years of service. Benefits are reduced by 3% for each year that early retirement precedes normal retirement. "Cliff vesting" occurs after 10 years; the worker is entitled before this time to no benefits and at 10 years to all benefits that accrue according to the formula described above. The early and normal retirement ages are 55 and 65, respectively. For a typical worker, I shall describe the annual increment to pension wealth as a percentage of the wage rate. Underlying the calculations is a representative lifetime age-earnings profile that assumes substantial growth in real wage rates between ages 30 and 50 and very little growth from 50 to 65. Consider first the pension accrual patterns for this plan if wage inflation is 6% and the nominal interest rate is 9% (3% real). The accrual pattern is shown in the top line of figure 1.3. (Kotlikoff and Wise, in this vol.). The other lines on the graph show the accrual profiles under different interest rate assumptions.

Three aspects of the accrual profiles need to be understood. First, there is no pension accrual before the year of vesting, and in the year of vesting there is an increase in pension wealth that varies from approximately 4% to 14% of wage earnings in that year depending on the interest rate. Sec-

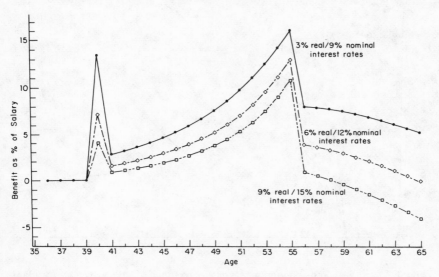

Fig. 1.3   Pension increments as a percentage of salary, by age, for a wage stream with 6% inflation discounted at real interest rates of 3%, 6%, and 9% (Kotlikoff and Wise, in this vol.).

ond, the rate of accrual increases slowly at first and then rather sharply until the age of early retirement. Thus pension wealth tends to be accrued during the later years of one's working life. Third, at the age of early retirement there is a sharp drop in the accrual rate, and the rate falls thereafter. The drop occurs because the early retirement reduction is less than an actuarially consistent reduction would be. That is, annual benefits are not reduced enough to offset the increase in the number of years that one will receive benefits if one retires early. In this case, two competing forces are determining accrual rates after age 55. On the one hand, benefits increase due to increases in wage rates with age and because of additional years of service. On the other hand, the worker gives up the option of taking benefits that are actuarially advantageous. After age 55, the rate of accrual continues to decline. Finally, note that the accrual pattern is substantially affected by the nominal interest rate. It is clear that the accrual due to vesting is affected by interest rates, but it can also be seen that if interest rates are high relative to the rate of inflation, then the accrual after age 55 can indeed be negative. In this case pension wealth could actually decline with additional years of work.

It is useful now to contrast a plan with an early retirement option with a plan that has no early retirement option or that uses an actuarially fair early retirement reduction formula. The difference is shown in figure 1.4 (Kotlikoff and Wise, in this vol.). Notice that without the early retirement option, benefits continue to increase to age 65. Indeed, in this case the

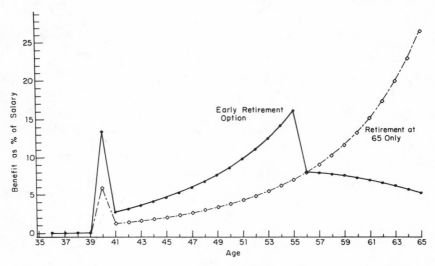

Fig. 1.4   Pension increments as a percentage of salary, by age, for plans with an early retirement option versus retirement at 65, assuming 6% wage inflation and a 3% real interest rate (Kotlikoff and Wise, in this vol.).

pension accrual rate is very much tilted toward the later years of a person's working career.

It should be clear from these graphs that the defined benefit formula seems to provide an increasing incentive to work at least to the age of early retirement. After this the incentive provided by the pension formula declines substantially. To the extent that retirement benefits provide an incentive to continue working, it is also clear that the incentive is much greater without the early retirement option than with it.

It is important to emphasize the impact of the interest rate on pension accruals. Suppose, for example, the graph in figure 1.4 were reproduced, assuming zero wage inflation and a 10% interest rate. Under these assumptions the pension accrual rate after the age of early retirement would indeed be negative. If a person worked an additional year, pension wealth would actually be lost at a rate approaching 15% of wage earnings at age 65 (Kotlikoff and Wise, in this vol.). While these assumptions are probably unrealistic, they demonstrate an important point.

Wage inflation is also important. While the general pattern of pension wealth accrual is not greatly altered by wage inflation, the increment to pension wealth at the time of vesting is very greatly affected by inflation. For example, with 2% wage inflation and a 5% interest rate, the increment to pension wealth in the year of vesting would be over 35% of the wage rate in that year. On the other hand, with 10% wage inflation and a 13% interest rate, the increment at the time of vesting would be only about 5% (Kotlikoff and Wise, in this vol.). Thus, while it is sometimes argued that vesting is not an important determinant of labor market behavior, it can be seen that the effect is likely to vary substantially with wage inflation.

Finally, in the majority of plans, pension accrual ceases once normal retirement age is reached. In many other plans, there are limits on additional accrual. Almost no plans make provisions for actuarial increases to compensate for the fact that late retirees will collect benefits over a shorter period. Typically, continued work after the normal age of retirement involves a substantial loss in pension wealth. Thus pensions typically provide a strong disincentive to work after the age of normal retirement.

What is the effect of pensions on job change? Figure 1.5 illustrates the cost in pension wealth of job change (Kotlikoff and Wise, in this vol.). The graph, for ease of exposition, assumes no early retirement option. The figure shows accrual rate profiles for workers joining the pension plan at ages 30, 40, and 50. The figure is constructed under the assumption that workers of the same age receive identical wage compensation, regardless of job change. Thus the diagram indicates the potential loss in accrued pension benefits for workers who switch jobs but receive the same wage compensation in the new job and are covered by the same pension plan. The top line of this graph shows the accrual rate for a person who

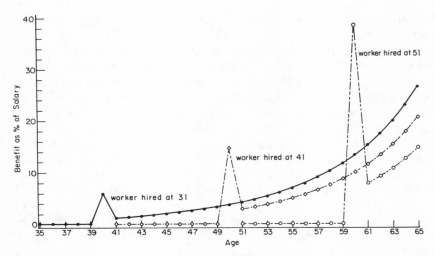

Fig. 1.5   Pension increments as a percentage of salary, by age, for an employee beginning work at 31, 41, 51, with no early retirement option, assuming 6% wage inflation and a 3% interest rate (Kotlikoff and Wise, in this vol.).

starts work at age 30 and does not change jobs thereafter (with 6% wage inflation and a 3% real interest rate). A person with one job change would accumulate benefits up to age 41 according to the top curve but then would accumulate benefits according to the curve labeled age 41. Note that no benefits would be accumulated for the first 10 years. The difference in accumulated pension benefits at age 65 reflects the difference in the areas under the two accrual paths. This difference could be very substantial and depends, of course, both on when job changes occur and how frequently they occur. It is important to note that the loss in this example is not due primarily to vesting. It results from the characteristics of many defined benefit plans that, in effect, index pension accumulation to increases in earnings. This indexation is uncoupled when a job change occurs. If the person were to change jobs at age 51, the loss would be greater. The loss would be greater still if the person were to change jobs twice, say at age 41 and then again at age 51. Individual pension accrual patterns with job change would of course depend on whether the worker becomes vested in earlier plans, but because of their relationship to final wage rates, benefits from the last plan are typically much more important than those from earlier plans.

This graph also shows that, even under moderate wage inflation and interest rate assumptions, vesting can be a very important component of compensation. For a worker hired at age 51, the increment in pension wealth in the year of vesting amounts to 40% of salary in that year.

In short, in inflationary times the benefit provisions of most defined benefit pension plans are in fact powerful deterrents to job switching even for the young and even if the alternative job offers identical wages and provides an identical pension plan. Thus the benefit provisions of defined benefit formulas not only serve as a strong deterrent to retirement prior to the early retirement age, they serve as a remarkably strong deterrent to job switching, even at very young ages. In addition, it appears that pension plans tend to encourage retirement after the age of early retirement and provide a very strong incentive to retire at the age of normal retirement. Whether such effects are intended or whether workers recognize them is yet another question.

We have examined the characteristics of a typical defined benefit plan. But what can one say about the average incentive effects implicit in the wide range of stipulations among actual plans? The accrual profiles implied by a very large number of plans described in the Bureau of Labor Statistics' Level of Benefits Survey look on average much like the hypothetical plans described above (Kotlikoff and Wise, in this vol.). The analysis of actual plans suggests that vesting may provide an important incentive for staying with a firm and that pension wealth accruals provide an important incentive for remaining until the age of early retirement. After this age the incentive for continued work provided by typical pension accruals declines rapidly. And it should be kept in mind that after age 65 the average accrual rate would indeed be negative, certainly encouraging retirement. It is also found, based on the analysis of actual pension plans, that job change can reduce pension benefits substantially. For example, consider accrued benefits at age 65 for persons hired at age 31, 41, or 51. Assume in addition that a person does not become vested in another plan prior to joining the firm. Based on the analysis of 700 plans and estimated wage profiles—and assuming 6% wage inflation and a 9% interest rate— the average aggregate of benefits of persons hired at age 51 are only about 50% of the benefits of those hired at 31. Persons hired at 41 would accumulate about 80% of the benefits of persons hired at 31. Benefits if hired at age 51 range from only 31% of the benefits if hired at 31 in retail trade, to 78% in manufacturing. The ratio among those hired at age 41 ranges from 65% in retail trade to 95% in transportation (Kotlikoff and Wise, in this vol.).

Implications that may be drawn from the above discussion are based directly on the structure of pension plans. In addition to the incentive effects of the plans, their structure also seems to provide substantial evidence for long-term contract versus spot market theories of the labor market (Kotlikoff and Wise, in this vol.). The next section summarizes the volume's more detailed empirical analysis of the determinants of pension coverage, the effects of pension on labor force participation, and important implications of the unfunded nature of the Federal Civil Service Retirement System. For convenience, papers that rely more heavily on a formal conceptual approach are summarized in the following section. The issues addressed include the use of pensions to select certain types of workers and to encourage early retirement, the importance of heterogeneity among workers in designing optimal plans, the incentive effects of particular job characteristics, and pensions as insurance. Simulation results on the riskiness of pension plans are also discussed in the section. The arbitrariness of the grouping, however, is revealed by the very substantial overlap in the issues addressed in the papers and their conclusions.

1.3   The Determinants of Pension Coverage and the Impact of Pensions on Labor Force Participation

The descriptive data above suggest a very substantial relationship between union membership and pension coverage and also suggest that typical defined benefit pension plans could have a potentially significant effect on labor force participation. While these data only suggest possible cause and effect, more detailed analysis points to the existence of a causal relationship.

Unions have a substantial effect on pension coverage, even after controlling for other determinants of coverage such as firm size, worker education, and the wage rate (Freeman, in this vol.). Unions increase the probability that establishments or workers will have a pension plan by sizable and statistically significant amounts, with estimates ranging from .17 to .32. Given the existence of a plan, however, the effect of unions on contributions to the plan is not substantial. Although estimates vary widely, the evidence suggests that for a nonunion worker to have the same probability of having a pension as a union worker, the wage rate of the nonunion worker would have to be at least twice as high as the wage rate of the union worker, given like other characteristics. While establishment size is a key determinant of whether a nonunion worker has a pension plan, it has only a modest effect on whether a union worker has a pension plan.

Not only do unions increase the allocation of funds to pensions, they affect the provisions of pensions as well. In particular, union pension plans are more likely to pay benefits on a flat rate dependent on years of service rather than on earnings. It may be argued that paying flat rate benefits is the pension equivalent of standard rate wage policies and reflects the redistributive goal of unions as a political organization. At the same time, because pension benefits are based on years of service, these plans tend to benefit older workers more than younger ones (Freeman, in this vol.).

The evidence on the structure of pension plans presented above suggests that defined pension plans could have a very substantial effect on retirement behavior. Because available data do not allow one to associate particular individuals with details of their pension plans, however, it is not possible to provide direct evidence on the effects of the characteristics of these plans on retirement. Reliable data that would reveal the potential interaction between wage rates and pension coverage, for example, have not been released. Pension coverage may not be exogenously determined. In addition, it is important to keep in mind that income after retirement is evidently the major reason for pensions, so if they lead to earlier retirement this should not necessarily be interpreted as an undesirable result. It may, however, be in conflict with other goals of society such as extension of the working life with increases in longevity. Nonetheless, the varied evidence that is available suggests a very substantial effect of pension coverage on the reduction in labor force participation of older workers. Summary data show that the proportion of preretirement income that is replaced by pension benefits is considerably higher for those who retire younger than for those who retire at an older age. For example, among those who retire between 50 and 54, 27% of preretirement is replaced by pensions, while for those who retire after age 65, approximately 17% of preretirement income is replaced by pension benefits (Ellwood, in this vol.). In general, those who retire later tend to have lower pension wealth (Taubman, in this vol.). The implication is that increased benefits may encourage workers to retire earlier. On the other hand, persons who want to retire at an early age could simply arrange to acquire higher pension benefits to accommodate their retirement goals. The circumstantial evidence provided by more detailed analyses, however, suggests that this effect probably is not the major explanation.

Compare, for example, the retirement behavior of federal civil service employees, who have very generous retirement benefits, with the retirement behavior of employees in the private sector. Over half of federal employees retire before the age of 60, whereas the comparable figure for the private sector is only 7% (Leonard, in this vol.). This seems clearly related to the provisions of the federal civil service retirement system. Consider the capitalized value of the pension received under the current federal civil service retirement system by an employee who joins the system at age 25 and who receives typical longevity salary increases over his or her lifetime. Suppose that such an employee were to attain a nominal salary of $25,000 at the age of 58. The value of pension entitlement for this illustrative employee accumulates slowly across his working life, reaching by age 54 an amount equivalent to about $130,000, given on his or her sixty-fifth birthday. The next year, when the employee qualifies for full retirement, the value jumps to the equivalent of $323,000. It stays at this level for a short time and then begins to fall, reaching $248,000 if the employee waits until age 65 before retiring (Leonard, in this vol.). It is clear that federal employees have a substantial, increasing incentive to work until they reach eligibility for full retirement. At this point, the equivalent of their entitlement peaks; if they continue working it starts to fall. Indeed, this illustrative individual would lose $75,000 in pension benefits if he retired at 65 instead of 55. The discontinuity in the entitlement at age 55 comes from the shift in the entitlement's value as the employee crosses the combination of age and experience that allows early retirement. This may be a rather extreme case because the civil service pension system is much more generous than the typical private pension plan. Nonetheless, the effect seems clear and the direction of the effect is substantiated by other analyses.

This very generous system is achieved only at very substantial cost and budget consequences. The unfunded liability of the federal civil service retirement system amounts to approximately $500 billion, a net liability approximately one-half the size of the current officially recognized national debt. Labor expenses recognized in the direct expenditures budget considered by Congress would have to be about 22% higher than they currently are to account for full funding of pension obligations occurred in each year. Thus a full accounting of pension obligations would imply considerably higher labor compensation for federal employees than is commonly recognized (Leonard, in this vol.).

Among California teachers in public schools, and after controlling for other individual attributes that may be related to retirement, the age of retirement shows that larger pension benefits are associated with earlier retirement. Analyzing a random sample of California schoolteachers, both retired and still teaching, we find a standard deviation increase in pension wealth is associated with an approximately one-year decrease in the age of retirement.[1]

If higher private pension benefits and provisions lead to earlier retirement, then one might suppose that greater social security benefits would also tend to encourage earlier retirement. The evidence on the effect of social security benefits on the age of retirement is indeed consistent with the evidence on the effect of private pension plans on retirement. Analysis of data collected in the Retirement History Survey, that follows for 10 years persons aged 58–63 in 1969, verifies two hypotheses about the likely effects of pension benefits (Hausman and Wise, in this vol.). The first is that, other things equal, persons who can retire with larger benefits are more likely to leave the labor force than those who would receive smaller benefits if they were to retire. The second is that persons who by working another year could increase the discounted value of pension benefits that they would receive in the future are more likely to continue working. Or, if working another year would reduce the present value of future benefits, the individual is more likely to retire early. This loss is analogous to the typical loss in private pension benefits if one continues to work after the age of early retirement, as demonstrated in the graphs above. In short, analysis of the Retirement History Survey shows both a strong effect of the increment in pension benefits on prolonging labor force participation and a strong effect of cumulated social security wealth on departure from the labor force. Indeed, the data suggest that a large proportion of the dramatic decrease in labor force participation of older workers between 1969 and 1979 can be explained by the large increases in social security benefits over this period (Hausman and Wise, in this vol.).

It can be argued, as mentioned above, that individuals choose jobs and associated pension plans, make savings decisions, and take account of expected social security benefits to provide retirement income consistent with preplanned desired age of retirement. In major part, however, this could not be said to be true of social security benefits, large portions of which must have been unexpected, in particular the very large increases in the early 1970s. Thus the relationship between social security benefits and age of retirement that is observed in the data must have been induced to a substantial degree by unexpected social security benefits and is not a reflection of retirement decisions based on expected benefits.[2]

Indeed, further analysis of the Retirement History Survey shows that retirees in this sample would receive three to four times as much in benefits as they made in contributions (Hurd and Shoven, in this vol.). Possibly more surprising, the wealthy received the largest transfers in absolute amounts, and in many cases they even received the highest rates of return on social security contributions (Hurd and Shoven, in this vol.).

The description of pension plan provisions presented above also suggested that, at least through the age of early retirement, pensions should tend to reduce job change. Although to date we have not undertaken detailed analyses of the effect of pension plan provisions on job change—again due to limitations of data available to us—summary data suggest that pension provisions do reduce job turnover. For example, whereas 73% of all workers aged 51–55 without pensions have less than 10 years' tenure, only about 33% of workers with pensions have been with their employer for less than a decade (Ellwood, in this vol.). The direction of this relationship holds for every age group. Of course, such data prove nothing. There is a host of possible explanations for these differences, some of which are emphasized in conceptual work referred to below. Still, the data do suggest that pensions may in fact have sizable impacts on job change.

1.4   More Formal Conceptual Results

Conceptual analyses of the effects of pension plans in general reinforce the implications suggested by the structure of the plans described above. In addition, these analyses provide insights that are not so readily discernible based on the structure of the plans.

Analysis of accrued benefits based on plan provisions presented above shows that job change is likely to be associated with a substantial cost in loss of pension benefits. Descriptive data mentioned above also show that turnover or job change among employees covered by pensions is much less than among those who are not covered. Consistent with this observation, theoretical analysis demonstrates that pensions can be important in reducing turnover among workers who are attracted to the firm (Viscusi, in this vol.). But, in the face of worker uncertainty about future job performance and turnover costs, pensions can also be important in self-selecting more stable employees. (Viscusi, in this vol.). This suggests, of course, that observed relationships between pension coverage and job turnover are likely to result at least in part from self-selection, by workers who would like to avoid job change, of firms with appropriate pension plans.

The structure of pension plans also suggests that most plans tend to encourage retirement after some age, in many instances after the age of early retirement and in almost all cases after the age of normal retirement. It is difficult to make contracts that commit workers to retire at a certain age, and it may be institutionally impractical to reduce wages commensurate with the reduction in productivity of older workers. It can be demonstrated, however, that pensions may be used to help induce appropriate retirement behavior, consistent with economic efficiency (Nalebuff and Zeckhauser, in this vol.). In addition, work heterogeneity has important implications for the design and effects of pension plans. In particular, heterogeneity among workers implies that the concept of actuarial fairness is illusive and much more ambiguous than is commonly recognized (Nalebuff and Zeckhauser, in this vol.). As demonstrated above, most defined benefit plans are apparently actuarially unfair to those who prolong their working lives. However, if workers can estimate their life span, those who expect to live longer may choose to retire later and the apparent pattern of actuarial benefits may be reversed. For example, a person who expects to live five more years may find that the increase in pension benefits that would be gained by working another year is not large enough to offset the reduction of one year in the number of years that benefits would be received. On the other hand, a person who expects to live 10 more years and thus would receive the incremental benefits over a longer period of time may find that it is worthwhile to prolong labor force participation for an additional year. The structure of a pension plan that is optimal for an individual, that is, one that maximizes ex ante expected utility, however, must make it actuarially unfavorable for the individual to retire later than some age (Nalebuff and Zeckhauser, in this vol.).

We know, of course, that typical pension plans cover large numbers of workers that may be dissimilar in many respects, in particular with respect to life expectancy. Some proposed pension reform proposals would indeed impose more similar plans on even more heterogeneous groups of workers. In a first-best situation, however, a separate pension plan would be designed for each homogeneous group of workers. The imposition of the same plan on nonhomogeneous groups of workers may be shown to work to the possible detriment of each of the groups. That is, it could turn out that under the common plan no group is better off than under the plan tailored to its particular characteristics (Nalebuff and Zeckhauser, in this vol.).

Given existing compensation arrangements, heterogeneity among individuals may in general have an important impact on the compensation that individual workers receive. A variety of economic models of compensation suggest that firms should allow workers to choose individually how they would like to have their compensation divided between wages and benefits. More compensation in the form of retirement benefits or health insurance benefits would be offset by reduced wage rates. In this case, there would be no reason for firms to try to attract certain types of workers. In practice, however, even among equally productive workers wages and benefits will not necessarily balance (Bulow and Landsman, in this vol.). Workers may, for example, receive the same wage rather than the same total compensation. Nonetheless, for labor as a whole, increases in aggregate benefits would be offset by decreases in wage compensation. Under these circumstances, firms that offer particular types of benefits should expect to attract workers likely to take advantage of these benefits. An important implication of this possibility is that we can say only a limited amount about the aggregate firm worker implicit labor contract by looking at individual compensation profiles (Bulow and Landsman, in this vol.).

It should be clear that defined benefit pension plans have potentially large incentive effects on labor participation. Whether they are efficient or not is another question. If the pension rule is taken to be exogenous, then many provisions of defined benefit plans are shown to have adverse incentive effects. For example, a large number of plans incorporate a 10-year cliff vesting provision, but complete and immediate vesting would be a necessary condition for fully efficient pension plans (Lazear, in this vol.). On the other hand, defined contribution plans, in contrast to defined benefit plans, always induce an efficient allocation of resources (Lazear, in this vol.).

An alternative to the analysis of the incentive effects of exogenously given pension plans is to consider the form that private pensions are likely to take when employers provide pensions—in contrast to an optimally formulated government pension policy, for example. In particular, workers may like to have insurance against many work-related contingencies: disability, future productivity, change in employment. Because these uncertainties are hard to verify, however, they cannot be the object of insurance directly. A worker may thus want to allocate some part of his current compensation to provide income in situations in which the income will be more important to him, and thus pensions may serve as insurance (Diamond and Mirrlees, in this vol.).

Finally, uncertainty about receipt of future pension benefits is an important aspect of the equivalent compensation value of the plans. This, of course, is not an attribute of plans that can be gleaned from the structure of the plans as described above. Several economically relevant events during a worker's lifetime, both macroeconomic events and individual-specific ones, are likely to affect the value of pension benefits actually received. Through simulation analysis, it is possible to compare the riskiness of alternative forms of defined benefit pension plans (Green, in this vol.). Results based on this methodology show that among four forms of defined benefit plan, a plan based on a percentage of final salary is least risky when compared to a plan that bases benefits on the highest 10 years of salary, a plan based on the worker's career average salary, and one that determines benefits by years of service only. It may be argued that the extent to which pension plans are risky has important implications for the effect of pension plans on other forms of individual saving (Green, in this vol.). The certainty equivalent value of a pension to the worker is likely to be much less than the value of the liability it represents to the firm. This is because part of the variance in pension wealth viewed by the worker is due to individual-specific risk that from the point of view of the firm is averaged out over many workers. Therefore it may be argued that pensions decrease the value of other forms of savings by workers by less than the increase in required saving by firms necessary to offset their pension liabilities. Thus the riskiness of private pensions may have substantial importance in studying the effect of private pensions on aggregate savings in the national economy (Green, in this vol.).

1.5   Conclusions

Over the past three decades pension coverage has expanded substantially; over the latter part of this period there has been a very dramatic reduction in the labor force participation of older workers. The typical defined benefit pension plan provides an increasing incentive for an employee to remain with the same firm until the age of early retirement; after that the structure of the typical plan provides less incentive to work, and indeed the stipulations of many plans imply actual losses in pension wealth accrual after the age of early retirement. After the age of normal retirement, almost all plans incorporate loss in pension wealth if the employee continues to work. Thus the structure of pension plans alone suggests that the increase in pension coverage may have had a good deal to do with the decline in the labor force participation rate of older workers. More detailed analysis of the relationship between pension coverage and age of retirement appears to confirm this possibility. In addition, empirical analysis suggests that the increases in social security benefits have played a substantial role in the decline in the labor force participation of older workers.

In addition to providing an incentive for older workers to retire, the typical structure of defined benefit pension plans imposes a substantial cost in pension wealth on workers who change jobs. The order of magnitude of these losses may not be widely appreciated, but the evidence available suggests that pension coverage reduces job change.

More formal analysis of pensions reinforces the apparent implications that can be drawn from the structure of the plans themselves. In particular, the use of compensation in the form of pension coverage can provide a mechanism for encouraging older workers to retire when institutional constraints may prevent employers from reducing the wage earnings of older workers in accordance with reductions in labor productivity. Theoretical analysis also demonstrates that pensions can be used to select more stable employees and to discourage job changing among those hired. In addition, conceptual analysis highlights the importance of heterogeneity among employees, suggesting that policies that encourage uniformity among pension plans may not necessarily increase the general welfare of employees.

Notes

1. These findings are from Steven I. Kutner, "Individual Attributes and Pension Acceptance Decisions: A Case Study." Although presented at the conference, the final version of the paper was not finished in time for inclusion in this volume.
2. This point is emphasized by Hurd and Boskin (1981).

References

Hurd, M., and Boskin, M. 1981. The effect of social security on retirement in the early 1970s. NBER Working Paper no. 659.
Kotlikoff, L. J., and Smith, D. E. 1983. *Pensions in the American economy*. Chicago: University of Chicago Press (for NBER).

2   Pensions and the Labor Market: A Starting Point (The Mouse Can Roar)

David T. Ellwood

Pensions have for some time been seen in the financial world as a major influence on capital markets. It is, after all, rather difficult to ignore the role of institutions that collectively hold assets that have grown in 1980 dollars from under $100 billion in 1950 to well over half a trillion dollars today (American Council of Life Insurance 1980). But until recently the possible labor market impacts of pensions have been largely ignored. The explanation perhaps lies in two different directions. First, pensions have often been treated by labor economists as one of many fringe benefits. If these have been considered at all, it has largely been in the context of how such benefits alter the total compensation paid by firms. A second possible reason may have been a conscious or unconscious acceptance of what Blinder has called a "Modigliani-Miller theorem for pensions" (Blinder 1982, p. 6). So long as capital markets are perfect, taxes are unimportant, and employees retain the full financial rights to whatever contributions are made on their behalf, it would seem that workers could always undo any effects of pensions.

If this Modigliani-Miller theorem breaks down, then, pensions could have very important effects in the labor market. With that much capital floating around, it certainly seems plausible that any peculiar characteristics of pension plans might cause dramatic changes in the incentives facing workers and their employers.

This paper is designed to serve as an introductory summary of the basic facts and figures involving private and public pensions with particular em-

David T. Ellwood is assistant professor at the John F. Kennedy School of Government at Harvard University and is a faculty research fellow at the National Bureau of Economic Research.

I am extremely grateful to David A. Wise for several discussions of the incentive effects of pension provisions. Daniel Smith provided excellent computer assistance.

phasis on those features of pensions which are likely to be of most significance for labor markets. The paper is divided into two main sections. The first examines both the historical and cross-sectional patterns of pension coverage and pension receipt in the United States. The second examines the magnitude of the incentives pensions might create in the labor market and the implications these incentives might have for retirement and turnover behavior of workers. It is my conclusion that these labor market effects could be quite large.

The emphasis in this paper will be on private pension plans. Publicly funded pension plans providing coverage for federal, state, and local employees will receive some attention. Unfortunately, data are often sparse, particularly for state and local plans, and rarely in a form comparable to those available for private employee plans. In part this is because the Employee Retirement Income Security Act of 1974 (ERISA) and other regulations generally do not apply to government plans. Social security receives no discussion except inasmuch as it interacts with other retirement plans. It has already received considerable attention elsewhere (see, e.g., Boskin and Hurd 1978; Blinder et al. 1980; Stein 1980). And although social security is arguably a pension plan, when I speak of such plans in this paper I refer to plans other than social security.

A large part of the facts presented here are taken from tables in the exhaustive (and exhausting) book by Lawrence Kotlikoff and Daniel Smith *Pensions and the American Economy*. Their sources for the figures used here typically are tabulations of a special pension supplement of the May 1979 Current Population Survey (CPS), of the income supplement of the March 1980 Current Population Survey, or of the 1977 Employee Benefit Survey (EBS1) which contains pension plan information required of employers by ERISA. Some additional tabulations of the May 1979 data are reported. Other sources are cited as they appear.

2.1 Pension Coverage and Pension Receipt

• Pension coverage and pension receipt have grown dramatically in the past three decades. Private pensions now cover at least 35% of the total civilian work force, government pensions another 10%-15%. Nearly 20% of all persons over 55 are receiving a private pension, and another 10% collect one from the government. Interestingly, the biggest growth in pension coverage came in the 1950s and early 1960s, while the growth in pension receipt has continued into the 1970s.

Figures 2.1 and 2.2 document the rapid growth in pensions. It appears that roughly 50% of the active work force now has some form of pension coverage and 20% of those over 55 collect some pension income. Still, perhaps the most intriguing feature of these figures is the fact that pension

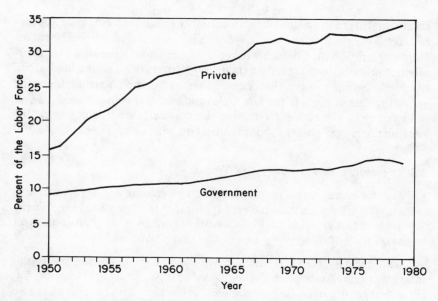

Fig. 2.1   Percentage of the labor force covered by pensions

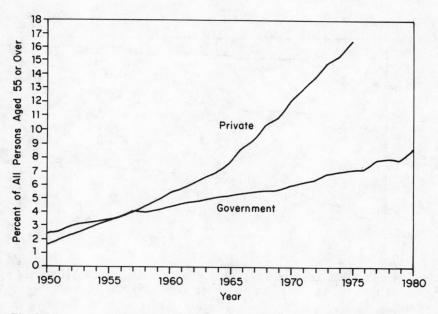

Fig. 2.2   Percentage of all persons 55 or over collecting pension benefits

receipt is still growing almost exponentially even though coverage appears to have leveled off in the past decade. The explanation lies in the rather lengthy gestation time before workers covered under a pension plan actually become eligible to receive benefits on retirement. And the large stock of elderly persons who retired before they had earned benefits under the growing pension plans in the late fifties and sixties is being diluted slowly.

In the next subsection I consider the correlates and determinants of pension coverage. Then I focus attention on pension receivers.

2.2   Pension Coverage of Active Workers

• Pension coverage is most common in the governmental sectors where at least 90% of workers are covered by some sort of pension plan.[1] In the private sector roughly half of all workers are covered. Pensions cover just under half of all private wage and salary workers.

Social security (OASDI) now covers virtually all private wage and salary workers. And although the real value of social security benefits has expanded greatly over the past decades, private pension coverage has also grown dramatically. For these workers pensions serve largely as a supplement. Many plans are explicitly integrated with the OASDI system. After periods of sharp growth in the 1940s and 1950s, private pension coverage appears to have leveled off in the 1960s and 1970s. Figure 2.3 shows that

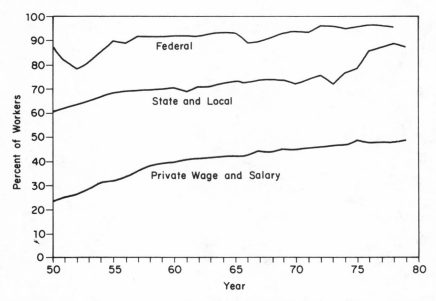

Fig. 2.3   Percentage of all workers with pension coverage by sector

between 1950 and 1960 coverage was extended from roughly 25% of the work force to over 40%. Coverage grew by about 5 percentage points in the sixties and 4 points in the seventies. By 1979 some 48% of all such workers had coverage.

By contrast, most federal workers and at least half of all state and local workers are not covered by social security during their employment in the public sector. Thus it seems plausible that these workers would be much more likely to have pension plans than other workers. Virtually all federal, state, and local employees have some form of coverage. State and local coverage climbed throughout this period and witnessed a sudden, and to my knowledge unexplained, growth spurt in the 1970s.

Coverage in the government sector is essentially complete, yet large portions of the private sector remain uncovered. One is naturally led to wonder why the growth in private pensions occurred in the fifties. The obvious place to look for answers is in the correlates of private sector coverage.

• Probably the single strongest determinant of pension coverage is union status. In 1979 nearly 80% of all union members reported that they were covered by a pension plan. By contrast only about a third of all nonunion workers reported such coverage.

Within industries, within income or age groups, within occupations, union members are much more likely to be covered by a pension plan than are nonunion workers. Figure 2.4 shows coverage of public and private wage and salary workers by one-digit industry and union status. In every industry union workers are much more likely to be covered. In a few the differences are quite dramatic. In construction, for example, over 80% of union workers are covered and less than 20% of nonunion workers are. It should be remembered, though, that since unions cover just 30% of all

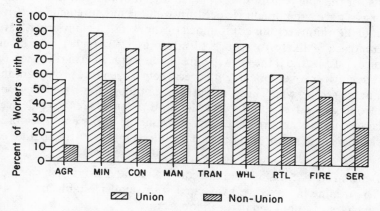

Fig. 2.4   Percentage of workers with pension coverage by industry and union status

workers, just over half of all workers covered by pensions are not union workers.

Another interesting feature of figure 2.4 is that industries that are disproportionately unionized also appear to have disproportionately high pension coverage, even in the nonunion sector. In the industries where unions have organized at least one-third of the work force (mining, construction, manufacturing, and transportation), union coverage typically exceeds 80%, and outside of construction, nonunion coverage is close to 50%. In other industries union coverage is typically less than 60% and nonunion coverage often falls below 30%. Apparently some of the same forces that favor unions also favor pensions.

It appears that the union market is largely saturated and has been so for some time. There is some evidence that the growth in pension coverage that has occurred has been most prominent in the nonunion sector. A study commissioned by Employee Benefit Research Institute (EBRI) reported that coverage growth rates for nonunion workers was twice that for union workers between 1968 and 1974 (Mathematica Policy Research 1979).

Traditional explanations for the high rate of union coverage look to both historical and economic influences. Unions may have used pensions as a way of gaining wage increases that were largely invisible to the general public and to wage and price control boards during the Second World War and the Korean War. Unions may also give more weight to older workers than the market does. Another factor may be economies of scale. Small firms may be forced to pay disproportionately high coverage and administrative costs. Unions could pool the employees of many firms and reap the economies.

The strong union component to coverage may have significant implications for the role pensions may play in the labor market. If pensions are seen as a device that might reduce turnover, the measurement of their impact in the union sector is confounded by the fact that many other features of unions are likely to reduce turnover as well (higher wages, more "voice," etc.). And if the growth of pensions is traced in part to their force in reducing turnover, one might expect them to be more prominent in the nonunion sector, which lacks at least some of the union-based methods of controlling turnover. On the other hand, if pensions are also a device for encouraging early retirement, their prominence in the union sector may indicate a greater desire on the part of union employers to separate older workers.

- Pension coverage is much more common in large firms than small ones. The decline in coverage associated with smaller establishment size is much less pronounced in the union sector.

Table 2.1 reveals that in the nonunion sector establishment size is an extremely powerful explanatory factor in pension coverage. Just 16% of

Table 2.1   **Percentage of Workers Covered by Pensions by Establishment Size and Union Status**

Establishment Size	Union (%)	Nonunion (%)
1–24	67.8	16.3
25–99	69.0	32.3
100–499	75.9	52.3
500–999	80.4	67.0
1000+	88.7	76.0
Total	76.4	33.7

Source: Tabulations of May 1979 CPS Survey.

workers in the smallest workplaces have coverage; 75% of those in the largest are covered. In the union sector the differences are much less pronounced. There is evidence that small firms are making the largest gains in coverage. The same EBRI study cited earlier found that between 1968 and 1974 coverage in the smallest establishments jumped by 13 percentage points. Coverage in the largest grew only 1 point.

There are abundant hypotheses that might be used to explain these findings. The most obvious focuses on the economies of scale just mentioned. Another would center on the mix of workers hired by small versus large firms. Yet another would be that larger firms are more fearful of unionization and thus seek to mimic benefits provided in the union sector.

It appears that union status and firm size are the two most prominent determinants of pension coverage. Whatever explanations are offered for the existence and growth of pensions ought to account for these key features.

• Younger, less educated, poorer, and female workers are all less likely to be covered by a pension plan. Nonwhite workers, on the other hand, seem just as likely to be covered as whites.

A familiar pattern emerges in figures 2.5, 2.6, and 2.7. Workers who gain lesser rewards typically are less likely to have pension protection. Lower rates of union coverage for these groups undoubtedly create some of these results. However, in results not reported here strong wage effects appear within the nonunion sector. Workers with higher wages are much more likely to be covered. It appears that pensions do little to equalize economic rewards. Indeed they appear to exacerbate existing differences.

One exception to this rule is in coverage of nonwhites. Overall white and nonwhites have very similar coverage rates. In figure 2.8 nonwhite men have slightly lower coverage rates and nonwhite women slightly higher ones than their white counterparts. The results for women are not too surprising since overall gross earnings no longer differ much by race. The results for nonwhite men may reflect their overrepresentation in unionized establishments.

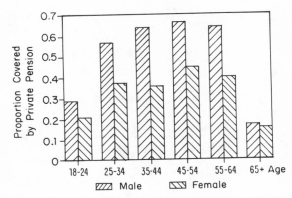

Fig. 2.5   Proportion of private sector workers covered by pensions by age

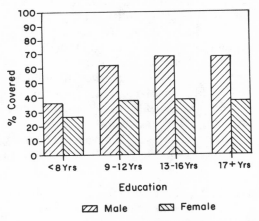

Fig. 2.6   Proportion of private sector workers covered by pensions by education

In summary, it does appear that pension coverage goes hand in hand with union representation, large establishment size, and the economic compensation in the labor market. The slowdown in growth in coverage during the 1970s may in part reflect the changing age, sex, industrial, and union mix of workers and employment. A simple back-of-the-envelope calculation I have done suggests pension coverage might have grown 3–5 percentage points more in this period had the mix been constant.

The collinearity of coverage with such important economic forces may make the effects of pensions in the labor market difficult to measure empirically. Nonetheless, for some workers, such as middle-aged men, pensions are quite common. Nearly two-thirds of all private wage and salary

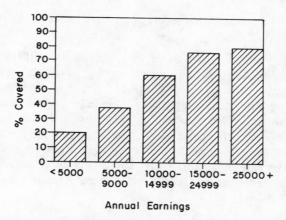

Fig. 2.7   Percentage of all private sector workers covered by pensions by annual earnings

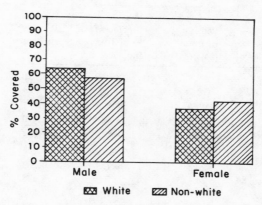

Fig. 2.8   Percentage of all private sector workers covered by pensions by race and sex

workers in this age group have coverage. As a result, it is certainly plausible that pensions have important influences in the labor market. Before addressing these issues, I shall consider the characteristics of pension recipients.

2.3.1   Pension Receipt

- Approximately one-quarter of all persons over age 65 receive some pension income. Among nonworking elderly males coverage reaches 41%. Patterns of pension receipt largely mimic patterns of coverage. Pension income accounts for only 15% of all income of persons over 65. But among pension receivers, benefits average 40% of income. Pensions appear to exacerbate rather than compensate for existing differences in old age income.

Differences in old age income, in large part, reflect differences in previous earnings. Not surprisingly, pension receipt, like pension coverage, is highly correlated with personal characteristics that are associated with higher earnings during working years. Table 2.2 shows that men are more likely than women, better educated are more likely than less well educated, and the well-to-do are more likely than the poor to have pension coverage. Perhaps the only surprise about coverage on table 2.2 is that whites and nonwhites fare quite differently. These differences suggest that relatively equal coverage among blacks and whites is a recent phenomenon or

Table 2.2   **Pension Income by Sex, Race, Age, Employment Status, Education, and Income, 1980**

	Population Aged 65+		Pension Recipients Aged 65+	
	Received Pension Income (%)	Pension Income as % of Total Income	Average Pension Income ($)	Pension Income as % of Total Income
Male	38.5	18.6	4,251	38.3
Female	18.2	10.6	2,913	34.3
White	27.7	15.1	3,725	36.6
Nonwhite	15.9	13.4	3,450	43.7
Age 65–69	28.7	15.3	3,948	37.4
Age 70+	25.3	14.8	3,555	36.6
Employed	20.5	6.7	4,163	24.4
Males	24.8	7.5	4,698	25.1
Females	13.4	4.1	2,525	21.1
Not employed	27.4	17.7	3,660	39.4
Males	41.7	24.1	4,190	41.8
Females	18.6	11.6	2,935	35.5
Education				
0–8 years	18.9	9.7	2,396	32.7
9–12 years	28.4	14.7	3,360	36.9
13–16 years	37.7	19.1	4,996	39.6
17+ years	56.3	23.5	6,862	37.6
Income				
$1,000–2,499	2.2	0.9	730	41.0
$2,500–4,999	11.4	3.2	1,033	25.6
$5,000–7,499	42.6	13.8	1,981	31.9
$7,500–9,999	54.0	20.9	3,352	38.5
$10,000–14,999	58.9	24.2	4,960	41.1
$15,000–19,999	52.2	22.3	7,319	42.9
$20,000+	45.2	16.3	11,443	35.5

Source: Kotlikoff and Smith (1983) based on tabulations of March 1980 CPS data.

that nonwhites are less likely to qualify for benefits even though they are equally likely to be enrolled in a plan (i.e., they fail to meet the minimum service requirements to get benefits). The more interesting numbers concern the significance of pension income.

With only one-quarter of all persons over age 65 receiving pension income, it cannot be surprising that pensions account for only 15% of income in this age group. Among pension recipients such income is much more significant, though, accounting for roughly two-fifths of all income. Average benefits in 1980 were just under $4,000 for those between 65 and 69 and $3,500 in older groups. Among those with pension income, there is surprisingly little variation in the benefits as a fraction of total income. Those with low incomes get low benefits if they get them at all. Those with high incomes get high benefits. Since the incidence of receipt varies inversely with income, pensions clearly heighten rather than reduce income inequality.

An alternative measure of the financial significance of pensions for the elderly is to treat pension and other income streams, like social security, as assets and to compare pension wealth to total wealth. Several authors have attempted to do so. Kotlikoff and Smith (1983) report that in 1969 pensions represented 8% of the "old age resources" of couples whose head was between the ages of 58 and 63. Hurd and Shoven (1982) report similar results in 1969, using the same data but a slightly different methodology. By 1975, when the heads had reached ages 64–69, pensions had grown to roughly 11% of the total, presumably because more of them had retired and were now collecting pensions. Neither sources report figures exclusively for pension recipients.

- Persons who receive pensions typically collect amounts equal to 20% of their average wage over the final five years of their career. This "replacement rate" varies little by sex, union status, or level of earnings in the period prior to retirement. However, younger retirees and those with more years of service have higher replacement rates.

Pension benefits, like social security benefits, are closely tied to prior earnings. In most pensions the links are quite explicit: benefits or contributions are a proportion of earnings. And pensions nearly always grow along with length of service. Table 2.3 was created by Kotlikoff and Smith (1983) using data from a matched file of benefit payments paid to persons receiving pensions from a sample of large firms which was matched with the recipients' social security earnings history. Although the sampling design is not representative, the results are revealing nonetheless. When the dust settles from the benefit process, workers seem to average benefits of roughly 20% of their preretirement earnings, regardless of union status or sex or earnings. Though these demographic factors sharply influence who gets pension coverage, among those who do, replacement rates look very similar.

Table 2.3   **Average Benefits and Proportion of Preretirement Income Replaced by Pension Benefits by Union Status, Sex, Age, Length of Service, and Preretirement Earnings**

	Average Benefit ($)	Average Replacement Rate
Union status		
Union	3,543	.20
Nonunion	3,741	.18
Sex		
Male	3,957	.19
Female	2,548	.18
Age		
50–54	5,960	.27
55–59	4,817	.23
60–64	4,576	.22
65–69	3,832	.18
70–74	3,389	.17
75–79	3,026	.17
80 and over	2,841	.17
Years of service		
1–5	540	.04
6–10	1,060	.08
11–15	1,598	.10
16–20	2,159	.14
21–25	3,239	.17
26–30	4,626	.22
31–35	5,401	.25
36 and over	6,184	.27
Preretirement income		
Under $7,500	1,225	.25
$7,500–8,499	1,296	.16
$8,500–9,499	1,287	.14
$9,500–10,499	1,470	.15
$10,500–11,499	1,628	.15
$11,500–12,499	1,896	.16
$12,500–13,499	2,093	.16
$13,500–14,999	2,450	.18
$15,000–24,999	3,591	.19
Over $25,000	5,550	.19

Source: Kotlikoff and Smith (1983), based on tabulations of the Survey of Private Pension Benefit Amounts.

Note: Preretirement earnings are defined as the average level of real earnings in the fifth to the third year prior to retirement.

As one would expect, replacement rates vary with length of service. Somewhat unexpected is the finding that younger retirees have higher replacement rates. Being younger, they ought to have had less opportunity to accumulate benefits. In most pension plans it is possible to retire early. As will be considered below, the benefits from such early retirement are often greatest for those with the longest service. Thus the results may indicate that some workers who have long service are electing to retire and claim their higher benefits. Those with lesser benefits accumulated tend to stay on until normal retirement age.

Old age income is in large part a reflection of previous earnings history. Since pensions are also tied to earnings, they do not ameliorate differences that result from past labor market outcomes. Persons who did better in the labor market typically have higher income when they are older, and they are more likely to have pension income. And, as noted above, among pension recipients, those with high income (even excluding the pension) have large pensions; persons with low income collect small pensions.

All of the results presented here indicate that pensions tend to heighten rather than compensate for differences in income among workers or the elderly. But their potential significance must not be missed. Half of the work force is enrolled in a plan that could provide 40% of their income when they are old. The important question that remains is, Do pension plans constrain strong incentives that might influence labor market behavior?

2.3   Market Impacts of Pensions

The most natural way for labor economists to examine the impact that pensions might have on the labor market is to view marginal pension wealth accumulation (or reduction) as an increase (decrease) in the effective wage. Because the true earnings profile differs from the observed wage payments, one would predict a variety of labor market responses by employees and employers that differ from those that might have been expected based only on the observed wages. The two types of behavior that have commanded the most attention in recent years are labor supply decisions, notably retirement behavior, but also work effort and labor turnover. Presumably pensions also influence hiring and layoff decisions of employers by changing the true cost of labor.

In this section I examine the provisions of pensions that might influence labor market behavior. I also provide some basic labor market data as background for the likely effects. The goal here is not to estimate the impact that pensions have on the labor market. Rather, I attempt to give the reader a rough idea of the magnitude of the incentives created by pensions and to point to the impact that various pension provisions have on these incentives. The effects that pensions might have on labor supply and on job changing are considered separately.

One other word of warning. Although I try to discuss provisions of both public and private pensions, the best data are available for private ones. Most of the calculations of the incentives created by pensions will implicitly assume a private pension plan is being considered.

2.3.2 Pensions and Labor Supply

• There has been a dramatic fall in the labor force participation rate of men over 55 in the past two decades. Participation of women in this age group was relatively stable, but the participation of younger women was increasing rapidly over this period. It may be that participation of older women also was depressed.

Figure 2.9 shows that between 1960 and 1980 the labor force participation rate for men aged 55–65 fell from 87% to 72%. For those over 65 rates fell from 35% to below 20%. The participation rates for women did not fall, but the contrast with the dramatic increases in paid economic activity for women in younger groups suggests that labor supply of these groups was also depressed. Several authors have attributed these declines largely to the increases in real social security benefits (e.g., Hurd and Boskin 1981), though others dispute the effects (e.g., Blinder et al. 1980; Gordon 1982). An obvious question is whether pension plans increase retirement incentives and whether the growth in pension plans contributed to this decline.

Pensions could have both a wealth and a substitution effect. Pensions add to the real wealth of workers who in turn may decide to consume more leisure, particularly late in their career. And they alter the effective wage. In general we tend to regard wealth as relatively fungible. Workers

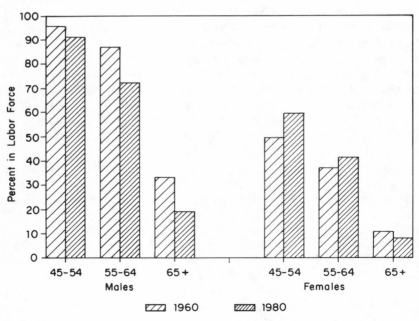

Fig. 2.9   Civilian labor force by race and age, 1960 and 1980

offered the choice between higher wages and pension benefits ought to be indifferent, unless there are tax advantages to pensions. Since there are such advantages, persons with pensions do make real income gains.

Pensions also distort the effective wage rate, and the impact of these distortions might be nontrivial. To understand these incentives we need to consider four key provisions of pension plans: the type of plan, the benefit formula, the normal retirement provisions, and the early retirement rules. Each will be considered and the impact that each has on pension wealth and the marginal returns to work will be reported for several hypothetical workers.

2.3.3 Plan Type

- Three-quarters of all persons and nearly 85% of all union members participating in private pension plans are enrolled in defined benefit plans where benefits are determined according to a specified formula. The remainder are enrolled in plans where benefits are directly related to contributions made on behalf of (and by) the employee and to the performance of the plan's investments portfolio. Virtually all government pensions are defined benefit plans.

Though their share of the pension market appears to have been declining in recent years, defined benefit plans still predominate. They seem to be most common for blue-collar workers in large firms. Defined contribution plans appear to be more common among professionals and highly paid white-collar workers. Profit-sharing plans and employee stock option plans are typically of this form. Smaller firms also are more likely to use this form of plan, perhaps to reduce the variability that a defined benefit plan can create. Blue-collar, and particularly union, workers seem most likely to have defined benefit coverage. Some union plans are actually a combination of the two, whereby employers make specified contributions to a union pension plan and then benefits are paid out according to some formula.

The type of plan has very important implications for the labor market impacts of a pension plan. Under defined contribution plans the employee typically gets out what has been put in for him. Once benefits are vested (once the employee can leave the firm and still collect his accrued benefits), the cost of leaving the firm is simply the value of lost contributions. The marginal cost of a year's lost contributions typically will be small in relation to total contributions for those with considerable service. In contrast, in "defined benefit" plans, benefit formulas are often such that benefits accumulate very rapidly late in a worker's career. The marginal cost of a year less service could be enormous.

- Most workers covered by defined benefit plans receive benefits based on a formula that increases pension benefits as length of service grows.

Union workers tend to receive a flat amount of money for each year worked. Nonunion workers tend to receive a percentage of average earnings in the last few years worked for each year of service.

The plethora and complexity of benefit provisions of defined benefit pension plans is overwhelming. The confusing nature of even a single plan suggests that economic actors are unlikely to respond exactly to the peculiar incentives of one or another plan. These complexities also raise interesting questions about the reasons for pensions. If pensions exist either to take advantage of tax benefits or to influence the economic behavior of workers and employers, then it is surprising that such complex institutional arrangements have developed.

Generally pension benefit provisions fall into one of two broad categories. Pattern or flat benefit plans pay a certain benefit per year of service. Kotlikoff and Smith (1983) estimate that the benefits averaged roughly $100 per year (plus or minus $70) for each year of service (though some plans have a formula whereby later years of service are compensated with greater pension increments). Thus a worker with 30 years of service would have received roughly $3000 per year in pension benefits had he retired in 1977. As shown on table 2.4, this type of plan is found almost exclusively in the private unionized sector.

Table 2.4   Benefit Formulas for Participants in Private Defined Benefit Plans

| | Percentage of Participants | | |
	Union	Nonunion	Total
Formula based on earnings and service	21.0	71.1	42.1
Earnings base Final or highest 3 years	2.4	2.7	2.5
Final or highest 5 years	9.0	43.0	23.3
Final or highest 10 years	.6	9.5	4.3
Career average	9.0	15.9	11.9
Flat rate based on service only	47.1	19.6	35.6
Flat rate not based on earnings or service	12.2	.2	7.1
Other	15.3	6.6	11.6
Not classified	4.4	2.4	3.6
Total	100.0	100.0	100.0

Source: Kotlikoff and Smith (1983), based on tabulations of the Employer Benefit Survey 1977.

It is tempting to conclude that flat benefit plans are quite susceptible to inflation. In general such a conclusion probably is not appropriate. Since flat benefit plans are found almost exclusively in the union sector, the retirement benefit is renegotiated with each contract. Benefits can be and are adjusted upward with the cost of living. Flat benefit plans probably do redistribute income somewhat from better-paid workers to lower-paid ones relative to plans based on earnings. Nonetheless, it should be remembered that many union contracts cover only a narrow class of workers where income increases primarily with seniority. Plans often compensate more senior workers with greater benefits per year of service.

Conventional or unit formula plans are found almost exclusively in the nonunion private sector and the public sector. Benefits are computed as a percentage of some earnings base, most commonly average earnings in the five years prior to departure. The percentage grows with service. So, for example, annual pension benefits might be 1% of average salary in the final five years times years of service. A 30-year veteran would thus receive 30% of his salary.

These formulas often are quite complex. Many are integrated with social security in some way, either by reducing benefits by some fraction of social security benefits or by providing higher benefits for that portion of earnings over the social security maximum. Integration is much more common in the private sector (75% of unit formula plans) than in the public (under 15%), in large part because a large fraction of public workers are not included in the social security system while employed by governments. Trying to generalize about these formulas is treacherous, but as a rough approximation it appears that benefits average between 1% and 1.25% of earnings per year of service for plans using average earnings of the last five years as the base.

The definition of the earnings base obviously sharply influences the sensitivity of benefits to changes in inflation. Recent changes in inflation appear to have influenced the benefit formulas used. According to the Bankers Trust Survey of large pension plans in 1960, career average earnings was used as the earnings base in the overwhelming majority of conventional pension plans and only about 15% used earnings bases of five years or less. By 1980 only 20% reported using career average earnings and 75% used bases of under five years (Mischo et al. 1980).

- Defined benefit pension plans sharply twist the earnings profile. The increase in the effective wage from pension increments is greatest in the years just prior to retirement age and for workers with the greatest service. Inflation lowers the pension increment dramatically for younger workers and raises it sharply for older ones and for those with long tenures.

For purposes of illustration throughout this section, it seems useful to look at the impacts of a "representative plan" on several "representative workers." The purpose here is not to describe the exact incentives pensions create taking into account all of their individual peculiarities.[2] Rather the goal is to provide the reader with the orders of magnitude of the possible incentive effects.

I will examine the incentives facing a worker currently earning $15,000 per year who expects to see no real wage increases for the remainder of his career. This wage growth assumption is not realistic, of course, but it greatly simplifies understanding the results. The worker faces a 3% real interest rate. The nominal interest rate grows one for one with inflation. Finally, he is enrolled in a plan where benefits are computed as 1% of earnings in the final five years before departure from the firm. Though this obviously is not a flat rate formula, if the flat rate were $150 now, and if retirees in subsequent years would get the same real flat rate, the unit formula would be essentially equivalent to a flat rate. Benefits are assumed vested at five years.[3] In this first example, assume benefits begin at age 65. No cost of living increases are granted to retirees.

Table 2.5 shows the present discounted value of pension benefits and the marginal increment in this present value associated with an additional year's work. In this relatively conservative example the value of pension benefits can be quite high. At age 65, a worker with 40 years of experience has accumulated over $50,000 in benefits in a noninflationary environment. Inflation obviously lowers the real value of benefits since they are fixed in nominal terms on retirement, but even with 7% inflation the value is nearly $35,000. A worker with half as much experience has half as much pension wealth.

The incremental gain in pension benefits from each year's additional work suggests that pensions do in fact create some important incentives. When there is no inflation, the gain from one year more work is $150 (1% of $15,000) per year in pension benefits on retirement. At 3% discount rate the value of these benefits is roughly $1300 at age 65. Thus for workers near retirement, wages are increased by roughly 10%. However, at young ages this $1300 must be discounted and thus the present value of the increment is smaller for younger workers. The benefit increment depends only on age—not on tenure—when there is no inflation.

Inflation alters this image quite sharply.[4] Staying an extra year now has two effects. The worker raises his benefits by 1% of the wage again. But since benefits are fixed in nominal terms, the benefits of that increment are much smaller. There is a second effect, though. By staying an extra year, the worker increases his wage base by the amount of inflation. At 7% inflation this amounts to a 7% increase in the value of the pension. For younger workers who have accumulated little pension wealth, this effect is small. For older workers, on the other hand, this effect is quite large. Notice that this effect is also dependent on tenure because workers with greater tenure will have accumulated more pension wealth at any age.

Table 2.5   **Present Value of Accrued Benefits and Marginal Change in Benefits for Hypothetical Worker with No Early Retirement**

	Present Value of Accrued Benefits ($)		Marginal Change in Present Value of Accrued Benefits from an Additional Year's Work ($)	
	0% Inflation 3% Discount	7% Inflation 10% Discount	0% Inflation 3% Discount	7% Inflation 10% Discount
Current age	Starting age 25			
30	2,274	144	455	41
35	5,271	463	527	82
40	9,167	1,120	611	158
45	14,169	2,404	708	297
50	20,532	4,840	821	546
55	28,563	9,354	952	988
60	38,631	17,575	1,104	1,768
65	51,181	32,349	1,242*	2,794*
Current age	Starting age 45			
50	4,106	968	821	275
55	9,521	3,118	952	552
60	16,556	7,532	1,104	1,065
65	25,591	16,175	1,242*	1,764*

Assumes: Worker currently paid $15,000 per year with no real wage growth; worker will retire at age 65; pension plan pays 1% of average salary in last five years times years of service; pension plan contains no early retirement provisions or makes correct actuarial adjustment for early retirees; benefits are vested after five years; real discount rate is 3%, nominal rate increases one for one with inflation.

Notes: * indicates value calculated for age 64 rather than age 65; all values are constant dollars.

Thus in an inflationary environment, a year's more work adds just $108 in pension wealth for a 35-year-old with 10 years of experience. If the worker stays until age 65, though, the last year's work adds nearly $3000 in wealth. If the worker had started at age 45 instead, the last year's work adds roughly $2000 in pension wealth.

Thus pensions rotate the wage profile, and they rotate it most when there is wage and price inflation. Under a realistic scenario, where there are both real wage growth of workers as they age and inflation, pensions cause real wages of younger workers to rise only slightly. But for older workers and for those with considerable service, real wages can be increased by 20% or more.

Until retirement age is reached, pensions actually serve as a strong deterrent to retirement. The value of benefits increases most for workers just reaching retirement age. After retirement age is reached, however, the incentives change quite dramatically.

- On reaching retirement age in defined benefit plans, benefits almost always are provided only for retired workers. Benefits rarely are adjusted upward for workers who retire late to account for the shorter period they will collect their benefits. In many plans pension benefits stop accruing at age 65. As a result there is often a strong incentive to retire at the normal retirement age.

Virtually all (90%) private retirement plans specify a normal retirement age of 65. About half of all participants are in plans that also have a minimum service requirement. These average roughly five years. Service-only requirements are essentially unknown. By contrast in the public sector, particularly in state-administered plans, the normal retirement age varies widely, but the mean is roughly age 60. However, most of these have longer service requirements, averaging over 10 years for state governments and nearly 15 years for local governments. When participants meet these requirements they can retire and normal benefits will begin.[5]

There is no broad-based data source providing information on accrual and benefits after normal retirement age is reached. Nonetheless it appears that in the majority of plans, accrual ceases once normal retirement age is reached. In many others there are limits on additional accrual. Virtually no plans seem to make provision for actuarial increases to compensate for the fact that late retirees will collect benefits over a reduced period. Almost two-thirds of the large single-employer pension plans surveyed by Bankers Trust in 1980 allowed no accrual after normal retirement (Mischo et al. 1980). Only 6% had actuarial increases. A 1979 Survey of Professional, Administrative, Technical, and Clerical Pay showed that roughly half of all pension plan recipients were covered under plans that prevented accrual after normal retirement and 25% more had accrual limits (Kotlikoff and Smith 1983).

As a result the large wage supplements created by pensions prior to retirement age rapidly become penalties. In the majority of cases, workers gain no additional pension benefits and lose a year's pension benefits for each year they continue to work. In the case of the hypothetical worker described above, a worker with 40 years of experience added $1200 to the value of his pension by working when he was 64. If he continued to work at 65, he would lose $6000 in benefits. A worker with 20 years of experience would lose half that amount. With this type of benefit formula one would certainly expect to see a large number of persons retiring at age 65.

One must be cautious in interpreting these results. Strong incentives are created to leave the firm at age 65. The worker still has the option of working somewhere else after this "retirement" and then collecting both salary and pension benefits.[6] Naturally in doing so he will have to endure whatever costs are associated with locating and adjusting to a new job. And the social security earnings test does tax such earnings rather heavily.

One might think that pensions had done enough to incentives with the provisions discussed thus far. But the effects of pension on retirement are further complicated by early retirement provisions contained in most plans.

• Although the normal retirement age under most plans is 65, over 80% of covered workers are in plans that make some provision for early retirement. And in the vast majority of these plans workers with service in excess of 20 years can retire early and collect pension benefits that are reduced either not at all or less than actuarially fairly in spite of the fact that the worker will collect benefits for a much longer period than one who retires at age 65.

Nearly all pension plans allow workers who have attained a certain age (typically 55) and have served for a minimum number of years (typically 10–15) to retire and collect benefits immediately. Because such workers will collect benefits for a longer period, their benefits ought to be reduced from what they would have been if the worker were retiring with the same length of service and salary at age 65. In defined contribution plans, where workers essentially get out what is contributed, such reductions are automatic. In defined benefit plans, on the other hand, where early retirement is available in plans covering 90% of all participants (Kotlikoff and Smith 1983), such reductions must be built into the benefit formula.

While data are not available for all plans, information from several sources indicates that very few plans reduce benefits by the full actuarially fair amount. The Bankers Trust survey reveals that in 1980 some 95% of the large defined benefit plans in their survey had early retirement plans that reduced benefits by less than the actuarially fair amount. And over 60% allowed some workers to retire early with full accrued benefits or greater (Mischo et al. 1980).

Accrual continues for nearly all workers eligible for early retirement if they elect not to take the early retirement option. As a result there are competing forces influencing the wage profile. On the one hand, the worker who keeps working continues accruing benefits and thus adds to his pension wealth. On the other hand, if benefits for early retirees are reduced by less than an actuarially fair amount, the value of the pension wealth he has already accrued actually declines because he loses out on some benefits he could otherwise receive. Which of these two effects is stronger depends on the benefit reduction formula and on the forces that influence the speed of pension accrual—namely, wage inflation and the benefit formula.

Table 2.6 shows what the marginal increments in pension wealth might be for our hypothetical worker if the pension plan allowed early retire-

Table 2.6   **Present Value of Accrued Benefits and Marginal Change in Benefits for Hypothetical Worker Early Retirement Allowed after Age 55 with Benefits Reduced Half Actuarially Fair Amount**

	Present Value of Accrued Benefits ($)		Marginal Change in Present Value of Accrued Benefits from an Additional Year's Work ($)	
	0% Inflation 3% Discount	7% Inflation 10% Discount	0% Inflation 3% Discount	7% Inflation 10% Discount
Current age	Starting age 25			
30	3,801	330	760	94
35	8,814	1,065	881	188
40	15,326	2,572	1,022	363
45	23,690	5,522	1,184	682
50	34,329	11,117	1,373	1,254
55	47,756	21,485	(665)	286
60	50,652	26,307	(1,174)	341
65	51,181	32,349	(1,598)*	461*
Current age	Starting age 45			
50	6,866	2,223	1,373	631
55	15,919	7,162	791	563
60	21,708	11,274	282	569
65	25,591	16,175	(141)*	628*

Assumes: Worker currently paid $15,000 per year with no real wage growth; worker will retire at age 65; pension plan pays 1% of average salary in last five years times years of service; benefits are vested after five years; real discount rate is 3%, nominal rate increases one for one with inflation.

Notes: * indicates value calculated for age 64 rather than age 65; all values are constant dollars; figures in parentheses are negative.

ment at age 55 and reduced benefits by just half the actuarially fair amount. In this example when there is no inflation, the pension system penalizes the worker with considerable service for working beyond early retirement. The penalty is over $600 at age 55 and it rises to $1600 by age 64.[7] When inflation is at 7% the benefit accrual is great enough to offset the depressing effects of the less than full actuarial reduction. And even in this case the incentives to remain at the firm created by the pension plan are diluted considerably.[8] For workers with less experience the depressing effects of early retirement are less severe, but strong nonetheless.

Based on these data, then, one is naturally drawn to the conclusion that for the 40% of the work force covered by defined benefit plans, benefit provisions could very well distort retirement decisions a great deal. Prior to early retirement age, pensions unambiguously increase the reward for work. This ought to reduce retirement (and, as we shall see, job switching) in these years. After early retirement age is reached, the impact is ambiguous. In general early retirement incentives are most powerful for workers in plans where benefit reductions for early retirees are smallest and in environments where wage inflation is the lowest. After normal retirement age is reached, the impact of pensions is again unambiguous. The presence of a pension serves as a substantial penalty for further work. It thus appears that the growth of pensions could, in fact, be a major contributing factor in the decline in labor force participation of older workers, particularly for men, where coverage is now quite common.

For those in defined contribution plans there may still be wealth effects, but it appears that these plans do little to alter the shape of the compensation schedule. That both workers and firms opt for the much more invasive defined benefit plans certainly raises the possibility that these incentives are created purposefully.

2.3.4   Pensions and Job Changing

In this section the impact that pensions might have on job changing is considered. The term "changing" is used in preference to turnover because turnover would be created within a firm both by job changing and by retirement of employees. Since the latter was discussed above, attention in this section is focused exclusively on the former. Figure 2.10, which is derived from May 1979 CPS data, helps illustrate the distinction be-

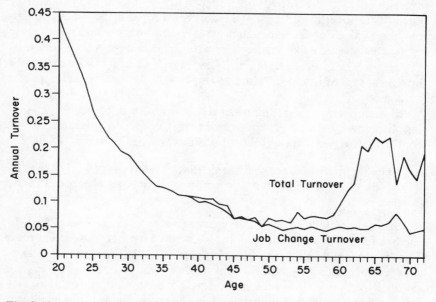

Fig. 2.10   Total turnover and job change turnover by age

tween turnover and job changing. The top line represents total annual turnover of male workers as seen by firms by age of workers. The lower line represents turnover created only by job changing.[9] That is, it reflects turnover created by workers changing jobs. In the later years there is a second effect—turnover is also created by persons leaving work and not returning. Thus employment for the cohort actually declines. At age 60 roughly 15% of male workers leave their firm. One-third that number show up the next year as new workers. Thus the remaining two-thirds leave employment.

- Total turnover is U-shaped, being high for young people due to job changing and high for older workers due to retirement. Job-changing turnover declines very sharply with age until age 55 when it increases somewhat. Job changing among persons over age 45, while considerably below the rate of younger workers, still affects between 10% and 15% of workers.

The figure suggests some important facts to consider when examining the potential usefulness of pensions in reducing turnover. Apparently turnover is a particularly serious problem for the young. Turnover is considerably less common among middle-aged workers, though whether the rates for these workers are low or high depends on one's perspective. Hall (1982) argues employment is quite stable at this stage. On the other hand, turnover rates of 10% imply completed employment spell durations which average only 10 years. Without independent evidence it is difficult to know if turnover of different aged workers is more or less costly to employers. If all turnover were equally costly, employers would presumably prefer that a vehicle like pensions have the greatest impact on turnover of younger workers. If job changing by experienced workers who have built up a great deal of job specific human capital is costly, the desired impact is ambiguous.

All the provisions that influence retirement also influence job changing. Moreover, two other features of pensions deserve attention in this context: initial pension eligibility provisions and vesting rules.

- Eligibility provisions are so minimal that virtually every worker over 25 with one year's service in a firm with a pension plan is enrolled in the plan.

ERISA essentially requires that every private worker over age 25 working in a firm with a pension plan for his class of worker must be covered. The law does allow persons who join the firm within five years of the normal retirement to be excluded, though three-quarters of all workers are enrolled in plans with no such exclusions. For older workers seeking a new job in a firm with a defined benefit plan, these provisions could be important because the cost to the employer of providing the defined benefits grows rapidly as retirement age approaches.

Government plans tend to be even more liberal than private ones. Most have no eligibility requirements; those that do tend to have lower age limits than private plans with some restrictions (Kotlikoff and Smith 1983).

- Virtually every worker enrolled in a pension plan is fully vested after 10 years of service. Thus, after 10 years of service, workers can leave the firm and still be assured of receiving on retirement all benefits they had accrued to the point of departure. Most workers lose all benefits if they leave prior to 10 years of service.

A worker whose benefits are fully vested can leave his firm and still collect, on retirement, all of the pension benefits he has accrued. A worker who is not vested typically loses all rights to pension benefits on departure. Prior to the passage of ERISA there was a proliferation of vesting provisions. ERISA imposed certain limits on the maximum length of time a worker could be employed before he was vested in a private pension plan. There remains some flexibility in the vesting formulas. ERISA provided several options and allowed plans to adopt even more liberal provisions. Largely as a result of the laws, over 90% of private pension participants are now fully vested after 10 years of service to the firm (Kotlikoff and Smith 1983).

Most private workers (73%) are covered by 10-year "cliff vesting" provisions. Workers in these plans lose all benefits if they leave the firm before 10 years, but after 10 years on the job they become entitled to all benefits accrued prior to their departure. Most of the remainder of pension participants are covered by plans that cliff vest earlier or gradually vest benefits (Kotlikoff and Smith 1983).

Vesting provisions for defined benefit plans tend to be much more liberal than those for defined contribution plans. Table 2.7 shows that while just 4% of private workers in defined contribution plans are fully vested after five years, 42% of those in defined contribution plans are vested by that stage and another 26% are partially vested.

Less complete information is available about public pension plans, but evidence from Arnold (cited in Kotlikoff and Smith 1983) suggests that vesting provisions are somewhat more liberal than those found in private defined benefit plans. For example, over half of all state-administered plans are fully vested after five years, 98% after 10.

- Vesting provisions serve as a moderately strong device for reducing turnover among all workers with less than 10 years of service in an inflation-free environment. But during inflationary times, vesting rules are likely to have only a small effect on job changing by younger workers. The impact on older workers could be large, though this effect is muted by the fact that most middle-aged and older workers have more than 10 years of service.

Workers who are not vested lose the present value of accrued pension benefits if they leave the firm. Table 2.8 shows that while the value of benefits can be quite large at very low discount rates, the value is relatively small for younger workers even with moderate discounting. Thus, contrary to popular belief, in the current inflationary times vesting probably does not serve as a strong deterrent to job changing by those under 40.

Table 2.7   **Vesting Provisions of Private Pension Plans Percentage of Workers Hired at Age 30 Who Would Be Vested by Length of Service (Participant Weighted)**

Length of Service	Defined Benefit (%)	Defined Contribution (%)	All Plans (%)
		Fully Vested (Partially Vested)	
1 year	.8 (.9)	18.1 (19.5)	4.8 (5.2)
3 years	2.0 (1.4)	23.8 (24.0)	7.0 (6.6)
5 years	3.6 (9.4)	42.6 (26.8)	12.5 (13.4)
10 years	92.5 (7.6)	91.7 (8.3)	92.3 (7.7)
15 years	100.0 (.0)	100.0 (.0)	100.0 (.0)

Source: Kotlikoff and Smith (1983), based on calculations from ESB1 File.

Table 2.8   **Present Value of Accrued Pension at Time of Vesting for Hypothetical Worker and Pension Plan by Age of Hire and Discount Rate**

Age When Hired	0%	5%	10%	15%
		Discount Rate		
25	$15,000	$2,680	$528*	$114
35	$15,000	$4,365	$1,370	$460
45	$15,000	$7,111	$3,553*	$1,861
55	$15,000	$11,583	$9,217	$7,528

Assumes: Hypothetical worker currently earns $15,000 per year, expects to retire at age 65 and live to age 75. Hypothetical pension plan pays 1% of final salary times years of service. Plan has 10-year cliff vesting.

Note: * these values differ slightly from the present value of accrued benefits after 10 years in the earlier example because average earnings over five years was used as the benefit base rather than final year's earnings.

On the other hand, for workers who join the firm at age 45 the value of benefits can be high even at moderate discount rates (or inflation levels). A worker using a 3% real discount rate in a time of 7% inflation (10% nominal discount rate) could lose the equivalent of nearly 25% of one year's salary by leaving his job.

Figure 2.11 demonstrates, however, that only about 20% of pension participants over 50 report that they are not vested, and another 10% are uncertain of their status. Among 40–50-year-old pension participants, just under 30% are sure that they are not vested. These are relatively small proportions, but those who are not vested may be more prone to job switching (hence their nonvested status), and vesting may provide the strongest incentives for those who are most likely to depart. In general, though, I would tend to conclude that vesting is not particularly important in times of high inflation. It is potentially most powerful for groups that generally are not affected by it and for groups in which turnover is already low.

Interestingly enough, although vesting may have very little effect on job changing in inflationary times, the other provisions of pensions can be very important, particularly when inflation is high.

- In inflationary times the benefit provisions of most defined benefit pension plans are in fact powerful deterrents to job switching even for the young and even if the alternative job offers identical wages and provides an identical pension plan.

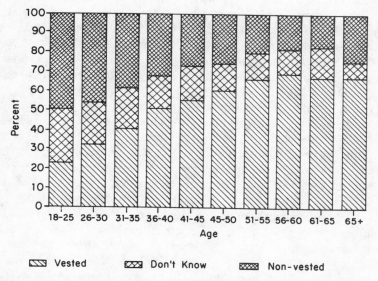

Fig. 2.11   Percentage of persons covered by pensions with vested and nonvested coverage by age

Consider a 35-year-old worker in 1983 with 10 years of experience working again at $15,000 per year in the "representative firm," which has a pension plan paying 1% of average salary in the last years at the firm times length of service. The worker intends to retire at age 65. If he stays with the firm until retirement he will be paid in annual retirement benefits 40% of his last salary. If he leaves now and finds a new job that offers him the same wage profile and an identical pension plan, it appears at first that he is just as well off. But note that at age 65 he will receive two checks: One from his new firm for 30% of his salary at age 65, and another from the first firm for 10% of his wage at age 35. If his wage at 65 is identical to the one at 35 he is equally well off. But if there has been even moderate nominal wage growth over this period, his wage at 65 will be vastly higher and the worker will lose a considerable amount in pension benefits. What he loses by switching jobs is the wage growth that would have pushed up the wage base used to calculate the benefits from the service already served at the old firm.

Table 2.9 indicates just how serious these losses can be. The magnitude is at first surprising since the marginal additions to pensions are small at younger ages. Remember, however, that when nominal wages are rising, the marginal value of increased pension wealth associated with one more year of work is related to both age and tenure. As a result, a job switcher who turns back the tenure clock is forced to accept a lifetime of smaller pension increments. The present value of all these lost increments can exceed $3000 for a 35-year-old with just 10 years of service even with no real wage growth and only 7% inflation. Obviously under stronger assumptions this $3000 would be low. In this case the incentive effects for older workers are just as great. A 55-year-old worker with 10 years of service also loses $3000. Although this worker loses increments over a shorter period, the losses are not discounted over nearly so long a period as are those for a younger worker.

There are still other reasons departure can be costly. Many pension plans offer early retirement with full benefits for some workers with long service. Since the value of these early retirement benefits can also be quite high, the worker again has an incentive to stay and accumulate service in only one firm. Finally, many benefit formulas are more generous for those with more years of service. For example, a plan might offer 1% of salary for the first 20 years and 1.5% for all years thereafter. Many union plans offer different flat rates for persons with short and long service records.

None of this applies to defined contribution plans. In these plans the worker has a certain amount set aside for him. Whether that money is in one employer's plan or another's ought to be a matter of some indifference. If he leaves one firm and joins a new one he retains his pension rights and loses no future benefits. One exception would arise if firms contributed more for workers with longer service.

Table 2.9 **Marginal Change in the Present Value of Benefits If Hypothetical Worker Works an Additional Year and Present Value of Lost Benefits If Worker Changes Jobs (No Early Retirement)**

	Marginal Change in Present Value of Accrued Benefits from an Additional Year's Work ($)		Present Value of Lost Pension Benefits If Change Jobs Now ($)	
	0% Inflation 3% Discount	7% Inflation 10% Discount	0% Inflation 3% Discount	7% Inflation 10% Discount
Current age	Starting age 25			
30	455	41	0	1,392
35	527	82	0	3,065
40	611	158	0	4,957
45	708	297	0	6,899
50	821	546	0	8,514
55	952	988	0	9,047
60	1,104	1,768	0	7,075
65	1,242*	2,794*	0*	2,007*
Current age	Starting age 45			
50	821	275	0	1,703
55	952	552	0	3,016
60	1,104	1,065	0	3,032
65	1,242*	1,764*	0*	978*

Assumes: Worker currently paid $15,000 per year with no real wage growth; worker will retire at age 65; pension plan pays 1% of average salary in last five years times years of service; pension plan allows no early retirement provisions or makes actuarially fair adjustment in benefits for early retirees; benefits are vested after five years; real discount rate is 3%, nominal rate increases one for one with inflation; if worker changes jobs he will work until age 65 at a new job which pays the same salary and offers an identical pension plan.

Note: * indicates value calculated for age 64 rather than age 65; all values are constant dollars.

Thus the benefit provisions of defined benefit formulas not only serve as a strong deterrent to retirement prior to the allowed age, they serve as a remarkably strong deterrent to job switching, even at very young ages. Whether such effects are intended or whether workers recognize them is yet another question. But in principle even young workers in relatively spartan plans lose a considerable amount of pension wealth by switching jobs even after the benefits are vested.

It is not the purpose of this paper to examine whether pensions do in fact reduce turnover. However, the data hint that such effects could be strong.

• Workers in pension plans have considerably longer tenure at every age.

Table 2.10   Workers with Less Than 10 Years of Tenure by Pension Coverage Status, 1979

Age	Covered (%)	Not Covered (%)
18–25	99.7	99.7
26–30	97.2	98.9
31–35	79.2	93.7
36–40	61.9	88.6
41–45	50.4	85.3
46–50	42.7	80.6
51–55	32.7	72.7
56–60	30.1	68.9
61–65	24.2	66.8
65 +	20.8	64.3

Source: May 1979 CPS.
Note: Workers who do not know if they are covered are excluded from this table.

Table 2.10 reveals that workers who report themselves covered by pensions do in fact have much longer tenures. Whereas 73% of all workers aged 51–55 without pensions have less than 10 years of tenure, only about 33% of workers with pensions have been with their employer for less than a decade. Of course, such a table proves nothing. There are many possible explanations for the differences observed here. Still, the data do suggest that pensions may have sizable impacts for those in defined benefit plans.

This table should serve as a reminder as well. It simply is not appropriate to think of all workers in pension plans as though they had joined the firm at age 25 (even though I occasionally may have succumbed to that temptation in discussion above). A large proportion of covered workers still have less than 10 years of tenure even late in their careers. Thus total value of pension plans is reduced for these workers and the incentives are often weaker, although in the example presented here job-changing incentives were just as great. One must avoid the trap of using the 25-year-old entrant as the typical worker.

It is also important to remember that defined benefit plans only cover just over one-third of the work force, and over half of these are union workers. The other distorting effects of unions may be so severe that it is hard to ferret out the independent effects of pensions, particularly on turnover.

2.4   Conclusion

Pensions may in fact be an important influence in the labor market. After reviewing this evidence several points strike me as being particularly pertinent for those interested in labor:

- Pensions are most common in unionized firms and in large establishments.
- Because both pension receipt and the level of benefits are closely related to income, pensions complement other forms of compensation or income. Pensions do nothing to equalize incomes across groups.
- Defined benefit pension plans effectively increase the reward to work quite dramatically in the period prior to retirement age and substantially penalize work afterward.
- Even though vesting provisions may not provide much incentive to remain with a firm, the way in which benefits are calculated often creates a very high penalty for switching firms in an inflationary environment.
- The effects of pensions are extremely sensitive to inflation.
- In sharp contrast to defined benefit plans, virtually no labor market distortions arise from defined contribution plans.

Pensions do not apply to all workers. Some pensions look relatively neutral in the labor market. But for the 35%–40% of the work force covered by defined benefit plans, pensions could play a very important role in labor market behavior.

Notes

1. When I refer to coverage in this paper I will be referring to persons who are participating in some form of pension plan. Workers in firms with pension plans who are not participants themselves are meant to be excluded from these figures.
2. For a discussion of the exact effects of actual plans, see Kotlikoff and Wise (in this volume).
3. Ten years is a much more common vesting period. In the current example, however, a five-year vesting period simplifies the tables and presentation without changing the results.
4. For an excellent discussion of many of the effects of inflation on pensions, see Bulow (1981).
5. The sources for these statements are Kotlikoff and Smith (1983) and Mischo et al. (1980).
6. Recent work by Gustman and Steinmeier (1983) suggests that "retired" persons often work for new employers.
7. Note that the present value of pension benefits for older workers is greater even though marginal increments to work are negative because the value of accrued pension wealth automatically rises as the time to retirement is shortened and the benefits are discounted over a shorter period.
8. For a more detailed discussion of the impact of early retirement provisions, see Bulow (1982).
9. This figure was derived by expanding a technique described by Hall (1982). The basic idea derives from the fact that employment of age cohort a' in year t' can be described as

$$E_{at} = E_{at-1} - \text{leavers}_{at-1} + \text{new hires}_{at}.$$

New hires can be inferred from the number of persons with less than one year of tenure, E_{at} is measured directly, and E_{at-1} can be estimated from E_{a-1t} with an adjustment for population. Thus, leavers can be inferred. Turnover is just leavers/employment. Net declines in the number of cohort members employed cause retirement turnover. The remainder is caused by job changing.

Comment   Zvi Bodie

You might be wondering why a financial economist is the first discussant at a conference on labor market aspects of pensions. The answer is that in the judgment of the conference organizers most of the basic scientific questions and policy issues regarding pensions cannot be properly addressed without considering financial and labor market aspects simultaneously.

Take, for example, an issue that arises immediately from David Ellwood's excellent analysis of defined contribution versus defined benefit pension plans: Why is defined benefit the most prevalent form? This question is puzzling to most economists because it would appear that an employer could always duplicate a defined benefit plan with a defined contribution plan costing the sponsor the same amount but offering the employee more options.

To illustrate this point, let us take Ellwood's numerical example in Table 2.5. A worker aged 30 earns a pension increment—a nominal deferred annuity—worth $41 under the defined benefit plan. For that same $41 cost to the firm the worker could be given a choice about how to invest the money in a defined contribution plan. His welfare would go up or at least stay the same (if he chose to invest in nominal deferred annuities) with no increase in cost to the firm. Isn't it in the best interest of all parties to have a defined contribution plan?

From a finance perspective I can think of four main reasons for the firm to prefer the defined benefit form.

1. *Funding.* Current IRS and ERISA rules allow firms considerable latitude in funding their accrued vested pension liabilities, which represent the only legally enforceable obligation the firm has to past and present covered employees. ERISA specifies minimum funding requirements designed to protect the PBGC against incurring a large liability for insured benefits on the termination of an unfunded plan, and the IRS sets maximum contribution limits to prevent the abuse of the tax advantages of pension plan overfunding. But these limits are quite broad, and in terms of the contribution to the fund in any given year they effectively allow the firm to contribute as little or as much as it wants.

Thus, should a normally healthy firm with a fully funded plan find itself in a short-term cash squeeze, it can always exercise its option to drastically reduce its pension contribution. The principal means at its disposal for doing so would be to alter its actuarial assumptions (e.g., raise its interest rate assumption), to produce a lower estimate of accrued vested

Zvi Bodie is professor of economics and finance at Boston University's School of Management and research associate, National Bureau of Economic Research.

benefits. Should the firm find itself in a more serious financial crisis, it has the option of drawing on this internal source of debt financing confident that even in the event of bankruptcy the PBGC will assume responsibility for most of the vested benefits of its employees. On the other hand, a healthy firm may want to exercise its option to overfund its plan and reap the benefits of the tax deferrals made possible thereby.

2. *Asset allocation.* Since the firm's liability to a worker under virtually all existing defined benefit plans is in the form of nominal deferred annuities, the firm could always hedge the risks associated with it by buying insurance contracts or by making equivalent investments in long-term fixed-interest securities. In fact, only a minority of sponsors choose to do so, and those that do tend to be the small plans.

Clearly, most sponsors try to earn "excess" returns on their pension funds, or, in their parlance, to reduce pension costs by superior investment performance. To be sure, if the investment results turn out to be truly superior, the sponsor can share the fruits with the plan participants by distributing ad hoc benefit increases. On the other hand, if investment results are poor and plan assets fall in value to levels below the vested accrued benefits, the PBGC may find itself with an underfunded plan on its hands.

3. *Accounting policies.* Under current rules of the Financial Accounting Standards Board, major corporations are required to state in their annual reports the market value of the assets in their pension funds, the accrued vested and nonvested pension liabilities, and the interest rate assumed in evaluating them. In principle, current and prospective shareholders and creditors of the firm as well as all other interested parties should be able to use these numbers to get a rough idea of the true magnitude of the firm's unfunded pension liabilities in order to compute adjusted debt/equity ratios and other measures of the firm's capital structure.

In an ideal informationally efficient capital market, the accounting treatment of these numbers should not matter to any of the parties making financial decisions relating to the firm. In reality, however, corporate financial officers and their creditors behave as if the accounting numbers do matter.

4. *Systematic overvaluation of defined benefits by employees.* Almost all defined benefit plans are extremely complex financial contracts requiring a fair degree of sophistication and knowledge in order to evaluate the benefits they provide. Although sponsors employ actuaries and other experts to enable them to compute the annual costs of benefits accruing under their plans, workers rarely are informed about how much they are actually earning in this form.

There is evidence that employees, particularly younger ones, are ill informed about the value of their accruing pension benefits and in some cases do not even know whether they are covered by an employer pension plan. An hypothesis that could explain in part why corporations prefer defined benefit to defined contribution plans is that workers might systematically overvalue their accruing benefits because of failure to discount them properly.

A common link among all four of these possible reasons for employers to prefer defined benefit plans to defined contribution plans is that in each case the firm is shifting part of the cost of its pension commitments to other parties: the IRS, the PBGC, the investor community, or its own employees. To the extent that these affected parties are unaware of this cost shifting, it may be a source of public policy concern.

With these considerations in the background, the natural question I am led to ask the labor economists at this conference is whether there are any reasons, suggested by the theory of labor contracting, to believe that defined benefit pension plans are a more efficient arrangement than defined contribution plans.

In my role as discussant of David Ellwood's paper I have very little to say beyond praise for a job well done. I think he has done a fine job of extracting from Kotlikoff and Smith's gargantuan volume, *Pensions in the American Economy*, the most salient facts relating to labor market aspects of pension plans in the United States, and I will not repeat them in my comments. The latter part of his paper presents a good introduction to the features of defined benefit pension plans that are most likely to affect the labor market behavior of individuals—retirement and job change turnover decisions. Since a more detailed empirical treatment of these issues is the subject of the paper by Kotlikoff and Wise, which I have also been asked to discuss, I will treat that paper and the second half of Ellwood's together (see pp. 000–000 below).

References

Blinder, A.S. 1982. Private pensions and public pensions: Theory and fact. NBER Working Paper no. 902.

Blinder, A.S.; Gordon, R.; and Wise, D. 1980. Reconsidering the work disincentive effects of social security. *National Tax Journal* 33:431–42.

Boskin, M.J., and Hurd, M. 1978. The effect of social security on early retirement. *Journal of Public Economics* 10:361–78.

Bulow, J.I. 1981. Early retirement pension benefits. NBER Working Paper no. 654.

———. 1982. The effect of inflation on the private pension system. In *Inflation: Causes and effects,* ed. R. Hall. Chicago: University of Chicago Press (for NBER).

Gordon, R.H. 1982. Social security and labor supply incentives. NBER Working Paper no. 986.

Gustman, A., and Steinmeier, T. 1983. Retirement flows. NBER Working Paper no. 1069.

Hall, R.E. 1982. The importance of lifetime jobs in the U.S. economy. *American Economic Review* 72:716–24.

Hurd, M.D., and Boskin, M. J. 1981. The effect of social security on retirement in the early 1970s. NBER Working Paper no. 659.

Hurd, M.D., and Shoven, J. B. 1982. The economic status of the elderly. NBER Working Paper no. 914.

Kotlikoff, L.J., and Smith, D. E. 1983. *Pensions in the American economy*. Chicago: University of Chicago Press (for NBER).

Kotlikoff, L.J., and Wise, D. A. 1985. Labor compensation and the structure of private pension plans: Evidence for contractual versus spot markets. In this volume.

Lazear, E.P. 1982. Pensions as severance pay. NBER Working Paper no. 944.

Mathematica Policy Research. 1979. *Review of Research on Retirement Income Programs, Section I*. Washington, D.C.: Employee Benefit Research Institute.

Mischo, W.J.; Chang, S.-K.; and Kaston, E. P. 1980. *Corporate pension plan study: A guide for the 1980s*. New York: Bankers Trust Co.

Munnell, A.H. 1982. *The economics of private pensions*. Washington, D.C.: Brookings Institution.

Stein, B. 1980. *Social security and pensions in transition: Understanding the American retirement system*. New York: Free Press.

3 Labor Compensation and the Structure of Private Pension Plans: Evidence for Contractual versus Spot Labor Markets

Laurence J. Kotlikoff
David A. Wise

What are the incentive effects of private pension plans? What is the cost in pension benefits of job turnover? How important is vesting? Is there a cost in pension benefits of forgoing the early retirement option? Do pension stipulations encourage early retirement? By analyzing the stipulations of pension plans, we are able to develop considerable evidence directed to these questions. At the same time, the structural features of private pension plans permit new and potentially strong inferences concerning the contractual nature of labor market agreements and the role of pensions in assisting such arrangements.

Understanding the contractual arrangements between workers and firms is important for a host of economic issues ranging from the degree of wage flexibility over the business cycle to the availability of human capital insurance within the firm. Discriminating between "spot" and "long-term contract" views of the labor market is also critical for evaluating numerous questions specific to private pensions. One such question is whether workers and employers fully appreciate how complex pension plan provisions alter a firm's total compensation package. Evidence that labor markets closely accord to the predictions of a spot market would suggest rather small information problems. Equally productive workers, in this case, receive identical total annual remuneration regardless of their current employer or the specifics of the employer's pension plan.

A second question involves proper disclosure and valuation of a pension plan's net financial liabilities. In a spot market setting an employer's

Laurence J. Kotlikoff is professor of economics, Boston University, and research associate, National Bureau of Economic Research, David A. Wise is John F. Stambaugh Professor of Political Economy, John F. Kennedy School of Government, Harvard University, and research associate, National Bureau of Economic Research.

We thank Gary Heaton for masterly and very extensive computer programming and Douglas Phillips for excellent research assistance.

net liability corresponds simply to the accrued value of vested pension benefits. Additional pension liabilities projected to arise from future employment, in such a setting, are matched dollar for dollar by future projected revenues associated with the worker's continued employment. The excess of projected over accrued liabilities should not, therefore, affect a firm's valuation and suggests no case for estimating and disclosing projected pension liabilities. Under a long-term contract arrangement, on the other hand, revenue from continued employment need not match the accrual of future pension liabilities, plus the payment of tenure wages, and the disclosure of projected rather than accrued liabilities is potentially more relevant for firm financial valuation.

A third question is the effect of pensions on labor mobility and hiring practices. In a spot market environment the particular and quite peculiar rates of pension benefit accrual with age described here would have no consequences for labor mobility, since offsetting increases or reductions in direct wage compensation would leave the worker indifferent between staying on the current job or switching to another job offering an identical amount of total compensation. A spot market would also entail flexibility in wage compensation sufficient to permit hiring equally productive old and young, black and white, male and female workers, despite differences in their accrual of vested pension benefits reflecting age, race, and sex-specific mortality probabilities. Long-term contractual agreements, in contrast, may leave less flexibility to accommodate differences in individual circumstances.

Given knowledge of a worker's current and previous level of earnings, and the benefit and retirement provisions of his pension plan, one could, in principle, directly test the spot market hypothesis by checking whether, in each year, the sum of the increment to a worker's accrued vested pension benefits plus his wage compensation equaled his marginal product.[1] Unfortunately, a worker's marginal product is unobservable and difficult to estimate. In addition new government data linking pension plan provisions and the earnings histories of participating workers have not yet been released.[2] These data limitations restrict, but by no means preclude, inferences about spot versus contractual labor market arrangements.[3]

While little is known about the typical profile of marginal productivity by age, it seems safe to assume that this schedule does not exhibit sharp discontinuities. In addition, while there is currently no publicly available means of matching particular earnings histories with particular pension plans, there is considerable information available concerning the typical shape of age-earnings profiles.

This paper calculates the pattern of accrual of vested pension benefits for alternative, but realistic, age-earnings profiles. These accrual profiles are computed for a large sample of plans contained in the Bureau of Labor Statistic's 1979 Level of Benefits Survey (BLS–LOB). These new pension data, based on a survey of 1469 establishments with 3,386,121 pension participants, provide extremely detailed information concerning pension benefits, vesting, and early retirement formulas, all of which are key inputs to the calculation of pension accruals.

The sum of the assumed age-earnings profile, measured in constant dollars, and the associated real pension accrual profile equals, under the spot market assumption, the age–marginal productivity profile. Hypothetical age–marginal productivity profiles derived in this manner exhibit rather sharp discontinuities at two critical ages, the age of full vesting, for plans with cliff vesting, and the early retirement age, for plans permitting early retirement on better than actuarially fair terms. For a large fraction of pension plans making reasonable assumptions concerning age-earnings profiles and interest rates, we find discontinuities as large as 50% of wage compensation depending on the worker's age at hire. An alternative statement of these findings is that for smoothly shaped age–marginal product schedules, wage compensation must potentially fall or rise by roughly 40% of the wage at the age of cliff vesting and other critical ages to satisfy conditions of spot market equilibrium. These figures appear sufficiently large to rule out the hypothesis of spot clearing for a large segment of the United States labor market.

In addition to the potentially large discontinuities in pension benefit accruals, the pattern of accruals also sheds considerable light on the role of pensions in discouraging worker turnover. In many instances even workers who change jobs with no loss in wage compensation and commence employment in a new firm with an identical pension plan lose a large amount in pension benefits.

The accrual patterns also permit inferences about incentives that pensions provide for early retirement. Under our actuarial assumptions we find positive pension accruals on average throughout the work span, that is, worker separation at any time prior to normal retirement typically involves a loss of remuneration in excess of the loss in wage compensation. These findings appear to differ from those of Lazear (1983), who finds that after the age of early retirement, continued work typically involves a loss in pension benefits. Part of the difference in results is due to differences in interest rate and nominal wage growth assumptions. In addition, we do not consider in this paper benefits for all plans covered by the LOB survey. In particular, all plans used in this analysis base benefits on wages.

As Lazear's (1983) insightful study points out, the present expected value of accrued pension benefits represents a form of severance pay for workers who choose to separate from the firm. Such severance pay would naturally arise in contractual settings in which workers are paid (in wages) less than their marginal products. The severance pay may be thought of as the return of the worker's bond, which he puts up to guarantee the quality and quantity of his work effort. As the worker ages, the value of this "severance pay" rises, according to our findings. In a contractual setting the implication of our finding of positive average pension accrual at all ages prior to normal retirement is that real wages represent a lower bound for the average marginal product of workers covered by our sample of plans. It is important to emphasize, however, that we find large deviations from the average, with large negative accruals after the age of early retirement under the provisions of many plans.

Finally, an additional implication of our findings is that compensating differential studies of the trade-off between wages and pension benefits, if they are to be meaningful, cannot be based on cross-section evidence at a point in time. To understand the relationship between compensation in the form of wages versus pension benefits, one must consider the receipt of both over a long period of employment.

The next section describes procedures used to calculate pension benefit accrual and presents illustrative accrual rates for a standard earnings-based defined benefit plan, but one that is not integrated with social security. This plan is also used to demonstrate the sensitivity of accrual rates to assumptions about wage inflation and interest rates. Section 3.2 presents evidence concerning age-earnings profiles, suggesting, in particular, that for fully employed workers between ages 55 and 65 who remain in a given firm, nominal earnings grow on average at rates commensurate with, if not greater than, inflation. The assumption of positive nominal wage growth after age 55 is crucial for generating positive pension benefit accrual between 55 and 65. Section 3.3 describes the BLS–LOB data set in more detail and examines the heterogeneity of accrual profiles for our sample of 1183 plans.[4] We conclude the section by drawing inferences from these data concerning the weight of evidence in favor of contractual as opposed to spot labor markets. Section 3.4 summarizes principal findings and suggests areas for future research.

3.1   Pension Benefit Accrual Formulas and Illustrative Graphs of Accrual Profiles

3.1.1   Accrual Formulas

To begin, consider the benefit accrual profiles shown in figure 3.1. The nominal wage growth incorporated in the top profile assumes moderate life-cycle growth in real wages plus a 6% rate of inflation. A 3% real interest rate (or 9% nominal rate) is also assumed. The lower graphs are based on 6% and 9% real (12% and 15% nominal) interest rates, respectively. In the paragraphs below we describe features of pension benefit formulas that produce the unusual shapes of these profiles.

Vested pension benefit accrual at age a, $I(a)$, equals the difference between pension wealth at age $a + 1$, $Pw(a + 1)$, and pension wealth at age a, $Pw(a)$, accumulated to age $a + 1$ at the nominal interest rate r:

(1) $$I(a) = Pw(a + 1) - Pw(a)(1 + r).$$

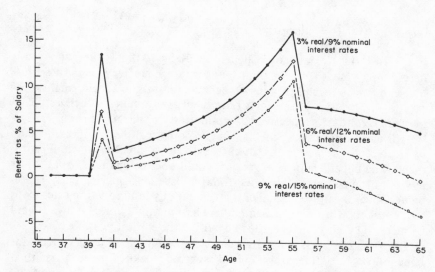

Fig. 3.1   Pension increments as a percentage of salary, by age, for a wage stream with 6% inflation discounted at real interest rates of 3%, 6%, and 9%.

Pension wealth at age a is defined as the expected value of vested pension benefits discounted to age a. Intuitively, $Pw(a)$ can be thought of as the worker's pension bank account. If $I(a)$ equals zero, the worker continuing employment with the plan sponsor at age a has exactly the same pension wealth at age $a + 1$ as an identically situated worker who terminates employment at age a. Pension accrual is thus the increment to pension wealth in excess of the return on the previously accumulated pension bank account.

If the labor market exhibits spot market equilibrium, $I(a)$ plus the worker's nonpension compensation at age a, $W(a)$, equals the worker's marginal product at age a, $M(a)$:

$$(2) \qquad M(a) = W(a) + I(a).$$

Obviously, if $W(a)$ is a smooth function of age and $I(a)$ exhibits sharp discontinuities, $M(a)$ must exhibit sharp discontinuities at these same ages to satisfy (2).

The source of discontinuities in age accrual profiles is clarified by considering a sample earnings-related defined benefit plan with "cliff vesting" at 10 years of service. Vested accrued benefits are clearly zero prior to the age at which the worker has 10 years of credited service in the plan. Let $R(a, t)$ denote the ratio of $I(a)$ to $W(a)$ for a worker age a with t years of tenure. Then $R(a, t)$ is zero for $t < 9$. If a person age a with nine years of service works an additional year, the ratio of the increment to the wage $W(a)$ is

(3) $$R(a, 9) = \frac{B(a, t)A(55)(1 + d)^{-10}(1 + r)^{-[55 - (a + 1)]}}{W(a)}$$

In (3), $B(a, t)$ is the retirement benefit available to the worker who termi-nates employment with the plan sponsor at age a after t years of service but who delays receipt of pension benefits until the plan's normal retire-ment age. The normal and early retirement ages assumed for this stylized plan are 65 and 55, respectively. Terminating workers are, however, eligi-ble for early retirement benefits. Our hypothetical plan reduces benefits by d percent for each year that early retirement precedes normal retire-ment. The benefit reduction rate, d, could be greater than, equal to, or less than the actuarial fair rate. Today most plans offering early retire-ment appear to stipulate smaller than actuarially fair reduction rates; con-sequently, the formulas presented here assume that workers always gain by receiving their vested accrued benefits at the earliest possible date.

The function $A(55)$ is the actuarial discount factor that transforms benefit flows initiating at age 55 into expected stocks of pension wealth at age 55. Expectations here are taken with respect to longevity. Thus $A(55)$ is the annuity value of a dollar's worth of pension benefits to be received each year until death, beginning at age 55. For simplicity assume that the probability of dying prior to age 55 is zero. Hence the present value at age a of $A(55)$ is $A(a) = A(55)(1 + r)^{-(55 - a)}$ for $a \leq 55$. If pension benefits are determined as a constant λ times the product of final year's earnings and service, and there is no offset for receipt of social security benefits, $B(a, t)$ is simply

(4) $$B(a, t) = \lambda W(a)t,$$

and

(5) $$R(a, 9) = \lambda(1 + d)^{-10}(1 + r)^{-[55 - (a + 1)]}A(55)10 \cdot \frac{W(a + 1)}{W(a)}.$$

$R(a, t)$, for t increasing pari passu with age, is zero prior to t equals 9 and jumps at t equals 9 to the value given in (5). Cliff vesting thus pro-duces spikes in the accrual profile such as that in figure 3.1 at 10 years of service. Between the age at cliff vesting and age 55, pension wealth $Pw(a)$ is given by

(6) $$Pw(a) = \lambda W(a)(1 + d)^{-10}(1 + r)^{-(55 - a)}A(55)t,$$

and the increment to pension wealth $I(a)$ divided by the wage $W(a)$ is given by

(7)
$$R(a, t) = \lambda(1 + d)^{-10}(1 + r)^{-[55 - (a + 1)]}A(55)t \left[\frac{W(a + 1)}{W(a)} \frac{t + 1}{t} - 1 \right].$$

Equations (7) and (5) suggest a drop in $R(a, t)$ as a increases to $a + 1$ concurrent with an increase in t from 9 to 10. Equation (7) will be positive if the term in brackets exceeds zero. This will be the case if the percent increase in the wage plus the percent increase in years employed ($1/t$) is greater than zero. Assuming the term in brackets is positive and is roughly constant, $R(a, t)$ will increase exponentially due to the exponential decline in the discount factor, $(1 + r)^{-[55 - (a + 1)]}$, as a approaches 55.

If the value of d is considerably less than actuarially fair, a discontinuity in $R(a, t)$ occurs at the early retirement age, 55. At ages 55 and 56 we have

(8) $$Pw(55) = \lambda W(55)(1 + d)^{-10}A(55)t$$

and

(9) $$Pw(56) = \lambda W(56)(1 + d)^{-9}A(56)(t + 1).$$

Hence,

(10)
$$R(55, t) =$$

$$\lambda(1 + d)^{-10}(1 + r) A(55)t \left[\frac{W(56)}{W(55)} \frac{t + 1}{t} \frac{A(56)}{A(55)} \frac{(1 + d)}{(1 + r)} - 1 \right].$$

Assuming wage growth at 54 is close to that at 55 and $A(56)$ approximately equals $A(55)$, then $R(55, t)$ primarily differs from $R(54, t - 1)$ because the first term in the bracket in (7) is now multiplied by $(1 + d)$, while the second term, -1, is multiplied by $(1 + r)$. Since r exceeds d by assumption, $R(55, t)$ can easily be less than $R(54, t - 1)$. Indeed, this change in the functional form of $R(a, t)$ can produce sharp drops in accrual rates at the early retirement age for a host of pension plans and a range of realistic economic assumptions. Figure 3.1 illustrates such discontinuities.

It is important to realize that the early retirement reduction, lower wages, and one less year of tenure yield lower benefits at 55 than at 56. The early retirement reduction reduces benefits at the rate d. But if benefits were taken at 55 they could accrue interest at the rate r. Thus by forgoing the early retirement option of receiving benefits at 55, a cost is incurred that depends on the difference $r - d$. If this loss is not offset by the increase due to wage growth and one year of additional tenure, there will be a drop in the benefit accrual rate between 55 and 56.

The same considerations pertain to benefit increments between 56 and 65. Recall that we have assumed a less than fair early retirement reduction so that benefits accrued before 55 are valued assuming receipt of benefits at the age that yields maximum pension wealth. The optimum time to receive benefits accrued between 55 and 56 is 56, between 56 and 57 is 57, and so forth. But to gain benefits from working another year, it is necessary to forgo the option of immediately taking accrued benefits at an advantageous reduction rate.

Between ages 56 and 65, $R(a, t)$ equals

$$(11) \quad R(a, t) = \lambda(1 + d)^{-(65 - a)}(1 + r) A(a)t$$
$$\left[\frac{W(a + 1)}{W(a)} \frac{(t + 1)}{t} \frac{A(a + 1)}{A(a)} \frac{(1 + d)}{(1 + r)} - 1 \right].$$

In contrast to the $R(a, t)$ formula in (7) applying to the period between cliff vesting and early retirement, (11) indicates that the actuarial reduction factor—rather than the interest rate r—imparts an upward tilt in the $R(a, t)$ profile between early and normal retirement, as long as the term in brackets is positive. In (11) as in (7) and (10) the accrual rate, $R(a, t)$ is an increasing function of the rate of nominal wage growth. Larger nominal interest rates reduce accrual rates at all ages, with a negative interaction with age prior to early retirement.

Finally, while equation (7) is unlikely to be negative, wide differences between wage growth and the interest rate r can yield negative increments in pension wealth after the early retirement age. To a first approximation, the bracketed term in equation (11) will be positive if $\Delta W/W + 1/t > r - d$ where $\Delta W/W$ is the percent increase in wages and $1/t$ the percent increase in tenure. It is easy to see, however, that low wage growth and high interest rates will yield negative increments. Thus actuarial increments after the early retirement age are very sensitive to assumed values for wage growth and the interest rate.

While the preceding formulas suggest the general shape of accrual rate profiles, there are few earnings-based plans with features as simple as the one considered here. In addition to more complicated rules for plan participation and vesting that often involve age as well as service requirements, there are a variety of methods of computing earnings bases, including career averages, and averages of earnings, possibly highest earnings, over a specified period or number of years. Reduction rates for early retirement are often a specified function of age, if not length of service. Some plans allow no further accrual after a given number of years of service. Roughly 30% of defined benefit participants belong to plans that are integrated with social security. There are two, not necessarily independent, important forms of "integration." One involves a "step rate" benefit formula that uses a different value for the percentage of the product of earnings times service for levels of earnings below and levels above specified values. The second is referred to as an "offset" formula that reduces pension benefits by some fraction of the participant's basic social security benefit. Many of the offset plans set ceilings on the extent of the offset. A minority of plans, in particular those with social security offset formulas, provide supplemental benefits for early retirees prior to their receipt of social security benefits. The supplemental benefit formulas can also be fairly involved, incorporating both the participant's age and service in the calculation. There are also plans that use one benefit formula to compute early retirement benefits and a different formula to determine normal retirement benefits. In addition to these earnings-related plans, a significant number of plans covering over 40% of defined benefit participants calculate benefits independent of the participant's earnings history (Kotlikoff and Smith 1983, table 4.5.1). These formulas can also be quite complex. There are other plans that are earnings related but provide differing flat benefit amounts based on the participant's earnings bracket. Finally, there are plans that specify minimum and maximum benefit levels.

Each of these additional features can significantly alter the profile of accrual rates by age, especially the extent of discontinuities in the profile. Our analysis in Section 3.4 of pension plans in the BLS–LOB sample takes account of a great number of these complexities. Two important exceptions in the current paper are plans with non-earnings-related benefit formulas and plans with supplemental benefit formulas. These plans will be considered in future research.

The assumption of constant nominal interest rates implies a quite different pattern of pension accrual than would occur with variable interest rates. Changes in long-term nominal interest rates produce capital gains and losses on previously accumulated pension wealth that do not directly affect pension accrual. However, as indicated in equations (5), (7), (10), and (11), accrual rates are also a direct function of the currently prevailing long-term interest rates. A time path of varying interest rates around a constant mean would produce a much more discontinuous age-pension accrual profile than those of figure 3.1 and other diagrams in this paper.

3.1.2 Illustrative Graphs of Accrual Profiles

Figure 3.2 depicts three accrual rate profiles for a worker who begins participating at age 30 in a defined benefit plan similar to that described above. The plan calculates normal retirement benefits as 1% of average earnings over the last five years of service times years of service. Benefits are reduced by 3% for each year that early retirement precedes normal retirement. Cliff vesting occurs after 10 years. The early and normal retirement ages are 55 and 65, respectively.

Nominal wage growth is determined by two factors, a cross-sectional profile of "merit" increases by age and an assumed economy-wide rate of wage inflation. The merit profile involves approximately a 50% growth in real wages between ages 30 and 50 and very little growth from 50 to 65. The rate of wage inflation incorporates both across-the-board increases in labor productivity and the price level. The three profiles in figure 3.2 differ both in their assumed rate of wage inflation and nominal interest rates. The 2% wage inflation profile discounts pension benefits at a 5% nominal

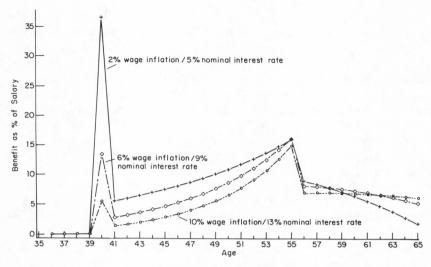

Fig. 3.2   Pension increments as a percentage of salary, by age, for wage
                               inflation of 2%, 6%, and 10%. Note: Benefits are discounted
                               at a 3% real interest rate.

rate, while the 6% and 10% wage inflation profiles use 9% and 13%
nominal interest rates, respectively.

These assumptions about wage growth and nominal interest rates produce "vesting spikes" ranging form 5% to 37% of wages at age 40. The intermediate wage and interest rate assumption produces a 14% spike at
cliff vesting. All three profiles indicate reductions in the accrual rate of
about 8 percentage points at age 56. In order to reconcile these profiles
with the dictates of spot market equilibrium, one must believe that marginal products rise abruptly by an additional 5% to 37% exactly at age 40
and then fall by an additional 3% to 31% exactly at age 41. In addition, an
abrupt decline in the worker's marginal product of close to 8 percentage
points exactly at age 56 that occurs neither before nor after 56 is required
for the theory of spot equilibrium.

One response to these profiles is that straight wage compensation,
rather than increasing smoothly through time, could adjust to meet the
spot market. Figure 3.3 suggests the implausibility of this view. Here accrual rate profiles for workers joining the pension plan at ages 30, 40, and
50 are presented based on the intermediate wage and interest rate assumptions of figure 3.2. The vesting spikes for the three profiles are 14%, 36%,
and 66% of the corresponding wage at ages 40, 50, and 60. While vesting
at these latter ages is much less common than prior to age 40, Kotlikoff
and Smith (1983, table 3.6.5) report that over a quarter of current defined
benefit pension recipients retired with 20 or fewer years of service.

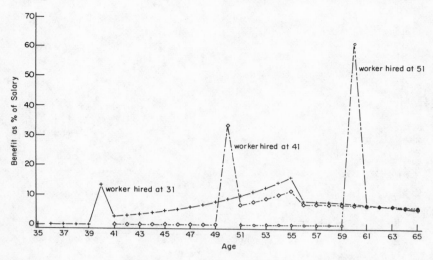

Fig. 3.3   Pension increments as a percentage of salary, by age, for an employee beginning work at 31, 41, 51. Note: 6% wage inflation, 3% real interest rate.

Figure 3.3 is constructed under the assumption that the workers of the same age receive identical wage compensation. Thus the diagram indicates the potential loss in accrued pension benefits for workers who switch jobs but receive the same wage compensation in the new job and are covered by the same pension plan. We present below a similar diagram, based on a plan like our base plan but without the early retirement option. In this case, the loss is substantially greater.

Figure 3.4 highlights the importance of the early retirement benefit reduction formula for pension accrual. The profile labeled "early retirement option" repeats the accrual profile from figures 3.2 and 3.3 based on intermediate economic assumptions. The "retirement at 65 only" profile indicates the pattern of accrual rates for the same plan but excludes the early retirement option. This profile could also be labeled "actuarially fair accrual rates" since, by definition, an actuarially fair early retirement reduction formula produces an accrual profile that is independent of the age at which benefits are first received.

To the extent that retirement benefits provide an incentive to continue working, the incentive is much greater without the early retirement option than with it. It is important to realize that the difference is only a matter of the pattern of accruals; for workers who retire at normal retirement, the total accumulation of accrued benefits is independent of whether the plan does or does not have an early retirement option.

In contrast to the "early retirement option," the actuarially fair "retirement at 65 only" profile exhibits a 6% rather than a 14% value for R

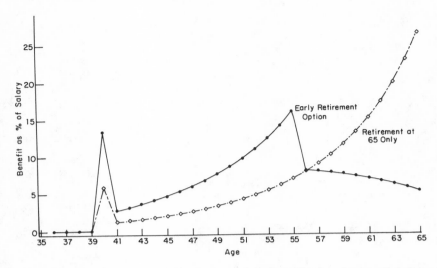

Fig. 3.4   Pension increments as a percentage of salary, by age, for plans
with an early retirement option versus retirement at 65. 6%
wage inflation, 3% real interest rate.

(a, 10) at cliff vesting. In addition there is no discontinuity at age 55 in the
latter profile. While these features of the actuarially fair profile are less
troubling for the spot market hypothesis, the very rapid rate of benefit
accrual between 55 and 65 presents other difficulties for this view of the
labor market. The merit schedule built into the nominal wage profile implies a quite limited growth in real wages of workers after age 55. If anything, this schedule appears to provide for too much growth in real wages
after 50. As described in the next section, cross-sectional profiles of earnings by age decline slightly after age 50 for virtually all classification of
workers by occupation and major industry. Since a 3% growth in real
wages due to economywide productivity growth is above historic averages, one might reasonably infer that real wage growth after age 55 is below 3%. The actuarially fair profile of figure 3.4, however, entails increases in total real pension remuneration of almost 20% of real wages
between ages 55 and 65. Needless to say, it is difficult to accept the spot
market implication that, in addition to productivity-induced real wage
growth, workers at age 65 are 20% more productive than they are at age
55. Thus the plan examined in figure 3.4 indicates that the difficulty in
reconciling pension accrual rates with a spot market is not simply the result of early retirement benefit provisions.

Figure 3.5 and figure 3.1 above demonstrate the sensitivity of the accrual profiles to assumptions about nominal wage growth and nominal
interest rates. Figure 3.5 repeats figure 3.4 under the assumption of a 10%
interest rate but no growth in wages by age. For the profile with the early

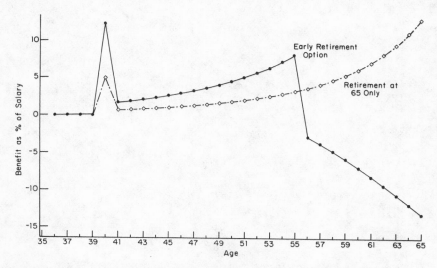

Fig. 3.5   Pension increments as a percentage of salary, by age, for plans with an early retirement option versus retirement at 65. 0% wage inflation, 10% real interest rate.

retirement option accrual rates after age 55 are substantially negative, approaching −15% of salary at age 65. With no early retirement option, on the other hand, accrual rates are always positive. The bottom profile in figure 3.1 incorporates 6% nominal wage growth but a 15% nominal interest rate. The intermediate profile in figure 3.1 is based on 6% wage growth and a 12% nominal interest rate. It yields increments at 65 that are approximately zero. These figures indicate that a considerable gap between nominal interest rates and wage growth rates is needed to produce negative accrual rates.

Finally, we illustrate in figure 3.6 the cost of job change with no early retirement option. It should be compared with figure 3.3. The plans represented in the two diagrams are the same except that in figure 3.6 the early retirement reduction schedule is assumed to be actuarially fair (or, that there is no early retirement option). Again, the top line of this graph shows the accrual rate under our plan for a person who starts work at age 30 (with 6% wage inflation and a 3% real interest rate). A person with one job change would accumulate benefits up to age 41 according to the top curve but then would accumulate benefits according to the curve labeled "age 41." Note that no benefits would be accumulated for the first 10 years. The difference in accumulated pension benefits at age 65 reflects both the difference in the areas under the two accrual paths and the interest rate used in accumulation of these flows. This difference could be very substantial and depends, of course, both on when job changes occur and how frequently they occur. It is important to note that the loss in accrued

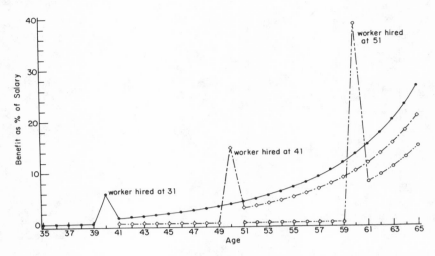

Fig. 3.6   Pension increments as a percentage of salary, by age, for an employee beginning at 31, 41, 51, with no early retirement option. Note: 6% wage inflation, 3% real interest rate.

benefits from job change in this example is not due solely to vesting; in figure 3.6, accrual in years after vesting occurs is larger for a worker remaining on the same job for 35 years than for a worker who changes jobs (literally pension plans). This lower accrual beyond vesting for later plan entrants results from the interaction of tenure and wage growth in earnings-based defined benefit pension formulas. To see the nature of this interaction, consider a plan with immediate vesting that pays 2% of final year's salary times years of service. For a worker experiencing positive wage growth who is employed for 30 years and retires at 60 the pension benefit is 2% of the age 60 salary times 30. If this same worker with the same wage growth were to change jobs each year, joining an identical plan, his benefit would equal 2% times the sum of the 30 annual salaries. Assuming positive wage growth, the pension benefit of the former worker, which is based on the age 60 salary, will exceed that of the latter worker whose benefit is primarily based on the lower earnings received in earlier years of his career.

3.2 Wage Rate Profiles

To calculate average pension benefit increments by industry-occupation group, for a given length of employment, we need estimates of age-wage profiles for each group. It is particularly important that assumptions about the wage profiles of older workers be as realistic as possible. Without lengthy longitudinal records on individuals, we have no completely satisfactory way of estimating age-wage profiles. The Retirement History Survey (RHS), however, does provide some longitudinal data for older workers.[5] We first discuss evidence from these data and then present estimated age-wage profiles based on the Current Population Survey (CPS) data. For older workers the two sources of data seem to provide roughly consistent evidence.

The age-wage profiles appropriate for determining pension accrual are clearly those pertaining to workers staying in the same firm. Thus tenure as well as age should be included in the analysis of earnings by age. Our accrual profiles also assume full-time employment. Hence, wage rates per unit of time is the appropriate earnings concept for our purposes. While conventionally computed age-earnings profiles sometimes show a downward trend for older workers, this appears due, in part, to a reduction in hours worked and in part to the mix of full-time and part-time workers in the sample.

3.2.1   Evidence from the Retirement History Survey

The RHS data are based on a sample of persons who were first surveyed in 1969 when they were between 58 and 63. These respondents were resurveyed every two years until 1979. Table 3.1 shows the means of hourly wages by age and year for persons who reported an hourly wage rate and who were not partially or fully retired in a given year. For a given calendar year, these data in general show little decline in wage rates at least through age 63 or 64. The number of observations per cell is fairly small since the cells only include older individuals who are still working. Possibly those whose wage rates would have fallen from one year to the next are less likely to be in the sample. Analogous calculations showing the median of annual salaries of persons who reported weekly, monthly, or annual salaries are presented in table 3.2. Here again, in the cross-section, there are relatively constant real salary levels through age 64 among persons who are not retired, although there seems to be some decline on average.

The accrual calculations require, however, nominal wage profiles. From both tables 3.1 and 3.2, it is clear that nominal wages of older workers increased rather rapidly over this period. A more precise indication of nominal increases is shown in table 3.3 for all persons who reported weekly, monthly, or annual salaries. The entry corresponding to age 58–60 and the year 1969–71 is the median salary increase between 1969 and 1971 over all persons who were 58 in 1969 and who reported salary figures in both 1969 and 1971. The other entries are calculated in an analogous manner. The table shows very substantial nominal increases over this period, on the order of 6% per year on average. (The entries pertain to a two-year interval.) Considering the average increments by age in the last column, there is

Table 3.1   **Means of Hourly Wages for Non-Self-Employed Males, by Age and Year**

Age	1969	1971	1973	1975	1977	1979	All Years
58	3.03 (134)						3.03 (134)
59	3.36 (159)						3.36 (159)
60	3.14 (155)	3.25 (154)					3.19 (309)
61	3.05 (130)	3.36 (149)					3.21 (279)
62	3.12 (125)	3.50 (134)	3.89 (107)				3.48 (366)
63	2.91 (93)	3.30 (115)	4.10 (103)				3.44 (311)
64		3.41 (74)	3.53 (80)	4.03 (61)			3.63 (215)
65		3.44 (44)	3.15 (34)	3.54 (41)			3.39 (119)
66			3.45 (24)	3.59 (24)	4.62 (18)		3.82 (66)
67			3.24 (21)	2.83 (13)	3.48 (22)		3.24 (56)
68				3.85 (14)	4.34 (14)	4.42 (8)	4.17 (36)
69				3.60 (6)	2.71 (9)	3.82 (7)	3.30 (22)
70					3.25 (10)	4.45 (7)	3.74 (17)
71					4.25 (7)	4.16 (4)	4.21 (11)
72						3.21 (7)	3.21 (7)
73						4.42 (2)	4.42 (2)

Source: Retirement History Survey. Excludes people who say they are partially or fully retired. The number of observations used to calculate the associated value is recorded in parentheses.

Table 3.2   **Medians of Annual Salary for Non-Self-Employed Males, by Age and Year**

Age	Year						All Years
	1969	1971	1973	1975	1977	1979	
58	7494 (666)						7494 (666)
59	7280 (733)						7280 (733)
60	7280 (683)	8372 (485)					7800 (1168)
61	7280 (690)	8100 (563)					7600 (1253)
62	7280 (591)	8216 (453)	9850 (322)				8008 (1366)
63	7225 (454)	8000 (413)	8800 (339)				7860 (1206)
64		8000 (403)	9100 (303)	10088 (246)			9000 (952)
65		7800 (179)	8200 (151)	9480 (146)			8320 (476)
66			8944 (110)	9200 (107)	11600 (76)		9663 (293)
67			8320 (91)	8942 (90)	11830 (56)		9048 (237)
68				9284 (70)	8541 (48)	6600 (18)	8998 (136)
69				8913 (54)	10089 (42)	4225 (8)	9360 (104)
70					7850 (30)	3750 (12)	6703 (42)
71					8525 (23)	4160 (10)	7380 (33)
72						3016 (13)	3016 (13)
73						7800 (9)	7800 (9)

Source: Retirement History Survey. Excludes people who say they are partially or fully retired. The number of observations used to calculate the associated value is recorded in parentheses.

Table 3.3   **Median Percentage Changes in Annual Salary for Non-Self-Employed Males, by Age and Year**

Age	Year					All Years
	1969–71	1971–73	1973–75	1975–77	1977–79	
58–60	13.0 (423)					13.0 (423)
59–61	12.5 (486)					12.5 (486)
60–62	12.5 (393)	12.6 (264)				12.5 (657)
61–63	11.7 (354)	11.0 (280)				11.1 (634)
62–64	11.3 (346)	11.7 (237)	13.3 (170)			11.5 (753)
63–65	10.4 (148)	11.1 (118)	11.1 (101)			11.1 (367)
64–66		12.9 (86)	12.1 (83)	10.5 (64)		12.2 (233)
65–67		9.5 (58)	12.5 (54)	11.4 (45)		10.8 (157)
66–68			10.8 (47)	12.8 (37)	12.9 (10)	11.8 (94)
67–69			6.4 (41)	10.1 (36)	6.2 (3)	8.3 (80)
68–70				10.6 (18)	29.8 (3)	13.3 (21)
69–71				12.5 (20)	17.5 (2)	12.5 (22)
70–72					13.1 (2)	13.1 (2)
71–73					15.4 (1)	15.4 (1)

Source: Retirement History Survey. Excludes people who say they are partially or fully retired. The number of observations used to calculate the associated value is recorded in parentheses.

some evidence that the increases declined somewhat with age. At least through 1977—after which our sample sizes are very small—it appears that salary increases for these older workers were in general keeping up with price increases. The percent increases in the Consumer Price Index (CPI) for the years 1969–77 were as shown in the unnumbered table on page 73.

Year	CPI
1969	6.1
1970	5.5
1971	3.4
1972	3.4
1973	8.8
1974	12.2
1975	7.0
1976	4.8
1977	6.8

In short, these data suggest substantial nominal wage increases for older workers, roughly consistent, on average, with overall inflation levels.

3.2.2 Wage-Tenure Profiles from the Current Population Survey

To estimate age-tenure profiles by industry and occupation group, we matched the May 1979 Supplement to the March 1979 CPS. The May Supplement provides tenure data, while the wage data come from the March tape. We were able to obtain the required wage, age, and tenure information for somewhat over 15,000 persons in the 24 industry-occupation groups distinguished in the LOB survey. Relevant cell sample sizes, however, were large enough to obtain "reasonable" estimates for only 16 groups, noted below.

After considerable experimentation with two-way tables showing average salary by age and tenure, we elected simply to obtain least-squares estimates of wage rates using the specification

(12) $$W = a_0 + a_1 A + a_2 A^2 + b_1 T + b_2 T^2 + cAT,$$

where W is the wage rate, A is age, and T is tenure. To estimate wage levels by age for a person who entered a firm at, for example, age 30 we calculated

(13) $$\hat{W} = \hat{a}_0 + \hat{a}_1 A + \hat{a}_2 A^2 + \hat{b}_1(A - 30) + \hat{b}_2(A - 30)^2 + \hat{c}(A)(A - 30),$$

for values of A between 30 and 65.

The estimated profiles for the total group, and by occupation over all industry groups, are presented in figure 3.7. These profiles are empirical counterparts of the "merit" scale used in the illustrative calculations in Section 3.1 above.

The cross-sectional age-earnings profile (13) for all groups combined increases by about 50% between age 30 and 52 when it reaches its maximum. Then it declines by about 10% over the next 13 years, or about .8% per year on average. Assuming a wage inflation rate of 6%, therefore, produces a nominal wage rate for older workers increasing at about 5%

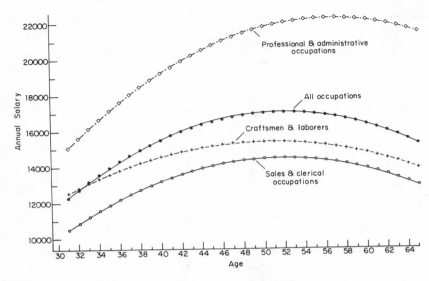

Fig. 3.7   Estimated real wage-tenure profiles by age

per year. For older workers this path of nominal wage growth seems to be in rough accord with the evidence from the Retirement History Survey.

In addition to the graphs of the cross-section wage profiles, summary indicators of their shapes are provided in table 3.4. It shows salary at age 30, maximum salary, the age of maximum salary, and salary at age 65, together with average percent increases between the end points and the maximum.

3.3   Accrual Rates from the BLS Level of Benefits Survey

The BLS–LOB (1979) establishments constitute a subsample of the 1979 National Survey of Professional, Administrative, Technical, and Clerical Pay. Based on the file's population weights, this subsample covers 17,965,282 private pension plan participants in the United States, which is slightly over half of all participants covered by private pensions. The subsample's universe consisted of all firms with over 100 employees with the exception of mining, construction, and retail trade establishments where the minimum firm size was 250 employees and service establishments where the minimum firm size was 50 employees. Sampled establishments were requested to report work schedules and information about 11 different types of fringe benefits. This information was provided for each of the three occupational groups. The BLS–LOB (1979) pension benefits tape consists of establishment records for each occupational group that detail features of pension benefit plans covering the particular occupational

Table 3.4   **Summary Statistics on Wage Profiles by Industry and Occupation Group**

Industry and Occupation	Salary at Age 30	Max Salary (Age)		Salary at Age 65	Average Percent Increase Age 30 to Maximum	Average Percent Decrease Maximum to Age 65
All	11848	17022	(52)	15216	2.0	−.8
All:						
Professional and administrative	14470	22232	(57)	21454	2.0	−.4
Sales and clerical	10112	14446	(52)	12890	1.9	−.8
Craftsmen and laborers	12228	15366	(51)	13866	1.2	−.7
Mining	18062	22676	(65)	22676	.7	−.0
Construction	15822	18036	(45)	13678	.9	−1.2
Manufacturing:						
Professional and administrative	16374	24634	(55)	23150	2.0	−.6
Sales and clerical	10670	14894	(56)	14380	1.5	−.4
Craftsmen and laborers	10960	14822	(52)	13294	1.6	−.8
Transportation:						
Professional and administrative	21466	25230	(65)	25230	.5	−.0
Sales and clerical	12284	16806	(48)	13128	2.0	−1.3
Craftsmen and laborers	13938	17630	(64)	17628	.8	−.0
Wholesale Trade	12644	18416	(48)	12908	2.5	−1.8
Retail Trade:						
Professional and administrative	11268	18844	(48)	12620	3.7	−1.9
Sales and clerical	8528	11932	(46)	7518	2.5	−1.9
Craftsmen and laborers	10974	13538	(49)	11816	1.2	−.8
Finance	12072	19552	(59)	19194	2.1	−.3
Services:						
Professional and administrative	13326	19246	(54)	17936	1.9	−.6
Sales and clerical	9230	10822	(54)	10514	.7	−.3
Craftsmen and laborers	11220	12810	(50)	11950	.7	−.4

Source: May 1979 Current Population Survey.

group in question. Unfortunately firm identifiers are intentionally excluded from the computer record; hence, it is impossible to reconstruct
the actual pension characteristics of the initial establishment. The data
can, however, be used to estimate industry-wide or occupation-wide values of pension variables.

In this section we examine accrual ratios for 1183 earnings-based defined benefit plans. Earnings-based plans account for approximately 80%
of BLS-designated usable plans from the survey and about 65% of plans
weighted by pension coverage.[6] Each of the 1183 plans stipulates cliff
vesting at 10 years, but the plans have different normal and early retirement ages. Other earnings-based plans with different vesting ages have accrual profiles similar to those that we shall describe, but for convenience
of exposition we have not included them in our analysis here. Of the 1183
plans, 508 are integrated with social security under an offset formula.

Table 3.5 presents weighted average accrual ratios for the 1183 plans by
early and normal retirement ages for workers hired at age 31. Our intermediate assumptions of 6% nominal wage growth and a 9% interest rate
are used in conjunction with the industry-occupation-age-earnings profiles discussed in Section 3.2. The spike at the age of vesting varies with
early retirement and normal retirement ages. It is 24% for plans with early
and normal retirement at 55. Among the plans with early retirement at 55
the vesting spike declines with the age of normal retirement, with a vesting
spike of approximately 12% for plans with normal retirement at 60 and a
spike of about 7% for plans with normal retirement at 65. For plans with
later early and normal retirement ages, the vesting spike is much smaller,
ranging from a little over 3% to about 5%.

A total of 356 plans have the same early and normal retirement ages,
that is, they do not permit early retirement. For example, there are 209
plans with both early and normal retirement at age 55. In this case, the accrual ratio is about 5% immediately after vesting and increases to about
15% by age 50. Between ages 50 and 55 the accrual ratio increases to almost 27%. A similar pattern is observed for the other plans in which the
normal and early retirement ages are the same, but the accrual ratios just
after vesting are no more than 1% in these cases. It may be noted that
these plans correspond to our earlier description of plans with no early retirement provision, as depicted, for example, in figure 3.4. We have not
calculated accrual ratios after the age of normal retirement, but it appears
that accrual after the normal retirement age in most cases is very small and
in some cases significantly negative. Hence, there appears to be a very
substantial discontinuous drop in the rate of pension accrual after the
normal retirement age for a significant fraction of private pension plans.
In subsequent work we shall describe in detail the accrual rates of plans
after the age of normal retirement.

Plans with early retirement typically exhibit a rather slow increase in accrual ratios after vesting until a few years before the age of early retire-

Table 3.5   **Weighted Average Accrual Rates for Percentage of Earnings Plans with 10-Year Cliff Vesting, by Early (E) and Normal (N) Retirement Age**
(N = Number of Plans)

Age	E = 55, N = 55 (N = 209)	E = 55, N = 60 (N = 152)	E = 55, N = 65 (N = 528)	E = 60, N = 60 (N = 78)	E = 60, N = 65 (N = 53)	E = 62, N = 62 (N = 19)	E = 62, N = 65 (N = 8)	E = 65, N = 65 (N = 50)
40	.239	.115	.069	.033	.047	.036	.054	.037
41	.046	.024	.013	.007	.010	.016	.009	.010
42	.052	.027	.016	.008	.010	.017	.010	.011
43	.059	.031	.108	.009	.013	.020	.011	.013
44	.067	.036	.020	.011	.015	.031	.013	.014
45	.077	.041	.023	.013	.017	.037	.014	.016
46	.087	.047	.026	.016	.019	.042	.015	.018
47	.099	.055	.031	.027	.022	.048	.017	.021
48	.113	.063	.034	.038	.025	.055	.019	.024
49	.128	.071	.040	.054	.029	.062	.021	.028
50	.145	.086	.046	.063	.034	.070	.023	.032
51	.163	.085	.042	.081	.040	.079	.026	.033
52	.184	.100	.062	.087	.051	.081	.029	.044
53	.209	.114	.072	.101	.060	.103	.032	.051
54	.235	.130	.083	.112	.068	.115	.036	.056
55	.269	.151	.097	.143	.083	.130	.039	.066
56		.110	.070	.163	.095	.146	.036	.069
57		.116	.074	.185	.107	.165	.039	.078
58		.120	.079	.215	.128	.188	.044	.091
59		.120	.081	.232	.147	.212	.049	.107
60		.215	.083	.259	.168	.245	.054	.121
61			.074		.119	.223	.060	.131
62			.070		.121	.252	.066	.148
63			.063		.122		.023	.167
64			.060		.123		.019	.190
65			.052		.121		.012	.216

Note: Plans with early or normal retirement supplements are excluded.

ment. There is often a sharp drop in the accrual ratio at that age, with either limited increases or gradual declines in accrual ratios thereafter. For example, of the 528 plans with early retirement at 55 and normal retirement at 65 the accrual ratio reaches about 10% at age 55 and then drops by about 30% to 7% at age 56. By age 65 the accrual ratio has fallen to 5%. The pattern exhibited by these plans is similar to the one described in figure 3.4 for a typical plan with a normal retirement provision.

A comparison of plans with and without a social security offset is presented in table 3.6, for plans with early retirement at 55 and normal retirement at 55, 62, or 65. There are two major differences in these plans: first, the within-group weighted average spike at vesting is very substantial for

Table 3.6 Weighted Average Accrual Rates for Percentage of Earnings Plans with 10-Year Cliff Vesting, and Early Retirement at Age 55, by Normal Retirement Age and Social Security Offset (N = Number of Plans)

Age	Normal Retirement at 55		Normal Retirement at 62		Normal Retirement at 65	
	Without Offset (N = 178)	With Offset (N = 31)	Without Offset (N = 124)	With Offset (N = 118)	Without Offset (N = 261)	With Offset (N = 267)
40	.258	.084	.174	.024	.120	.016
41	.050	.014	.036	.009	.022	.004
42	.057	.017	.041	.012	.025	.005
43	.064	.021	.046	.015	.029	.006
44	.072	.025	.052	.019	.033	.008
45	.082	.031	.066	.024	.037	.010
46	.093	.042	.067	.027	.040	.011
47	.105	.054	.077	.035	.048	.014
48	.119	.063	.089	.041	.051	.017
49	.134	.078	.103	.050	.058	.020
50	.151	.092	.115	.065	.065	.026
51	.171	.097	.131	.078	.072	.031
52	.193	.116	.146	.096	.080	.042
53	.218	.137	.169	.113	.090	.053
54	.246	.162	.190	.132	.101	.064
55	.278	.196	.218	.156	.115	.078
56			.099	.129	.080	.061
57			.101	.128	.080	.068
58			.111	.143	.079	.079
59			.107	.147	.077	.085
60			.100	.148	.073	.094
61			.096	.105	.076	.071
62			.090	.095	.066	.074
63					.054	.073
64					.047	.074
65					.032	.073

Note: Plans with early or normal retirement supplements are excluded.

plans without social security offset, ranging from 12% to 26% and is very small for plans with a social security offset with the exception of plans with normal retirement at age 55. In this case the average spike at vesting is about 8%. Second, the discontinuity in accrual ratios at the age of early retirement is much larger for plans without a social security offset than for plans with an offset. For example, among plans with normal retirement at age 62, there is a 55% drop in the accrual ratio between ages 55 and 56, while for plans with a social security offset the drop is about 17%.

The smaller reduction in the accrual ratio at age 55 for these social security offset plans appears to be explained as follows. Because workers experience faster wage growth prior to their mid-fifties, their social security Primary Insurance Amount, a key determinant of the benefit offset, grows at a faster rate for younger workers. This factor plus the ceilings on the offset amount established by many of these plans means that social security offsets reduce accrual ratios prior to a worker's mid-fifties by a greater percentage than after his or her mid-fifties. As a consequence, the reduction in the accrual ratio at age 55 is proportionally smaller in offset plans than in nonoffset plans.

To demonstrate the wide variation among plans with the same early and normal retirement ages, we have reproduced in table 3.7 the accrual ratios for plans with normal retirement at 55 and early retirement at 65, together with the minimum and maximum accruals among these plans for each age. Almost half of the plans have these early and normal retirement ages.

Table 3.7   **Weighted Average and Minimum and Maximum Accrual Rates for Percentage of Earnings Plans, with 10-Year Cliff Vesting with Early Retirement at 55 and Normal Retirement at 65**

Age	Average	Minimum	Maximum
40	.069	.000	.388
41	.013	−.025	.072
42	.016	−.025	.081
43	.018	−.027	.092
44	.020	−.026	.104
45	.023	−.079	.118
46	.026	−.028	.133
47	.031	−.025	.164
48	.034	−.020	.169
49	.040	−.021	.191
50	.046	−.011	.215
51	.052	−.020	.243
52	.062	−.018	.274
53	.072	−.015	.309
54	.083	−.014	.348
55	*.097*	*−.005*	*.409*
56	.071	−.065	.431
57	.074	−.063	.355
58	.079	−.050	.252
59	.081	−.046	.309
60	.083	−.064	.351
61	.074	−.157	.347
62	.070	−.155	.334
63	.063	−.194	.320
64	.060	−.221	.471
65	.052	−.326	.350

Note: Plans with early or normal retirement supplements are excluded.

The average accrual ratios, as noted above, rise to about 10% by the age of early retirement and then fall to about 5% by the age of normal retirement at 65. But there is a very large variation among the plans. In particular, a large number of plans exhibit negative rates of pension accrual after the age of early retirement, while others have much higher accrual ratios than the average. For example, at 65 the accrual ratios range from a low of a negative 33% to a high of about 35%. These differences highlight the potential importance of joint consideration of wage rates and pension accruals, a task that we shall pursue in the future if appropriate data can be obtained.

Table 3.8 shows how average accrual ratios vary across industries. An important difference among the five industry groups is the proportion with specific early and normal retirement ages. Approximately 60% of plans in manufacturing have early retirement at 55 and normal retirement at 65, while in retail trade more than 90% are in this group. Over 60% of plans in manufacturing, on the other hand, have early retirement as well as normal retirement at 55. Very few plans in retail trade, finance, or services have normal retirement at 55.

Plans with early and normal retirement at 55 have approximately the same weighted average accrual patterns in each of the industry groups, with a spike at vesting close to 25% and the accrual ratio at 55 ranging between 20% and 27%. The typical plan with normal retirement at age 62 exhibits a substantial drop in the accrual ratio at the early retirement age of 55. The drop is about 35% in manufacturing and in finance and over 50% in transportation.

Plans with normal retirement at 65 typically exhibit an accrual pattern that is much flatter than the pattern exhibited by the other plans in each industry. These plans exhibit a drop in the accrual ratio at the age of early retirement that ranges from a low of 14% in services to a high of 35% in retail trade. The average accrual rate at 65 is -6% in retail trade and $+11\%$ in finance. It is approximately 6% in services and transportation and 7% in manufacturing.

Early and normal retirement supplements lead to widely varying accrual patterns, and we have not tried to summarize them here. We will, however, present details of these plans in a subsequent paper. We shall also describe in future work the accrual pattern of flat rate plans with benefits based only on years of service. Approximately 35% of the BLS–LOB pension plans weighted by coverage are of this type. They typically exhibit negative accrual ratios after the age of early retirement.

Job change can reduce pension benefits substantially. For 749 plans we calculated accrued benefits at age 65 for persons hired at 31, 41, and 51. In these calculations, we assume that a person does not become vested in another plan prior to joining the firm. For each plan we calculate accrued benefits, using the associated industry-occupation wage profiles, for each of the hiring ages. The comparison of benefits of persons hired at 31 with

Table 3.8   Weighted Average Accrual Rates for Percentage of Earnings Plans with 10-Year Cliff Vesting, by Industry and by Early (E) and Normal (N) Retirement Ages (N = Number of Plans)

Age	Manufacturing E=55, N=55 (N=49)	E=55, N=62 (N=137)	E=55, N=65 (N=264)	Transportation E=55, N=55 (N=145)	E=55, N=62 (N=46)	E=55, N=65 (N=37)	Retail Trade E=55, N=55 (N=2)	E=55, N=62 (N=6)	E=55, N=65 (N=90)	Finance E=55, N=55 (N=5)	E=55, N=62 (N=25)	E=55, N=65 (N=77)	Services E=55, N=55 (N=5)	E=55, N=62 (N=5)	E=55, N=65 (N=33)
40	.220	.082	.056	.252	.156	.120	.021	.001	.080	.102	.061	.071	.266	.161	.068
41	.040	.018	.011	.049	.035	.021	.020	.001	.014	.032	.017	.016	.049	.030	.013
42	.045	.022	.013	.056	.040	.024	.019	.001	.016	.039	.020	.019	.055	.033	.015
43	.052	.025	.015	.063	.045	.027	.018	.001	.018	.046	.023	.022	.063	.038	.017
44	.059	.030	.017	.072	.051	.030	.017	.002	.019	.055	.028	.025	.071	.042	.020
45	.067	.036	.020	.082	.073	.034	.015	.002	.021	.065	.032	.029	.080	.048	.023
46	.078	.040	.023	.092	.068	.035	.016	.002	.024	.077	.038	.032	.090	.054	.027
47	.091	.048	.027	.105	.077	.040	.016	.003	.026	.091	.044	.037	.102	.061	.030
48	.102	.058	.030	.118	.087	.045	.016	.003	.029	.106	.052	.043	.115	.069	.035
49	.116	.070	.036	.133	.099	.051	.094	.007	.032	.121	.063	.049	.129	.078	.041
50	.132	.078	.042	.151	.112	.059	.112	.015	.035	.144	.099	.057	.146	.088	.048
51	.150	.090	.047	.171	.130	.067	.127	.020	.039	.103	.115	.065	.164	.099	.065
52	.169	.101	.053	.193	.149	.080	.142	.022	.043	.148	.148	.090	.185	.112	.065
53	.192	.117	.063	.218	.178	.098	.165	.025	.047	.170	.168	.102	.209	.127	.076
54	.218	.133	.074	.246	.203	.111	.174	.081	.050	.199	.192	.120	.235	.143	.087
55	.250	.157	.088	.279	.230	.127	.198	.099	.056	.232	.219	.143	.266	.161	.098
56		.102	.069		.105	.094		.089	.035		.139	.094		.129	.084
57		.102	.074		.115	.098		.086	.034		.139	.098		.127	.089
58		.107	.081		.144	.104		.116	.028		.145	.106		.124	.102
59		.107	.085		.146	.109		.110	.020		.144	.112		.119	.110

Table 3.8 (continued)

Age	Manufacturing			Transportation			Retail Trade			Finance			Services		
	E=55, N=55 (N=49)	E=55, N=62 (N=137)	E=55, N=65 (N=264)	E=55, N=55 (N=145)	E=55, N=62 (N=46)	E=55, N=65 (N=37)	E=55, N=55 (N=2)	E=55, N=62 (N=6)	E=55, N=65 (N=90)	E=55, N=55 (N=5)	E=55, N=62 (N=25)	E=55, N=65 (N=77)	E=55, N=55 (N=5)	E=55, N=62 (N=5)	E=55, N=65 (N=33)
60		.103	.087		.147	.114		.099	.019		.140	.114		.113	.114
61		.083	.079		.119	.098		.072	.014		.076	.108		.144	.083
62		.075	.079		.106	.093		.047	.004		.067	.109		.178	.077
63			.077			.070			−.015			.110			.071
64			.076			.069			−.025			.113			.066
65			.074			.066			−.057			.110			.057

Note: Plans with early or normal retirement supplements are excluded.

those hired at 41 and 51 is made in two ways. The first is to sum age 65 accrued benefits over all plans for each age of hire and calculate the ratio of the sum of the benefits if persons were hired at 41 (or 51) to the sum if the same persons were hired at 31. The second comparison is the average of the ratios calculated for each plan, with each ratio weighted by the number of persons covered by the plan. The results are shown in table 3.9.

Table 3.9   **Accrued Benefits at Age 65 for Persons Hired at Aged 41 and 51, as Percentage of the Benefits of Persons Hired at Age 31**

Plans Included and Age When Hired (N = Number of Plans)	Ratio of the Sum of Benefits	Weighted Average of the Plan Ratios
All plans (N = 749)		
Hired at 41	.82	.89
Hired at 51	.54	.62
Plans without social security offset (N = 488)		
Hired at 41	—	.79
Hired at 51	—	.50
Plans with social security offset (N = 261)		
Hired at 41	—	.86
Hired at 51	—	.52
Mining (N = 20)		
Hired at 41	.83	—
Hired at 51	.49	—
Construction (N = 7)		
Hired at 41	.79	—
Hired at 51	.48	—
Manufacturing (N = 346)		
Hired at 41	.80	—
Hired at 51	.50	—
Transportation (N = 86)		
Hired at 41	.95	—
Hired at 51	.78	—
Wholesale trade (N = 25)		
Hired at 41	.83	—
Hired at 51	.57	—
Retail trade (N = 127)		
Hired at 41	.65	—
Hired at 51	.31	—
Finance (N = 100)		
Hired at 41	.84	—
Hired at 51	.50	—
Services (N = 38)		
Hired at 41	.90	—
Hired at 51	.57	—

The aggregate benefits of persons hired at 51 are only about 50% of the benefits of those hired at 31. Persons hired at 41 would accumulate about 80% of the benefits of persons hired at 31. There is little difference between plans with and without a social security offset, based on the weighted average of plan ratios. Variation among occupations is not striking, but there is substantial variation across industries. Benefits if hired at 51 range from only 31% of the benefits if hired at 31 in retail trade to 78% in manufacturing. The ratio if hired at 41 ranges from 65% in retail trade to 95% in transportation.

Thus job change can impose a very large cost in pension benefits. While these calculations do not incorporate vesting on one job before changing to another, we believe that such calculations—more in line with the illustrations in Section 3.1—would not substantially alter the order of magnitude of the benefit losses. Because we used accrued benefits at age 65, the calculations also incorporate some negative accruals after the age of early retirement. It may be more appropriate to use maximum accrued benefits for each age of hire.

3.4 Concluding Comments

In our view the magnitude, patterns, and variations in pension accrual ratios are strikingly at odds with the view of spot clearing in labor markets. While market clearing in longer-term contracts seems the only equilibrium theory consistent with these findings, it strains our credulity to ascribe optimizing behavior to the choice of pension accrual profiles. It seems much more likely that employees and employers rough tune rather than fine tune in their choice of pension plans, if there is any tuning whatsoever.

In our future research we intend to examine the ratio of accrued vested benefits to straight wages after the age of normal retirement. Preliminary evidence suggests very sizable potential work disincentives after the normal retirement age because of a sharp decline in pension benefit accrual. We will also focus on the particular plan features having the greatest effect on accrual profiles. Plans with non-earnings-related benefit formulas as well as plans with early and normal retirement supplemental benefits will also be studied. Given the appropriate data, we wish to investigate the relationship between individual earnings profiles and associated pension plans. In particular, we would like to know the extent to which wages adjust in accordance with pension plan provisions. A second important issue is the extent to which pension accrual patterns affect retirement decisions as well as turnover prior to vesting, early retirement, and normal retirement.

Notes

1. This assumes no other explicit or implicit fringe benefits.
2. We are hopeful that the Department of Labor's extremely valuable survey of Private Pension Benefit Amounts will be released in the near future.
3. Bulow (1979) appears to be the first discussion of these discontinuities. Lazear (1981, 1983) presents empirical analysis of this issue.
4. The BLS–LOB survey contains 3248 plans of which the BLS labeled 2492 as "usable." Our master sample consists of 2343 of these 2492 plans, although this study only examines 1183 plans.
5. We make no use here of the truncated earnings data contained in the RHS social security earnings records.
6. The 1183 earnings-based plans with cliff vesting account for 51% of plans weighted by pension coverage.

Comment   Zvi Bodie

Laurence Kotlikoff and David Wise try to accomplish two goals in their paper. The first is to describe the age-tenure profiles of pension benefit accruals over a worker's career implied by the provisions of actual defined benefit plans, and the second is to test whether those profiles are consistent with a "spot market" theory of labor contracting. According to this theory the total compensation—wages plus the present value of pension benefits—paid to a worker in each year of employment must equal the expected value of his marginal product in that same year. In the context of this theory, the present value of pension benefits earned through continued service during any year must be evaluated as if the worker's employment were to be terminated at year's end.

If wages follow a smooth trajectory over a worker's career, then the stipulations of a typical defined benefit plan with "cliff" vesting and early retirement benefits that are better than actuarially fair imply that the profile of earned pension increments will have two spikes in it, one in the year vesting occurs and one at the age of early retirement. Because Kotlikoff and Wise assumed that the age-tenure profiles of both wages and the unobservable marginal product are smooth, they interpret these spikes as strong evidence against the spot market theory.

I want to begin my critical comments by saying that I think Kotlikoff and Wise are to be congratulated for undertaking the enormous task of programming the stipulations of these plans and systematically analyzing

Zvi Bodie is professor of economics and finance at Boston University's School of Management and research associate, National Bureau of Economic Research.

them. Defined benefit plans are extremely complicated because there are so many dimensions along which they can differ, and I think the Kotlikoff-Wise paper helps us to understand the quantitative impact of these differences.

At the same time I have some reservations and questions about what they have done. My first three comments relate to the purely descriptive aspects of their work, while my last is directed at their tests of the spot market theory.

First, they have assumed for all 522 plans in their sample that if a worker terminates employment prior to the age of early retirement he is still entitled to early retirement benefits. I believe that this is not true for many, if not most, plans. This feature makes a big difference for the profile of pension increments. If a plan provides early retirement benefits only to participants who remain with the firm until early retirement age, then relative to the profiles shown by Kotlikoff and Wise in their figure 3.1, for example, (1) the spike at vesting (age 40) is smaller; (2) the spike at early retirement age (55) is much larger; and (3) the whole profile of pension increments up to age 54 is much lower.

Second, in generating their nominal wage trajectories Kotlikoff and Wise ignore secular growth in real wages that might arise from trend growth in labor productivity. In effect the pension increment profiles they show all implicitly assume that this growth rate is zero. While this may have been true for many sectors of the United States economy in the decade of the 1970s, it certainly was not true before then, and even if Kotlikoff and Wise think zero the most likely number, I believe it is still worth showing the effect of a positive growth rate.

Third, I find one aspect of the results reported in table 3.5 absolutely mystifying. The next to the last column in that table presents the minimum accrual rates among the plans in the sample. How can these be negative at all ages? I can understand their turning negative for some plans after the age of early retirement, but not earlier.

My remaining comments deal with Kotlikoff and Wise's methodology for testing the spot labor market theory. While I agree that the spikes in the profile of pension benefit accruals, particularly the one at early retirement age, are difficult to explain in the context of a strict spot market theory, I do not think that they have provided a real test of that theory in its less strict and perhaps more credible form.

Granting their assumption that the age-tenure profile of marginal product of labor is smooth, a real test of the theory would compare the wage and total compensation profiles of workers in firms with defined benefit pension plans to those of workers without such plans. Lacking appropriate data to perform such a comparison, Kotlikoff and Wise have simply assumed a smooth wage profile for workers with such plans (they fit a quadratic functional form to the wage data, thus guaranteeing smoothness) and therefore, given the vesting and early retirement provisions, the pension accrual and the total compensation profiles must exhibit spikes. A proper test of the spot market theory would also require information on the age-tenure profile of other forms of labor compensation in addition to wages and pension benefits.

Kotlikoff and Wise are aware of the shortcomings of their data set for testing the spot market theory, and they are attempting to get data on wage and benefit profiles for workers controlling for the characteristics of the pension plan they participate in. They also plan to explore further the disincentives to job change turnover implicit in the stipulations of the plans in their current data set. David Ellwood in his table 2.9 presents some illustrative calculations of the present value of lost benefits if a worker changes jobs, and they appear quite significant under reasonable assumptions about the rate of inflation.

In conclusion I again congratulate David Ellwood and Kotlikoff and Wise for a difficult job done well.

References

Bulow, J. 1979. Analysis of pension funding under ERISA. NBER Working Paper no. 402.

Lazear, E.P. 1981. Severance pay, pensions, mobility, and the efficiency of work incentives. Mimeographed. University of Chicago.

———. 1983. Pensions as severance pay. In *Financial aspects of the United States pension system,* ed. Z. Bodie and J. B. Shoven. Chicago: University of Chicago Press (for NBER).

Kotlikoff, L.J., and Smith, D.E. 1983. *Pensions in the American economy.* Chicago: University of Chicago Press (for NBER).

4   Unions, Pensions, and Union Pension Funds

Richard B. Freeman

Pension plans have long been a concern of organized labor. Some of the earliest pension plans for blue-collar workers were originated by unions.[1] Following the 1949 *Inland Steel* decision by the Supreme Court, pensions became a mandatory bargaining topic and the subject of nearly all collective negotiations.[2] Some 30 years later union concerns with pensions expanded from issues relating to worker benefits to the use of pension fund money in the capital market, raising new economic and legal questions relating to union economic power.

This paper examines what unions do to pensions and pension plans in the context of the "two faces" model of unionism, which treats unions as institutions of monopoly power and of collective voice. It argues that the effects of unionism on pensions are better understood by this model than by the simple monopoly perspective that permeates much economic thinking about unions. Section 4.1 sketches out the implications of union monopoly power and of union voice on pensions. Section 4.2 presents a detailed analysis of the impact of unionism on the provision of pension plans, using data from both establishment and worker surveys. It shows that, other factors held fixed, unionism has a significant and sizable effect on the probability that blue-collar workers are covered by pension plans and that unionization also alters the factors determining coverage. Section 4.3 contrasts the provisions of union and nonunion pension plans. Section 4.4 shows how union pension plans alter the age-earnings profile of union workers and thus estimates how unionism affects the earnings of workers of different ages. Section 4.5 explores the recent efforts of unions to direct pension fund investments away from nonunion firms into pro-

Richard B. Freeman is professor of economics at Harvard University, the Fairchild Scholar at the California Institute of Technology, and research associate, National Bureau of Economic Research.

jects beneficial to unionized workers. The paper concludes with a brief summary. The Appendix describes in detail the various data sets used in the analysis.

4.1 What Unions Should Do to Pensions

The potential impact of unionism on the provision of pensions can be decomposed into two separate effects: the effect of unionism on pension spending that results from union monopoly power raising costs of labor, and the effect of unionism on the pension share of a given compensation package. Formally, let p = expenditures on pensions per hour, c = total compensation per hour, x = diverse other factors that affect pensions, and u = unionism.

Then, using standard regression formulas, the impact of unionism is

$$(1) \qquad bpu \cdot x = bpu \cdot cx + bcu \cdot x \; bpc \cdot ux,$$

where $bpu \cdot x$ = total effect of unionism on pensions (holding fixed controls x), $bpu \cdot cx$ = effect of unionism on the pension share of labor cost (since c is fixed), $bcu \cdot x$ = effect of unionism on total compensation, and $bpc \cdot ux$ = effect of compensation on pensions, holding unionism fixed.

Differentiating between the union impact on the *share* of compensation going to pensions *(bpu · cx)* and the impact on the level of compensation *(bcu · x)* and through it on demand for pensions *(bpc · ux)* is important because the forces that determine the pension share are likely to differ from those determining total compensation and its associated pension spending. Whereas the impact of unionism on total compensation is readily analyzable in the context of the standard monopoly "face" of unionism in which union market power is used to raise pecuniary rewards to workers, the impact of unionism on the pension share is not so readily explicable. An increase in spending on pensions with total compensation fixed necessarily means a decrease in spending on wages or other fringes. A simple monopoly model does not tell us whether a union would prefer pensions to wages, or vice versa. To understand the preferences of unions for one or the other requires analysis of the "voice" face of the institution and the factors that might lead a collective democratic organization to be more (or less) willing than workers in a competitive setting to forgo dollars of wages for pension benefits.

4.1.1 The Voice Model

In a world in which some workers are more or less permanently attached to firms while others are movable, there are good reasons to expect the political nature of unions to lead to greater preferences for pensions than would be expressed by workers in a competitive market. The most important reason is that in general the union will give greater weight to the preferences of the older, relatively permanent employee relative to those of younger, more mobile one than will a competitive market in which the desires of the marginal employee set the compensation package. In the context of a median voter model, the union would represent the tastes of the median worker as opposed to the marginal worker. If older, presumably less mobile workers have greater desires for pensions, the demand for pensions will then be greater under collective than individual bargaining. Hence, firms that engage in collective bargaining are likely to allot a greater share of compensation to pension benefits.

Formally, I represent the postulated differential attachment of workers to firms by an upward-sloping supply schedule dependent on wages and pensions:

(2) $$L(W, P), \; L_W > 0, \; L_P > 0,$$

where L = the number of workers supplied to the firm. $L_W(L_P)$ is the partial derivative of L with respect to $W(P)$.

The inverse function of (2), relating wages to pensions and employment, defines the supply price of pensions:

(3) $$W, (P, L), \; W_P < 0, \; W_L < 0.$$

Cost minimization by the firm faced with this supply price requires, for any given L, an interior solution P^* such that a dollar of pensions reduces the marginal wage cost of labor by one dollar:[3]

(4) $$W_P(P^*, L) = -1.$$

The firm will provide pensions when at the optimal value P^* the reduction in wages covers variable costs and the fixed cost (C) of instituting the program:

(5) $$L[W(0, L) - W(P_i^*, L)] \geq P_i^* L + C,$$

where $W(0,L)$ is the wage paid in the absence of pension and $W(0,L) - W(P_i^*,L)$ is the savings of wages from introducing pensions. According to equation (4), expenditures on pensions in a nonunion setting depend on the marginal evaluation of pensions by the marginal (L^{th}) worker, $W_P(P, L)$. According to equation (5) initiation of a particular benefit depends on the change in wages $W(0, L) - W(P_i^*, L)$ exclusive of any potential inframarginal "worker surplus."

By contrast, the supply price set by the union will depend on the operation of the union as a political entity and the resultant union maximand. In this paper I consider two schematic models of union behavior: a median voter model and an optimizing cartel model. Under both models, and reasonable mixtures or variants thereof, it can be demonstrated that worker demand for pensions will be higher under unionism.

Consider first the case in which the union seeks to maximize the preference function of the median worker. If all workers are ordered from zero to L in terms of greatest to least attachment to the firm, the value of pensions to workers will be $W(P, L/2)$.[4] Cost minimization by the firm leads to the interior solution, P^m, that satisfies

(6) $$W(P^m, L/2) = -1$$

and to the condition for introducing the pension, P, of

(7) $$L[W(0,L/2) - W(P, L/2)] > LP_i^m + C.$$

If, as assumed, marginal workers have less desire for pensions than inframarginal workers, $W_P(P, L/2) < W_P(P, L)$. As a consequence, $P^m > P^*$ and the union firm will be more likely to introduce pensions than the nonunion firm.

As an alternative, consider the behavior of a union that, for reasons of logrolling and internal redistribution of benefits among members, operates like an optimizing cartel.[5] Such a union will be assumed to maximize total worker surplus, defined as the area above the supply curve:

(8) $$LW(P, L) - \int_0^L W(P, X)dX.$$

Maximization requires an interior solution, P^C, that satisfies

(9) $$W_P(P^C, L) - 1/L \int_0^L W_P(P^C, X)dX = 0,$$

where $1/L \int_0^L W_P(P^C, X)$ is the average value of the pension and the condition for providing it is

(10) $$1/L \int_0^L W(P_i, X)dX > P_i^C + C/L.$$

When the average value is greater (in absolute value) than the marginal value, P^C will exceed P^*. When the "average surplus," $1/L \int_0^L W(P_i, X)dX$, exceeds the saving in wages $W(0, L) - W(P_i, L)$, the union firm will be more likely than the nonunion firm to initiate particular programs. Both of these conditions hold when $W_{PL} < 0$, that is, when, as postulated, marginal workers have less desire for pensions than inframarginal workers.

Although both the median voter and optimal cartel models represent polar cases, which ignore numerous complexities of union behavior, they shed light on the difference between the demand for pensions under collective and individual bargaining. The prediction of greater allocation of funds to pensions under unionism does not depend on the precise model of union behavior but rather on the broad principle that, as political institutions, unions are likely to weigh more heavily than will nonunion firms the preferences of inframarginal workers who tend to be especially desirous of pensions.

4.1.2   Additional Routes of the Union Effect

Trade unionism is likely to raise demand for pensions in several other ways as well. First, by increasing the length of the attachment between workers and firms (raising job tenure and lowering quit rates) unionism will increase the likelihood that workers will receive pensions. As a result, the value to workers will be greater under unionism, raising the willingness of workers to forgo wages to obtain these pensions (Freeman 1980).

Second, in sectors of the economy in which workers are attached to occupations rather than employers (e.g., construction), or in which firms are relatively small (trucking), unions provide the type of large permanent market institution needed to operate most pension programs. Without unions (or some comparable structure) the probability that workers would receive deferred benefits would be too small and the employer's start-up costs too high for most benefits to be economically sensible. Multi-employer programs, of the type initiated by unions in the aforementioned industries, are needed, with portability across employers and the size to reduce average set-up costs.

Third, as argued by Freeman (1976), Hirschman (1976), and Nelson (1976), unions may elicit more accurate information about workers' preferences than can be gained from individual bargaining, which may also lead to greater provisions of pensions. Conceptually, the adversary relation between employers and employees—the fact that the level as well as allocation of the compensation package is at stake—argues for circumspection by workers in providing their employer with information about their preferences. If employers had complete knowledge of employee preference functions, they would seek to extract all of the worker surplus, striking a bargain that would leave workers at their minimum acceptance point. This provides a motivation for nonunion employees to withhold information about preferences. As the agent of workers, on the other hand, unions should obtain a more accurate revelation of preferences through their internal process of bargaining over the pay package that will be acceptable to the majority of members; in this way, unions may play an especially important role in eliciting employees' desire for pensions.

Fourth, the complexities involved in evaluating the costs and prospective benefits of pensions may make workers more willing to "buy" them when they have a specialized agent, like a union, evaluating and monitoring employer claims and programs. Significant investments in knowledge that lie beyond the purview of individual workers are needed to judge the true cost and future benefits of alternative compensation packages. Union lawyers, actuaries, and related experts are one institutional mechanism by which workers can obtain the expertise to bargain over these diverse benefits.

4.1.3   Effects on Provisions of Pension Plans

In addition to influencing whether or not a firm's workers have a pension plan, unionism is likely to affect the provisions of plans: the way workers receive pensions, the amount of vesting and eligibility requirements, the requirements on firms to fund plans. Potential differences in the provisions of union and nonunion pension plans provide important tests of the role of collective voice and monopoly factors in the impact of unions on pensions. In the framework of a simple monopoly model where unions try to obtain " more and more" of all benefits, one could expect the provisions of union pension plans to be more "liberal" than those of nonunion pension plans in such areas as eligibility, vesting, and related rules. In the framework of a more complex "voice" model under which older, more senior workers have a greater say in what unions do, one expects the opposite: benefit provisions tilted in favor of more senior employees. One further expects union pension plans to be more income redistributive than nonunion plans, making pensions less dependent on earnings and more on seniority. Indeed, one gets an entire set of testable predictions about pension provisions under unionism by comparing the provisions desired by the "median" worker with those desired by the marginal worker whose preferences determine competitive contracts (see sec. 2.4).

4.2   Empirical Analysis: Provisions of Pensions

The first and most fundamental question is whether unions do, indeed, increase firm expenditures on pensions: Is there a union pension effect, and if there is, how does it compare to the union impact on wages?

To answer these questions I have analyzed five surveys that contain information on unionism, pensions, and related other economic factors likely to influence pensions. One—the Expenditures for Employee Compensation survey of the Bureau of Labor Statistics—is an establishment survey that reports whether an establishment has a pension plan and the amount of employer contributions put into the plan. Three of the others surveyed individual workers to discover whether they are covered by pensions. The last survey, of pension plans, contains information on the years the plan has existed, providing a different picture of the union impact by dating the creation of the plan. While none of the surveys is perfect, with the establishment data lacking information on the personal characteristics of workers and the individual surveys lacking information on employer spending, together they present a fairly comprehensive and uniform picture of the union impact on pensions.

Table 4.1 presents the basic results of my analysis of these various surveys. Column 1 gives the mean value of the pension variable in each survey; column 2 gives the coefficient and standard error on unionism in the pension equation; column 3 gives the coefficient and standard error on log wage in the same equation. The regressions examine four dependent variables: cents per hour spent on pensions; provision of a pension plan; cents per hour spent for those having a plan; and the number of years the plan has been in operation. All of the equations are estimated by ordinary least squares; experiments with more sophisticated techniques yield comparable findings. All of the calculations control for the wages paid workers, industry of employment, occupation, and size of establishment where available; the analyses of individual workers also control for the demographic features of the workers.

Table 4.1   Estimates of the Effect of Collective Bargaining on Provision of Pensions and of Employee Contributions to Pension Funds and of the Age of Pension Plans

		Coefficients and Standard Errors	
Data, Years, Observations	Sample Mean	Collective Bargaining	Log Wages
Establishment survey			
1. Expenditures for employee compensation, private industry, production workers 1973–77 (7316)			
Pension coverage	64%	.20 (.01)	.26 (.02)
Dollars per hour, all firms	.19	.08 (.01)	.32 (.01)
Dollars per hour, firms with pensions	.30	.002 (.007)	.08 (.002)[a]
2. Expenditures for employee compensation, private industry, production workers 1967–72 (10,888)			
Pension coverage	63%	.29 (.01)	b
Dollars per hour, all	.09	.04 (.04)	b
Dollars per hour, firms with pensions	.15	.003 (.005)	b
Person survey			
3. May Current Population Survey, 1979 (7964) blue-collar workers			
pension coverage	47%	.32 (.01)	.23 (.01)
4. National Longitudinal Survey of Older Men, 1976 (1438)			
pension coverage	68%	.26 (.02)	.14 (.02)
5. Quality of Employment Survey, 1977 (983)			
pension coverage	68%	.25 (.03)	.27 (.03)

Table 4.1 (continued)

Data, Years, Observations	Sample Mean	Coefficients and Standard Errors	
		Collective Bargaining	Log Wages
Pension plans			
6. Employee Benefit Survey, 1977 (4878)			
Age of pension plan, single employer	10.4	6.3 (.4)	—
Age of pension plan, multiemployer	13.4	1.6 (1.1)	—

a Wages, not log wages.

b Included in regression but not reprinted in published article.

Sources: Calculated from various tapes by ordinary least squares with additional controls as follows:

1. EEC 1973–77, 63 industry controls, 3 region controls, year dummies, and log employment.
2. EEC 1967–72, as reported in Freeman (1981).
3. CPS, 4 firm size dummies, age, tenure, tenure^2, years of schooling, sex and race dummy variables, eight industry, three region, three marital status, and eight occupation controls.
4. NLS, 10 industry dummies, 9 occupation dummies, 7 experience, experience squared, race, and education.
5. QES, six industry controls, tenure, tenure squared, experience, race, education.
6. Department of Labor, EBS-1 files, no additional controls in regressions.

The figures tell a clear story about what unions do to pensions: they *increase* the probability that establishments or workers have a pension plan by sizable and statistically significant amounts and therefore raise the contribution of firms to pension plans. In the EEC data the union impact on the probability of a pension plan varies from .17 in the 1973–77 tapes to .29 in the 1967–72 tapes. In the surveys of individuals the union impact ranges from .24 to .32. Given the mean levels of the provision of pensions these are all very substantial impacts. The negligible union coefficient on pension contributions by firms with pension plans shows, moreover, that the union effect occurs largely on whether a firm has a plan, rather than on contributions to a plan. This suggests that the absence of data on contributions or levels of pensions is not a serious drawback: if virtually all of the union effect takes the form of increased coverage, the "are you covered by a pension plan?" questions capture everything of interest.

How does the union impact on pensions compare to the impact of wages on pensions? The final column in the table shows the estimated response of the pension variables to a change in wages. In the linear probability equations these coefficients range from 30% higher than the coefficient on unionism (line 1) to about half the estimated union coefficient (line 4), depending on the survey. In the former case, the numbers suggest that for a nonunion worker to have as good a chance of having a pension as a union worker with the same characteristics his or her wage must be 116% higher than that of the union worker. In the latter case, the required difference is over 500%. The expenditures regressions tell a similar story, although here unionism has the same impact as a 28% wage increase. The reason for the smaller relative impact of unions on expenditures is that unions have very little effect on the pensions expenditures by firms that have plans. Even so, the estimated impact of unions is very large; taking the ratio of the coefficient on collective bargaining in the expenditure regression in line 1 to the mean expenditure yields .42, which is over twice the estimated impact of unionism on wages in these data (.18). I interpret the large impact of unions on pensions (with wages fixed) compared to wages as indicating that what unions do to pensions involves much more than a simple exercise of union monopoly power coupled with standard income elasticities of demand for pensions.

The regression models used to generate the union impacts in table 4.1 seek, as far as is possible, to compare workers with similar characteristics. They answer the question, What does unionism do to the pensions of otherwise comparable workers? Related but somewhat different questions are, What do unions do to the determinants of pensions? and Does unionism have a differential impact on the pensions of different types of worker? On the basis of the first section, one could expect differences in both respects: the impact of unionism ought to be larger among smaller firms, and it ought to reduce the effects of personal characteristics on pension coverage, as the desires of "marginal" workers are dominated by the preferences of "average" workers. To examine these possible relationships I have estimated pension equations separately for union and nonunion workers in the CPS (both blue- and white-collar workers included), compared the relevant coefficients, and estimated the union impact on workers with the average characteristics of union members and of union nonmembers from the separate equations. The results, given in table 4.2, show the expected differences. The most striking difference in the impact of variables on pensions is size of establishment, which is a key determinant of whether a nonunion worker has a pension but a modest factor in whether or not a union worker has a pension. Panels A and B of figure 4.1 highlight this important result by showing the differential union impact on small as opposed to large firms. In the CPS file unions raise the probability that a worker in a firm of less than 100 persons has a pension by 46 percentage points compared to a bare 8 points in a firm with 1000+ workers. In the EEC file unions raise expenditures on pensions by 60% in firms with less than 500 workers compared to an increase of 6% in firms with more than 500 workers. This is consistent with the notion that where firms are small, viable pension programs require a large permanent market in-

Table 4.2   **Determinants of Pension Coverage, Union versus Nonunion Workers or Establishments (Current Population Survey)**

Variable	Mean Values		Estimated Impacts and Standard Errors	
	Union	Nonunion	Union	Nonunion
Pension	.83	.39		
Firm size				
≤25	.16	.45	−.04 (.02)	−.26 (.02)
25–99	.21	.21	.02 (.02)	−.15 (.01)
99–599	.11	.06	.04 (.02)	.09 (.02)
1000+	.24	.10	.07 (.02)	.10 (.01)
Sex (female = 1)	.23	.48	.00 (.02)	−.06 (.01)
Education	11.64	12.4	.009 (.003)	.011 (.002)
Log wage	1.93	1.62	.21 (.02)	.12 (.01)
Nonwhite	.11	.08	−.02 (.02)	−.01 (.01)
Other controls (dummy variables)				
Industry			41	41
Region			3	3
Marital status			3	3
Occupation			8	8
Age			3	3
Tenure			3	3
R^2			.22	.38
			Predicted Pension Probabilities	
Worker with union characteristics			.82	.60
Worker with nonunion characteristics			.65	.39

Source: Calculated from May 1979 CPS separately for union and nonunion workers, with 3249 union and 11,884 nonunion workers.

stitution such as unions to provide deferred compensation. Other factors whose impact on pension coverage between union and nonunion workers differs noticeably are sex, with being female having a smaller impact on pension coverage in the union sector, and occupation and industry, which tend to have a smaller impact on pension coverage under unionism. The smaller role of industry factors under unionism, measured by variation in coverage rates by detailed industries in figure 4.2, represents the general "standardization" effect of unionism on personal differentials, which is also found in studies of union wage effects (see Freeman 1976; Hirschman 1976; Nelson 1976).

The only variable that has a greater effect under unionism is wages: in the Current Population Survey wages have a higher elasticity on coverage among unionists; however, in the EEC data, they have the same elasticity, while in my analysis of earlier EEC data (1967–72), I found a lower elasticity of wages for unionists, leading to no clear conclusion about its effects (see Freeman 1981). Even with the ambiguous wage coefficients, however, the overall pattern of differences in pension determination in union and nonunion settings is clear: standard personal and job factors matter less under unionism.

Finally, the summary differences at the bottom of table 4.2 record the results of applying the estimated coefficients from the equation for one group to the mean values of characteristics of the other groups to determine predicted coverage for workers of different characteristics under the two regimes. They show that unionism raises the coverage of workers with the characteristics of union workers by 22 points and raises the coverage of workers with the characteristics of nonunion workers by 26 points.

From the calculations in tables 4.1 and 4.2 I conclude that unionism has a positive effect on pensions that is greater for workers with the characteristics of union workers but that is still sizable for workers with the characteristics of nonunion workers. Moreover, in pension coverage, as in wages, unionism reduces the effect of personal and sectoral characteristics on the determination of the outcome.

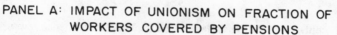

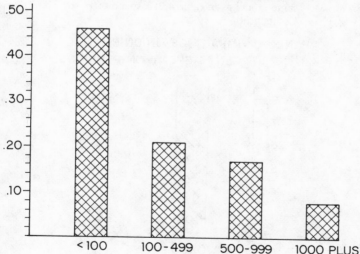

Fig. 4.1   Differential effects of unionism on pensions of different-sized establishments or firms. *A,* Firm size (Number of workers); calculated from the surveys using the same model as in table 4.2, Current Population Survey.

PANEL B: IMPACT OF UNIONISM ON FRACTION
OF WORKERS COVERED BY PENSIONS

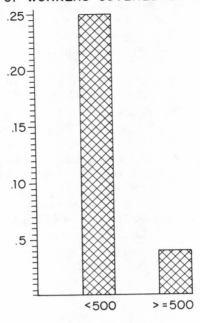

Fig. 4.1 (cont.)   *B,* Establishment size; calculated from the surveys using the same model as in table 4.2, Expenditures for Employee Compensation.

PANEL C: IMPACT OF UNIONISM ON
CENTS SPENT ON PENSIONS

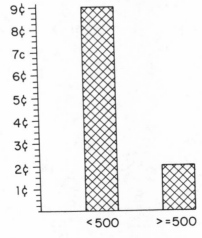

Fig. 4.1 (cont.)   *C,* Establishment size; calculated from the surveys using the same model as in table 4.2, Expenditures for Employee Compensation.

PANEL D: PERCENTAGE IMPACT OF UNIONISM
ON PENSION EXPENDITURES

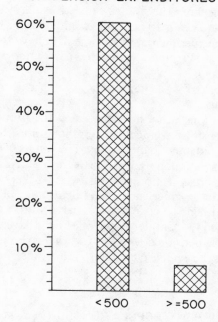

Fig. 4.1 (cont.)   *D,* Establishment size; calculated from the surveys using the same model as in table 4.2, Expenditures for Employee Compensation.

4.2.1   Additional Evidence

Cross-section comparisons like those in tables 4.1 and 4.2 show that union workers or establishments are more likely to be covered by pensions than nonunion workers or establishments, but do they in fact show that unionism *causes* the observed differences? Maybe unions just happened to organize firms with pension plans and have no real impact on pension coverage. In recent years, objections of this form have often been raised about the diverse nonwage effect of unionism as well as about cross-sectional union/nonunion wage differences. The force of the objections depends on the extent to which analyses control for the independent impact of variables related to unionism and the likelihood that omitted "unobservables" that determine the outcome are correlated with unionism. If one controls for numerous other factors and if omitted factors either have a random effect on the outcome or are uncorrelated with unionism, the cross-section estimates are valid. If these assumptions are not met, the estimates will be biased.

One way of checking the unions-cause-pension interpretation of the cross-section differences is to examine longitudinal or before/after data. While like all nonexperimental data these data have their own problems (for a discussion, see Freeman, in progress), it is important to confirm our union effect on them.

Do firms or workers who change union status also experience a change in pension coverage?

To answer this question I have tabulated the proportion of workers gaining/losing pension coverage as their union status changes in the 1973–77 Quality of Employment panel survey. The results of the analysis, given in table 4.3, reveals a union impact on coverage of a magnitude similar to that found in the cross-section analysis, with workers who go from nonunion to union status experiencing a 34 percentage point net increase in the probability of pension coverage compared with essentially no change for other groups in the sample. While one might have expected an analogous decline in the pension coverage of workers who went from union to nonunion status, the evidence here shows that those workers experienced

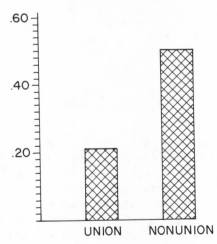

A: CURRENT POPULATION SURVEY, MAY 1979

Fig. 4.2   Coefficients of variation for industry differences on pension coverage, union versus nonunion status. *A*, CPS, based on 44-industry coverage figures as reported in Kotlikoff and Smith (1983), table 3.2.9. The average coverage in the union sector was .74, the standard deviation was .15. The rate of coverage in the nonunion sector was .46, the standard deviation was .23.

B: EXPENDITURES FOR EMPLOYEE COMPENSATION

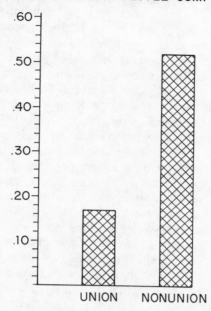

Fig. 4.2 (cont.)   *B,* EEC, based on 63 industries for nonunion and 61 industries
for union, with industries having less than 5 firms deleted. The
rate of coverage in the union sector was .89, the standard
deviation was .15. The rate of coverage in the nonunion sector
was .47, the standard deviation was .24.

Table 4.3   **Changes in Whether a Worker Has a Pension Plan, by Changes in
                   Union Status, 1973–77**

Status of Worker (Number of Workers)	Workers Gaining Pension (%)	Workers Losing Pension (%)	Net Change (%)
Union 1973, union 1977 (182)	3	3	0
Union 1973, nonunion 1977 (64)	11	13	−2
Nonunion 1973, nonunion 1977 (407)	15	10	5
Nonunion 1973, union 1977 (44)	41	7	34

Source: Tabulated from Panel data, 1973–77 Quality of Employment Survey. Based on 687
workers.

only a slight change. The reason: workers who give up a union job move to jobs with higher coverage than the typical nonunion job. In the sample covered, 77% of union leavers went to jobs with pensions compared to 70% pension coverage among workers who were always nonunion.

Information on pension coverage in newly organized firms supports the finding that unionism raises coverage in longitudinal as well as cross-section data. In a study of recently unionized white-collar workers, the Conference Board reported that immediately after organization 35% of the firms improved their pension programs. (Curtin 1970, p. 63).

A related way of testing the union impact of pensions is to compare the likelihood that blue-collar workers have pensions in establishments where white-collar workers do or do not have pensions. If one believes that, rather than inducing firms to set up pension programs, unions organize "good employers" who offer such plans for their entire work force, non-union and union blue-collar workers should be equally likely to have pension plans when the white-collar workers in their establishment have a plan and equally (un)likely to have a plan when the white-collar workers do not have a plan. The tabulations in table 4.4 dispel this possibility and show that much of the union impact takes the form of unions' establishing pension plans in companies that do not have plans for their white-collar workers. Regressions of the difference between the likelihood of a company's having a plan for blue-collar as for white-collar workers yields a positive significant union coefficient of .12, which is only .05 points lower than the union coefficient estimated in table 4.1.[6] While there may be something to the company employment policy argument, it is not the dominant factor behind the estimated union impact.

We conclude that unions do indeed increase pension coverage. The increase is *not* due to the union wage effect and the normal effect of higher wages on the purchase of pensions, or to unions' organizing firms that happen to have pensions before organization.

4.3 Pension Provisions

Because unions are collective organizations whose goals are influenced by majority rule, it is reasonable to expect not only the existence (level) of

Table 4.4   **An "Establishment Brothers" Test of the Union Impact on Pensions**

White-Collar Workers Have a Pension Plan	Union Blue-Collar Workers Have a Pension Plan (%)	Nonunion Blue-Collar Workers Have a Pension Plan (%)
Yes (4435)	97	91
No (2120)	62	2

Source: Tabulated from Expenditures for Employee Compensation Surveys with 2594 blue-collar union establishments and 3961 blue-collar nonunion establishments.

pensions to differ between union and nonunion settings but also the provisions of plans. Broadly, unionized plans should reflect the preferences of "inframarginal," older or senior workers to a greater extent than should nonunion plans and should also reflect other union policies, such as standardization of rates of pay, use of arbitration to decide disputes, and so forth.

To analyze differences between the provisions of union and of nonunion pension plans, I have pulled a random sample of nearly 5000 plans from the ESB-1 file of the U.S. Department of Labor and estimated the impact of unionism on 12 important provisions, with other potential determinants of provisions (size of plan, industry, occupation of workers) held fixed.[7] In the sample are 4666 single-employer plans, of which 12% are union plans; and 212 multiemployer plans, of which 61% are union plans. Because choice of whether a plan is of the defined benefit type (where workers are promised a given amount at retirement) or of the defined contribution type (where a given amount is put into the plan for each worker, who then obtains an amount dependent on the return) often dictates other provisions, I report estimates of the union impact for all plans and then for all plans with a dummy variable controlling for type of plan. In the single-employer sample 41% of the plans are defined benefits plans; in the multiemployer sample 71% are defined benefits plans, but not of the standard form since employers' obligations are limited to contributing to the fund.[8] In addition to analyzing the full set of plans, I have also examined separately the multiemployer, single-employer, and defined benefit and defined contribution plans and will report differences among them that are lost in the regressions for all plans.

Table 4.5 summarizes the results of analysis of the impact of unionism on four basic aspects of pension plans: the type of plan and method of payment; eligibility requirements; dispute resolution; and the nature of contributions. The analysis shows sizable differences between the provisions of union and of nonunion plans, with the bulk of the differences consistent with the "collective voice" interpretation of what unions do.

4.3.1   Rules of Pension Plans

1.   Benefit type and payments. Union pension plans are much more likely to be defined benefit than defined contribution plans. There are two "voice" reasons for this: first, defined benefit plans permit redistribution of benefits from workers who leave the company to those who stay and from the young to the old, particularly when plans are first established; second, defining benefits rather than contributions puts the risk of fluctuations in the market value of pension fund assets onto employers rather than workers.

Union pension plans are more likely to pay benefits on a flat rate, dependent on years of service rather than on earnings. Paying flat-rate bene-

Table 4.5   Estimates of the Impact of Unionism on Provisions of Single-Employer Pension Plans

	Mean Values		Estimated Union Effect, Standard Error	Holding Fixed Type of Plan
	Union	Nonunion		
Benefit type and payments				
1. Defined benefit	.89	.35	.33 (.03)	—
2. Flat rate	.50	.03	.31 (.01)	.29 (.01)
3. Integrated with social security plan	.07	.09	−.01 (.02)	−.08 (.01)
Eligibility requirements				
4. Vesting more liberal than required by law	.08	.47	−.12 (.03)	.00 (.03)
a. in defined benefit				−.04 (.03)
b. in defined contribution				.23 (.09)
5. Age and service requirements for receipt of pension	.56	.21	.27 (.02)	.21 (.02)
6. Age and service requirements for receipt of desirability insurance	.19	.04	.11 (.01)	.08 (.01)
7. Hours worked required				
a. For vesting of full benefits	690	565	70 (30)	40 (41)
b. For receipt of full benefits	790	510	178 (34)	113 (34)
Dispute resolution				
8. Use arbitration	.24	.08	.14 (.02)	.14 (.01)
Nature of contributions				
9. Employer contribution related to profits	.37	.03	−.26 (.03)	−.08 (.02)
10. Employer contribution related to actuarial	.31	.67	.22 (.03)	−.04 (.02)
11. Voluntary employee contributions	.46	.06	−.21 (.03)	−.10 (.03)
12. Employer contributions	.22	.08	.08 (.02)	.09 (.02)
Other characteristics				
13. Plan size	2865	295	—	—

Source: Tabulated from EBS-1 forms of Department of Labor with regressions including eight industry dummies, plan size, whether plan for salaried or hourly workers (as opposed to both), age of plan, and ratio of beneficiaries to workers, and a dummy for multiemployer plans.

fits is the pension equivalent of standard rate policies in wages and reflects the redistributive goal of unions as a political organization.

Controlling for type of plan, union pension plans are less likely to take advantage of "social security integration" possibilities than nonunion plans. Since integrating a plan with social security allows an employee to tilt defined benefits in favor of higher-paid workers by deducting from the employer's obligation social security benefits, one could expect unions to oppose such schemes. The data show they do. Consistent with our results, Kotlikoff and Smith (1983) find that only 11% of union defined benefit plans compared to 60% of nonunion defined benefit plans use social security integration formulas.

2. Eligibility requirements. The findings with respect to eligibility are especially interesting because here a simple monopoly perspective leads to quite different predictions than does the collective voice analysis. As noted in section 4.1, a simple monopoly model leads one to expect union plans to have more liberal vesting and eligibility requirements than nonunion plans. In fact, the opposite is true: union plans have vesting provisions that tend to be only as liberal as required by law, have both age and service requirements (as opposed to separate age or service requirements) not found in nonunion plans both for normal retirement and for disability, and require more rather than fewer hours worked for workers to be eligible for vesting or for receipt of full benefits. Of these findings, the frailest appears to be that pertaining to liberal vesting, which is significant only if one does not control for type of plan. When I examined the defined benefit and defined contribution plans separately, however, I found that unionism reduced liberal vesting in the defined benefit plans but raised it in defined contribution plans, as can be seen in the final column of table 4.5.[9] What explains the general increased eligibility requirements under unionism and the divergent effect on vesting in defined benefit and defined contribution plans? Why do unions not use their monopoly power to extract better eligibility provisions in all cases? The voice explanation is that the eligibility rules are set to benefit the "average" union member at the expense of the benefits. The increased liberality in union defined contribution plans can be explained by the fact that, there, the absence of any such transfer among workers means that all will favor more liberal vesting.

Finally, I have also examined the portability provisions of plans—that is, the rules governing when employees carry their service credits to a new employer—and found differences between multiemployer and single-employer defined benefit plans. Unionism increases all forms of portability in multiemployer plans by significant amounts, while among single-employer plans, unionism reduces portability by significant amounts (see unnumbered table on p. 108).

	Multiemployer		Single Employer	
	Mean	Estimated Impact of Unionism	Mean	Estimated Impact of Unionism
Portable among employers in plan	.77	.16 (.09)	.24	− .11 (.03)
Portable within other employers	.37	.21 (.11)	.10	− .02 (.03)
Portable with both participating and nonparticipating employers	.78	.17 (.09)	.28	− .10 (.03)

Here again we can gain insight into the causes of differences from comparing what an "average" worker would want with what a marginal worker would want. An average employee in an industry with high mobility such as construction, where union multiemployer plans predominate, would want portability. An average employee in a factory, where mobility is modest and single-employer plans are found, would by contrast have no concern for portability. Hence the divergent results. As for the rigid eligibility rules under unionism, exclusion of marginal workers will lower the actuarial cost of pensions to the firm, permitting the senior union workers who are eligible to obtain large defined benefits.

4.   Dispute resolution. While neither union nor nonunion pension plans make extensive use of arbitration to resolve disputes about claimed pension benefits, union plans are far more likely to rely on arbitration than are nonunion plans.

5.   Nature of contributions. Union pension plans also differ significantly in the nature of employer's and employee's contributions to the pension fund. Union plans are much less likely to relate contributions to profits than are nonunion plans and are much more likely to make employer contributions a fixed bargained amount or determined by the actuarial rate for the plan. (The effect on actuarial contributions is due to the choice of a defined benefit plan.) On the worker side, union plans are less likely to involve voluntary worker contributions, largely though not exclusively by having fixed benefit plans in which worker contributions do not affect benefits.

In sum, union pension plans differ greatly from nonunion plans in ways that are, in general, explicable by the "collective voice" face of the institution.

4.3.2   Levels of Benefits

Thus far I have discussed various aspects of pension plan provisions but not actual pension benefits received. Do union pensioners get more? This is a difficult question to answer because surveys of retirees rarely ask about the prior union status of the retirees. In the one survey that does contain such information, the Department of Labor's 1979 Survey of Private Pension Benefit Amounts, Kotlikoff and Smith (1983, table 3.8.1) find that union pensioners do about as well as nonunion pensioners. Among male workers, the ratio of pension benefits to preretirement earnings is .194 for union workers compared to .180 for nonunion workers and among women, .198 (union) and .170 (nonunion). This is consistent with the table 4.1 finding that union employers contribute to pension plans an amount (wages fixed) similar to that contributed by nonunion employers who have pension plans.

In inflationary times a key aspect of pension plans is the extent to which benefits of retired workers are adjusted for inflation. While few private plans in the United States contain formal provisions for cost-of-living adjustment (COLA), it is common to grant such adjustments.

For example, the 1980 Bankers' Trust study of pension plans showed that 69% of the plans surveyed offered some cost-of-living adjustment to retirees between 1975 and 1980. For workers who retired in 1965, the adjustment was 20% of their promised pension. For workers who retired in 1970 (and whose pay and therefore pensions were higher) the average gain was 17% whereas for workers who retired in 1975 it was 8% (Bankers' Trust 1980, pp. 53, 55). As inflation in the period was 63%, however, even the oldest group suffered serious loss in the value of their retirement pay.

Whether union plans are more or less likely to adjust upward the benefits of retired workers is unclear: on the one hand, the current workers who generally ratify contracts will prefer a dollar of wage today to a dollar of retirement benefit for retirees; on the other hand, current workers will also prefer to have *their* retirement pay indexed in some fashion. In some unions, moreover, retired workers vote for union leadership, while in at least one (the United Mine Workers) they vote on contract acceptance as well.

Evidence on the adjustment of pensions to inflation by union status of the pension plan has been provided to me by Steven Allen, Robert Clarke, and Daniel Summer of North Carolina State University. Table 4.6 shows that, in their data, unionized workers were given better inflation protection after they are retired than nonunion workers, implying that the desire of current workers to index retirement pay dominates their desire to spend more on themselves and less on retirees.

Table 4.6   Number of Increases for 1973 Beneficiaries, 1973–78, and Percentage Increase in Value of Pensions, by Union Status

Number of Increases	Union	Nonunion
Zero	19.4	32.0
One	8.9	19.1
Two	17.9	21.0
Three	4.8	17.5
Four	4.8	8.3
Five	10.3	0.9
Six	33.9	1.3
	Value of Pension, 1973–78 (%)	
All	27.1	18.1
Only those with increases	33.6	26.6
Rate of inflation of CPI	63.3	63.3

Source: Steven Allen, Robert Clark, and Daniel Sumner, "Pension Benefits and Inflation," work in progress, North Carolina State University.

4.4 Implication for Earnings Profiles

One of the most puzzling results of union wage studies is the finding that the shape of age-earnings profiles rises less rapidly for union than for nonunion workers, despite the presumed greater influence of older (more senior) workers in union settings. To what extent does this puzzle reflect the failure of the wage studies to take account of the greater pension coverage under unionism and the greater value of defined benefit pensions to older workers?

To answer this question I estimate the present value of expected pension benefits for workers of different ages and then add the *increment* in the present value in a year to their income in that year. If the increment in present value divided by the wage is greater for older workers than for younger workers, the result will be a tilt favorable to older workers, and contrarily if the increment in present value over wages is greater for younger workers. The simplest formula for estimating the present value of pension wealth (PW) is

$$(11) \qquad PW = \lambda_t WR_t/(1 + r + m)^{65-t}$$

where λ = ratio of present value of pension earnings received as retiree at time of retirement (lump sum equivalent of pension receipts) to final year earnings; WR_t = real earnings at year of retirement for workers t years before retirement; m = probability of *not* receiving pension due to mortality or mobility; and t = years before receipt of pension. Assuming that λ is fixed and that the wage at retirement rises with the growth of real earnings, we obtain

(12) $$PW \approx \lambda W_t / (1 + r - g + m)^{65-t},$$

where W_t is the worker's current wage.

Then, for ease of analysis let W be the same for workers of different ages—a reasonable assumption for blue-collar labor—and take the first difference of (12) to obtain the annual increment in PW:

(13)$\Delta PW \approx \lambda W[1/(1 + r + m - g)^{65-t-1} - 1/(1 + r - g + m)^{65-t}]$,

which yields

(14) $$\Delta PW/W \approx \lambda[1/(1 + r + m - g)]^{65-t}(r + m - g).$$

As long as $r + m - g > 0$, the increment in present value is positive (that is, as long as growth of real wages does not exceed the discount and mobility factors). Regardless of the sign of $r + m - g$, the change in present value is greater for older workers since $[1/(1 + r + m - g)]^{65-t}$ is greater for them when $r + m - g$ is positive and smaller when $r + m - g$ is negative. Hence, in this model, unions tilt the profile toward older workers, with the tilt rising exponentially.

To provide order of magnitude estimates of the tilt, assume that $\lambda = 2$, so that the lump sum value of pensions is twice a year's final pay in that year, and let $r + m - g$ take values ranging from .03 to .10. Table 4.7 presents the resultant estimates of the impact of the changes in discounted value of pensions on the earnings of workers at different ages. At low values of $r + m - g$, the differences in the changes by age are smaller (they are zero when $r + m - g$ is zero); at higher values, the gains to older workers are substantial.

What happens if older workers have, as seems plausible, lower mobility rates or are vested and thus do not lose their pension rights when mobile? We can read the answers to these questions in the table by applying different values of $r + m - g$ to the different age groups. When older workers are less mobile, the value of m for them will be smaller than for younger workers, reducing the relevant increase in pension wealth for the older workers. When a worker is vested and leaves, m is zero but so too is g, so

Table 4.7   **Changes in Earnings Due to Increments in Pension Wealth**

Age	Earnings	Values of $r + m - g$			
		.03	.05	.07	.10
25	1.00	1.9%	1.4%	.9%	.0%
35	1.00	2.5%	2.3%	1.8%	1.1%
45	1.00	3.3%	3.8%	3.6%	3.0%
55	1.00	4.4%	6.1%	7.1%	7.7%
65	1.00	6.0%	10.0%	14.0%	20.0%

Source: Based on formula $\Delta PW/W = \lambda(1 + r + m - g)^{t-65}(r + m - g)$.

that the value of his pension wealth will depend solely on the discount factor. Depending on the assumptions one makes, one will obtain different magnitudes for the increment in pension wealth by age, with, however, a general pattern of greater increases for older workers, as can be seen by comparing the maximum increase for the youngest group (1.9% in the column under .03) with the minimum increase for the oldest group (6.0% in the same column).

Finally, is the change in earnings at different ages due to increments in pension wealth enough to overturn the puzzling greater impact of unionism on the wages of young as opposed to older workers?

To answer this question I have estimated the effect of unions on log wages for blue-collar workers in four different age groups, using the Current Population Survey, and then adjusted the union coefficients for the omission of pensions by multiplying the estimated impact of unionism on

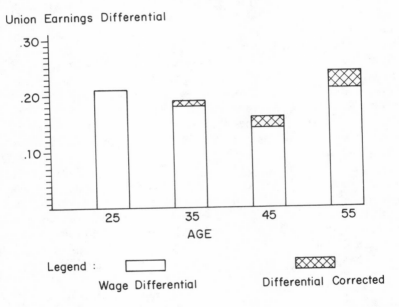

Union Earnings Differential

Legend :   Wage Differential   Differential Corrected

Differential corrected for pensions assuming minimum impact (R+M–G=.03)

Fig. 4.3   Estimates of the union wage differential and the differential corrected for the increased income worth of pensions, by age. *Source:* Estimates of the union wage advantage from May Current Population Survey 1979, with control variables for demographic and industry characteristics, as reported in Freeman and Medoff (1984). Estimates of union impact on pension value obtained by multiplying values in table 4.7 by .30, where .30 is an aproximate estimate of the impact of unions on the provision of pensions from table 4.1.

pension coverage by the minimum table 4.7 estimates of the income value of the pensions by age. The results, shown in figure 4.3, suggest that in these data at least the union pension impact does not quite reverse the finding of a flatter age-earnings profile for union than for nonunion workers, though it has a noticeable effect on the estimated union advantage among the oldest group of workers. While the greater provision of pensions under unionism does not completely reverse the flatter age-wages profile under unionism, analyses of the impact of the full spectrum of union seniority advantages (including health, vacation, job security) may overturn this result. Pensions are part of the union seniority package but not the whole.

4.5 Union Use of Employee Pension Funds: New Tool in Labor's Arsenal?

The assets of our pension fund represent the deferred wages of our members, and we believe that the union should have an equal voice in managing those assets. [A UNION LOCAL PRESIDENT][10]

Goals for Union Participation in Pension Fund Management Established by AFL-CIO Executive Council (AFL-CIO 1981)

To increase employment through reindustrialization including manufacturing, construction, transportation, maritime and other sectors necessary to revitalize the economy.

To advance social purposes such as workers' housing and health centers.

To improve the ability of workers to exercise their rights as shareholders in a coordinated fashion.

To exclude from union pension plan investment portfolios companies whose policies are hostile to workers' rights.

Proposed use of union pension funds to "advance social purposes" and to strengthen unionism represents the major innovation in the union pension area in the 1980s, with potentially important consequences for the economy and unionism. Because private pension funds are major factors in capital markets, owning upward of 12% of corporate equities and 27% of corporate and foreign bonds in 1980 and increasing their share over time, and because union pension funds constitute perhaps one-half of the total, many analysts and unionists have viewed them as a potentially important weapon in the union's arsenal (Kotlikoff and Smith 1983, table 5.5.7). The press, including business publications, have called for greater innovation in traditionally conservative pension fund investments. In 1978 Randy Barber and Jeremy Rifkind wrote an important book advocating that union pension fund moneys be invested in unionized parts of the economy, rather than in nonunion sectors, endangering jobs of members. Indicative of the importance unions now attach to pension fund investments, in 1980 the AFL-CIO's Industrial Union Department began publishing a bimonthly journal, *Labor and Investment,* dealing with issues of pension fund investments. In Fall 1981, the *Journal of Labor Research* published a symposium on "Union Use of Employee Pension Funds," one indication of growing academic interest.

There are two important questions regarding union pension fund investments: (1) Does investment in "socially desirable" areas or exclusion "from union pension plan investment portfolios of companies . . . hostile to worker rights" require union pension funds to take lower returns than they otherwise could earn? (2) Are some investments in lower return projects desirable to unionized workers and, if so, are these investments legal?

Because of the newness of the issues and the consequent paucity of data, I can offer only tentative answers to these questions, with far less documentation than in the other parts of this study.

4.5.1   Returns from Union Pension Fund Investments

Both theory and empirical evidence suggest that union pension funds can shun the stocks of anti-union firms without lowering returns to portfolios. In theory, if the stock exchange is an efficient market union pension funds should be able to earn normal returns, with normal risk, by excluding a moderate number of companies from their portfolio. If it is widely recognized in the market that certain nonunion firms offer, for whatever reason, better profit prospects, their stock prices will reflect this, so that a fund will not lose by shunning them. In a "thick" market with the equity of thousands of companies for sale, one ought to be able to obtain the same valued portfolio by choosing the stock of predominantly union firms rather than those of comparable nonunion firms.

Limited empirical evidence on the returns from investments of pension funds that do or do not shun major nonunion companies provides support for this argument. In 1978 the Corporate Data Exchange analyzed the portfolios of 75 union-related pension plans and 20 employer-controlled plans and found that the former held half as much of their portfolio in the stocks of 15 major predominantly nonunion companies such as McDonald's, Sears, and Texas Instruments.[11] How did the stocks of these companies fare in the market? From 1977 to 1982, a weighted average of those stocks *did worse* than the market averages: excluding Sears Roebuck, which performed especially poorly, and which is bought in large amounts by the Sears Pension Fund, the nonunion companies earned a 36% return compared to a 45% gain in the Standard and Poor's 500; including Sears, the return on the nonunion firms' stock was 19% (Dreben 1983). Over this five-year period, the union-related plans did well to shun the stocks of these firms. More generally, comparison of median rates of return for some union plans (Taft-Hartley multiemployer plans) and nonunion plans by A. G. Becker Company of Chicago show rough similarities in returns on equity for the two, with union plans earning slightly more in half the years and slightly less in half the years (see table 4.8).

The evidence thus supports the "efficient market" argument that unions can direct investment funds away from certain stocks without sacrificing returns. By the same token, however, one expects such a policy to have essentially no real economic impact. In a market with millions of investors, the decision to shun certain companies is unlikely to have any permanent effect on their stock prices. In short, excuding from union pension plan portfolios nonunion companies will harm neither the pension fund nor those firms. Its only impact will be psychic.

Does this mean that union influence on pension fund stock market investments is a mere chimera?

Not necessarily. If union pension fund ownership of the shares of a company were used to pressure management through the board of directors, ownership could prove to be a tool in labor's arsenal. However, to do this the unions would have to invest in, rather than shun, the stocks of major nonunion firms. Barber and Rifkind (1978, pp. 156–57) report the results of just such an effort in 1954 when the Teamsters used their Montgomery Ward stock in the midst of a proxy fight to convince management to agree to collective bargaining. Similarly, James Bennett and Manuel Johnson (1982, p. 187) point out union use of pension funds to pressure the bankers, insurance company executives, and boards of organization that held much of the debt of the J. P. Stevens Company to get the company to stop blatant, illegal efforts to prevent unionization. In both of these situations, it was pension fund ownership (or influence on the owners) of company equity or debt that allowed the unions to influence com-

Table 4.8   **Median Rates of Return on Equity Portion of Pension Plan Portfolio, 1973–82**

Year	Taft-Hartley (Union)	Corporate Plans
1973	−21.7	−22.2
1974	−31.0	−31.6
1975	33.0	33.1
1976	20.3	19.1
1977	7.1	−7.8
1978	7.4	7.1
1979	18.9	21.2
1980	30.9	32.7
1981	−3.1	−5.0
1982	25.3	21.9

Source: A. G. Becker Co., telephone interview, March 3, 1983.

pany behavior. If union pension funds follow the suggestion of the AFL-CIO Executive Council they will reduce, not enhance, the impact of unions on management.

4.5.2 Actual Investment Projects

It is in the area of specific investment projects, such as investments in unionized construction designed to "create" jobs, where union pension plans might accept, for good reason, lower returns. This is because such investments will increase employment of organized labor only if the pension fund offers the firm more attractive loan terms than can be gotten elsewhere. Under some circumstances union investments in projects that earn a lower return than could otherwise be gotten but that create jobs for union workers *may* benefit union members.

First, some of the wage bill of unionized firms will go into the pension fund, which may offset lower returns and enhance the financial position of the fund. Because the greater employment may also create added obligations for the plan, however, one cannot in general conclude that this will be the case. In the case of construction industry pension funds, the issue depends on eligibility rules (How much of the increased work force will stay in the sector long enough to be vested?) and on benefit rules (How many hours per year earn workers credits for pensions?) and on the rates of contribution and the benefits paid out, as well as on the difference between rate of return from the investment and the best alternative. Some pension plans may likely to do better as a result of the greater contribution while others will not. Those that do can justify taking lower returns.

The second and more important reason for unions to take lower returns is to "create" or "save" union jobs. If a union takes a slightly lower return on a pension fund investment that employs workers at union rates, the *total* return to members, consisting of the lower return in the capital market and the higher return on the labor market (the union wage effect), could exceed the higher return the fund could earn with its moneys. If the goal of the union investment is to maximize the wealth of members, taking a lower return on the caital side can be justified. The criterion for the investment should not be the return on capital with labor valued at the union wage but rather the return on capital with labor valued at the nonunion wage rate. In project analysis terms, this is the "shadow cost" of labor.

The strategy may be justifiable, but is it optimal? Should not the union reduce wages to create jobs rather than offer investment funds at an attractive rate?

Unless the union sets employment as well as wages, it may be better to offer capital funds at a lower return. This is because by controlling the amount of the investment, as well as the return, the union can manipulate the employer to the "optimal" discriminating monopolist point, which it cannot do by determining wages. In the simplest situation, where capital-labor ratios are fixed, the union can invest enough capital in a project to hire the same number of workers the firm would hire in a competitive market and can extract all of the "quasi rent" from the firm via higher wages. From this perspective, use of pension fund capital can augment union power in the labor market.

Whether investment strategies for the purpose of raising employment are legal under the Employment Retirement Income Security Act of 1974 (ERISA) is, however, unclear. Plan fiduciaries are obligated to act "solely in the interest of participants and beneficiaries" for the "exclusive purpose of providing benefits" to them.[12] If the workers who obtain the high-wage union jobs were identical with the beneficiaries, perhaps such an investment strategy would be legal. But in general the workers will be younger employees and the beneficiaries older employees, and it may be that a strategy that benefits employed union members but is possibly harmful to pension beneficiaries is illegal. On the other hand, the enhanced monopoly power due to strategic use of pension fund investments could be used to benefit beneficiaries as well, even when the pension fund return is lower. It could do this by bargaining for higher defined benefits at the expense of the union wage differential.

Have union pension plans sacrificed returns to enhance employment prospects?

The limited data I have seen suggests that they have not, at least noticeably. AETNA Insurance, which manages a large Union Separate Account for investment in union construction, reports earning returns above those that could be obtained in the bond market.[13] My discussions in Southern California with pension fund officials suggest similar good returns, thus far, with concern over fiduciary impossibilities making officials wary of taking lower returns for the sake of union jobs.

4.6 Conclusion

This paper has examined the role of trade unions in pension coverage, expenditures by firms for pensions, the provisions of pension plans, the impact of pensions on age-earnings profiles, and pension fund investments. It has four basic findings:

1. Unions greatly increase pension coverage and alter the determinants of coverage in ways that go beyond the monopoly wage effects of unionism.

2. Unions alter the provisions of pension plans in ways that benefit senior workers and that equalize pensions among workers.

3. Estimates of the age-earnings profile of union members are flawed by failure to take account of the union impact on pensions, which enhances the earnings of the oldest groups.

4. Union pension funds can and do shun the stocks of nonunion firms without lowering the value of the portfolio. Investments in actual projects

that take lower returns are, up to a point, justifiable in terms of the full economic benefits accruing to workers.

Notes

1. The first union retirement plan was established in 1905 by the Granite Cutters' International Association of America, according to American Council of Life Insurance, *Pension Facts, 1978–1979,* p. 37, as cited by Munnell (1982).

2. In the *Inland Steel Company* case (1948), a National Labor Relations Board ruling that pensions were a mandatory subject was upheld by the Seventh Circuit. Inland Steel Co. v. NLRB, 170F 2d 247, 22 LRRM 2505 (CA 7, 1948), *cert. denied,* 336 U.S. 960, 24 LRRM 2019 (1949).

3. If C is the fixed cost in instituting the program, the total cost function $TC = C + WL + PL$. Differentiation with respect to P yields $W_P L + L = 0$. This model assumes that the firm is indifferent between paying pensions or paying hourly rates.

4. The assumption that ordering workers by attachment to the firm also orders them by preferences for pensions is the key assumption in the analysis. In the model all workers of the same tenure with a firm are treated as if they had the same preference for pensions, making the difference in tenure the sole cause of different desires. When worker preferences for pensions differ for reasons unrelated to attachment to the firm, the competitive market will produce different sets of compensation packages, with more pensions in some establishments than in others to attract those preferring pensions. Variation of this type is ignored to concentrate on the situation in which preferences differ by potential mobility or tenure in the firm.

5. For a detailed discussion of this maximal in the context of work quality, see Viscusi (1980).

6. This regression was performed for all of the 4668 establishments with the same controls as those used in table 4.1, line 1.

7. This work builds on the earlier analysis of Engberg, (1980).

8. These so-called Taft-Hartley plans are defined benefit plans from the perspective of the worker who is promised a fixed pension, but not from the point of view of the firm.

9. In the Kotlikoff-Smith examination of the EBS-1 file (which did not control for other factors, but which includes the full sample) they found union plans to be less generous with vesting. Fifteen percent of nonunion plans in their sample have full and immediate vesting compared to a bare 3% among union plans; 52% of nonunion plans have partial or complete vesting after three years of service compared to a bare 7% of union plans (Kotlikoff and Smith 1983, table 3.8.1).

10. Labor and Investments citation by local president of International Association of Machinists.

11. Corporate Data Exchange, stock held by 101 selected pension funds in 32 companies identified as "socially controversial," as reported in Barth and Cordes (1981).

12. 29 U.S.C. 1104 (a) (1). For a discussion of legal issues see Bredloff (1982).

13. See AETNA Life Insurance, first Annual Report on Union Separate Account (1983).

Comment   Albert Rees

This paper consists of three parts of unequal length: a short first part discusses why unionism might increase the probability of pension coverage, a much longer second part presents evidence that it does, and a short

Albert Rees is president of the Sloan Foundation.

third part deals with the investment policies of union pension funds. The principal argument of the first part is that unions are more likely than employers to give heavy weight to the views of older workers in dividing compensation between wages and pensions. Employers are most interested in recruiting and retaining young workers, who may place a relatively low value on pensions because they discount the distant future heavily. Older workers are easier to retain than young workers because their natural mobility is lower and they have other benefits related to seniority. The median voter in a democratic union will be closer to retirement age than the new recruit and will therefore place a higher value on pension benefits. If the union is autocratic, the controlling group is probably even older, and more concerned with pensions, than the median voter. I find this argument novel and convincing, although as Freeman states it is not the only explanation of the positive association between unions and pension coverage.

The second part of the paper demonstrates by analyzing a variety of data sets that unions do indeed increase pension coverage by large amounts. The principal way in which they do so is by increasing the pension coverage of small firms. The creation of collectively bargained multi-employer pension funds creates a convenient mechanism through which the small employer can offer pension coverage at low administrative cost. Given that a firm has a pension plan, Freeman finds that unions do not have a substantial effect on the cost of the plan. The use of data from a variety of sources and of different types makes this part of the paper highly convincing.

The principal point of the third part of the paper is that union pension funds avoid investing in the securities of leading nonunion employers and that this restriction has not lowered their mean return on investment. This argument is sound as far as it goes but is subject to serious limitations. The restriction on investments in union pension plans may have maintained mean yields only at the cost of higher variance in returns, a possibility that is not considered. More important, the avoidance of nonunion firms is only one possible union objective in setting investment policy. Others include promoting the employment of union members, avoiding firms with operations in the Union of South Africa, and promoting socially desirable investments such as low-cost housing. Pursuing several of these goals at once could have a pronounced effect in lowering rates of return or raising risks.

In the multiemployer plans set up under the Taft-Hartley Act with both union and management trustees, the obligations of the individual employer are fulfilled by making the required contributions. The investment performance of the fund over a long period will determine the size of the pensions that can ultimately be paid. If the trustees sacrifice only a little yield, the working of compound interest over a worker's life will transform this into a large difference in outcome.

The paper does not discuss the cases in which the trustees of Taft-Hartley pension plans have conspicuously departed from sound investment practices. Although these may be few, they are not unimportant.

The most conspicuous case is that of the Teamsters Central States, Southeast, and Southwest Area Pension Fund.[1] As of the mid-1970s, this fund covered 400,000 working teamsters and 70,000 retirees and had large unfunded liabilities. The District Director of the Internal Revenue Service in Chicago found "trust funds invested for a return not commensurate with prevailing rates" and "trust funds invested against the advice of professional advisers retained by the trust." As of 1975, when its total assets were $1,363 million, the fund had nine "questionable" loans totaling $332 million in hotels, casinos, and undeveloped land. In 1983 a former trustee of the fund, Roy L. Williams (also president of the International Brotherhood of Teamsters), was found guilty by a federal jury of defrauding the fund.

In passing the Taft-Hartley Act, Congress no doubt thought that the presence of both union and management trustees of multiemployer funds would serve as protection against this kind of abuse. In the Central States Teamsters fund, management trustees appear to have played a passive role because they feared retaliation in collective bargaining if they insisted on orthodox investment policies.

References

Aetna Life Insurance Co. 1983. First annual report on union separate account.

American Federation of Labor and Congress of Industrial Organization. 1981. *Investment of union pension funds.* Washington, D.C.: AFL-CIO.

Bankers' Trust Co. 1976. *Corporate pension plan study: A guide for the 1980's.* New York: Bankers' Trust.

Barber, R., and Rifkind, J. 1978. *The nation will rise again.* Boston: Beacon.

Barth, J., and Cordes, J. J. 1981. Nontraditional criteria for investing pension assets: An economic appraisal. *Journal of Labor Research* 2:219–47.

Bennett, J., and Johnson, M. 1982. Union use of employee pension funds: Introduction and overview. *Journal of Labor Research* 2:181–90.

1. For a thorough discussion of the investment policies of the Central States fund, see James and James (1965). A more recent if less scholarly discussion may be found in Teamsters for a Democratic Union (1977). The data cited above are from this source.

Bredloff, E. 1982. Another look at ERISA. *Labor and Investment* (July-August), pp. 3–8.

Curtin, E. 1970. *White collar unionization*. New York: National Industrial Conference Board.

Dreben, R. 1983. Investment of union pension funds. B.A. thesis, Harvard College.

Engberg, J. 1980. Differences in benefit structure among defined benefit pension plans. B.A. thesis, Harvard College.

Freeman, R. B. 1976. Individual mobility and union voice in the labor market. *American Economic Review* 66:361–68.

———. 1980. The exit-voice tradeoff in the labor market: Unionism, job tenure, quits, and separations. *Quarterly Journal of Economics* 94:643–73.

———. 1981. The effect of unionism on fringe benefits. *Industrial and Labor Relations Review* 34:489–509.

Hirschman, A. 1976. Some uses of the exit-voice approach—discussion. *American Economic Review* 66:386–89.

Kotlikoff, L. J., and Smith, D. E. 1983. *Pensions in the American economy.* Chicago: University of Chicago Press (for NBER).

Munnell, A. H. 1982. *The economics of private pensions.* Washington, D.C.: Brookings Institution.

Nelson, R. L. 1976. Some uses of the exit-voice—discussion. *American Economic Review* 66:389–91.

Teamsters for a Democratic Union. 1977. *You and Your Teamster Union.* Teamsters Rank and File Educational and Legal Defense Foundation, September.

Viscusi, W. K. 1980. Unions, labor market structure, and the welfare implications of the quality of work. *Journal of Labor Research* 1:175–92.

5   Determinants of Pension Benefits

Paul Taubman

The life-cycle consumption-saving model of Modigliani, Brumberg, and Ando (MBA) has long been recognized as a major strand in the postwar developments on consumption and saving behavior. Recently its use or misuse in the public finance literature has given this model even more attention than the related permanent income hypothesis (Kotlikoff and Summers (1981). The essence of the life-cycle model is that individuals save primarily to maintain a smooth (or smoother) consumption than earnings path. Earnings received during a person's lifetime fluctuate greatly because of business cycles, systematic variations in earnings with age and work experience, and retirement or reduced labor force participation. A major emphasis in this model is that individuals will acquire assets while working and dissave while retired when earnings will be low or zero.[1]

The MBA model was developed in the early and mid-1950s to help explain consumption data drawn from earlier periods. In those earlier periods, however, retirement, the driving force in this model, was rare and relatively short lived. Table 5.1 contains data on life expectancy and labor force participation of men of various ages for the period 1950–80. In 1950, 70% of the men who were 65 participated in the labor market and had a remaining life expectancy of only 13 years. The corresponding participation rate and remaining life expectancy for a 70-year-old was 50% and 10 years. In 1980 only 35% and 21% of the men who were 65 and 70 years old were in the labor force and the remaining life expectancy was 14 and 11 years. Since pension plans are made at earlier ages, it is useful to note that the remaining life expectancy of a 50-year-old male has risen

Paul Taubman is professor of economics at the University of Pennsylvania and a research associate of the National Bureau of Economic Research.

Table 5.1   Participation Rates and Life Expectancy at Selected Dates for Men

Year	Age 60		Age 65		Age 70	
	LFPR*	Remaining Life Expectancy†	LFPR	Remaining Life Expectancy	LFPR	Remaining Life Expectancy
1950	84.7	15	71.7	13	50.0	10
1960	85.9	16	56.8	13	37.3	10
1970	83.9	16	49.9	13	30.2	11
1980	74.0	17	35.2	14	21.3	11

Sources: Participation rates from Burkhauser and Turner (1982), p. 305. Life expectancy from various Vital Statistics.
*Labor force participation rate.
†Remaining life expectancy.

from 23 years in 1950 to 25 years in 1980. Life expectancy of women has risen even more than that of men during this time interval.[2]

Several major factors that contribute to the increase in nonparticipation of the elderly are the size of the benefits paid by social security relative to wages from working (Parsons), the actuarial fairness in social security and private pension (Lazear), and mandatory retirement ages set in private pension plans whose use has grown over time.

Whatever the reason for retirement, the increase in the expected length of time in retirement should influence both the volume of savings and its composition.

In this paper, I will use The Retirement History Survey (RHS) to determine how the non–social security pensions (hereafter, private pensions) vary across sociodemographic groups and how the present discounted value of pensions taken over expected remaining life span correlate with expected retirement years. Public and private pensions should be good substitutes for the individual. But as Samuelson has pointed out, the pay-as-you-go feature of social security can reduce total savings. Thus I will also study the interrelationship of the two pensions to get at a set of issues initially examined by Feldstein. In addition I examine the relationship with number of children, who are often thought of as an alternative source of funds during retirement.[3] Finally I will examine the relationship of pensions to total financial wealth and income derived thereon. The results obtained on some of these hypotheses at times may be affected by my desire to study the socioeconomic differences. For example, it is of some interest to learn that those without pensions are more likely to be working after age 65. It is not really possible to distinguish, however, if the lack of a pension caused these people to continue to work or if they selected an occupation which they knew would let them work until they died and thus did not require a pension.

The RHS has been used by Blinder, Gordon, and Wise (BGW) to study a number of issues related to pensions. Our data set and analyses differ in several important ways from theirs. They used primarily the 1971 survey and restricted themselves to white males. BGW also estimated dollar amounts of pensions for people not yet receiving or reporting amounts and social security wealth based on four reported wage figures.

I use the 1977 survey and include women and nonwhites. By 1977 every head of household is at least 66 and almost everyone eligible for a pension is receiving it. We calculate social security wealth from benefits received or from the social security earnings records, which have been matched to the file.[4] I also allow for differential life expectancies for different groups. All these differences contribute to substantial differences between averages shown in the two studies.

BGW started off with a tightly specified life-cycle savings model in which an intertemporal utility function was maximized. As their paper indicates, during their study they sustained doubts about the validity or usefulness of this model. (See also Blinder 1982.) My model is more loosely structured in part because we wish to examine demographic and other socioeconomic differences. It reaches conclusions more favorable to the life-cycle model.

5.1   The Model

One can, of course, treat the question raised above as being descriptive in nature and obtain the answers without recourse to economic theory. In "Pensions and Mortality" (Taubman 1981), however, I demonstrate how it is possible to have a worker demand for pensions and a firm supply of pension funds that can be solved to obtain a reduced-form equation that depends on the sociodemographic variables I am studying here that does not have to include the price or after-tax rate of return on pensions. Thus the following model can be thought of as an approximation to such a system:

(1) $$PB = F(SSB, \mathbf{X}, W),$$

PB = dollar amount of pension benefits, SSB = present discounted value of the dollar amount of social security benefits calculated over remaining expected lifetime, $\mathbf{X}$ = a vector of sociodemographic characteristics, W = financial wealth.

5.2   Data

In 1969 the Retirement History Survey (RHS) was established. At that time a random sample of heads of households 58–63 years old was surveyed. The same group of people or their surviving spouses were scheduled to be reinterviewed every second year through 1977, though there was attrition because of death and other reasons. Two valuable features of the RHS are that the sample has been linked to social security records and there is a breakdown of previous year's income by source. Unfortunately, because the man is automatically designated as the head of the household, the only women who are respondents in 1969 are widowed, divorced, separated, or never married.

By 1977, the youngest respondent is 67 years old and most pensions are being drawn. Because the pension amounts for the previous year are reported, I do not make use of the 1975 reinterview. The mean and variance of some important variables in that year are given in table 5.2 separately for men and women. In 1977 the men are about 68 years old; they have financial net worth exclusive of pensions of about $28,000; their average family income is about $10,000; about 28% were in the labor force; 83% received social security benefits; half received or expected to receive a pension; the average amount of the pension for all men was $1675 but for those with a pension was $3793; and their pension and social security wealth was $20,676 and $40,377, respectively. The numbers for women heads of households are similar except that wealth, family income, and pensions are about one- to three-quarters the size of men's.[5]

The data for 1977 have the advantage that everyone is at least 66 and likely to have retired and thus able to provide accurate dollar amounts for pensions. However, there has been sample attrition that may not be random and 216 people with pensions did not report the amount in 1977. Moreover, in 1977 about 7% of the men and women who expect to receive a pension still do not have one.

5.3   Methodology

Because most people in the sample do not receive a pension, the use of the OLS on the whole sample causes statistical problems. To surmount this difficulty, I estimate probit equations on the probability of having a pension (or having and expecting to have a pension) and OLS regressions on pension amount for those with positive pensions. While this is not the only method for handling the issue,[6] it is appropriate and lets me look at two issues of concern, that is, who has pensions and how big are the pensions of recipients. The two estimates can be combined to obtain estimates of the effect of various variables and differences in pension holdings for various groups in the total sample.

5.4   Results

Probit equations for the probability of receiving a pension are given in tables 5.3A and 5.4A for males and females. Corresponding equations for the sum of respondents receiving or expecting to receive a pension are given in tables 5.3B and 5.4B.

Table 5.2   **Means of Selected Variables in 1977 RHS Survey**

Variable	Males	Females
Financial wealth*	$27,889	$12,608
Age 77	68.3	67.2
Family income†	8,266	3,890
Nonwhite	.10	.14
Receives or expects to receive pension 77‡	.51	.42
Receives pension	.44	.26
Receives social security 77	.83	.70
Social security amount	2,460	1,681
Social security wealth	40,377	17,266
Pension amount	1,675	737
Pension amount, recipients	3,794	2,879
Pension wealth	20,676	5,467
Labor force participation	.28	.20
Married 77	.82	
Widowed 77	.06	.57
Div/sep 77	.04	.12
Number§	4,997	2,996

Definition of Variables

Nonwhite	0 = white	1 = otherwise
LFP	1 = participating in labor force	0 = otherwise
Prof	1 = professional worker	0 = otherwise
Clerk	1 = clerk	0 = otherwise
Skill	1 = skilled worker	0 = otherwise
Manager	1 = manager	0 = otherwise
Self	1 = self-employed	0 = otherwise
FEarn 77	Family earnings—pension income	
SS 77	Social security income	
Rec SSN	1 = receive social security income	0 = otherwise
Widowed	1 = widowed	0 = otherwise
Div/sep	1 = divorced or separated	0 = otherwise
Educ 69	Education (in years) in 1969	
Wea 77	Wealth	
Kids	Number of children	
LifePen	Lifetime value of pension income	
Life SS	Lifetime value of social security income	
Married	1 = married	0 = otherwise
Assup	Expected years of retirement from 1977 (0 = still in labor force)	
PEN 77	Pension income in 1977	
ERecPen	Receiving *or* expecting to receive a pension	
RecPen	Receiving a pension	

*Excludes pensions and social security benefits.
†Includes social security benefits.
‡Some recipients expect to receive another pension in the future.
§If information is not reported, missing data are set equal to mean.

Table 5.3.A   Dependent Variable: Currently Receiving Pension, Males

Variable	Maximum Likelihood Estimate	t-Value	Maximum Likelihood Estimate	t-Value	Maximum Likelihood Estimate	t-Value	Maximum Likelihood Estimate	t-Value
Constant	-.40	-5.08	-.57	-6.94	-.82	-8.85	-.24	-2.92
Widowed	.20	1.93	.20	1.87	.25	2.30	.15	1.41
Div/sep	.036	.30	.023	.19	.048	.39	.0059	.05
Nonwhite	-.28	-4.49	-.30	-4.81	-.09	-1.36	-.30	-4.76
Married	.31	3.83	.33	4.05	.30	3.67	.36	4.25
Educ 69					.042	8.82		
FEarn 77			.000070	-3.43				
SS 77								
Prof								
Clerk								
Skill								
Manager								
Self								
LFP							-.74	-17.37
Rec SSN								
Log likelihood function	-3399.94		-3341.46		-3360.30		-3242.21	

	(1)		(2)		(3)		(4)	
Constant	-.74	-8.25	-.81	-9.57	-.16	-1.97	-.88	-7.88
Widowed	.19	1.83	.14	1.33	.18	1.64	.20	1.81
Div/sep	.22	.18	.14	0.11	.18	0.01	-.03	-0.21
Nonwhite	-.27	-4.29	-.17	-2.65	-.40	.0020	-.030	-0.10
Married	.30	3.68	.24	2.88	.36	4.40	.38	4.25
Educ 69							.07	11.68
FEarn 77							.000002500	-1.02
SS 77			.00019	15.67			.00019	10.39
Prof					-.71	-12.13	-.66	-9.89
Clerk					-.28	-3.63	-.31	-3.77
Skill					-.20	-4.53	-.18	-3.85
Manager					-.62	-10.01	-.67	-9.96
Self					-1.25	-8.96	-1.30	-9.27
LFP							-.61	-12.89
Rec SSN	.41	8.35					-.23	-3.04
Wea 77							.00000078	1.52
Kids							-.03	-3.84
Log likelihood function	-3364.28		-3274.00		-3252.52		-2968.39	

Table 5.3.B Dependent Variable: Currently Receiving or Expecting to Receive Pension, Males

Variable	Maximum Likelihood Estimate	t-Value	Maximum Likelihood Estimate	t-Value	Maximum Likelihood Estimate	t-Value	Maximum Likelihood Estimate	t-Value
Constant	-.07	-1.03	-5.45	-5.97	-.05	-.61	-.37	-4.53
Widowed	.12	1.13	.16	1.56	.11	1.10	.067	.63
Div/sep	.11	-.93	-.10	-1.83	-.12	-.99	-.14	-1.18
Nonwhite	-.25	-4.09	-.04	-.57	-.27	-4.33	-.17	-2.70
Married	.33	3.84	.32	3.69	.27	3.14	.27	3.08
Educ 69		2.05	.05	9.81				
FEarn 77					.00000500	-2.42	.00013	11.24
SS 77								
Prof								
Clerk								
Skill								
Manager								
Self								
LFP								
Rec SSN								
Log likelihood function	-3399.88		-3300.82		-3346.93		-3285.85	

	(1)		(2)		(3)		(4)	
Constant	−.17	−2.10	−.10	−1.21	−.17	−1.97	−.23	−2.11
Widowed	.08	.74	.06	.55	.11	1.08	.14	1.24
Div/sep	−.16	−1.30	−.15	1.22	.12	−.99	−.13	−1.00
Nonwhite	−.37	−5.97	−.27	−4.37	−.25	−4.03	.04	.34
Married	.21	2.62	.08	2.47	.16	1.99	.26	2.96
Educ 69							.069	12.44
FEarn 77							−.0000013	−.53
SS 77							.00017	−9.43
Prof	−.76	−12.99					−.72	−10.86
Clerk	−.23	−2.88					−.28	−3.34
Skill	−.19	−4.07					−.15	−3.15
Manager	−.61	−10.01					−.69	−10.37
Self	−1.21	−9.62					−1.28	−9.72
LFP			−.72	−17.27			−.65	−13.88
Rec SSN					.11		−.56	−7.12
Wea 77						2.25	.00000090	
Kids							−.04	−4.91
Log likelihood function	−3199.41		−3196.29		−3347.35		−2917.96	

Table 5.4.A   Dependent Variable: Recipient—Currently Receiving, Females

Variable	Maximum Likelihood Estimate	t-Value	Maximum Likelihood Estimate	t-Value	Maximum Likelihood Estimate	t-Value	Maximum Likelihood Estimate	t-Value
Constant	−.30	−4.65	−.36	−4.80	−1.35	−11.02	−.19	−2.86
Widowed	−.31	−4.21	−.30	−4.05	−.20	−2.56	−.33	−4.39
Div/sep	−.33	−3.30	−.32	−3.18	−.28	−2.74	−.32	−3.20
Nonwhite	−.54	−5.56	−.52	−3.63	−.30	−2.93	−.54	−5.54
Educ 69					.093	10.30		
FEarn 77			.000012	1.56				
SS 77								
Prof								
Clerk								
Skill								
Manager								
Self								
LFP							−.66	−7.31
Rec SSN								
Log likelihood function	−1190.74		−1099.51		−1132.37		−1161.27	

Constant	−.56	−6.39	−.89	−10.47	−.40	−5.42	−1.23	−8.31
Widowed	−.32	−4.27	−.29	−3.76	−.25	−3.32	−.03	−.29
Div/sep	−.34	−3.43	−.31	−3.03	−.27	−2.64	−.07	−.65
Nonwhite	−.52	−5.35	−.35	−3.46	−.43	−4.33	−.06	−.58
Educ 69							.07	6.46
FEarn 77							−.00002	−2.06
SS 77	.00028	11.46					.0005	10.55
Prof					.61	5.62	.41	3.31
Clerk					.20	2.50	.10	1.17
Skill					−.25	−2.76	−.17	−1.71
Manager					−.22	−1.37	−.51	−2.87
Self					−.30	−.96	.02	.07
LFP							−.69	−6.80
Rec SSN	.33	4.46					−.82	−6.20
Wea 77							.0000030	2.46
Kids							−.07	−3.93
Log likelihood function	−1180.51		−1121.93		−1163.29		−1002.57	

Table 5.4.B   Dependent Variable: Currently Receiving Pension or Expecting to Receive Pension, Females

Variable	Maximum Likelihood Estimate	t-Value	Maximum Likelihood Estimate	t-Value	Maximum Likelihood Estimate	t-Value	Maximum Likelihood Estimate	t-Value
Constant	−.17	−2.68	−1.17	−9.94	−.25	−3.30	−.64	−7.68
Widowed	−.23	−3.13	−.12	−1.60	−.22	−2.92	−.21	−2.77
Div/sep	−.33	−3.39	−.29	−2.90	−.32	−3.28	−.32	−3.13
Nonwhite	−.52	−5.72	−.28	−3.00	−.50	−5.42	−.37	−3.92
Educ 69			−.089	10.33				
FEarn 77(000)			.000015					
SS 77(000)					.00022	1.96	9.23	
Prof								
Clerk								
Skill								
Manager								
Self								
LFP								
Rec SSN								
Log likelihood function	−1258.54		−1200.48		−1256.68		−1214.89	

	(1)		(2)		(3)		(4)	
Constant	−.27	−3.66	−.08	−1.15	−.31	−3.53	−.96	−6.81
Widowed	−.17	−2.26	−.25	−3.32	−.23	−3.16	.02	.23
Div/sep	−.27	−2.75	−.33	−3.34	−.39	−3.43	−.126	−1.15
Nonwhite	−.43	−4.53	−.53	−5.77	−.51	−5.59	−.11	−1.05
Educ 69							.068	.73
FEarn 77							−.000010	−1.14
SS 77							−.00037	9.03
Prof	.66	5.92					.44	3.54
Clerk	.16	2.01					.06	.68
Skill	−.22	−2.63					−.125	−1.37
Manager	−.11	−8.02					−.32	−2.00
Self	−.48	−1.52					−.23	−.73
LFP			−.54	−6.40			−.58	−6.27
Rec SSN					.17	2.31	−.78	−6.27
Wea 77							.00000200	1.78
Kids							.05	−3.33
Log likelihood function	−1130.69		−1236.91		−1255.84		−1106.77	

The first equation contains only marital status and race variables. As shown in the first column in table 5.3A, married and white men are significantly more likely to have pensions than single or nonwhite men. The last column in the table contains my most comprehensive equation. The coefficients that have a positive and significant effect on the probability of having a pension are social security benefits, years of schooling, and being married. The negative and significant impacts flow from receiving social security benefits, being a labor force participant in 1977, and being self-employed and in any (longest) occupation versus an unskilled or blue-collar laborer.[7]

These results, while often subject to several interpretations, bear on a number of important issues. First, it is well known that married men have higher earnings.[8] In this equation I have controlled for financial wealth and for education, current earnings, social security benefits, and longest occupation, all of which are proxies for permanent earnings. Yet married men continue to be more likely to have a pension. This suggests that married men have a lower rate of time preference than single men.[9]

Second, the nonwhite coefficient is no longer significant. The inclusion of earnings and education has reduced the significance of this variable. Thus nonwhites are not discriminated against directly in the provision of pensions though this can hardly be a comfort if they are discriminated against with respect to wages and other determinants of pensions.

Third, the labor force participation rate variable has the largest t statistic. Presumably this coefficient reflects two forces. Some people (e.g., college professors) will not draw their pension until they retire at some later age. In addition, those people who plan to work without retiring are less likely to acquire pensions. However, when the same set of variables is used in a probit function for "expect to receive pension in the future and not currently have one," the labor force participation variable is significant at about the 1% level and has a negative coefficient. That is, they are less likely to expect a future pension. Thus this finding is more consistent with the life-cycle model.

Fourth, a person who receives social security is significantly less likely to receive a pension. This is consistent with Feldstein's substitution hypotheses.[10] But the higher his social security wealth, the more likely he is to receive a pension. This result can be explained in terms of social security benefits' being a proxy for permanent earnings.

Family income net of private pension benefits is negatively related to the probability of having a pension, but the results are not significant. Of course, at this point in the life cycle, current income should be a poor proxy for permanent income.

Table 5.4A contains the corresponding results for the women heads of household. While they are qualitatively similar, there are some important differences. For example, in equation 1, never-married women are much more likely than widows to receive a pension even though some widows receive payments from their husband's pension plans. This is probably due to the greater labor force participation of single women, the incomplete use of joint and survivor pensions, and a spouse's dying before vesting occurs. These coefficients become statistically insignificant in the more complete equations, which have various proxies for work experience.

In my most recent equation, I obtain results qualitatively similar to those for men except that professionals and net worth have positive and significant coefficients, the family income variable has a significant negative coefficient, and some occupations are not significant.

In tables 5.5 and 5.6 I present OLS regressions for males and females who receive one or more pensions in 1977.[11] Because some of the signs change as I move from less to more inclusive equations, I show some of the less inclusive versions. In my discussion I concentrate on the most inclusive equations. For women, the equation explains over 60% of the variance in the amount of pensions received. Clerks receive smaller pensions than unskilled workers who may be more likely to unionize. Widows and divorced and separated women receive noticeably smaller amounts than single (never-married) women who were more likely to be in the labor force and not dependent on a husband's choosing joint and survivors' insurance or on alimony provisions.

Various proxies for family permanent income and wealth reveal a mixed picture for women. Pension amounts increase significantly with family income and education. However, both the receipt of and dollar amount of social security benefits lead to reduced pensions. This may reflect Feldstein's substitution argument; however, many private pensions contain provisions that reduce pension payments by a portion of social security benefits. While this mechanism is also one of substitution, it is not the mechanism Feldstein speaks of. Moreover, some of these provisions are designed to concentrate pensions among high-income individuals who are in the higher marginal tax brackets while letting the plan qualify as a deductible expense in the IRS code (see Munnell 1982).

Men continuing in the labor force have much lower pensions. Professional and skilled workers are receiving smaller pensions than the unskilled. Divorced and separated men did not sign away their pensions. Family income and respondent's education have large positive effects. Finally, dollar amounts of social security benefits are negatively related to amount of pension received. (See above for a discussion of why.) While there are some differences between the male and female equations, there is substantial agreement.

I am often more interested in the present discounted wealth than in the dollar amount of pensions. I have converted the pension benefits into a wealth measure in which the benefits are drawn during the person's ex-

Table 5.5   Males with Positive Pensions (*t*-Statistics below Coefficients)

SBPR. NO.	NWHITE 1	LFP 2	PROF 3	CLERK 4	SKILLED 5	MANAG 6	SELF 7	MARR 8	WIDOW 9	DIV/SEP 10
1.	-770.2847							567.50007	262.8037	346.2207
	-2.2101							1.2236	.4482	.4942
2.	-770.3345	9.9386						567.1951	263.0195	146.6331
	-2.2097	.0392						1.2225	.4484	.4964
3.	-901.0171							671.1428	233.6219	326.2542
	-2.6222							1.4688	.4045	.4729
4.	-609.336							469.8147	375.4016	641.898
	1.7620							1.0229	.6465	.9328
5.	-1119.9470							725.7759	310.9895	258.7063
	-3.2432							1.5893	.5390	.3753
6.	495.3103							546.8975	425.7163	520.6323
	1.4055							1.2191	.7504	.7681
7.	-629.3474		1629.0618	403.7642	-1114.7139	1897.9219	338.8010	540.2017	305.3132	360.9309
	-1.8439		4.9855	1.0620	-5.2566	5.7106	0.3310	1.1917	.5334	.5274
8.	107.377	-1143.33	370.617	-187.333	-720.463	986.04	305.55	550.210	497.202	286.073
	.3126	-3.689	1.110	-.508	-3.508	-2.957	.311	1.254	.905	1.194

SBPR. NO.	RECSS 11	FEMPEN 12	SS77 13	EDUC69 14	WEA77 15	INTRCEPT 16	KIDS 17	R-SQUARE 18	F-STATS 19
1.						3333.2886 7.4962		.0034	1.8524
2.						3331.9675 7.4704		.0034	1.4816
3.	−2334.3254 −8.3096					5314.6641 10.6587		.0338	15.3379
4.		.0840 6.7937				−2721.88 6.0586		.0239	10.7432
5.			−0.5200 −8.5784			4714.6016 10.1135		.0358	16.2491
6.				296.4890 12.3264		194.1917 0.3885		.0680	31.9722
7.						326.1150 7.5301		.0529	13.5650
8.	−888.75 −2.336	.034 2.601	−.3922 −4.828	214.729 8.305	.0185 5.979	2516.776 4.533	−35.839 −.84	.143	22.5258

Table 5.6   Pensions of Women with Positive Pensions (*t*-Statistics below Coefficients)

SBPR. NO.	NWHITE 1	LFP 2	PROF 3	CLERK 4	SKILLED 5	MANAG 6	SELF 7	WIDOW 8	DIV/SEP 9	RECSS 10
1.	-601.4692							-2156.0823	-2205.6345	
	-1.3280							-7.9522	-5.7758	
2.	-616.5217	743.2588						-2162.5237	-2207.0276	
	-1.3635	1.7455						-7.9898	-5.7900	
3.	-889.3832							-2212.5000	-2054.4351	-1989.0146
	-2.8231							-8.4468	-5.5607	-6.4617
4.	-505.69							-2109.7	-2155.4	
	-1.10							-7.7268	-5.6225	
5.	-982.6653							-2342.1174	-2259.4697	
	-2.1873							-8.7492	-6.0462	
6.	55.7803							-1683.7561	-1983.0435	
	0.1276							-6.3835	-5.4607	
7.	-563.7683		1658.1133	-599.1079	-1288.5254	-1008.7683	3011.5210	-1977.8240	-1958.0813	
	-1.2871		4.9551	-2.0798	-3.5067	-1.5837	2.2832	-7.5570	-5.3283	
8.	-405.566	283.554	1053.223	-408.633	-459.983	-822.263	3315.526	-1461.858	-1400.647	-1824.149
	-.9760	.720	3.223	-1.523	-1.301	-1.336	2.683	-5.481	-3.949	-3.887

SBPR. NO.	FENPEN 11	SS77 12	EDUC69 13	WEA77 14	INTRCEPT 15	KIDS 16	R-SQUARE 17	F-STATS 18
1.					4512.6117 23.4508		.1147	24.2265
2.					4458.4062 22.9154		.1195	18.9980
3.					6217.4805 19.2667		.1761	29.9284
4.	.048 1.36				4264.4		.1176	18.6624
5.		-.4403 -5.1245			5731.4883 18.8946		.1543	25.5531
6.			243.2953 8.0008		1387.2935 3.2179		.2055	36.2143
7.				.0092 3.233	4410.9648 19.3356		.2043	17.8480
8.	.0369 1.0720	-.129 -.956	185.577 5.959	.0092 3.233	3629.749 7.126	-172.718 -2.838	.3372	18.5208

pected lifetime and discounted at a rate of 1%. The expected lifetime, whose derivation is given in the appendix, varies by characteristics. Because I have changed the dependent variable in the OLS equation nonproportionality and because I have also converted social security benefits to a lifetime wealth measure, I have reestimated my most inclusive equations, which are shown in table 5.7. The coefficients are similar to those already discussed.

The total effect of any exogenous variable on dollar amount of pension received depends on the probability of receiving the pension and the impact on the pension conditional on receiving one. I have calculated these numbers evaluated at the means of the other variables. The results are given for my most inclusive constructs in tables 5.8–5.10.

The first entry in table 5.8 indicates that a married professional male has a pension with an expected present discounted value that is $6555 less if he receives social security benefits. (The footnote means that a pension in a specific occupation was used and not the actual distribution across occupations.) While the impacts of receiving social security are always negative, the amounts vary substantially by marital status and occupation. It is perhaps surprising that blue-collar workers do better than anyone else, but this is consistent with other data.

The impact of self-employment is always negative. Many of these people can continue to work longer, can often acquire large amounts of financial asset by selling their business, and generally acquire more financial

Table 5.7   **Pension Wealth Equations for Males**

Variable	Probability of Receiving Pension		Amount of Pension Wealth If Positive	
	MLE	t	Coefficient	t
Constant	− .48	− 9.04	− 23157.00	− 3.40
Married	.079	.80	58623.00	10.37
Widowed	.033	.29	43133.00	6.62
Div/sep	− .139	− 1.06	41059.00	5.33
Nonwhite	− .007	− .11	− 621.76	− .16
Educ 69	.07	11.74	2991.2	9.97
FemPen	− .000005	− 2.01	.356	2.37
Life SS	.000009	8.49	− .282	− 5.16
Prof	− .67	− 10.01	3151.00	.82
Clerk	− .30	− 3.63	− 1857.2	− .44
Skill	− .16	− 3.36	− 7783.00	− 3.29
Manager	− .64	− 9.45	12915.00	3.36
Self	− 1.29	− 9.21	− 3352.0	− .30
LFP	− .65	− 13.68	− 10071.00	− 3.52
Wea 77	.0000008	1.58	.188	5.27
Kids	− .033	− 3.75	− 448.14	− .911
Log likelihood	− 2907.48		$R^2 = .1823$	

Table 5.8 Total Marginal Effects of Various Variables on Dollar Amount of Lifetime Pensions

				Males					
	Receives SS	Self-Employed	Nonwhite	Labor Force Participant	2-Year ΔED	Kids	Life sS Δ100	Femmpen Δ100	Wealth Δ100
Married professionals[a]	−6554.7	−1107.4	−277.15	−10487.0	1859.94	−576.91	5.27	2.73	6.39
Widowed professionals[a]	−5242.8	−6740.1	−227.47	−7146.3	1495.61	−394.54	.655	4.96	5.67
Div/sep professionals[a]	−4249.1	−5083.5	−182.52	−5687.6	1172.38	−318.53	.656	3.88	4.54
Married clerks[a]	−8262.2	−1367.2	−364.53	−12266.0	2289.09	−650.94	1.73	7.43	8.90
Widowed clerks[a]	−6811.9	−784.5	−308.12	−8321.3	1826.87	−444.09	−3.45	9.91	8.17
Div/sep clerks[a]	−5766.0	−613.72	−258.67	−6906.5	1548.72	−374.56	−2.77	8.23	6.85
Married skill[a]	−8520.2	−1272.4	−384.12	−1165.8	2316.43	−610.08	−1.76	10.47	9.88
Widowed skill[a]	−7064.6	−643.8	−326.97	−7601.3	1851.12	−400.62	−6.98	12.97	9.04
Div/sep skill[a]	−6194.8	−5649.9	−283.48	−6778.7	1635.12	−363.04	−5.28	10.68	7.76
Married manager[a]	−7432.2	−1406.1	−310.72	−12730.0	2136.83	−698.31	8.30	1.30	6.89
Widowed manager[a]	−6085.4	−9467.4	−259.55	−9260.1	1710.57	−509.97	3.53	3.60	6.15
Div/sep manager[a]	−5012.1	−7335.7	−211.18	7541.6	1411.11	−421.62	3.24	2.67	4.97

[a]Versus unskilled workers of the same marital status and other variables at their mean.

wealth to cover widely fluctuating incomes. While most of these reasons are controlled for in this analysis, the results are obtained by evaluating the probit function at the sample mean of these variables.

The impact of race on expected pension wealth is almost zero. As noted earlier, there is little difference in payments once other variables are controlled for though substantial difference in the raw numbers.

Those still working, who have less need for a pension in the life-cycle view, expect to receive from $5600 to $12,300 smaller pensions. Each additional two-year change in education adds $1200–$2300 in pension wealth. Each child reduces expected wealth by $300–$700. Since variation in schooling is likely to be larger than in family size, the Barro explanation may not be quantitatively important. Each $100 increase in social security wealth has effects ranging from a decrease in pension wealth of $5 to an increase of $5. These are modest effects.

The impact of current family income is positive but only ranges from $1 to $13 with each $100 change. Financial wealth is positively related to pension wealth with impacts of about the same size.

The differences between marital status are given in table 5.9A, evaluated at the means. The comparisons are with never-married men. Married men do better than widows, who do better than divorced men, who do better than the never married. These results occur because of differentials both in life expectancy and in lifetime earnings.

The results for women are given in tables 5.10A and 5.10B. For the most part they are similar to those for men. However, the coefficient on self-employment has changed signs and is large; the effect of children is doubled, the effect of social security wealth is much increased, ranging between $10 and $26 per hundred-dollar change in this wealth; the impact of changes in financial wealth is muted; and marital status differences are smaller.

These results are derived from equations in which the labor force participation variable is included. As noted earlier, it is possible that pension wealth and retirement decisions are determined or planned for simultaneously. If so, it would be appropriate to eliminate the participation variable from the pension equations.

Doing so we obtain tables 5.9B, 5.9C, 5.10C, and 5.10D. The effects are somewhat different quantitatively. For example, for males the effects

Table 5.9.A	Marginal Effects of Marital Status, Single Is Comparison State			
	Males			
Marital Status	Professional	Clerk	Skilled	Manager
Div/sep	9343.52	14791.5	17338.8	9326.72
Widowed	11202.7	1689.1	19204.7	11770
Married	15925	23711.1	26795.1	16821.1

Table 5.9.B   Total Marginal Effects of Various Variables on Dollar Amount of Lifetime Pensions, Labor Force Participation Variable Excluded

Males

Group	Receives SS	Self-Employed	Nonwhite	2-Year ΔED	Kids	Lifetime SS Ben Δ100	Earn Δ100	Wealth Δ100
Married professionals	−5076.1	−10477	−568.36	3497.84	−592.71	8.0585	−8.0583	5.45279
Widowed professionals	−4499.9	−7153.8	−465.65	2942.07	−439.6	2.9242	−3.028	5.36766
Div/sep professionals	−3563.6	−5295.7	−368.03	2361.3	−349.59	2.5357	−2.6117	4.19705
Married clerk	−6858.6	−13677	−727.63	4431.21	−698.74	5.3036	−5.4442	8.17088
Widowed clerk	−6160.8	−8725.5	−60.28	3760.53	−508.53	−1.0199	.75406	8.06147
Div/sep clerk	−5136.3	−6764.6	−499.75	3178	−426.29	−.5574	.34306	6.65251
Married skill	−7577.9	−13778	−768.76	4684.6	−687.67	1.4857	−1.7475	9.62166
Widowed skill	−6855.4	−8010	−635.23	3991.4	−488	−5.2339	4.7318	9.50535
Div/sep skill	−5950.4	−6967.6	−558.02	3540.67	−442.43	−3.3555	3.04167	8.0288
Married manager	−5899.1	−13791	−682.75	4133.57	−736.54	11.5937	−11.54	6.07478
Widowed manager	−5302.7	−10258	−576.05	3558.17	−577.36	6.25912	−6.3129	5.98717
Div/sep mangaer	−4285.3	−7833.2	−466.61	2920.76	−472.81	5.55211	−5.5819	4.74371

Table 5.9.C   **Marginal Effects of Marital Status, Single Is Comparison State, Labor Force Participation Excluded**

	Males			
	Professional	Clerk	Skill	Manager
Div/sep	8877.39	14564.5	18089.3	9252.35
Widowed	10895.6	16878.7	20255.3	11971.7
Married	14404.8	22478	27091.7	15729.8

of receiving social security are generally substantially closer to zero and the educational effects are larger. For females the self-employment effect is reduced, presumably because many of the labor force participants are self-employed.

The amount of pension and savings required to finance retirement depends on how long the person expects to be retired. This period can differ because of variation in life expectancy and date of retirement. (The variations in life expectancy also influence the value of social security wealth.)

I have calculated average life expectancy and average retirement age in the following way. First using the RHS I have calculated probit equations for the probability of having died by a given year. The equations, which are given in the appendix, include as explanatory variables age, race, sex, education, and marital status. Let P_{jt} be the probability that a person with the jth set of characteristics will die in year t. The probability of surviving through year t is $(1 - P_{jt})$. The probability of surviving through year $t + k$ is $\pi (1 - P_{j,t}) (1 - P_{j, t+1}) \ldots (1 - P_{j}, t + k)$. The average life expectancy is found by dividing the π term, evaluated from age 60 to age 110, by k, or 51 years. The probit equations tell us how the P's vary as characteristics change.

The average retirement age was calculated in two ways. The first is an expectational view. I used unpublished March 1975 CPS tabulations on employment, unemployment, and nonparticipation by age, race, sex, and education to find average expected number of years of nonparticipation. The age groupings were in 10-year intervals beginning at 45. The average age of nonparticipation was subtracted from the average life expectancy. The second method uses age in 1977 and adjusts for being not retired then. I then estimate the probability of having a pension and the dollar amount of the pension on the average retirement period.

The equations include expected social security wealth and financial wealth since all three can be used to finance retirement though not bequests. Labor force participation is included because I assume that the 18% who are still working in 1977 will have an expected length of retirement of zero. This dummy variable permits me to correct any mistake in this assumption. As shown in table 5.11, the coefficient on actual retirement time (expected date of death minus current age is retired) is positive

Table 5.10.A   Total Marginal Effects of Various Variables on Dollar Amount of Lifetime Pensions

Lifetime

	Receives SS	Self-Employed	Nonwhite	Labor Force Participant	2-Year Δ100	Kids	Lifetime Δ100	Femmpen Δ100	Wealth Δ100
				Females					
Widowed professional[a]	−6658.0	6385.66	−2823.8	−8297.2	2341.15	−1101.4	25.85	22.78	3.47
Div/sep professional[a]	−6608.4	6444.81	−2529.2	−7333.0	2122.04	−984.8	24.71	23.61	2.27
Widowed clerk[a]	−4904.6	4648.94	−1811.1	−5042.7	1594.70	−711.17	18.27	17.65	2.27
Div/sep clerk[a]	−4861.9	4705.74	−1552.5	−4237.9	1391.21	−607.63	17.25	18.40	1.93
Widowed skill[a]	−3207.0	2785.22	−1480.7	−4061.8	1343.68	−590.18	13.15	10.31	1.92
Div/sep skill[a]	−3174.9	2837.93	−1270.0	−3432.1	1170.14	−504.99	12.31	10.96	1.64
Widowed manager[a]	−2799.2	2462.82	−1141.5	−3062.4	1064.49	−455.3	10.96	9.56	1.48
Div/sep manager[a]	−2769.5	2509.84	−952.77	−2506.9	9060.34	−378.71	10.02	10.14	1.23

[a]Versus unskilled workers of the same marital status and other variables at their mean.

and highly significant. The labor force participation dummy is significant and has a coefficient of $11,560, which is far less than the $15,800 average in the sample. Of course, the expected date of death is used in calculating the expected pension wealth, and this can lead to spurious correlation with retirement time. However, this correlation would be negative and would bias the retirement time coefficient downward. Moreover, dollar amounts of pensions are positively related to expected number of retirement years (equation not shown).

The above results are encouraging in that they indicate people who need more assets to maintain consumption over longer retirement periods have the assets, controlling for other types of wealth. However, pension wealth is generally accumulated over long periods of time. It is quite possible that choice of lifetime occupations occurs much earlier when one's post-65 health is unknown. Thus there is some interest in redoing the equation using years of retirement expected as of age 45. Separate estimates of nonparticipation were made by race, sex, and education (0–8, 9–11, 12, 13–15, and 16 and more years of schooling). Estimated year of death was also calculated for each group. Unfortunately, when the expected retirement years were included in the equation, it had a negative, significant coefficient and yielded a higher R^2 than in the first equation.

I then decided to separate out the retirement time from the expected death date. The results are shown in column 3. The variable for expected date of death is insignificant, while the expected years of retirement variable is negative and highly significant. Much of the variation in retirement is correlated with education and low wages. (See Parsons 1980). Apparently I am picking up the early retirement of this group whose wages and earnings base were low. The lower pensions and pension wealth may not represent a large decline in consumption or utility.

Victor Fuchs has suggested that people might use disability payments as an alternative source of funds while not working. I have used the 1973 CPS-SSA Exact Match Sample to estimate for those 45–65 a probit function for the probability of receiving (in 1976) disability payments from social security. (After 65 you switch to regular old age benefits.) The equation was then evaluated for various configurations and an average probability of being on disability was calculated for each different race, sex, education, and marital status possibility. When this variable is included in

Table 5.10.B   Total Marginal Effects of Marital Status, Single Is Comparison State

	Females			
	Professional	Clerk	Skilled	Manager
Div/sep	2086.1	1664.46	1017.87	9492.83
Widowed	3564.36	2720.51	1751.41	1569.29

Table 5.10.C   Total Marginal Effects of Various Variables on Dollar Amount of Lifetime Pensions, Labor Force Participation Variable Excluded

Females

Group	Receives SS	Self	NonWhite	2-Year ΔED	Lifetime SS Ben Δ100	Δ100 Earnings	Δ100 Wealth	Δ100 Kids
Widowed professionals	-6048.1	1087.25	-2981.4	2276.67	27.2323	-.0401	3.159	-1087.4
Div/sep professionals	-5964.5	2119.29	-2659.2	2057.92	25.6793	2.937	2.819	-968.48
Widowed clerk	-4520.6	1520.14	-1926.7	1560.74	19.268	2.747	2.0855	-707.87
Div/sep clerk	-4453.2	19792.21	-1645.3	1358.7	17.8801	5.44	1.779	-602.56
Widowed skill	-2988.4	480.994	-1584.9	1320.7	14.3003	-1.9945	1.765	-591.9
Div/sep skill	-2937.8	712.166	-1351.6	1145.28	13.138	.3265	1.505	-503.62
Widowed manager	-2177.2	429.898	-1028.1	897.486	9.939	-.2295	1.164	-386.09
Div/sep manager	-2136.3	609.65	-844.5	753.668	9.005	1.6326	.955	-315.99

Table 5.10.D   Marginal Effects of Marital Status, Single Is Comparison State

	Females			
	Professional	Clerk	Skilled	Manager
Div/sep	1673.49	1412.91	838.897	683.052
Widowed	3150.33	2408.9	1594.48	1212.65

Table 5.11   Expected Lifetime Pension and Retirement Times

	Coefficient	t-Value	Coefficient	t-Value
Constant	− 6956.6	(3.9)	19051.6	(1.2)
Expected date death			157.8	(.8)
Expected number retirement			− 2425.4	(16.5)
Years before 65				
Expected date death—actual age	1931.7	(10.2)		
Expected social security wealth	.097	(4.9)	.018	(.9)
Financial wealth 1977	.086	(7.5)	.058	(5.1)
Labor force participant 1977	11560.7	(5.4)	− 11485	(11.3)
$\bar{R}^2$	.05			.09

the pension or pension wealth equations, it is highly signficant statistically but changes other significant coefficients by only modest amounts.

5.5   Conclusions

In this paper I have used the Retirement History Survey to study how pensions are distributed among the elderly. Combining probit estimates for having a pension and OLS regressions for dollar amount of pensions and converting to pension wealth by discounting such benefits over remaining expected life, I find that the groups that have substantially less pension wealth are those receiving social security, the self-employed males, labor force participants, and those with many offspring. Those groups having substantially more pension wealth include currently or previously married men and women, the more educated, blue-collar workers, and self-employed females. I also find that those with greater expected realized retirement years have more pension wealth (controlling for other forms of nonhuman wealth) available. This last result is not attributable just to spurious correlation.

In a sense, I find that the predictions of Barro (1976), Feldstein (1974), Ando and Modigliani (1953), and Modigliani and Brumberg (1954) are all correct. There is behavior consistent with parents choosing smaller pensions and more current consumption if there are children available to help them. Recipients of social security, per se, have much less pension wealth. Moreover, pensions rise with social security benefits but the amounts are far less than dollar for dollar and total savings fall. The basic essence of the life-cycle model seems to be correct. People who are not retiring save less, and the amount available for retirement increases as the length of retirement grows.

Appendix

I first estimated the probit specification for 1971, 1973, 1975, and 1977 data with dead versus alive as dependent variables.

Using the estimated coefficients from above for each year, I computed the probability of dying for different configurations of individual characteristics. For each configuration I computed the probability of dying for each age within the age range of the sample for that year. Thus in 1971 I computed for a black married male the probability of dying at age 60, 61, . . . 65. This was done for 1971, 1973, 1975 and 1977 samples.

Thus, for each characteristic combination there are 24 probabilities of dying (each with a corresponding age). (For widowed black males I dropped 71 data because results are improbable.)

With the 24 probabilities derived above, I specified

$$\ln \text{prob} = \alpha + \beta \text{age} + e.$$

Using OLS (since TSCS regression [error comp] yielded almost identical results) I estimated $\hat{\alpha}$, $\hat{\beta}$. This was done for each characteristic combination. Using $\hat{\alpha}$, $\hat{\beta}$ I then computed expected life by evaluation of

$$i = \frac{\sum_{61}^{110} (1 - e^{\alpha + \hat{\beta}i})\, i}{\sum_{i=61}^{110} 1 - e^{\hat{\alpha} + \hat{\beta}i}}$$

for each combination of characteristics. If the probability of being alive $(1 - e^{\alpha + \beta \text{Age}})$ became less than zero, I stopped the iteration at the age $- 1$.

The above results were used only to measure differences between married, widowed, divorced, or separated.

From Vital Statistics (1977) I found the expected remaining years of life for white males, white females, black males, and black females in 1977.

Since I guessed that a large proportion of these people were married, I used these numbers as reflecting married white males, etc. I then adjusted these numbers for being divorced, widowed, etc., by subtracting the differences found above.

Table 5.A.1   **Probability of Dying**

Variable	1971 MLE	1973 MLE	1975 MLE	1977 MLE
Race	.38	.14	.081*	.034*
Sex	−3.06	−.36	−.16	−.044*
Educ 69	−.0025*	−.011	−.014	−.016
Widowed	3.49	.55	.60	.63
Div/sep	−.0087*	−2.45	−2.22	−2.58
Married	−.40*	−2.22	−2.07	−2.39
Age	.034*	.030	.019*	.018*
Constant	−3.21	−2.69	−2.09	−2.10

*Not significant at the 5% level.

To compute lifetime social security I combined the spouse's social security benefits with those of the husband or wife. Based on age, marital status, sex, and race, I added on the expected number of years they have to live using the numbers from above.

I then computed

$$\sum_t \frac{SS77 + SPSS77}{(1 + r)^t} = \text{lifetime SS} \quad r = .01$$

$$\text{expected life} - \text{age 77}$$

$t = 1$ for age in 1977.

The identical procedure was followed for pension variable.

Notes

1. While the original model assumed zero expected terminal wealth, the model can be modified to incorporate bequests. There is an empirical issue of whether the elderly dissave.

2. These numbers probably understate the increase since the methodology used by the Census Bureau assumes everyone dies by age 85. There are more people living beyond this age now than in the past.

3. See Barro (1976); however, children's presence may induce a person to accept a job with higher current salary and lower pension if capital markets are not perfect.

4. For some purposes my treatment will cause more simultaneous equations problems.

5. The estimates of labor force participation for males are in line with those in table 5.1.

6. For a discussion of the problem and a comparison of alternative treatments, see Duan (1982), pp. 20–24. His appendix A shows that the method is consistent even if errors in the two equations are correlated.

7. A few farmers are included in the omitted category.

8. See Behrman et al. (1980). It is not known if this result occurs because they work harder, have more responsibilities, specialize more, or if higher-ability males are more attractive mates.

9. Higher earnings are subject to larger marginal tax rates; however, married and single people face different tax rate schedules, and it is not clear who faces the higher tax rate. This

is important since pensions generally allow a person to transfer income to a year with lower expected tax rates.

10. Feldstein may have revised that hypothesis, for the *New York Times* reports that he does not generally think of his pension holding as part of his wealth.

11. About 200 people, or less than 10% of the sample, received a pension in 1977 but did not report an amount. I omitted these people from the analysis.

Comment   Victor R. Fuchs

This paper is an extension of Taubman's NBER Working Paper 811 (December 1981), "Pensions and Mortality." The principal objectives are (1) to describe how pensions vary across socioeconomic groups; (2) to pay special attention to relations between private pensions, social security, and total financial wealth; and (3) to explore the relation between pension wealth and length of retirement.

The paper partially succeeds on all three counts, but I have some reservations concerning the data set, omitted variables, and the interpretation of results.

The Data

Given the advanced age of the persons in the sample, some attention to possible biases introduced by selective attrition would be desirable. Consider the possibility of selective survival. For every nonwhite man in this sample in 1977 there was at least one other who died after the age of 30. (I estimate the survival rate for this cohort at about 460 from 1000 at age 30.) The estimated survival for white men is much higher—about 600 out of 1000 at age 30. The greater selectivity among the surviving nonwhite men means that these results could be giving a biased picture of the relation between race and pensions. Survival is also highly correlated with years of schooling, raising the possibility of bias for this variable as well.

The other attrition problem concerns losses from the sample for reasons other than death (e.g., change of location, illness, refusal to continue participation). My impression is that these losses were substantial between 1969 and 1977. One wonders who was lost and why. These losses from the sample may be a particular problem in the probability of death regressions. In these equations divorced and separated men have as low a probability of death as married men. This is contrary to all previous results, including earlier studies based on the Retirement History Survey.

Another question about the data concerns the size of pension wealth relative to social security wealth. For 1971, Blinder, Wise, and Gordon (1981) estimated social security wealth as 60% of the total of social secur-

Victor R. Fuchs is professor of economics at Stanford University and program director for health economics at the National Bureau of Economic Research.

ity, pension, and financial wealth, and estimated pensions at 11%. In this paper the proportions are 45% and 23% respectively.

Also, why do so many more women than men "expect" to receive a pension, though they are not receiving it in 1977? For every hundred women receiving a pension in 1977, 69 others expect to receive one. For every hundred men receiving a pension in 1977, only 16 others expect to receive one.

Missing Variables

Although a great many variables are included in the analyses, at least two potentially important ones are missing. It is well known that unionized workers have greater pension benefits than nonunionized ones and that union status is correlated with several of the variables that are included. Which relations dominate? Also, disability payments have not been considered. Such payments could play an important role as a supplement to pension wealth for men who retire at an early age. Explicit attention to disability payments might help clarify the relation between pension wealth and years of retirement. The analysis of the relation between pensions and social security wealth would probably benefit from explicit attention to the distinction between government and private wage and salary workers.

Interpretation of Results

Are the right-hand-side variables really exogenous, as stated explicitly once and implicitly throughout? There are good reasons to believe that many of the important ones are not. The exogeneity of labor force participation is highly questionable: many papers based on the RHS data use pensions to *explain* labor force participation. Self-employment is also suspect as an exogenous variable. I used the RHS data in a longitudinal mode to study switching from wage-and-salary status to self-employment and found that the absence of a private pension was the strongest and most significant predictor of switching (Fuchs, 1982).

Problems of endogeneity aside, there is still a serious problem of how to interpret a correlation between pension benefits and various socioeconomic characteristics. Suppose one had a variable that was certified by the AEA Executive Committee as truly exogenous (e.g., height). Suppose that, ceteris paribus, this variable was highly correlated with pension benefits. Does this mean that tall men take a larger share of their compensation in the form of pensions, or do their higher pensions reflect additional compensation? The paper seems ambivalent on this question. At one point we read that the fact that married men are more likely to have a pension suggests that they have a lower rate of time preference than single men. This sounds like they are taking a larger share of their compensation in pensions. Later on, the married men are described as "doing better" than others, as evidenced by the larger pensions. This sounds like they are getting greater compensation. I believe that Taubman leans toward the first interpretation, but a more explicit discussion of this question would be welcome.

Why would some men choose to take a larger share of their compensation in pension form? The pension literature suggests two principal reasons: to avoid taxes, and as part of an optimal labor contract that benefits both employer and employee by reducing turnover during the worker's most productive years and then inducing retirement when productivity falls. I would underscore a third reason. Some workers (and their wives) probably like the forced saving or precommitment aspect of pensions. They want to save for their old age but doubt their ability to do it on their own. Moreover, the rate of return on a group pension may be more favorable than could be obtained through individual purchase of an annuity. A fourth possibility is paternalism, or concern about reputation. This might help explain why large firms and unions are particularly eager to include pensions in the compensation package.

How do these reasons relate to the regressions reported in this paper? The connection is not clear. To make further progress, it will be necessary to develop models that permit some discrimination among alternative explanations. One possibility is to introduce variables that are closely tied to a particular explanation. For instance, it should be possible to identify men who face different tax schedules (perhaps because of marital status) to test whether tax considerations play an important role. State of residence affects taxes because some states do not have any income taxes and rates vary among the other states. If tax avoidance is an important explanation for pensions, state of residence should matter. Furthermore, it should matter more for high-income workers, that is, there should be an interaction effect.

My final comments concern the relation between social security and pension wealth. For men, the larger the social security benefit, the more likely they are to be receiving a pension. But conditional on receiving a pension, the larger the social security benefit, the smaller the size of the private pension. This is an unusual result. Most variables have the same sign in the probability of receiving a pension and the size of pension regressions, for example, education, labor force participation, occupation. What's happening? One possibility is that government workers are a much larger proportion of those with private pension than they are of the total population. The pensions of government workers are larger, on average, than those of private sector workers, but their social security benefits are probably much smaller. It is possible that social security benefits and pension benefits are positively correlated for both government workers and private sector workers, but that the inclusion of both classes in the same regression produces a negative relation. (See fig. 5.C.1.) It might be desirable to do separate analyses for government workers and for private

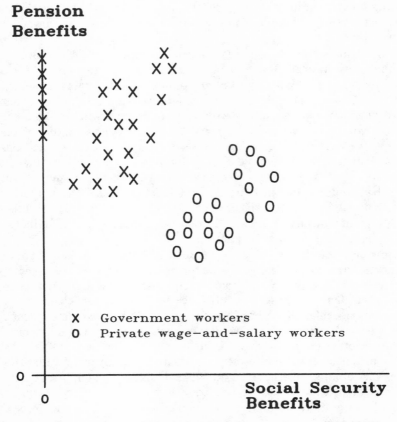

Fig. 5.C.1   Hypothetical relationship between private pensions and social security benefits.

sector employees. Similarly, it probably would be helpful to drop the self-employed, since it is highly unlikely that the other variables work the same way for self-employed as for wage-and-salary workers. The same might be done for farmers.

In general, one way to tease more out of the data might be through disaggregation. It may be possible to discriminate among competing explanations by looking at differences in the way certain variables work for some groups compared to others.

References

Ando, A., and F. Modigliani, 1953. The "life cycle" hypothesis of saving: Aggregate implications and tests. *American Economic Review* 53: 55–84.

Barro, R. 1976. Are government bonds net wealth? *Journal of Political Economy* 84: 1095–1117.

Behrman, J., et al. 1980. *Socioeconomic success: A study of the effects of genetic endowments, family environment and schooling.* Amsterdam: North-Holland.

Blinder, A. 1982. Private pensions and public pensions: Theory and fact. NBER Working Paper, no. 902.

Blinder, A.; Gordon, R.; and Wise, D. 1981. Social security, bequests, and the life cycle theory of saving: Cross-sectional tests. NBER Working Paper no. 619.

Duan, N. 1982. Appendix A. In *A comparison of alternative models for the demand for medical care* by N. Duan, W. Manning, C. Morris, and J. Newhouse. Santa Monica, Calif.: Rand Corp.

Feldstein, M. 1974. Social security, induced retirement, and aggregate capital accumulation. *Journal of Political Economy* 82: 905–26.

Fuchs, Victor R. 1982. Self-employment and labor force participation of older males. *Journal of Human Resources* 17: 339–57. (NBER Reprint 318.)

Kotlikoff, L., and Summers, L. 1981. The role of intergenerational transfers in aggregate capital accumulation. *Journal of Political Economy.* 89: 706–32.

Lazear, E. 1979. Why is there mandatory retirement? *Journal of Political Economy* (November/December) 87:1261–84.

Modigliani, F., and Brumberg, R. 1954. Utility analysis and the consumption function: An interpretation of cross section data. In *Post Keynsian economics,* K. Kurihara, ed., Rutgers, NJ: Rutgers University Press.

Munnell, A. 1982. *The economics of private pensions.* Washington, D.C.: Brookings Institution.

Parsons, D. 1980. Racial trends in male labor force participation. *American Economic Review* (December).

Samuelson, P. 1958. An exact consumption loan model of interest with or without the social contrivance of money. *Journal of Political Economy* 66: 467–82.

Taubman, P. 1981. Pensions and mortality. NBER Working Paper no. 811.

6 Social Security, Health Status, and Retirement

Jerry A. Hausman
David A. Wise

As people age they would like to work less. We observe, however, that for most persons, retirement is abrupt. The typical person retires from a job at which he was working full time, although many work part time on another job after retirement. Because retirement is a discrete outcome, it is natural to think of it in a qualitative choice framework. But retirement also has a time dimension, age, which not only characterizes retirement but affects the desire for it as well. Thus it is natural to describe retirement within the context of a continuous time qualitative choice model. In this spirit, we pursue a probability model of time to retirement (age of retirement).

We shall begin with a failure rate or hazard model specification common in the statistical and biometric literature (see Cox 1972 or Kalbfleisch and Prentice 1973, for example). Such a model was recently used by Lancaster (1979) to describe the duration of unemployment. Our model parallels his, with some slight extensions.[1] This model is essentially a reduced-form specification. In particular, it seems to have no natural utility maximization or first choice interpretation common to qualitative choice models in the econometric literature (e.g., McFadden 1973; Hausman and Wise 1978).

We then pursue another continuous time model of retirement that we hope will ultimately lend itself to a more structural interpretation but which also maintains the advantages of the hazard model. The central idea is to specify disturbances that follow a continuous time Brownian

Jerry A. Hausman is professor of economics, Massachusetts Institute of Technology, and research associate, National Bureau of Economic Research. David A. Wise is John F. Stambaugh Professor of Political Economy, John F. Kennedy School of Government, Harvard University, and research associate, National Bureau of Economic Research.

We are grateful for the extensive research assistance of Andrew Lo, Douglas Phillips, Lynn Paquette, and Robert Vishny.

motion (or Wiener) process. (See, e.g., Cox and Miller 1965; Karlin and Taylor 1975.) This leads to retirement likelihoods that have much in common with probit qualitative choice models while capturing the continuous time hazard idea as well. The specification of this model as we have set it up differs substantially from the hazard model. In particular, we make explicit use of hours worked before retirement, a consideration that plays no role in the hazard model. To date, however, the specifications of this model have not yielded entirely plausible results. We present the model nonetheless, in the hope that our experience will be of interest to others facing similar problems.

Empirical analysis is based on the Longitudinal Retirement History Survey (LRHS). The survey began in 1969 with over 11,000 persons who were aged 58–63 at that time. A series of follow-up surveys were used to obtain information on these persons at two-year intervals through 1979. We use all six surveys. The LRHS provides detailed labor supply, social security, earnings, health, and other information about those surveyed. To motivate the development below, we shall have in mind observations on each individual at selected ages.

The empirical focus of the paper is the effect of health and social security wealth, or social security payments, on retirement. Labor force participation fell significantly during the period of our data; the participation rate of men fell particularly substantially. The rates for 60–64-year-olds and those 65 between 1969 and 1979 were as shown in the unnumbered table below.[2]

Year	60–64	65 +
1969	75.8	27.4
1971	74.0	26.3
1973	68.9	23.4
1975	65.4	21.9
1977	62.6	19.9
1979	61.1	20.3

Part of this decline may have resulted from real increases in social security benefits, at least between 1969 and 1975. But counteracting influences were provided by increased real earnings during the beginning of the period and by large increases in future social security benefits from continued work. This latter effect has been emphasized by Blinder et al. (1980). Our models attempt to distinguish the effects of these influences.

The estimates based on both of the models that we use suggest a strong effect of social security benefits on the probability of retirement, with the increase in benefits between 1969 and 1975 accounting for possibly a 3%–5% increase in the probability of retirement for men 62–66. Both models suggest that increases in real earnings decrease the probability of retirement. Results based on the hazard model indicate that increases in future social security benefits decrease the probability of retirement, while the initial results of the Wiener model suggest the opposite. Because the Brownian motion model is in the early stages of formulation and the results are preliminary, it may be premature to attempt to explain the differences in results.

We begin by setting forth the hazard model. Then we present descriptive statistics that help motivate our specification of this model. For convenience, we also present data that help to understand our formulation of the Brownian motion alternative. After presenting estimates based on the hazard model, we describe a continuous time model of retirement based on a Brownian motion process and then present initial estimates based on this model.

6.1 The Proportional Hazard Approach

6.1.1 The Model

Suppose the probability that a person *has* retired by age t is given by

$$(1) \qquad G(t) = 1 - \frac{1}{\exp[\int_0^t \theta(\tau)d\tau]}$$

where $\theta > 0$. This is a convenient probability specification with the intuitive property that the probability of retirement goes to one as t gets large. For example, if θ were a function only of age, with $\theta(t) = f(t) = t^{\alpha-1}/\alpha$, $\alpha > 0$, then $G(t)$ would be $1 - \exp[t^\alpha/\alpha^2]^{-1}$, with $\exp[\cdot]^{-1}$ going to zero as t increases. Note that $f(t)$ is increasing with age if $\alpha > 1$ and decreasing with age if $0 < \alpha < 1$.

Associated with this "cumulative distribution" function is the density function

$$(2) \qquad G'(t) = g(t) = \frac{1}{\exp[\int_0^t \theta(\tau)]d\tau} \cdot \theta(t) = [1 - G(t)] \cdot \theta(t) ,$$

describing the likelihood of retirement at ages t ($0 < t < \infty$). The "instantaneous" hazard rate describes the conditional likelihood of retirement at age t, given that the person has not retired before t. It is simply

$$(3) \qquad \frac{g(t)}{1 - G(t)} = \theta(t) .$$

To make the distribution function $G(t)$ a function of individual attributes, the instantaneous hazard rate θ is parameterized in terms of attributes $\mathbf{X}$, in this case including age itself. For expository purposes, it is useful to develop the specification in stages. Suppose first that θ is a function of age t and of individual attributes $\mathbf{X}_1$ that do not change with age such that $\theta(t) = e^{X_1\beta} \cdot f(t) = e^{X_1\beta_1} \cdot t^{\alpha-1}/\alpha$, where β_1 is a vector of parameters and X_1 a vector of attributes. In this case, the probability of being retired by age t is $G(t) = 1 - \exp[e^{X_1\beta_1} \cdot t^\alpha/\alpha^2]^{-1}$.

Now suppose that there are unobserved as well as observed determinants of retirement. A convenient way to allow for unobserved individual attributes is to specify a random individual-specific term ν that enters θ such that

(4) $$\theta(t) = \nu \cdot e^{X_1\beta_1} \cdot t^{\alpha-1}/\alpha.$$

Note that ν is time invariant; it simply induces a proportional shift in the hazard function $\theta(\cdot)$ over all values of age t. The same is true for differences in X_1.

If we assume that ν has a gamma distribution over individuals $(0 < \nu < \infty)$, we can obtain a closed-form solution for $G(t)$.[3] In particular, the probability that a person with attributes X_1 has retired by age t is given by

$$G(t;X_1) = {}_0\!\int^\infty [G(t;X_1,\nu)]\,f(\nu)d\nu\ ,$$

$$= 1 - {}_0\!\int^\infty \exp\left[- {}_0\!\int^t\theta(\tau)d\tau \right] f(\nu)d\nu\ ,$$

(5)

$$= 1 - {}_0\!\int^\infty \exp\left[- \nu\exp(X_1\beta){}_0\!\int^t f(\tau)d\tau \right] f(\nu)d\nu\ ,$$

$$= 1 - [\,1 + \sigma2\exp(X_1\beta_1)\cdot t^\alpha/\alpha^2]^{-1/\sigma2}\ ,$$

with the last term obtained after some manipulation. Although this expression is not defined for $\sigma^2 = 0$, as the variance goes to zero, $G(t;X_1)$ goes to $1 - \exp(e^{X_1\beta} \cdot t^\alpha/\alpha^2)^{-1}$, the result with no random term.

Finally, suppose that there are some measured individual attributes X_2 that change with age. We again specify θ in a separable manner as

(6) $$\theta(t) = \nu \cdot e^{X_1\beta_1} \cdot X_2(t) \cdot f(t)\ .$$

Now the probability of retirement by age t becomes

(7) $$G(t;X) = 1 - [1 + \sigma^2\exp(X_1\beta_1) \cdot {}_0\!\int^t X_2(\tau) \cdot f(\tau)d\tau]^{-1/\sigma^2}\ .$$

The specification is completed by describing the integral

(8) $${}_0\!\int^t X_2(\tau) \cdot f(\tau)d\tau\ .$$

Since we do not have continuous observations on X_2, which would presumably allow integration over the function $X_2(t)$ determined by such a path, we specify the integral using the piecewise linear formulation

(9) $${}_0\!\int^t X_2(\tau) \cdot f(\tau)d\tau = \sum_{p=0}^{N} \bar{X}_2(p)\beta_2 \cdot \int_{t0(p)}^{tf(p)} f(\tau)d\tau\ ,$$

where p denotes the period. For example, $p = 0$ indicates the period between age 54 and the age at the time of the first survey, $p = 1$ indicates the period between the first and second survey, and so on. Note that 54 is taken as an arbitrary starting point, implicitly assuming that no one would have retired before this age. The variable $\overline{\mathbf{X}}_2(p)$ is the average of $\mathbf{X}_2$ during period p, and $t_0(p)$ and $t_f(p)$ are the initial and final ages, respectively, of the person during period p. (A discretely changing variable, like married or not, is taken to be the value of the variable the next time it is observed. If the variable is continuous, like income, the average is obtained by assuming that the variable followed a linear path over time.) We can also alter the specification of θ to allow for a discontinuous jump in the hazard rate at any age t. For example, $\mathbf{X}_1$ can include dummy variables that assume nonzero values at particular ages.

Given $\theta(t)$ and $G(t)$, it is straightforward to specify the likelihood of a variety of sample observations (see, e.g., Lancaster 1979). In particular, in our case there are three possibilities: the person was retired when first surveyed at age $t(1)$ with corresponding probability $G[t(1)]$, the person had not retired by the last (Nth) survey period at age $t(N)$ with probability $1 - G[t(N)]$, or the person retired between the nth and mth surveys, when he was aged $t(n)$ and $t(m)$, respectively, with probability $G[t(n)] - G[t(m)]$. The likelihood function obtained from these terms may be maximized to obtain estimates of the coefficients β on the variables $\mathbf{X}$ and on age, as well as the variance σ^2 of v.

6.1.2 Some Descriptive Statistics

Before we discuss estimates based on this model, we shall present summary statistics that help to motivate the model and our particular specification of it. Although our estimates are based on non-self-employed males, for comparative purposes, we also present descriptive data for self-employed men and for women. Empirical hazard rates for non-self-employed men are shown in table 6.1, by age and survey year. Tables 6.2 and 6.3 contain analogous data for self-employed men and for women, respectively. These data show the proportion of those not retired in a given year who retired during the next two-year interval. First we observe that the pattern of rates for self-employed men is quite different from the pattern for the non-self-employed. In particular, the jump at age 62 is much less pronounced for the self-employed, and the rates thereafter are much lower. The rates for women, however, are not strikingly different from those for men. This suggests that the availability of social security at 62 for the non-self-employed may play a substantial role in retirement behavior.

The hazard rates for men are graphed in figure 6.1. While the rates increase rather smoothly to age 62, we observe substantial jumps between ages 63 and 65 and then very little increase in the hazard rates after 65. This pattern would appear to be inconsistent with a hazard rate $\theta(t) = f(t) = t^{\alpha-1}/\alpha$ that depends only on age and is always increasing in age for $a > 1$. Thus we allow the hazard rate $\theta(\cdot)$ to depend on individual attributes $\mathbf{X}$,

Table 6.1   Retirement Hazard Rates for Non-Self-Employed Males, by Age and Year

Age	Year 1969	1971	1973	1975	1977	All Years
58	10.7 (782)					10.7 (782)
59	12.0 (872)					12.0 (872)
60	24.6 (826)	30.5 (662)				27.2 (1488)
61	32.4 (819)	36.2 (723)				34.2 (1542)
62	29.1 (717)	34.8 (604)	33.9 (445)			32.3 (1766)
63	57.3 (546)	64.6 (534)	60.3 (438)			60.7 (1518)
64		72.9 (480)	68.1 (398)	65.1 (321)		69.2 (1119)
65		58.9 (236)	56.7 (701)	55.6 (193)		57.3 (630)
66			45.8 (144)	52.0 (150)	49.1 (110)	49.0 (404)
67			52.6 (116)	50.0 (110)	51.7 (87)	51.4 (313)
68				58.2 (98)	51.5 (68)	55.4 (166)
69				52.3 (65)	48.3 (60)	50.4 (125)
70					52.0 (50)	52.0 (50)
71					50.0 (32)	50.0 (32)

Note: The hazard rate in year t is the ratio of the number of people who retire between years t and $t + 2$ to the number of nonretired people in year t, in percent. Numbers in parentheses are numbers of observations used to calculate hazards.

as well as on age. In particular, this pattern motivates the assumption of the unobserved random terms v that induce proportional shifts in the hazard rate, given **X** and t.

The percentage of non-self-employed men that is retired is shown in table 6.4 and for each age and year. Figure 6.2 presents the same data graphically. The most striking feature of these data is the very marked increase between 1969 and 1973 in retirement rates of men 62–65. For example, 31% of 62-year-olds were retired in 1969; by 1973, almost 42% of this

Table 6.2   **Retirement Hazard Rates for Self-Employed Males, by Age and Year**

	Year					
Age	1969	1971	1973	1975	1977	All Years
58	9.6					9.6
	(187)					(187)
59	11.6					11.6
	(172)					(172)
60	29.2	28.2				28.7
	(171)	(174)				(345)
61	30.4	24.8				27.7
	(184)	(177)				(361)
62	29.6	33.0	29.8			30.7
	(145)	(118)	(121)			(384)
63	54.9	44.5	46.6			49.0
	(142)	(119)	(131)			(392)
64		58.0	43.2	66.7		55.7
		(112)	(74)	(60)		(246)
65		37.9	37.3	44.9		39.6
		(66)	(59)	(49)		(174)
66			44.2	35.0	27.3	36.8
			(52)	(40)	(33)	(125)
67			36.2	33.3	57.6	42.0
			(47)	(27)	(33)	(107)
68				26.9	51.4	41.3
				(26)	(37)	(63)
69				40.7	34.4	37.3
				(27)	(32)	(59)
70					51.8	51.8
					(27)	(27)
71					31.8	31.8
					(22)	(22)

Note: The hazard rate in year t is the ratio of the number of people who retire between years t and $t + 2$ to the number of nonretired people in year t, in percent. Numbers in parentheses are numbers of observations used to calculate hazards.

age group were retired. Note that the limited evidence provided in these data suggests little change in retirement rates after 1973. About 79% of 65-year-olds were retired in both 1973 and in 1975.

The estimates we present below depend in part on our definition of retirement. We assume that a person is retired when he says that he is fully or partially retired. Although this may seem an obvious choice, on reflection, it becomes clear that retirement status is ambiguous. For example, our definition does not correspond to zero hours of work. While many

Table 6.3   Retirement Hazard Rates for Women, by Age and Year

Age	Year 1969	1971	1973	1975	1977	All Years
58	16.9 (231)					16.9 (231)
59	22.8 (272)					22.8 (272)
60	32.5 (274)	38.4 (198)				35.0 (472)
61	34.6 (243)	40.4 (220)				37.4 (463)
62	31.8 (242)	31.0 (187)	35.0 (117)			32.2 (546)
63	52.4 (185)	54.8 (168)	58.6 (133)			54.9 (486)
64		55.2 (181)	68.6 (137)	65.4 (78)		61.9 (396)
65		60.7 (107)	61.2 (85)	61.2 (67)		61.0 (259)
66			49.4 (89)	61.1 (54)	42.8 (35)	51.7 (178)
67			61.2 (49)	46.2 (39)	58.8 (34)	55.7 (122)
68				59.6 (52)	47.8 (23)	56.0 (75)
69				50.0 (26)	53.3 (30)	51.8 (56)
70					44.8 (29)	44.8 (29)
71					61.1 (18)	61.1 (18)

Note: The hazard rate in year *t* is the ratio of the number of people who retire between years *t* and *t* + 2 to the number of nonretired people in year *t,* in percent. Numbers in parentheses are numbers of observations used to calculate hazards.

people who are retired by our definition do not work at all, many do. In practice, our definition corresponds closely to retirement from a full-time or primary job. It is important to realize the significance of this distinction. It is possible, for example, that social security benefits have effects on retirement, by our definition, that are different from their effects on work after retirement. If hours of work are used to define retirement, the two types of effect are confounded. We have chosen to try to separate them. (Although we had intended to consider both retirement and work after retirement, we have been able to address only the first in this paper.

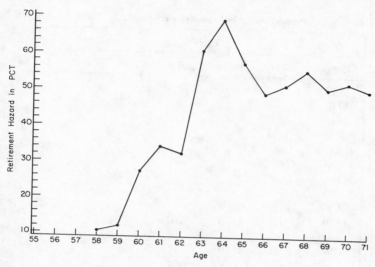

Fig. 6.1   Conditional retirement probabilities (hazards) by age for non-self-employed males.

In subsequent work we have addressed work after retirement. See Burtless and Moffitt [1983].)

The data in tables 6.5 and 6.6 help to clarify the distinction. Mean hours of work per week by retirement status and age, as well as employment status and sex, are shown in table 6.5. The first two columns of the table pertain to non-self-employed men. Notice that mean hours of work per week decline with age if those who are fully or partially retired are included in the sample. But among those who are not retired, there is virtually no decline between ages 58 and 63 and very little decline thereafter. Thus almost all of the reduction in hours is due to zero or reduced hours of work among those who are retired.[4] The same is true for self-employed men and for women. Most of the numbers in table 6.5 represent averages over two or three survey years. The details by year are shown in tables 6.A.1 through 6.A.6. In addition to little decline in hours worked per week among the nonretired, table 6.A.6 shows that there is also very little decline in weeks worked per year among men who are not self-employed and not retired.

While this empirical fact is not inconsistent with the hazard model specification of retirement, it is at variance with the standard form of the Brownian motion specification that we shall consider subsequently.

6.1.3   Hazard Model Parameter Estimates

The variables used in our analysis are defined as follows:

Social security (SS) payments: The monthly payments a person would receive were he to retire at a given age.

Table 6.4   **Proportion Retired for Non-Self-Employed Males, by Age and Year**

Age	Year						All Years
	1969	1971	1973	1975	1977	1979	
58	12.7 (879)						12.7 (879)
59	16.0 (1016)						16.0 (1016)
60	19.1 (1026)	19.2 (790)					19.2 (1816)
61	23.5 (1076)	24.0 (924)					23.8 (2000)
62	31.3 (1029)	37.1 (935)	41.9 (725)				36.2 (2689)
63	40.5 (912)	45.9 (978)	49.6 (841)				(45.2) (2731)
64		50.4 (959)	55.8 (864)	60.2 (683)			54.9 (2506)
65		72.9 (834)	79.3 (878)	78.9 (786)			77.0 (2498)
66			84.9 (881)	84.1 (805)	85.3 (632)		84.7 (2318)
67			85.6 (764)	88.8 (814)	89.7 (712)		88.0 (2290)
68				90.0 (834)	91.4 (734)	89.2 (576)	90.3 (2144)
69				91.8 (684)	92.2 (743)	92.5 (664)	92.2 (2091)
70					94.0 (749)	93.7 (695)	93.8 (1444)
71					95.0 (622)	94.2 (678)	94.6 (1300)
72						94.3 (683)	94.3 (683)
73						95.3 (567)	95.3 (569)

Note: The number in parentheses is the number of observations used to calculate the associated mean.

Change in (Δ) social security payments: The increment to monthly social security payments were a person to work for another year and then retire.
Social security wealth: The present discounted value of social security payments were a person to retire at a given age.

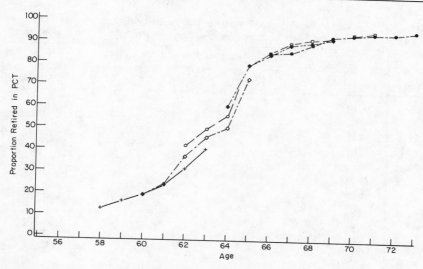

Fig. 6.2   Proportion retired by age and year for non-self-employed males.

Table 6.5   **Mean Hours of Work per Week by Age, Sex, Employment Status, and Retirement Status**

| | Men | | | | Women | |
| | Not Self-Employed | | Self-Employed | | | |
Age	Total[a]	Not Retired	Total[a]	Not Retired	Total[a]	Not Retired
58	42.4	42.8	48.7	50.0	38.1	38.5
59	42.3	42.8	47.2	49.6	37.1	38.0
60	41.8	42.2	47.5	49.4	37.3	38.7
61	41.5	42.1	46.7	49.0	36.5	38.2
62	41.0	42.1	45.3	48.8	35.8	38.6
63	40.8	42.4	43.0	48.2	34.7	38.0
64	39.3	41.5	42.0	49.2	33.5	37.8
65	36.5	41.3	37.7	47.4	30.5	36.4
66	33.8	41.2	37.6	45.6	28.5	35.9
67	32.2	39.6	35.3	46.0	26.7	35.2
68	30.0	38.8	37.0	47.0	26.8	34.8
69	29.8	39.4	32.6	43.5	24.8	34.3
70	28.2	37.1	34.7	47.2	25.5	34.9
71	28.9	36.9	31.9	41.4	24.0	29.5
72	25.9	35.6	31.6	43.1	28.1	33.9
73	29.8	36.0	30.6	35.8	21.1	29.9

[a]Includes fully or partially retired.

Table 6.6   Mean of Weeks Worked per Year for Non-Self-Employed Men, by Age and Year[a] Excluding Fully or Partially Retired

Age	1969	1971	1973	1975	1977	1979	All Years
			Year				
58	51.3 (248)						51.3 (248)
59	51.2 (265)						51.2 (265)
60	50.4 (242)	49.9 (656)					50.0 (1898)
61	51.0 (242)	50.2 (730)					50.4 (1972)
62	51.1 (222)	50.4 (610)	50.2 (449)				50.4 (1281)
63	50.9 (162)	50.1 (551)	49.7 (449)				50.0 (1162)
64		50.1 (492)	49.7 (401)	49.6 (318)			49.8 (1211)
65		50.2 (229)	49.4 (195)	49.4 (196)			49.7 (620)
66			49.5 (142)	47.2 (142)	50.0 (98)		48.8 (382)
67			47.7 (117)	48.6 (113)	48.6 (80)		48.2 (310)
68				49.5 (89)	47.6 (63)	39.7 (26)	47.4 (178)
69				48.8 (66)	46.9 (53)	35.6 (14)	46.6 (133)
70					48.6 (53)	39.9 (19)	45.9 (61)
71					46.0 (33)	38.8 (13)	44.0 (46)
72						40.4 (21)	40.4 (21)
73						41.1 (12)	41.1 (12)

[a]For 1971–79, the variable is one-half the number of weeks worked in the past two years, while the 1969 variable is usual weeks per year. The number in parentheses is the number of observations used to calculate the associated mean.

Change in social security wealth: The change in the present discounted value of social security payments were a person to work for another year and then retire.

Bad health: One if the person reported that poor health "limited the kind and amount of work" he could do, zero otherwise.

Earnings: Estimated earnings were the person to work for an additional year.

Liquid assets: Total of liquid assets.

Pension eligibility: One if the person would receive a private pension were he to retire, zero otherwise.

Education: Years of schooling.

Dependents: Number of completely supported children.

Age: Years old.

Because of limitations and apparent inaccuracies in reporting nonliquid assets in the RHS that, in particular, make it difficult to compare these assets from one year to the next, we have not used these values in our analysis. After more concerted data cleaning and estimation, we will probably be able to include nonliquid assets in future work.

The results of four alternative specifications are presented in table 6.7. The first two use social security payments as an explanatory variable, while the next two use social security wealth instead. Liquid assets are used in one of each of these groups.

To interpret the parameter estimates it is helpful to consider a case simpler than ours, with the hazard $\theta(t) = e^{X_1\beta_1} \cdot t^{\alpha-1}/\alpha$. In this case, the time T to retirement is given by $E(T) = \exp(-X_1\beta_1\cdot\alpha)$, with $\ln[E(T)] = -X_1\beta_1\cdot\alpha$, so that a unit increase in X_1 yields a percentage change in $E(T)$ equal to $-\beta_1\cdot\alpha$. Our model is more complicated, so that this simple result does not hold, but it is still a useful guide to interpretation. To obtain a better idea of the effects of changes in the variables in our model we must present simulation results. We do this after discussing the parameter estimates themselves.

First we find that an increase in monthly social security payments increases the likelihood of retirement after age 62, while larger increments in payments prolong work. The relevant parameters are measured with considerable precision. Thus our results appear to confirm the hypothesis of Blinder et al. (1980), although they think of this increment as an addition to the wage. We obtain comparable results when we use social security wealth instead of payments. According to the likelihood values, however, the social security wealth specification appears to fit the data much better than the payments version.

Poor health reduces the age of retirement substantially, by 1%–2% according to our estimates. Its effect is approximately equivalent to an increase of $70 per month in social security payments between the ages of 62 and 64, according to our results. Poor health has a somewhat greater effect than a $10,000 increase in social security wealth between 62 and 64, based on specifications (3) and (4). Liquid assets also are associated with earlier retirement, but because we have not calculated the annuity value of

Table 6.7   **Hazard Model Parameter Estimates (Standard Errors in Parentheses)**

Variable	Specification			
	(1)	(2)	(3)	(4)
SS payments, age 62–64 (100s)	.595 (.067)	.594 (.067)	—	—
SS payments, age ≥ 65	1.702 (.068)	1.731 (.069)	—	—
Δ SS payments	−1.020 (.148)	−1.022 (.150)	—	—
SS wealth, age 62–64 (10,000s)	—	—	.598 (.048)	.603 (.048)
SS wealth, age ≥ 65	—	—	1.357 (.089)	1.386 (.091)
Δ SS wealth	—	—	−8.265 (.611)	−8.244 (.613)
Bad health	.394 (.100)	.407 (.100)	.699 (.133)	.780 (.133)
Earnings (10,000s)	−.474 (.109)	−.567 (.113)	−.154 (.155)	−.301 (.160)
Liquid assets (10,000s)	—	.060 (.009)	—	.078 (.025)
Pension eligibility	.033 (.076)	.029 (.076)	−.089 (.098)	−.097 (.099)
Education	−.476 (.025)	−.481 (.026)	−.453 (.029)	−.457 (.030)
Dependents	−.608 (.078)	−.608 (.079)	−.558 (.095)	−.559 (.096)
Age parameter α	2.695 (.165)	2.739 (.170)	2.807 (.217)	2.860 (.223)
Standard deviation of ν	1.509 (.067)	1.525 (.068)	1.970 (.090)	1.991 (.091)
Likelihood value	−3559.9	−3553.6	−3213.1	−3208.5
Sample size	2000	2000	2000	2000

these assets their effect cannot be directly compared with the effects of social security payments or wealth.

Finally, we see that the more educated tend to retire later. An additional year of education is associated with about a 1.3% increase in the age of retirement. For example, suppose a person with 12 years of education would retire at age 60. We predict that a like person with 16 years of education would retire at age 63, all else equal. People with more dependent children are less likely to retire.

The only anomalous result is the statistically insignificant effect of private pension eligibility. The RHS provides no details of private pension plans, and we suspect that the limited information that is available may simply be inadequate to reveal, even in a gross way, the effects of pension availability.

It could be argued that since social security is dependent in large part on earnings, it may in principle be difficult to distinguish their effects. This possibility seems not to be evident in our results. All the relevant parameters have theoretically plausible signs, with currently available assets increasing the likelihood of retirement and monetary rewards to working decreasing the likelihood of retirement.

To give a better idea of the effects of social security on retirement, according to our estimates, we have performed several illustrative simulations. All of them begin with our sample of persons who were 60 years old and not retired in 1969. For this group, we first calculate the average probability of being retired by ages 62, 64, and 66. Estimates are obtained using both specifications (2) and (4) from table 6.7. These estimates are shown in the first column of table 6.8.

The next column presents estimates with all of the social security values reduced by amounts reflecting the increases in primary insurance benefits between 1969 and 1975. According to these calculations, if benefits had been maintained at the 1969 level approximately 3% fewer people would have been retired at age 64 (in 1973) and about 5% fewer at age 66 (in 1975).

These figures may be compared with the labor force participation rates shown in the introduction. The labor force participation rates of men 60–64 fell 9% between 1969 and 1973 and 13.7% between 1969 and 1975. For men over 65, labor force participation fell 14.5% between 1969 and 1973 and 20% between 1969 and 1975. Thus the increase in social security benefits over this period may account for possibly one-third of the decrease, according to our estimates. Our estimates pertain to retirement status, of course, and a substantial number of retired persons are in the labor force.

Table 6.8	Simulated Probabilities of Retirement, by Age, for Selected Changes in Social Security Provision			
Age	Current Law	SS Maintained at 1969 Level	No SS 62–64	No SS and No ΔSS
	Using SS Wealth (Specification 4)			
62	.288	.288	.221	.305
64	.496	.481	.320	.418
66	.686	.655	.613	.655
	Using SS Payments (Specification 2)			
62	.324	.322	.288	.278
64	.510	.493	.411	.407
66	.712	.674	.653	.650

Our estimated effects of social security appear also to be somewhat lower than those of Hurd and Boskin (1981), although their definition of retirement corresponds more closely to labor force participation than ours does. A good deal of the effect they estimate could pertain to persons who are retired by our definition.

We also simulated the effects of a much grosser change in social security, allowing payments to begin at 65 instead of 62, but for persons 65 and over assuming the benefits that were actually available to this age group. The results are shown in columns 3 and 4 of tabulation 1, assuming in the third column that social security wealth (or payments) is zero for persons 62–64 and in the fourth column that the increment as well is set to zero. This simple procedure probably makes most sense with respect to payments. According to this specification, such a scheme would reduce retirement rates at age 64 by about 20% and at 66 by about 8%. Thus these estimates suggest that changes in social security benefit amounts and in particular the age at which they are awarded could have very substantial effects on retirement behavior.

6.2   A Brownian Motion Retirement Process

6.2.1   The Model

The hazard model of retirement ignores one potentially important piece of information. No use of hours worked is made in that specification. We attempt to utilize this information in an alternative formulation of the retirement process, based on changes in "desired hours" of work. In this specification, changes in desired hours of work occur with changes in health status, social security wealth, age, and the monetary return to working. The basic idea is that if desired hours decrease to a sufficiently low level, the person chooses to stop working altogether or to change jobs. Because of fixed costs of working, desired hours do not need to fall to zero for this change in job status to occur. We use hours worked information by specifying observed retirement status at time t as a function of observed hours as well as other variables at time $t - 1$.

To begin, we shall think of retirement occurring when hours of work fall below zero. We later relax this assumption. The analysis of a Brownian motion process depends on whether it is possible to move back and forth between the retired and non-retired states. If not, the process is said to be absorbing. For expository purposes, we shall first present the ideas assuming that retirement is not absorbing. Then we shall assume that it is. It is the second version that we estimate. (In practice, typically retirement from a primary job is absorbing, but after retirement, it is possible to move among levels of work status, including zero hours.) Then we shall relax the implications inherent in this specification by considering desired hours of work versus potential hours of work on a primary job. This specification is motivated by the evidence in tables 6.5 and 6.6 that suggest little reduction in observed hours of work as one approaches retirement. Finally, we present parameter estimates, which must be considered preliminary at this stage.

If Retirement Is Not Absorbing

Suppose that the time path of hours worked by an individual who works $H(0) = H_0$ hours at some starting age is described by the graph in figure 6.3. The slope u of the solid line represents the "drift" in hours worked as the person ages. The random deviation ϵ from the drift is assumed to follow a Brownian motion (Weiner) process. That is,

- Every increment $e(t + d) - \epsilon(t)$ is normally distributed with mean zero and variance $\sigma^2 d$; and
- The increments for every pair of disjoint time intervals are independent.

It is common to refer to $H(t)$ as a Brownian motion process with drift u. The assumptions imply that at any time t, $\epsilon(t)$ is normally distributed with mean zero and variance $\sigma^2 t$. And because the *increments* in the process are assumed independent, hours worked at time $t + d$, given $H(t)$, is a function only of hours worked at time t (and the drift u). Given H_0, the increment by time t is normally distributed with mean ut and variance $\sigma^2 t$, that is,

$$(10) \qquad\qquad H(t) \sim N(H_0 + ut, \sigma^2 t),$$

where in our example u is negative.

If retirement means that $H \leq 0$, the probability that the person is retired at age t, given H_0, is simply

$$(11) \qquad \mathrm{pr}[H(t) < 0 \mid H(0) = H_0] = \phi \left[\frac{-(H_0 + ut)}{\sigma \sqrt{t}} \right].$$

In other words, this is the probability that at time t the process was at least H_0 lower than it was at time zero, where the expected fall is ut and the variance of the change is $\sigma^2 t$.

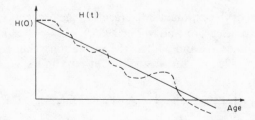

Fig. 6.3

Differences in individuals are accounted for by parameterizing the drift u. In theory, u could depend on H_0, as well as other individual attributes like health. Because the values of variables like pension eligibility change with age, presumably the drift u will also change. Thus we propose a piecewise linear drift with kink points that correspond to ages at the time of the surveys. The graph of $H(t)$ might then look something like figure 6.4, where the first survey is at age t_1. Now, given that the individual was working H_1 hours at age t_1, the probability of retirement at age t_2 is

$$(12) \quad \Pr[H_2 < 0| \ H(t_1) = H_1] = \phi \left[\frac{-(H_1 - u_1 (t_2 - t_1))}{\sigma\sqrt{t_2 - t_1}} \right].$$

Analogous expressions apply to subsequent age intervals. Note that the age of the first survey varies among individuals.

The simplicity of this analysis results first from the conditioning on initial hours of work and second from the assumption that retirement is not absorbing. In practice, however, retirement from a primary job is probably absorbing for most people; it is typically not possible to return to work on that job. We shall thus develop a specification analogous to the one above, but with retirement assumed to be absorbing. We shall not estimate the model above to describe retirement but shall return to it in subsequent work to describe work "after retirement." In this case, the assumptions below seem more plausible to us.

If Retirement Is Absorbing

Again we condition on initial observed hours H_0, where more generally initial time is when the first of any two consecutive surveys was conducted. Because the density vanishes at zero, the process is no longer normally distributed at period t but obeys the probability density function

$$(13)$$
$$p(H,t;H_0) =$$
$$\frac{1}{\sigma\sqrt{2\pi t}} \exp\left[- \frac{(H - H_0 - ut)^2}{2\sigma^2 t} \right]$$
$$- \exp\left[- \frac{2uH_0}{\sigma^2} - \frac{(H + H_0 - ut)^2}{2\sigma^2 t} \right],$$

where the second of the exponentiated terms in the brackets is the result of the "sink" at zero. (See Cox and Miller 1965.)

Again paralleling Cox and Miller, the probability that retirement has occurred at age t, given H_0 and absorption at zero hours, is

$$(14)$$
$$G(t|H_0, 0) = \phi\left[\frac{-H_0 - ut}{\sigma\sqrt{t}} \right] + \exp\left[- \frac{2uH_0}{\sigma^2} \cdot \phi \frac{-H_0 + ut}{\sigma\sqrt{t}} \right].$$

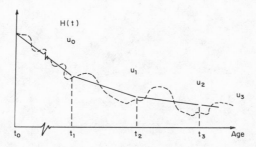

Fig. 6.4

This is analogous to the function $G(t)$ in section 6.1. The probability density function corresponding to the time of absorption is then given by

$$(15) \quad G'(t|\cdot) = g(t|\ H_0, 0) = \frac{H_0}{\sigma\sqrt{2\pi t^3}}\ \exp\left[-\frac{1}{2}\frac{(-H_0 - ut)^2}{\sigma\sqrt{t}}\right]$$

$$= \frac{H_0}{\sigma t^{3/2}}\cdot\phi\ \frac{-H_0 - ut}{\sigma\sqrt{t}}$$

This is the counterpart to the proportional hazard density in equation (2).

The likelihood function for this model is formed from the expression for $p(\cdot)$ in equation (13) and $G(\cdot)$ in equation (14). That is, the person either is working at level H, with likelihood $p(\cdot)$, or has retired, with probability G. Observations from the first survey are used only to condition the observed outcome at the time of the second survey. (In future work we shall enter an expression for the likelihood of the first-survey outcome.) Persons are followed only through the survey period in which they retired, at which point they are presumed to have been absorbed into the retirement state.

This analysis is based on the implicit assumption that hours of work can be reduced continuously until the person no longer wants to work at all; then retirement occurs. But suppose that the alternative to retirement is working the customary hours on a primary job, as suggested by the summary data presented above. The specification in the next section is intended to address this concern.

If Desired Hours Diverge from Production Practice

Suppose now that we think of *desired* hours of work decreasing with age, like actual hours of work in the section above. We use H to indicate desired hours. Suppose that actual observed hours, denoted by $\tilde{H}$, may diverge by an amount d from desired hours. Assume that observed hours before retirement represent required hours on the primary job. Finally, suppose that an individual retires if desired hours fall below a. These ideas are reflected in figure 6.5.

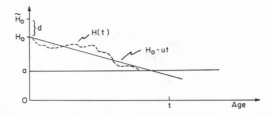

Fig. 6.5

The person will retire by t if during this period $H(t)$ falls from $\tilde{H}_0 + d$ to a, that is, if the process falls by an amount $(\tilde{H}_0 + d) - a$. Of course, we do not observe d or a, only $\tilde{H}_0$. To develop the likelihood of this outcome, we shall begin by writing out the probability that the process $H(t)$ falls from $H(0)$ to the level a by t. First we write the probability density function for H at age t, given the initial position H_0 and the absorbing barrier at a, as

$$p(H,t;H_0, a) =$$

(16)
$$= \frac{1}{\sigma\sqrt{2\pi t}} \exp\left[-\frac{H - H_0 - ut)^2}{2\sigma^2 t}\right]$$
$$- \exp\left[\frac{2u(a - H_0)}{\sigma^2} - \frac{(H - H_0 - 2(a-H_0) - ut)^2}{2\sigma^2 t}\right].$$

The probability that retirement has occurred by t is given by

$$G(t|H_0,a) =$$

(17)
$$= 1 - 1 - \phi\left[\frac{a - H_0 - ut}{\sigma\sqrt{t}}\right]$$
$$+ \exp\left(\frac{2u(a - H_0)}{\sigma^2}\right) 1 - \phi\left[\frac{-(a - H_0) - ut}{\sigma\sqrt{t}}\right]$$
$$= \phi\left[\frac{a - H_0 - ut}{\sigma\sqrt{t}}\right]$$
$$+ \exp\left(\frac{2u(a - H_0)}{\sigma^2}\right) \cdot \phi\left[\frac{a - H_0 + ut}{\sigma\sqrt{t}}\right].$$

If $a = 0$, equations (16) and (17) reduce to equations (13) and (14), respectively. Note that G gives the probability that the process falls from H_0 to a, sometime before t.

We would like to know the probability that the process falls from $\tilde{H}_0 + d$ to a. If we substitute $\tilde{H}_0 + d$ for H_0 in equation (17), then the terms $a - H_0$ in (17) become $a - d - \tilde{H} = b - \tilde{H}$. We of course know neither a nor d. Suppose, however, that b varies randomly across individuals. In this instance it is natural to assume that b is distributed normally, say with mean vb and variance σ_b^2. If this density is denoted by f, then the probability of retirement for an individual with unknown b is obtained integrating over all values of b, giving

$$(18) \qquad\qquad G(t) = {}_b\!\int G(t - \tilde{H}_0, b)f(b)db.$$

At least the deviation $d = H_0 - \tilde{H}_0$ is likely to depend on age. Thus in principle we should allow shifts in v_b with age. The estimates below, however, allow only for a single b.

6.1.2 Estimates

At its current stage of development the outstanding weakness of the model is that it does not allow for permanent unobserved individual effects. We intend to extend the specification to the case of unobserved individual effects in subsequent work. We give the first set of results in table 6.9. The results in columns 1 and 3 are based on the equations (13) and (14) in section 6.2 above. Those in columns 2 and 4 are based on the specifications in section 6.3, and allow the absorbing barrier to be estimated. The variable definitions coincide with the definitions used in table 6.7 for the hazard model. The results are considerably easier to interpret than the hazard results because the implicit left-hand variable is desired weekly hours.

In the first column note that the size of social security payments has an important effect on desired hours, with the size of payments after age 65 having a larger effect. But the change in social security payments has a negative sign—indicating that, contrary to expectation, desired hours fall with expected increases from working. The effect is estimated very precisely. The effect on desired hours of work, however, is very small, less than one hour per $100 increase in the payment increment, for example. Earnings have the expected effect, although the size of the effect is again small. Bad health and pension eligibility both have large and significant effects on desired hours. In column 2 we estimate a more general specification by allowing the absorbing barrier to differ from zero as in our second model. The estimate of the barrier is about four hours, which leads to a small decrease in the magnitude of the other coefficient estimates. However, the relative magnitudes remain constant for the effects of the right-hand-side variables.

In column 3 we replace social security payments and their change with social security wealth measures. The model does not fit the data as well, in contrast to our findings for the hazard model. Neither social security wealth before age 65 nor earnings significantly affects desired hours. Furthermore, the change in social security wealth again has the "wrong" sign, although its effect on desired hours is small. The effects of bad health, pension eligibility, and the socioeconomic variables are quite similar to the results for the model with social security payments instead of social security wealth.

Table 6.9   **Brownian Motion Process Parameter Estimates (Standard Errors in Parentheses)**

	Specification			
Variable	(1)	(2)	(3)	(4)
SS payments, age 62–64 (100s)	− 3.35 (1.77)	− 3.15 (1.60)	—	—
SS payments, age ≥ 65	− 6.38 (1.32)	− 5.87 (1.19)	—	—
Δ SS payments (100s)	− .583 (.072)	− .543 (.064)	—	—
SS wealth, age 62–64 (1000s)	—	—	.019 (.065)	.023 (.063)
SS wealth, age ≥ 65	—	—	− .306 (.050)	− .290 (.048)
Δ SS wealth (1000s)	—	—	− .128 (.046)	− .125 (.045)
Bad health	− 8.58 (1.53)	− 7.68 (1.37)	− 6.86 (1.51)	− 6.574 (1.432)
Earnings (1000s)	.161 (.103)	.139 (.117)	− .019 (.132)	.031 (.127)
Pension eligibility	2.40 (1.40)	− 2.20 (1.27)	− 3.30 (1.41)	− 3.083 (1.355)
Education	.660 (.191)	.592 (.172)	.594 (.195)	.568 (.187)
Dependents	.542 (.767)	.495 (.692)	1.90 (.821)	1.806 (.785)
Constant	− 13.42 (3.40)	− 11.81 (3.40)	− 20.2 (2.77)	− 19.405 (2.639)
Absorbing barrier	—	3.96 (.025)	—	1.982 (.018)
Standard deviation	30.25 (1.01)	27.44 (.868)	30.42 (1.09)	29.08 (1.02)
Likelihood value	− 12598.5	− 12387.8	− 12962.1	—
Sample size	2000	2000	2000	2000

6.3   Conclusions

Our results suggest a strong effect of social security benefits on the probability of retirement. Increases in real earnings decrease the likelihood of retirement. Increases in future social security benefits decrease the probability of retirement, according to the results we find the most reliable. Our major conclusions are based on a hazard model specification of retirement. We also presented a Brownian motion formulation of retirement and presented some initial results based on it. Our hope is that future work will yield a more satisfactory version of the model.

Notes

1. Other recent applications of the hazards model are Diamond and Hausman (1982) and Flynn and Heckman (1982).
2. From selected issues of *Employment and Earnings*, table A-4.
3. We standardize by setting the mean of the distribution equal to one. Sensitivity of the results to the distribution assumptions is investigated by Lancaster (1979), Lancaster and Nickell (1980), Baldwin (1983), and Heckman and Singer (1984).
4. See Gustman and Steinmeier (1981) for similar evidence.

Comment   Gary Burtless

This paper contains a careful assessment of alternative mathematical representations of the retirement process. Contrary to the promise implied by its title, the paper is only tangentially concerned with effects of health and social security on retirement. Its main concern is accurate statistical representation of processes that occur over time. Two representations are considered. The first section contains an analysis using a hazard-rate model. The second contains a novel representation of continuous time processes, which the authors refer to as a "Brownian motion" model.

There are several fundamental problems in modeling the retirement process. Unlike consumption of margarine or housing or trips to Disneyland, there is no natural translation of retirement into a consumption rate per unit of time. One either is or is not retired. And in most cases retirement, like death, is an "absorbing" state: one seldom returns.

This would present no special problems if all the factors affecting retirement were constant, or at least reasonably so, before the actual date of retirement. In that case, exogenous variables relevant to estimation would essentially be fixed at the start of the lifetime or working life. The analyst could proceed with estimation exactly as he does in estimating an ordinary demand relationship, with "fraction of expected lifetime devoted to retirement" being the dependent variable instead of consumption of margarine or housing services or whatever.

Of course, there are a couple of special problems. Retirement must be defined, which is not an easy task when some individuals define themselves as retired even though working 40 hours a week, while others persist in saying they're not retired even though they have not worked full time for years. Another problem is that we do not observe expected lifetimes, nor do we necessarily observe retirement ages for all persons in a cohort. Some respondents have not retired by the last survey date, so their retirement ages are unobserved. Death also interferes with unbiased estimation. If a respondent dies before he retires, the analyst is denied the oppor-

Gary Burtless is a senior fellow at the Brookings Institution.

tunity of observing a retirement age. From the point of view of the analyst—though not of the respondent—this is an inconvenience much like the case of nonretirement.

The problems just mentioned can be surmounted using due care as well as modern statistical models that handle sample censorship. In fact, except for the now trivial problem of censorship, with sufficiently good observations one could estimate demand for retirement using ordinary least squares.

But the major problem in estimation is the fact that most factors affecting retirement are changing, even as the retirement decision is being made. Someone previously in good health has a heart attack at age 55. Someone steadily employed on a $10-an-hour job is unexpectedly laid off, perhaps permanently. Unanticipated inflation erodes the value of a pension entitlement. These changes alter the economic trade-offs involved in retirement. The margarine consumer can take the price of margarine as well as other relevant factors to be fixed in making his weekly or monthly purchases, and the economist can analyze this consumption behavior accordingly. But the case of retirement is much less straightforward.

A common way to get around this problem is to analyze retirement over only a very short period, such as a year. The idea is that the variables affecting retirement are unlikely to change much over this period, so unanticipated changes can be safely ignored. The obvious problem with this strategy is that the sample of nonretirees at the beginning of some interesting year—say age 62—is highly self-selected. It excludes all individuals whose tastes or circumstances caused them to retire before age 62. So the results cannot be generalized to the whole population without strong untested assumptions. Considering all individuals' statuses—rather than *changes* in status—at age 62 causes a different kind of problem. The characteristics that initially caused retirees in this sample to retire may have changed by age 62, although their retirement status obviously has not. Consequently, the factors inducing retirement are only partially observed.

The contribution of Hausman and Wise is to offer two mathematical formulations of the retirement process that get around these problems. They essentially observe 10 years of individuals' lives and then try to model the dynamic process that causes them to retire before, during, or after that interval.

Their first model is based on the hazard or time-to-failure model first popularized in the biometrics literature, and subsequently applied in sociological work on marital separations and in economic research on the duration of unemployment spells. It is assumed that consumers have two choices at any point in time, to remain at work or to become retired. In any unit of time a certain fraction of individuals will choose to retire. By selecting a convenient mathematical representation of that probability density, the authors can easily compute the finite probability that retirement will occur between any two arbitrarily selected points. The method of maximum likelihood estimation finds those parameter values that most closely fit the observed retirement patterns in the sample, including retirees, nonretirees, and the deceased. It is then straightforward to modify this density function to take account of variables such as race and sex that are fixed over time. Essentially these factors have a proportional impact on the probability density, raising or lowering the chance of retirement as the case may be. The authors further modify their specification to permit these variables to have impacts that vary in different time periods—before and after age 65, for example. Individual-specific random differences are also introduced, though I wonder what practical effect this has on the parameter estimates.

To take care of time-varying variables—such as wealth, wages, and social security entitlements—the authors essentially divide up the individual's lifetime into short time periods—two-year intervals—and then assume that in each period the variable has an effect on retirement probabilities that is proportional to its average value in that period.

The estimates from this model indicate that social security has an extremely modest effect. They show that the 20% increase in real benefit levels in 1972 reduced the fraction of men working at age 64 by 1.5 percentage points, from around half to slightly less than half. It reduced the fraction working at age 66 by about 3 percentage points. These results are very similar to those recently obtained by Robert Moffitt and me (Burtless and Moffitt 1985). In obtaining our results we used the same data set as Hausman and Wise but a substantially different representation of the retirement process.

But the authors are unsatisfied with the economic underpinnings of the hazard rate model, so they go on to estimate a "Brownian motion" model. The idea here is that retirement takes place when an unobserved index of work preferences falls below a critical threshold value. They call this unobserved index "desired hours," and they assume the index trends downward during advanced age, though it also has random disturbances that may cause it to rise temporarily at certain ages. Estimates from this ingenious model are not very satisfactory, and I find them less easy to interpret because they are expressed in terms of unobserved desired hours rather than in more natural units of measurement, for example, average retirement ages or retirement probabilities per year. The sign of one of the social security coefficients is opposite to the one expected. This coefficient shows, contrary to the earlier result, that as the gain in future social security benefits from extra work rises, nonretirees desire to work *fewer* hours.

I shall give my reactions to the two models in reverse order. The second model does not seem to me an improvement over the first, so I am not sure

Table 6.A.1   **Mean Hours of Work per Week for Non-Self-Employed Men, by Age and Year, Including Fully or Partially Retired**

Age	Year						All Years
	1969	1971	1973	1975	1977	1979	
58	42.4 (794)						42.4 (794)
59	42.3 (889)						42.3 (889)
60	42.1 (842)	41.4 (670)					41.8 (1512)
61	41.7 (832)	41.3 (741)					41.5 (1573)
62	41.3 (723)	41.0 (657)	40.8 (490)				41.0 (1870)
63	41.4 (589)	40.4 (617)	40.6 (505)				40.8 (1711)
64		39.2 (564)	39.8 (461)	38.8 (383)			39.3 (1408)
65		38.3 (299)	35.7 (283)	35.5 (295)			36.5 (877)
66			32.8 (259)	34.3 (236)	34.7 (155)		33.8 (650)
67			33.0 (202)	31.6 (233)	32.2 (157)		32.2 (592)
68				29.8 (197)	29.6 (146)	30.5 (135)	30.0 (478)
69				30.6 (147)	29.6 (125)	29.1 (127)	29.8 (399)
70					28.0 (117)	28.4 (122)	28.2 (239)
71					30.1 (89)	27.9 (109)	28.9 (198)
72						25.9 (100)	25.9 (100)
73						29.8 (73)	29.8 (73)

Note: The number in parentheses is the number of observations used to calculate the associated mean.

why the authors felt it was needed. They state or imply that the economic rationale for the first model is unconvincing, but they do not show why the second model is better. In a future version of the paper, their reasoning needs to be made clearer.

I do not see why unobserved "desired hours" are a better way to model retirement than the simpler on/off representation implicit in the hazard

Table 6.A.2   Mean Hours of Work per Week for Non-Self-Employed Men, by Age and Year, Excluding Fully or Partially Retired

Age	1969	1971	1973	1975	1977	1979	All Years
58	42.8 (774)						42.8 (774)
59	42.8 (854)						42.8 (854)
60	42.4 (818)	41.8 (641)					42.2 (1459)
61	42.4 (789)	41.7 (712)					42.1 (1501)
62	42.3 (665)	42.0 (597)	42.1 (441)				42.1 (1703)
63	42.5 (531)	42.3 (542)	42.2 (444)				42.4 (1517)
64		41.4 (482)	41.5 (395)	41.7 (314)			41.5 (1191)
65		42.1 (222)	41.4 (192)	40.2 (192)			41.3 (606)
66			41.5 (139)	41.0 (142)	40.8 (96)		41.2 (377)
67			39.1 (115)	40.3 (114)	39.2 (80)		39.6 (309)
68				40.3 (91)	38.5 (63)	37.0 (61)	38.8 (215)
69				40.9 (63)	38.9 (53)	38.2 (51)	39.4 (167)
70					37.6 (43)	36.6 (41)	37.1 (84)
71					40.1 (33)	34.3 (40)	36.9 (73)
72						35.6 (36)	35.6 (35)
73						36.0 (31)	36.0 (31)

Note: The number in parentheses is the number of observations used to calculate the associated mean.

rate model. As the authors' own statistics on average weekly hours show, there is no tendency for actual (as opposed to desired) hours to decline prior to retirement. Why assume that the underlying process causing retirement is any different from the process we typically observe? What we observe is a steady level of work effort until the retirement age, at which point work effort drops significantly.

Table 6.A.3   **Mean Hours of Work per Week for Self-Employed Men, by Age and Year, Including Fully or Partially Retired**

Age	Year						All Years
	1969	1971	1973	1975	1977	1979	
58	48.7 (167)						48.7 (167)
59	47.2 (176)						47.2 (176)
60	46.4 (159)	48.5 (174)					47.5 (333)
61	46.4 (172)	47.0 (187)					46.7 (359)
62	45.4 (176)	45.8 (131)	44.7 (130)				45.3 (437)
63	42.7 (172)	43.2 (145)	43.0 (150)				43.0 (467)
64		42.6 (153)	40.8 (109)	42.4 (86)			42.0 (348)
65		37.7 (137)	36.9 (114)	38.7 (83)			37.7 (334)
66			38.6 (94)	39.7 (72)	34.5 (83)		37.6 (249)
67			35.8 (103)	33.6 (73)	36.3 (79)		35.3 (255)
68				35.5 (57)	40.4 (65)	35.2 (71)	37.0 (193)
69				33.2 (68)	31.8 (71)	33.0 (56)	32.6 (195)
70					33.9 (63)	35.5 (56)	34.7 (119)
71					31.3 (64)	32.7 (48)	31.9 (112)
72						31.0 (43)	31.6 (43)
73						30.6 (45)	30.6 (45)

Note: The number in parentheses is the number of observations used to calculate the associated mean.

Their hazard rate model is extremely well implemented and explained, although I think they should go into more detail in explaining their representation of time-varying variables: What are the implications of their particular specification?

Table 6.A.4   **Mean Hours of Work per Week for Self-Employed Men, by Age and Year, Excluding Fully or Partially Retired**

Age	Year						All Years
	1969	1971	1973	1975	1977	1979	
58	50.0 (147)						50.0 (147)
59	49.6 (148)						49.6 (148)
60	48.5 (133)	50.2 (155)					49.4 (288)
61	48.5 (145)	49.5 (157)					49.0 (302)
62	48.7 (137)	49.8 (95)	48.0 (102)				48.8 (334)
63	47.5 (125)	50.0 (97)	47.2 (116)				48.2 (338)
64		48.7 (104)	50.3 (60)	48.9 (55)			49.2 (219)
65		45.7 (63)	48.8 (54)	48.4 (41)			47.4 (158)
66			43.8 (48)	47.0 (38)	46.7 (28)		45.6 (114)
67			45.8 (41)	45.4 (25)	46.9 (33)		46.0 (99)
68				44.6 (25)	50.7 (36)	44.8 (36)	47.0 (97)
69				44.0 (25)	43.9 (33)	42.5 (26)	43.5 (84)
70					43.0 (26)	52.0 (23)	47.2 (49)
71					41.6 (25)	41.2 (19)	41.4 (44)
72						43.1 (12)	43.1 (12)
73						35.8 (18)	35.8 (18)

Note: The number in parentheses is the number of observations used to calculate the associated mean.

My final comment should not be taken as a criticism of this work but as a statement of how far we still need to go in this kind of research. The main problem with these models, it seems to me, is that they take full account of a worker's history but no account of his potential history. For ex-

Table 6.A.5   **Mean Hours of Work per Week for Women, by Age and Year, Including Fully or Partially Retired**

Age	Year						All Years
	1969	1971	1973	1975	1977	1979	
58	38.1 (215)						38.1 (215)
59	37.1 (260)						37.1 (260)
60	37.0 (281)	37.7 (200)					37.3 (481)
61	37.3 (266)	35.5 (220)					36.5 (486)
62	36.2 (264)	35.0 (216)	36.1 (137)				35.8 (617)
63	35.9 (224)	34.3 (193)	33.6 (155)				34.7 (572)
64		35.2 (194)	31.5 (165)	33.5 (106)			33.5 (465)
65		31.2 (139)	31.3 (114)	28.3 (84)			30.5 (337)
66			32.2 (110)	24.4 (96)	28.4 (60)		28.5 (266)
67			27.8 (76)	26.2 (79)	25.9 (53)		26.7 (208)
68				28.7 (77)	23.6 (53)	27.4 (46)	26.8 (176)
69				27.0 (56)	24.3 (46)	22.8 (47)	24.8 (149)
70					26.7 (48)	24.1 (42)	25.5 (90)
71					24.3 (29)	23.7 (31)	24.0 (60)
72						28.1 (36)	28.1 (36)
73						21.1 (22)	21.1 (22)

Note: The number in parentheses is the number of observations used to calculate the associated mean.

ample, consider the social security entitlement. The hazard rate model integrates over all *past* values of potential social security entitlements the worker might have had up to his observed age at retirement. All potential entitlements he might receive from working one extra year in the future, or two or 10 extra years, are ignored. But of course these *potential* entitle-

Table 6.A.6   **Mean Hours of Work per Week for Women, by Age and Year, Excluding Fully or Partially Retired**

Age	1969	1971	1973	1975	1977	1979	All Years
			Year				
58	38.5 (206)						38.5 (206)
59	38.0 (244)						38.0 (244)
60	38.3 (261)	39.2 (180)					38.7 (441)
61	39.0 (240)	37.4 (200)					38.2 (440)
62	38.9 (222)	37.8 (180)	39.4 (110)				38.6 (512)
63	38.8 (181)	37.8 (156)	37.0 (125)				38.0 (462)
64		38.5 (154)	36.6 (125)	38.5 (80)			37.8 (359)
65		37.4 (90)	37.3 (72)	33.8 (56)			36.4 (218)
66			38.3 (76)	30.7 (46)	38.0 (28)		35.9 (150)
67			35.7 (40)	36.9 (34)	32.6 (28)		35.2 (102)
68				34.9 (45)	31.3 (20)	37.3 (25)	34.8 (90)
69				38.3 (24)	32.9 (24)	30.1 (15)	34.3 (63)
70					36.8 (21)	32.1 (15)	34.9 (36)
71					29.2 (11)	29.8 (12)	29.5 (23)
72						33.9 (20)	33.9 (20)
73						29.9 (8)	29.9 (8)

Note: The number in parentheses is the number of observations used to calculate the associated mean.

ments and their rate of change may be exactly the factors motivating the worker when he chooses to retire. Consider the worker who retires at age 64, perhaps because he was laid off. Why does he not attempt to find another job? Why does he choose, instead, to retire? Perhaps because the rate of return from added work, in terms of added social security wealth, drops sharply at age 65. His decision is motivated by the *future* drop in social security entitlements rather than by the change he is now experiencing or has experienced in the past.

This is just a special case of the nonlinear budget constraint problem that Hausman and Wise understand very well: Since the price of retirement is not constant, to properly model the consumer's choice the analyst should include all the relevant prices—including the prices the consumer chooses not to face. By ignoring future retirement prices, the hazard model may misrepresent the retirement process. However, in view of the progress this paper represents over most past models of retirement, this should be considered a relatively minor quibble.

References

Baldwin, R. H. 1983. Army recruit survival functions: Estimation and strategy for use. Ph.D. dissertation, Massachusetts Institute of Technology.

Blinder, A.; Gordon, R.; and Wise, D. E. 1980. Reconsidering the work disincentive effects of social security. *National Tax Journal* 33:431–42.

Boskin, M., and Hurd, M. 1981. The effect of social security on retirement in the early 1970's. NBER Working Paper no. 659.

Burtless, G., and Moffitt, R. A. 1983. The effect of social security on labor supply of the aged: The joint choice of retirement date and post-retirement hours of work. Mimeographed. Rutgers, N. J.: Rutgers University, University of Wisconsin and Mathematical Policy Research.

———. 1985. The just choice of retirement age and postretirement hours of work. *Journal of Labor Economics* 3 (April).

Cox, D., and Miller, H. D. 1965. *The theory of stochastic processes*. New York: Chapman & Hall.

Diamond, P. A., and Hausman, J. A. 1982. Individual retirement and savings behavior. Mimeographed. Cambridge: Massachusetts Institute of Technology, Department of Economics.

Flynn, C., and Heckman, J. 1982. New methods for analyzing structural models of labor force dynamics. *Journal of Econometrics* 18:115–68.

Gustman, A., and Steinmeier, T. 1984. Partial retirement and the analysis of retirement behavior. *Industrial and Labor Relations Review* 37:403–15.

Hausman, J., and Wise, D. 1978. A conditional probit model for qualitative choice: Discrete decisions recognizing interdependence and heterogeneous preferences. *Econometrica* 42:403–26.

Heckman, J., and Singer, B. 1984. The identifiability of the proportional hazard model. *Review of Economic Studies*.

Kalbfleisch, J. D., and Prentice, R. L. 1980. *The statistical analysis of failure time data*. New York: Wiley.

Karlin, S., and Taylor, H. 1975. *A first course in stochastic process*. New York: Academic Press.

Lancaster, T. 1979. Econometric methods for the duration of unemployment. *Econometrica* 47:939–56.

Lancaster, T., and Nickell, S. 1980. The analysis of re-employment probabilities for the unemployed. *Journal of the Royal Statistical Society* 143A, pt. 2: 141–65.

McFadden, D. 1973. Conditional logit analysis of qualitative choice behavior. In *Frontiers in econometrics*, ed. D. Zarmbka. New York: Academic Press.

7 The Distributional Impact of Social Security

Michael D. Hurd
John B. Shoven

7.1 Introduction

Although social security retirement benefits often are thought of as a repayment of past contributions, it is now becoming a matter of general knowledge that the generation currently retired is receiving far more in retirement annuities than its members contributed in taxes during their working lives (see Aaron 1977; Burkhauser and Warlick 1981; Leimer and Petri 1981; Boskin et al. 1983). This is partly due to the state of the social security system: the retired generation is still receiving windfall start-up gains. These gains will diminish as the system matures and approaches a steady state. The excess of benefits over taxes for the presently retired is also due to the generosity of Congress in the early 1970s. Between 1968 and 1974 benefits were raised at a rate considerably higher than the rate of inflation; therefore, if the system had been actuarially fair in real terms prior to 1968, it certainly would not have been after 1974.

A natural question is, What is the magnitude of the gains or transfers (i.e., benefits less contributions in expected present value terms) of the elderly and how are they distributed? If the transfers are exceptionally large or concentrated among the affluent, a reform of the social security system might logically include the present retired generation giving up some of their gains. It is likely that additional funds or payout reductions will be required in the next 10 years and that major adjustments are necessary to operate the system over the next 75 years. The revenue sources or saving

Michael D. Hurd is professor of economics, State University of New York, Stony Brook, and is a research associate of the National Bureau of Economic Research. John B. Shoven is professor of economics, Stanford University, and is a research associate of the National Bureau of Economic Research.

We thank Beth Van Zummeren for her splendid and exhaustive research assistance. Without her extraordinary work, the paper would have not been possible. We have also greatly benefited from the extremely efficient and capable assistance of Steve Galatis and Harry Paarsch.

193

could include an increase in payroll taxes for workers, an advancement of the retirement age, or a decrease in the benefits of some of the currently retired. These measures to ensure the financial solvency of social security will have intergenerational effects. Raising the taxes of workers or increasing the retirement age will reduce the rate of return of the present working generation; cutting benefits, perhaps by making them taxable, will lower the gains of today's elderly. Because a substantial fraction of the elderly are far from wealthy, an across-the-board reduction in benefits is probably neither socially desirable nor politically feasible. However, the benefits of the wealthy retired could be reduced without causing undue economic hardship. If they have received large windfall gains through the social security system, fairness in restoring the financial soundness of the program would dictate a reduction in their benefits.

In this paper we calculate the present value of lifetime contributions to the social security system of a sample of the elderly and the present value of their expected benefits. The difference between the two we call social security transfers. We also compute for each family in our sample the internal rate of return to the retirement program. That is, we determine the discount rate that equates the present value of taxes to the present value of benefits. Our data are the Social Security Administration's Retirement History Survey. It originally interviewed slightly over 11,000 households in 1969. The head of household was between 58 and 64 years of age in 1969. These households were reinterviewed every two years through 1979. In this paper we calculate social security transfers and internal rates of return for the sample in 1969, 1975, and 1979 but use the other interview years to fill in missing values for our three years of primary interest.

Our primary results are that social security transfers and rates of return were very high for this population in 1969 and remained high throughout the decade. People in our sample could expect to receive three to four times as much in benefits as they made in contributions, even using a 3% real rate of time discount and calculating death probabilities using current life tables. Further, and more surprising, we find that the wealthy received the largest transfers, and in many cases they even had the highest rates of return. One must conclude that the social security system as now constituted has a substantial transfer element and that much of the transfer is from average workers to the wealthy retired.

We have attempted to calculate how the rates of return and transfers of the social security system will evolve as the system matures over the next 40–50 years. We have done this by creating some synthetic work and retirement histories for six different age cohorts and examining how the social security program, as currently constituted, would treat them. The households in this synthetic file are subject to the life hazards given by the 1969 life tables. We do not project changes in life expectancies that may occur. We find that the transfer components monotonically decrease with each succeeding cohort (spaced in age by 10 years) and that the median two-earner household of the cohort now aged 38 will receive negative transfers. This simply implies, of course, that they experience an internal rate of return lower than the 3% real rate we used in calculating transfers.

7.2 Methods and Data

The Retirement History Survey interview data have been merged with the Social Security Administration's Earnings Record (through 1974). We have extended the earnings history of each household by using the 1975, 1977, and 1979 interview responses. We then seek to calculate social security transfers and internal rates of return for this cohort of households as of 1969, 1975, and 1979. However, we want to calculate the ex ante rate of return and transfers for the cohort with only the path of the social security program taken as given. As far as we know, no one has pointed out that calculations of transfers to the currently retired overstate transfers to the cohorts of the retired, because the calculations do not take into account taxes paid by members of the cohort who did not live to retirement age. The currently retired are the winners in the annuity gamble; to study the intergenerational transfer component of social security, we need to account for all the taxes and benefits of cohort members whether they are alive at the time of the sample or not. As we shall see, for some groups among the retired this is quite an important adjustment, substantially lowering our estimates of their rate of return from social security. Our method of accounting for taxes paid and benefits received by deceased members of the cohort is described in some detail in the Appendix, but it may be briefly summarized here.

From sex- and race-specific life tables and actual social security contribution data of married survivors, we estimate taxes paid by deceased married members of each cohort. Some of these taxes are allocated to widows to reflect the taxes paid by deceased husbands on their behalf. The remainder are allocated to the surviving couples. Each single person's history is similarly adjusted upward to account for deceased singles from the same cohort. Benefits received are treated in the same manner. That is, benefits already received by deceased members of this cohort are attributed to the survivors. In this way, we examine how an entire cohort (in this case, alive in 1937 at the start-up of the system) has fared with social security. These adjustments treat the future and the past symmetrically: future benefits are discounted, weighted by the probabilities of living to collect the benefits, and then summed to get the discounted expected discounted present value; past benefits are multiplied by the appropriate interest rates and by a multiple reflecting cohort size at the time benefits were collected. In

1969, for example, the taxes paid by the cohort and the benefits received and to be received by the cohort are assigned to the surviving members of the cohort.

7.3   Results

The first of our results are shown in tables 7.1–7.3, where we report social security taxes paid and transfers received by race and marital status for 1969, 1975, and 1979. The taxes are calculated according to earnings records to the interview year, and the benefits under the assumption that the person makes no more contributions to social security. Table 7.1 shows that the life table adjustment makes little difference for couples in the sample. This is because extra taxes are attributed to interviewed couples according to the probability that both partners of an original couple died before 1969, and this event has low probability. However, the taxes of widows and widowers (referred to in this paper as widows only because females predominate) are more than doubled. This occurs because the Social Security Earnings History only records the widows' own earnings record and contribution profile. When we attribute to widows the contributions made by their deceased spouses, it naturally raises substantially the total taxes assigned to widows. Even so, all groups, including widows, have substantial transfers both in absolute value and in the return ratio, the ratio of the present value of benefits to the present value of taxes. However, widows have smaller transfers and lower return ratios than other groups: they only receive the husband's benefit rather than the husband's and wife's benefit. In most cases the taxes paid by the widow herself do not contribute to her benefit because the husband's benefit is larger. It should be noted that if account is not made of taxes paid by deceased husbands, one gets a completely different impression of the return ratio of widows. For example, if average actual taxes and average benefits are

Table 7.1	Social Security Taxes and Transfers by Marital Status and Race, 1969 (1968 Dollars)				
	Taxes (Life Table Adjusted) ($)	Actual Taxes ($)	Mean Benefits Less Life Adjusted Taxes ($)	Median Return Ratio	Median Rates of Return
Married	7,203	7,046	16,422	3.35	8.39
Widows and Widowers	5,406	2,345	6,011	2.03	6.01
Other singles	3,844	3,398	6,863	2.91	7.80
White	6,536	5,764	13,345	3.14	7.97
Nonwhite	4,249	3,198	7,690	2.91	7.66

Table 7.2   **Social Security Taxes and Transfers by Marital Status and Race, 1975 (1974 Dollars)**

	Taxes (Life Table Adjusted) ($)	Actual Taxes ($)	Mean Benefits Less Life Adjusted Taxes ($)	Median Return Ratio	Median Rates of Return
Married	16,222	15,282	40,041	3.58	8.76
Widows and Widowers	12,947	4,999	15,224	2.11	6.38
Other singles	9,871	7,632	15,879	2.73	7.63
White	14,752	11,609	30,422	3.23	8.19
Nonwhite	11,029	7,002	19,116	2.85	7.58

Table 7.3   **Social Security Taxes and Transfers by Marital Status and Race, 1979 (1978 Dollars)**

	Taxes (Life Table Adjusted) ($)	Actual Taxes ($)	Mean Benefits Less Life Adjusted Taxes ($)	Median Return Ratio	Median Rates of Return
Married	26,778	23,719	58,865	3.34	8.32
Widows and Widowers	22,335	7,499	23,118	2.04	6.24
Other singles	17,335	11,528	21,544	2.41	6.82
White	24,466	16,815	42,319	2.84	7.55
Nonwhite	19,400	9,991	27,457	2.52	6.95

used, the return ratio is 4.9, higher than that of couples. If average adjusted taxes are used, the return ratio is 2.03.

The internal rate of return is that interest rate that will equate the real life-table-weighted stream of taxes to the real life-table-weighted stream of benefits, assuming future benefits will be paid according to the law in effect. The median rate of return of couples in 1969 was 8.39. This is a real rate of return and is very much greater than what is generally assumed to be offered by other investments. For example, in our present value calculations for the first three columns of these tables, we have used a 3% real rate; the social security actuaries often use a 2.5% real rate. Over a number of years the difference between such rates and our calculated internal rate of return is enormous. For example, a 60-year-old in 1969 would have been 28 in 1937, the year in which social security taxes were first paid. At a real rate of 2.5%, a dollar contributed in 1937 would have grown to $2.20 in real terms by 1969; at a real rate of 8.39%, a dollar contributed in 1937 would have grown to $13.17 in real terms by 1969. At 6.01%, the widow's rate of return, it would have grown to $6.47. Over the 70 years that some people will be paying to or receiving from the social security system, even small differences in the rates of return will produce large differences in the present values. In interpreting the very high internal rates we calculate, one should also note that social security contributions and benefits are very heavily sheltered from the personal income tax. The benefits are completely tax free, the "compounding" is done on a tax-free basis, and only half the contributions (the employee's share) are subject to personal income tax.

In 1969 the rate of return of couples was the highest of the marital groups. Many researchers have stressed how the system discriminates against two-earner couples in the sense that the contributions of the wife are wasted in that they do not increase the benefits of the family. Certainly this is true relative to one-earner couples. However, married couples as a group obviously do at least as well as singles since they are offered their choice at time of retirement between being treated as two singles or calculating their benefits as a married couple. As a group, the married couples receive the highest rates of return from social security.

Nonwhites have slightly lower rates of return than whites and significantly lower absolute transfers. These outcomes are caused by the higher mortality rates of nonwhites, meaning that fewer live to collect benefits. Our calculations that attribute taxes of deceased cohort members to the living is more important for nonwhites. Nonwhites also have lower earnings records on average (reducing the size of the absolute transfer), and a larger fraction of nonwhite couples have two earners, which tends to reduce the rates of return.

Tables 7.2 and 7.3 show social security taxes, transfers, and rates of return for 1975 and 1979 by race and marital status. By 1975, taxes and transfers of all groups had risen. The rate of return of whites had increased even further, yet the rate of return of blacks had fallen slightly. The difference is undoubtedly due to the difference in mortality: a higher fraction of nonwhites than whites in our sample died before reaching retirement age between 1969 and 1975. The difference between life-table-adjusted taxes and actual taxes of widows continues to be large, and it begins to widen for other categories. By 1979, the rates of return had begun to fall for reasons to be discussed later. It was still the case that couples had higher rates than the other marital groups and that whites had higher rates than nonwhites. The life table adjustment has become important for all groups. The 1979 samples are those aged 68–74 years, and these are certainly a sample of winners in the annuity game.

Tables 7.4–7.6 present results on taxes and transfers by age in 1969, 1975, and 1979. In general, the internal rates of return and the absolute transfers are higher for the older households in the sample in all three interview years. This is presumably due to the maturing of the social security system. The older members of this population enjoyed more of the start-

Table 7.4	Social Security Taxes and Transfers by Age, 1969 (1968 Dollars)				
Age of Household Head	Mean Taxes (Life Table Adjusted) ($)	Mean Actual Taxes ($)	Mean Benefits Less Life Adjusted Taxes ($)	Median Return Ratio	Median Rates of Return
58	6,087	5,471	10,024	2.75	6.99
59	6,367	5,707	10,529	2.71	7.05
60	6,384	5,647	11,754	2.98	7.57
61	6,635	5,534	12,514	3.12	7.92
62	6,270	5,414	13,466	3.26	8.30
63	6,363	5,477	14,896	3.47	8.80
64	6,024	5,043	15,617	3.73	9.40

Table 7.5	Social Security Taxes and Transfers by Age, 1975 (1974 Dollars)				
Age of Household Head	Mean Taxes (Life Table Adjusted) ($)	Mean Actual Taxes ($)	Mean Benefits Less Life Adjusted Taxes ($)	Median Return Ratio	Median Rates of Return
64	14,986	12,325	28,241	3.0	7.8
65	15,119	12,616	29,004	3.1	8.0
66	14,939	12,106	28,737	3.1	7.9
67	14,457	11,440	29,541	3.2	8.2
68	14,225	11,082	30,496	3.3	8.3
69	14,077	10,749	31,216	3.4	8.6
70	13,269	9,820	32,228	3.7	9.2

Table 7.6	Social Security Taxes and Transfers by Age, 1979 (1978 Dollars)				
Age of Household Head	Mean Taxes (Life Table Adjusted) ($)	Mean Actual Taxes ($)	Mean Benefits Less Life Adjusted Taxes ($)	Median Return Ratio	Median Rates of Return
68	24,515	17,709	37,815	2.7	7.2
69	24,786	18,766	39,459	2.7	7.3
70	24,905	18,208	40,043	2.8	7.4
71	23,954	16,755	42,200	2.9	7.7
72	23,911	16,325	43,589	3.0	7.8
73	23,954	15,702	45,677	3.1	8.1
74	22,484	14,077	47,438	3.3	8.5

up gains of a pay-as-you-go retirement plan. The difference is most striking in 1969. Recall our assumption that no future contributions are made to the system. In 1969, the youngest cohort must wait four years to retire, so discounting has a substantial effect.

Table 7.7 collects some of the rate-of-return results from tables 7.4–7.6. It shows that the real internal rate of return to social security increased from 1969 to 1975 for the younger cohorts in our sample, even when both

Table 7.7   **Rate of Return by Cohort**

Cohort	1969		1975		1979	
	Rate	Age	Rate	Age	Rate	Age
7	7.0	58	7.8	64	7.2	68
6	7.0	59	8.0	65	7.3	69
5	7.6	60	7.9	66	7.4	70
4	7.9	61	8.2	67	7.7	71
3	8.3	62	8.3	68	7.8	72
2	8.8	63	8.6	69	8.1	73
1	9.4	64	9.2	70	8.5	74

taxes and benefits are life table adjusted. The real return decreased for the oldest two cohorts between 1969 and 1975 and also decreased for households of all ages between 1975 and 1979. The net change was an increase in the rate of return between 1969 and 1979 for the youngest two cohorts and a fairly sharp decline for the oldest three. These differences are probably the result of two factors: first, changes in the law between 1969 and 1975 increased the rates of return, but after 1975 changes in the law only increased the future real payments of workers through double indexing. This, however, had no effect on the real payments of retired people. Second, because delayed retirement between ages 62 and 65 is roughly actuarially fair at a 3% real interest rate, a delay in retirement will decrease the internal rate from the high values shown here. Of course, the internal rate will decrease even faster when someone works after the age of 65.

Tables 7.8–7.10 show social security transfers, return ratios, and internal rates of return by wealth quartile and by age in 1969, 1975, and 1979. The wealth variable is quite comprehensive in that it includes the value of home, business, and farm equity, other real property, stocks, bonds, bank accounts, pensions, and capitalized value of welfare payments, and the capitalized insurance value of Medicare. It excludes social security wealth and human capital. Table 7.8 indicates that social security transfers increase sharply by wealth quartile, especially if taxes are adjusted by the life tables. We feel such an adjustment is necessary to get a true picture of the way a cohort has fared with social security. The median life-table-adjusted transfer to those in the top wealth quartile is more than $6000 higher than that to those in the lowest wealth quartile, a 69% difference. The reason that the increase with wealth is greater for the life-table-adjusted numbers is that widows are heavily represented in the lower part of the wealth distribution, and the tax adjustment for mortality is much greater for them than for other groups. The increasing transfers with wealth are also due to the greater contributions of the wealthy to social security, a system that offered this generation a rate of return far greater than our 3% discount rate. The importance of using life-adjusted taxes is also shown in the return ratios: with unadjusted taxes, it appears that the lowest wealth quartile has a somewhat higher ratio of benefits to taxes than the other quartiles, yet when account is made of taxes paid by the deceased, the return ratio is almost flat across the quartiles.

Finally, the rates of return shown in table 7.8 are almost the same for the wealth groups. Most researchers would find this result surprising because the social security benefit schedule has considerable progressivity. Apparently that is neutralized by the taxes paid by the deceased and, possibly, by a different time pattern of contributions. For example, holding constant total undiscounted nominal contributions, the rate of return will increase if the contributions are made late in life rather than early.

Table 7.8 also shows how the transfers, return ratios, and rates of return vary by age within quartiles. It is important to disaggregate by age because both wealth and the rate of return vary positivity by age. Table 7.8 shows that at each age the transfers to those in the wealthiest quartile are much greater than the transfers to those in the lowest wealth quartile. In fact, for a couple of age groups the transfers are almost twice as great to the wealthy as to the poor. Table 7.8 shows that the internal rates of return are fairly flat across wealth quartiles; the highest rate of return recorded is for the upper wealth quartile among our eldest cohort, the 64-year-olds.

Table 7.9 contains similar results for 1975. The wealth and transfer figures are in 1974 dollars. The difference between adjusted and unadjusted taxes has become more important as reflected in the difference between the two transfer measures. Even more than in 1969, the unadjusted median return ratio gives a substantially different impression than the adjusted median return ratio: the one indicates that in percentage terms the poorer elderly gained more than the wealthy elderly, whereas the second indicates they did worse. The life-table-adjusted transfers to the wealthiest quartile are roughly double the transfers to the poorest quartile at every age except 70. Even their rates of return are highest at every age.

The results for 1979 as shown in table 7.10 are similar to the 1975 results: the adjustment for taxes according to the life table is important and, in fact, removes the negative correlation of the median return ratio with wealth quartile. The internal rates of return are down somewhat from 1975, most particularly for those in the wealthiest quartile. The apparent explanation is that those who worked past age 65 lowered their rates of return and that more of the relatively wealthy did that than those in the lower wealth quartiles. The overall result of tables 7.8–7.10, however, still remains that among the current elderly the wealthy have enjoyed the same high rate of return from social security as the poorer members of their age cohort.

Table 7.8   Social Security Transfers and Rates of Return by Non-Social-Security, Non-Human-Capital Wealth Quartiles, 1969

	Wealth Quartiles			
	$W \leq \$16{,}572$	$\$16{,}572 < W \leq \$32{,}188$	$\$32{,}188 < W \leq \$64{,}691$	$\$64{,}691 < W$
	Median Actual Transfers			
58	8,570	12,700	13,035	13,300
59	8,472	12,398	14,266	13,683
60	9,594	13,899	15,599	15,321
61	10,597	14,215	15,805	16,005
62	10,626	15,809	16,997	18,135
63	12,251	17,227	19,410	20,899
64	14,237	18,947	20,702	19,135
Entire Sample	10,542	14,508	15,830	15,802
	Median Life Table Adjusted Transfers			
58	8,108	11,678	12,851	13,222
59	7,529	11,999	14,123	13,414
60	8,310	13,230	15,233	15,241
61	9,185	13,708	15,418	15,678
62	9,164	15,211	16,535	17,838
63	11,056	16,348	18,944	20,573
64	12,818	18,117	19,871	18,248
Entire Sample	9,230	13,868	15,504	15,567
	Median Actual Return Ratio			
58	3.3	3.0	2.8	3.0
59	3.4	2.9	2.8	3.0
60	3.5	3.3	3.1	3.2

61	3.8	3.5	3.3	3.4
62	4.2	3.7	3.4	3.6
63	4.5	4.8	3.7	3.8
64	4.7	4.1	4.0	4.5
Entire Sample	4.0	3.5	3.3	3.4

Median Life Table Adjusted Return Ratio

58	2.9	2.7	2.6	2.8
59	2.8	2.7	2.7	2.8
60	2.9	3.0	3.0	3.0
61	3.2	3.1	3.0	3.2
62	3.3	3.4	3.2	3.2
63	3.6	3.4	3.5	3.5
64	3.7	3.6	3.7	4.0
Entire Sample	3.1	3.1	3.1	3.2

Median Internal Rate of Return (Life Table Adjusted)

58	7.1	7.0	6.9	7.0
59	7.1	7.1	6.9	7.2
60	7.4	7.6	7.6	7.5
61	8.1	7.8	7.7	8.0
62	8.3	8.5	8.0	8.2
63	9.0	8.7	8.7	8.4
64	9.6	9.0	9.4	9.8
Entire Sample	8.0	7.9	7.8	8.1

Note: Wealth and transfer amounts are in 1968 dollars. The number of households is 10,715.

Table 7.9 Social Security Transfers and Rates of Return by Non-Social-Security, Non-Human-Capital Wealth Quartiles, 1975

	Wealth Quartiles			
	$W \leq \$19,752$	$\$19,752 < W \leq \$43,678$	$\$43,678 < W \leq \$83,804$	$\$83,804 < W$
	Median Actual Transfers ($)			
64	23,522	31,911	36,793	39,541
65	23,371	29,155	39,858	42,435
66	21,959	31,762	39,574	41,643
67	25,289	29,524	39,313	41,531
68	28,152	31,317	39,455	42,554
69	27,418	31,298	37,632	43,631
70	30,271	38,189	40,639	38,933
Entire sample	25,563	30,701	40,639	41,477
	Median Life Table Adjusted Transfers ($)			
64	18,420	27,905	34,207	38,519
65	19,082	26,734	38,618	41,611
66	15,496	29,454	38,304	40,361
67	19,314	27,221	37,942	40,458
68	21,641	28,632	37,423	41,568
69	23,185	29,411	35,910	42,084
70	25,363	36,140	39,511	37,253
Entire sample	20,066	27,541	36,102	40,050
	Median Actual Return Ratio			
64	4.2	3.7	3.2	3.4
65	3.9	3.5	3.4	3.5

66	3.6	3.4	3.8	4.3
67	3.8	3.6	3.9	4.5
68	4.0	3.6	5.1	4.9
69	4.0	3.9	4.4	5.3
70	4.4	4.0	4.9	5.9
Entire sample	3.7	3.6	4.0	4.8

Median Life Table Adjusted Return Ratio

64	3.1	2.8	3.1	3.0
65	3.2	3.1	3.0	3.1
66	3.4	3.0	3.4	2.6
67	3.5	3.2	3.0	3.1
68	3.5	3.2	3.3	3.0
69	3.6	3.4	3.4	3.3
70	4.0	3.4	4.1	3.6
Entire sample	3.4	3.1	3.2	3.0

Median Internal Rate of Return (Life Table Adjusted)

64	8.0	7.6	7.9	7.8
65	8.3	8.0	7.9	8.1
66	8.2	7.9	8.3	7.1
67	8.7	8.2	7.8	8.2
68	8.7	8.1	8.3	8.4
69	9.2	8.7	8.3	8.5
70	9.5	8.8	9.5	9.2
Entire sample	8.5	8.0	8.0	8.1

Note: Wealth and transfer amounts are in 1974 dollars. The number of households is 8070.

Table 7.10 Social Security Transfers and Rates of Return by Non-Social-Security, Non-Human-Capital Wealth Quartiles, 1979

	Wealth Quartiles			
	$W \leq \$19,797$	$\$19,797 < W \leq \$50,548$	$\$50,548 < W \leq \$103,511$	$\$103,511 < W$
	Median Actual Transfers ($)			
68	39,618	44,030	47,245	51,808
69	38,888	38,477	49,842	53,643
70	38,977	45,507	46,972	52,251
71	44,741	42,266	52,542	49,430
72	51,341	46,162	47,541	50,907
73	52,099	44,097	50,156	51,073
74	61,877	46,068	47,144	48,087
Entire sample	46,499	41,854	47,733	50,631
	Median Life Table Adjusted Transfers ($)			
68	27,171	35,901	42,525	48,059
69	25,877	32,452	44,583	49,697
70	26,951	37,885	41,081	47,985
71	33,703	32,805	44,358	46,256
72	39,610	36,223	40,359	45,193
73	41,473	36,121	42,690	48,139
74	46,532	34,853	41,624	42,101
Entire sample	34,042	32,802	40,354	45,814
	Median Actual Return Ratio			
68	5.2	3.9	3.2	3.1
69	4.2	3.7	3.3	3.3

70	4.5	4.0	3.3	3.2
71	5.2	3.9	3.6	3.8
72	5.5	4.3	3.4	3.4
73	5.7	4.5	3.8	3.8
74	6.3	5.3	4.0	4.0
Entire sample	5.4	5.2	3.5	3.5

Median Life Table Adjusted Return Ratio

68	2.4	2.9	2.7	2.5
69	2.7	2.7	2.8	2.8
70	2.6	3.1	2.6	2.8
71	3.0	2.8	2.9	3.1
72	2.9	3.2	2.9	2.9
73	3.1	3.0	2.9	3.2
74	3.5	3.2	3.0	3.3
Entire sample	2.9	2.8	2.7	2.9

Median Internal Rate of Return (Life Table Adjusted)

68	7.2	7.6	7.3	7.0
69	7.4	7.1	7.3	7.6
70	7.3	7.9	7.2	7.4
71	8.1	7.4	7.5	7.9
72	8.2	8.1	7.3	7.7
73	8.4	7.9	7.5	8.3
74	9.2	8.2	7.9	8.2
Entire sample	7.9	7.4	7.2	7.6

Note: Wealth and transfer amounts are in 1978 dollars. The number of households is 7137.

7.4   Simulations

In this section we calculate the projected transfers and rates of return for six age cohorts, four household types, and three levels of earnings histories. This gives us some information about the intergenerational transfers implied by the social security system and predicts how the intragenerational transfers will change for later cohorts. It also shows the effects of the maturing of the system on the rate of return it offers.

The household types examined are single males, single females, and one- and two-earner married couples. We have collected data on median annual earnings for men and women by age from 1937 to 1977. These data were extended through the year 2020 with the assumption that median earnings grow at 10% from 1977 to 1982 and 6% thereafter. The accuracy of this assumption is not critical to our analysis because we use it only to generate the nominal earnings histories of our simulated households; that our profiles exactly match median values is relatively unimportant. We project 2% productivity growth, and therefore 4% CPI inflation, beyond 1982. For the simulated single men and women, we create three earnings profiles from age 20 to age 65, or, for the older cohorts, from 1937 until retirement at age 65. The low earnings profile is set at one-half the median earnings pattern, while the high earnings profile is set at the maximum earnings level subject to social security payroll taxes or five times the median, whichever is less. The one-earner married couples are assigned earnings histories equivalent to the single males, while the taxes of the two-earner married couples are the sum of those of a low-earning single male and female, a median-earning male and a low-earning woman, and, finally, a high-earning male and a median-earning woman. All told, there are 12 simulated households in each age cohort; three earnings profiles for each of four household types. The age cohorts are people who reach age 65 in 1970, 1980, 1990, 2000, 2010, and 2020. Husbands and wives are assumed to be the same age.

Unlike in the previous section, our simulations do not include widows. The single households have been life-long singles and their taxes reflect their own contributions plus the contributions of singles who, according to the life tables, die before age 65. The taxes of marrieds are also life table adjusted, but only for married couples where both spouses fail to reach age 65. After retirement, assumed to take place at age 65, we keep track of the joint survival probabilities of married couples and credit the benefits received during the resulting widowhood after the death of the first spouse.

Table 7.11 shows the internal rates of return for the 12 simulated households in six age cohorts. Several clarifications are necessary before these can be properly interpreted. First, these rates of return are done in an "ex ante" sense from age 65. By that we mean that individuals assume that the annuities they receive will remain constant in real terms (except for re-

Table 7.11   **Projected Internal Rates of Return by Household Type and by Age Cohort**

Demographic Status	Earnings Profile	Year in Which Head of Household Becomes 65						
		1970	1980	1990	2000	2010	2020
Single males	Low	7.5	5.3	3.2	2.4	2.2	2.1
	Median	6.3	4.5	2.4	1.6	1.3	1.3
	High	5.4	4.0	2.3	1.4	.9	.7
Single women	Low	10.7	7.7	5.9	5.0	4.5	4.4
	Median	9.1	6.6	4.6	3.8	3.4	3.3
	High	6.7	5.1	3.5	2.6	2.1	1.8
Married couples	Low/zero	9.7	7.4	5.3	4.3	4.1	4.0
	Median/zero	8.5	6.7	4.5	3.6	3.3	3.2
	High/zero	7.5	6.0	4.4	3.5	2.9	2.6
Married couples	Low/low	8.8	6.4	4.4	3.5	3.3	3.2
	Median/low	7.7	6.0	3.9	3.1	2.7	2.6
	High/median	6.7	5.1	3.4	2.6	2.2	1.9

Note: Benefits and taxes were projected according to the law at time of retirement except in 1970 where inflation indexation was assumed.

duced survivor benefits), and they do not take into account changes which may take effect ex post. The second, and similarly, the benefits and taxes paid out and collected after 1983 in our calculations are those projected in the Annual Statistical Supplement of the Social Security Bulletin (1980). Thus, these are not adjusted for changes that appear to be necessary to balance aggregate social security retirement benefits and taxes. The effect of the proposed changes will be to drive down the real rates of return for the younger cohorts, almost certainly making them negative for high-earning single males and some two-earner couples. The rates of return reported in table 7.11, then, should be taken as absolute upper bounds for these households and age cohorts since all signs indicate that they will pay more taxes and receive lower benefits than those officially projected in the Social Security Bulletin and used in these calculations.

The internal rates of return calculated for the 1970 cohort are consistent with our earlier examination of the Retirement History Survey population. Again, it should be emphasized that our simulated singles do not include widows. Within each household type the higher-earnings household has a lower rate of return. However, our earlier results indicated that this did not imply that wealthier retired households had lower rates of return on social security. The projected decline with cohort age in real internal rates of return is monotonic and substantial. For example, the median single female retiring in 1970 has an expected real rate of return of 9.1%. If she reached age 65 in 2000, however, she would only enjoy an expected 3.8% return. Single women earn higher rates than single men, not only due to their longer life expectancy but also due to their lower earnings profiles.

The results of table 7.11 indicate that those reaching age 65 in 1970 and 1980 were among those receiving windfall gains from the start-up and expansion of a pay-as-you-go social security scheme. The 1970 cohort enjoyed higher rates partly because it had a shorter history of tax payments (this generation was 32 years old in 1937). The 1980 cohort and to a lesser extent the 1990 cohort did well because social security tax rates were low during a substantial fraction of their work lives. Consistent with the results of the previous section, we find that the start-up and expansion gains are diminishing but that they extend over a longer period than is commonly realized. Those who retired on social security from 1940 to 1990 will enjoy some of these gains, and a noticeable fraction of the elderly population will be in this category until the year 2010.

The life-table-adjusted expected social security transfers in 1970 dollars are shown in table 7.12 for our simulated households. Again, the results are roughly in accord with our examination of the Retirement History Survey population. As in the previous section, the real discount rate used in the transfer calculations was 3%. For the households retiring in 1970, social security was "a good deal," and in most cases the higher earnings

Table 7.12   **Projected Transfers by Cohort (1980 Dollars)**

| Demographic Status | Earnings Profile | Year in Which Head of Household Becomes 65 | | | | | |
		1970	1980	1990	2000	2010	2020
Single males	Low	20,980	20,718	2,524	−12,556	−19,052	−25,410
	Median	25,615	23,994	−13,690	−48,670	−69,237	−88,482
	High	23,332	18,748	−19,301	−64,713	−121,610	−179,654
Single women	Low	25,784	28,270	23,746	22,255	21,513	24,649
	Median	32,027	34,660	21,169	14,915	9,825	9,377
	High	41,861	45,819	13,921	−17,324	−56,982	−96,659
Married couples	Low/zero	46,077	60,296	45,282	38,150	36,693	42,649
	Median/zero	63,425	87,293	51,960	30,664	16,596	16,596
	High/zero	63,907	88,025	53,996	27,707	−7,351	−41,365
Married couples	Low/low	47,704	55,587	33,651	19,139	11,759	10,858
	Median/low	58,052	76,031	33,758	5,250	−17,564	−25,915
	High/median	59,384	68,934	19,265	−23,122	−75,670	−126,388

Note: Benefits and taxes were projected according to the law at the time of retirement except in 1970 where inflation indexation was assumed.

households received larger transfers because they were allowed to participate in this good deal to a greater extent. This effect offset the somewhat lower internal rate earned by households with higher earnings profiles, as shown in the previous table. For the younger cohorts, the level of transfers is much lower (and in some cases negative), and their pattern across earnings profiles is very different. Consider the higher-earnings households retiring in the year 2010 or later; rather than being allowed to participate in a larger extent in a good deal (which was the case for the high earners earlier), those with high earnings in the later cohorts are forced to participate to a larger extent in a program that offers them a poor return. Each of our high-earnings household types retiring in the year 2010 has negative transfers. The progressive nature of the program, which has had essentially no impact on those who have retired to date, is strongly evident by the year 2010. The reforms currently being discussed will not only further lower the transfer numbers of the young cohorts but may add to the strong progressive pattern of the transfer figures already projected for them under current law.

7.5 Conclusion

We have examined the real rates of return and the transfers in the retirement (OASI) component of social security. Most of our analysis uses the Retirement History Survey population, which ranged in age from 58 to 64 in 1969 and which was interviewed six times from 1969 to 1979. Our primary result is that this generation did extremely well on social security, earning a real rate of return of roughly 8%. We calculated this number taking into account the taxes paid by the unfortunate cohort members who did not live to retirement age, and found this to be an important correction. Without it, we would get even higher rates of return for the RHS household population.

We examined the rates of return and transfers by marital status, race, and age. The results were that the married couples had higher rates of return than singles in the RHS population and that nonwhites did less well than whites. The lowest rates of return were for widows when account is taken of the taxes paid by the deceased spouses.

Perhaps our most interesting result, other than the high rate of return itself, is that the rate of return does not decline with wealth for this population sample. In fact, the wealthy in the RHS population have earned roughly the same high rate of return as their poorer cohort members and have enjoyed far higher absolute transfers.

In the final section of the paper we simulated the evolution of the impact of the social security system on 12 household types. We project that the high rates of return would have declined monotonically and significantly even before the social security changes now contemplated. The transfer components become negative for some households; for example, the negative transfer is projected at $180,000 (1980 $) for high-income single males currently age 27. The intergenerational transfers are extremely large and the intragenerational distribution of transfers is quite different (more progressive) for the currently young than it is for the presently elderly.

The results of this paper should be useful in assessing how the social security system could be revised. It indicates that the idea that all current retirees should be protected from cuts and only those who will retire in 20 or more years should be asked to rescue the system would lead to a policy of protecting those who have done well at the expense of those who are already projected to do poorly. Of course, this consideration must be weighted against the financial flexibility of the young relative to the currently elderly.

Appendix

Calculation of Present Value of Taxes and Benefits, and Rate of Return

The basic principle is that all taxes paid and benefits received by a cohort will be allocated to surviving members of the cohort. Unless this is done the survivors will appear to have received above-average rates of return even under an actuarially fair annuity system. We distingish groups according to marital status (married, single, or widowed), sex, and race.

Consider first a single person of age A with a stream of past taxes, t_i, and of past benefits, b_i. Let P_i be the probability that a person will live to age A given that he has reached age i. Thus, for each person of age A there were $1/P_i$ persons living at age i. There were on average $t_i(1/P_i - 1)$ taxes paid at age i by people who died before reaching age A and who had similar tax histories to the surviving person in the sample. The present value of these taxes over all ages less than A is

$$\sum_{i=1}^{A} t_i(1/P_i - 1)\, \beta_i(1 + r_i)^{A-i},$$

where β_i is the price level adjustment. r_i was taken to be a constant 3%. This number was added to the present value of taxes actually paid to get the total of taxes paid by the person in the sample and by similar people who did not survive until age A. Because the sample is self-weighting, aggregating over all singles will give a good estimate of total taxes paid by the cohort, provided mortality rates are independent of tax contributions. The mortality probabilities are race and sex specific; they are calculated from the 1969 life tables.

The present value of past benefits received by the cohort is calculated in a way symmetric to the calculation of taxes.

Now consider a widow in the 1969 sample. The data only include her tax contributions, which will be treated in the same way as the taxes of a single person. However, in almost all cases her benefits are based on the taxes of her deceased husband, and a rate-of-return calculation should take those into account. This is done by allocating part of the taxes paid by deceased husbands to the widows. The general reasoning is that for each surviving couple there were additional couples who paid taxes but did not survive as couples. Some survived as widows, some as widowers, and some had no survivors. From the life tables and our data on the tax histories of husbands, we can calculate taxes paid by deceased husbands in the same way as was done for singles. That amount multiplied by the probability that the wife survived is allocated to widows; the remainder is allocated to surviving couples. More specifically, if t_i is the tax stream of a husband in the sample, $ET = \sum_{i=1}^{A} t_i(1/P_i - 1) \beta_i(1 + r_i)^{A-i}$ is the present value of taxes paid by deceased husbands who were similar to the surviving husband. ET multiplied by the probability the wife survives until the survey year is allocated to widows, and the remainder is allocated to married couples in the sample. The allocation for widows is summed over all couples. That amount divided by the number of widows is added to the life-table-adjusted taxes actually paid by each widow on her own earnings record. In principle, the taxes paid by deceased wives should be similarly allocated between the couple and widowers, but for simplicity we allocated all of them to the couples: wives have small tax contribution histories, and the probability that the husband outlives the wife is small. Again, it is assumed that the mortality rates are independent of taxes. In addition, we assume independence between mortality rates of husbands and wives. Past benefits are treated symmetrically to taxes.

The present value of future benefits uses the 1969 life tables. Mortality probabilities of husbands and wives are assumed to be independent. The following provisions of the law were taken into consideration: actuarial reduction for early retirement; 1% benefit increase for work past age 65; a wife may draw on her own record or her husband's record; a widow may draw at age 60 at a reduced fraction of her husband's PIA, but at age 62 she can switch to her own record if it yields a higher benefit; the PIA calculation is based on the law in effect in the year of the calculation; a widow's benefit is reduced if her former husband drew benefits before he was 65 or if she draws benefits before she is 65.

The rate of return in year T is calculated in the following way. Let t_i and b_i be the life-table-adjusted real stream of taxes and benefits of an individual. The t_i will be zero prior to year of employment and after retirement. The b_i will be zero before retirement; after T, they will be calculated according to the social security law in effect in year T. The rate of return in year T solves the equation $\sum_{i=0}^{N} b_i(1 + r)^{T-i} = \sum_{i=0}^{T} t_i(1 + r)^{T-i}$, where N is the maximum age and $0 < T < N$.

Comment   Henry J. Aaron

Social security annually receives about 5% of gross national product in taxes and pays out roughly the same amount in benefits. In any year there is little overlap between taxpayers and beneficiaries. At some time during their lifetimes, however, most workers are both taxpayers and beneficiaries.

Most economists agree that an annual perspective is not useful for measuring such redistribution as may occur under social security. It is inadequate because any kind of insurance would appear redistributive from an annual perspective, even if premiums and benefits were set according to strict actuarial rules. Thus, redistribution would appear where none was occurring over time or among risk groups.

Hurd and Shoven argue that the lifetime is the appropriate period over which to measure the amount of redistribution that occurs under the social security system. They focus on the lifetime not of individuals but of age cohorts of individuals. They calculate the present value of the total taxes paid by various cohorts and of the benefits that they will receive, discounted at a 3% real interest rate. By focusing on cohorts they deal automatically with the fact that not everyone survives to receive the retirement benefits to which their own earnings entitle them or to which the earnings of others might entitle them.

Under the social security system, of course, death of a covered worker or retiree often triggers survivor benefits for surviving relatives; and early withdrawal from the labor force because of disability, followed by death before age 65, triggers first disability and then survivor benefits. These benefits flow not only to spouses but also to children and sometimes to others. Hurd and Shoven disregard disability and survivor benefits paid to relatives other than surviving spouses; presumably they also exclude the portion of payroll taxes that cover these benefits. In the case of couples of

Henry J. Aaron is professor of economics at the University of Maryland and a senior fellow at the Brookings Institution.

different ages, Hurd and Shoven assign to the surviving widow (or widower) the benefits paid after a spouse's death and a portion of the taxes imposed previously on the spouse. They do not explain in their paper how the division of taxes is made, but I assume that they assign a portion of the total taxes paid by the active worker equal to the ratio of the present value of taxes paid to the surviving spouse to the present value of all benefits paid to the surviving spouse and to the couple before the spouse's death. They make no mention of dependents or survivors benefits in addition to those paid to workers and their spouses. After describing the results, I shall comment on the assignment of benefits and taxes in analyzing the distributional consequences of taxes and transfers.

Hurd and Shoven find that the internal rate of return has been handsome for cohorts reaching retirement age in time to be interviewed in the 1969 Retirement History Survey. Couples did better than other aged persons, with internal rates of return of more than 8% and median ratios of benefits to costs of more than 3.3. Whites did slightly better than blacks, despite the progressivity of the benefit formula and the lower average earnings of blacks, because blacks die before receiving benefits more often than do whites.[1] These rates increase somewhat in the 1975 survey, presumably because Congress liberalized benefits in 1972. They decline in the 1979 survey and will continue to decline, unless benefits are liberalized again, because the sustained payment of benefits greater than the growth of the labor force and real wages is not possible in a pay-as-you-go social security system. This fact shows up in the tables presenting results for individual age cohorts, which reveal that older age groups enjoy higher ratios of benefits to costs and higher median rates of return than do younger cohorts. Hurd and Shoven adopt a computational simplification that contributes to this result. They exclude expected tax payments between date of interview and expected retirement and discount expected benefits to present values.

Hurd and Shoven also find that the absolute difference between benefits and costs increases with wealth. The transfer to the top and next-to-the-top cohorts are about equal in 1969, but both are larger than that received by the second quartile, which is larger than that received by the first. Much the same situation obtains in 1975, although the top quartile begins to do a bit better than the one just below it. By 1979, the absolute transfer to the bottom quartile has moved past that going to the second quartile but remains below those of the top two quartiles. One would expect that with the passage of time, as the internal rate of return declined, the pattern of transfers at a 2.5% discount rate would reverse; eventually the bottom wealth classes will receive algebraically larger transfers than do the top wealthy classes. As of now, however, low-wealth workers may receive higher rates of return or higher ratios of benefits to costs than do high-wealth workers; but because the marginal benefit in the social security system has exceeded the marginal cost (because the benefits to early participants in a pay-as-you-go social security system have overwhelmed everything else), the wealthy receive larger absolute transfers.

One may approach the analysis in this paper from one or more of three standpoints. Are the analytical techniques innovative and worth studying for future use? Are the results novel and interesting? Do the results have clear relevance to important questions of policy?

Methods of Analysis

The methods of analysis that Hurd and Shoven use are well established in most respects. Both Leimer and Petri (1981) and Aaron (1977) analyzed the distributional effects of social security on cohorts. Burkhauser and Warlick (1981) found that the excess of the present value of benefits over costs rose irregularly with permanent income. Like Hurd and Shoven, Aaron also took account of differences in life expectancy by income, race, and education.

Hurd and Shoven emphasize the importance of viewing the effects of social security ex ante with respect to mortality. But this adjustment raises other difficult questions. Ex ante, say at age 18, few people know whether they will reach retirement single, married, widowed, or divorced. Few know with certainty where life's vicissitudes will bring them in the distribution of permanent income. About all that they know for sure is their race, sex, and birthdate. A consistent ex ante calculation would require the specification of the ex ante probabilities not just of death but of all events relevant to the calculation of the present value of social security benefits and taxes.[2] In short, a true ex ante calculation of redistribution is likely to be damnably difficult, and Hurd and Shoven have not done it.

Even worse, such a calculation would shed no light on many of the questions about redistribution in which most of us are interested. As a practical matter, we are interested as well in ex post outcomes and ex post redistribution. We *do* want to know how various income classes fare, how one- and two-earner couples are treated relative to single, divorced, or widowed persons, and so on. To measure ex post redistribution, we need to measure the record of completed payments for people who actually move through the system. It makes sense within such an ex post framework to compare the relative treatment of couples, single persons, widows, and widowers. But it makes no sense within an ex ante framework, unless one is prepared to shoulder the monumental task of calculating ex ante probabilities of marriage, divorce, death of a spouse, and earnings achievement.

One may view the Hurd and Shoven calculations as ex post calculations, except with respect to mortality. But ex post calculations have imperatives of their own—for example, survivors and disability benefits, a topic that Hurd and Shoven try to skirt (like virtually everyone else), raise similar problems. Despite the progressivity of the social security benefit formula and relatively low average lifetime earnings, blacks according to Hurd and Shoven receive a smaller internal rate of return than do whites.[3] The reason for this result is that mortality rates for blacks are higher than for whites up to about age 65. Blacks, therefore, have a lower probability than whites of claiming retirement benefits. But the fact of higher mortality and the correlated higher incidence of disability means that blacks are disproportionate beneficiaries of survivor and disability benefits. Simply subtracting a proportion of payroll taxes from taxes paid that equals the average cost of survivors and disability benefits does not help at all. The essence of the problem is that complementary programs produce complementary benefits that exactly undo one of the more striking and misusable results.[4] And what sense does it make to compute separate rates of return for widows and widowers separately from those for couples in a life-cycle contest, as widowers and widows, by definition, were once part of a couple and some will yet be. This distinction is a speck of "annual perspective" clogging the gears of a life-cycle calculation.

Thus, the most useful framework for analysis probably is ex post. But proper application requires that one measure all of the benefits a cohort receives. Furthermore, such measurement requires that one hypothesize what would happen in the absence of the program. For example, if social security replaces privately financed transfers, from the covered worker to spouses or other dependents that would be made in the absence of the public program, the benefits as well as the costs accrue to the worker. If the benefits are in addition to those the worker would have provided voluntarily, the benefits accrue to the spouse or dependent and the tax to the worker. Here may be the reason Hurd and Shoven and others have focused on retirement benefits—they accrue to one or both members of a couple which we feel more comfortable treating as a unit in the life-cycle framework. Of course, such benefits may replace or increase intergenerational transfers, as Barro has pointed out. This possibility underscores once again that analysis of redistribution through social security and other programs usually implies a particular underlying framework of utility maximization and makes sense only within it.

Results

The results that this paper generates are not new, but they are an example of a product all too rare in economics, the confirmation of previous findings with a new set of data.[5]

The findings are in the "it's-not-surprising-when-you-think-about-it" class. If benefits rise with earnings, then the first cohort to receive benefits in a pay-as-you-go system will receive very high internal rates of return, and the excess of benefits over costs to that cohort will rise with income and, very likely, with wealth. In a mature pay-as-you-go system, the internal rate of return will equal the sum of the rates of growth of population and of real wages, subject to variations in life expectancy, labor force participation rates, retirement ages, and other factors that might affect the ratio of the number of active workers to beneficiaries. There will be no transfer component, if benefits and taxes are discounted at this internal interest rate, other than intracohort redistribution that arises from nonproportionality of the benefit formula. Of course, internal rates of return may vary widely over time depending on variations of birth rates, productivity, and other factors, and among households at any given time, depending on the benefit formula and personal characteristics.

Between opening day and maturity, rates of return will drop and, if the benefit formula is progressive, like that in social security, the bonus to high-income (and relatively wealthy) beneficiaries will reverse. Stated this way, the result is not surprising.

Policy

The most important question is, having been shown this result, how much the man on the street or his elected representative would have learned that is relevant to public policy. Hurd and Shoven stated that they think he would have learned a lot: "If [the wealthy retired] have received large windfall gains through the social security system, fairness in restoring the financial soundness of the program would indicate a reduction in their benefits."

I am not sure quite what this statement means, quite apart from the implicit allusion to an accepted metric for measuring fairness. Should benefits be reduced for the 70-year-old newly retired dentist? The 65-year-old formerly disabled steelworker? The 85-year-old rich widow? At least some beneficiaries in each of these classes will be receiving above-average benefits and, as Hurd and Shoven show, above-average net transfers. If their benefits are to be cut, how is it to be done? By a comprehensive wealth test? By an income test and, if so, repeated how often? By a retroactive cut in the benefit formula? Or should the cut be applied only to those who have not yet claimed benefits, presumably on the ground that people should be given some warning? But how much warning? Not 20 years, we are told. One year? Five? Ten?

These questions are rhetorical, but they raise a serious point. As economists we are much and properly concerned with property rights. The Constitution protects certain forms of property from seizure without due process of law. An extensive literature exists analogizing various features of the economic arrangements to property in which people have rights somehow defined. Tax reformers are alert to the problem of capitalization and to the limitations that it places on optimal changes in tax laws. As Feldstein (1976) pointed out, optimal tax reform may depend sensitively on the course of previous tax legislation. Capitalization may take the form of changes in market prices, which are then ratified by transactions, a possibility that undergirds the saying, sometimes suggestive, sometimes wrong, that an old tax is a good tax. But capitalization may also take the form of investments in human capital or acquired habits that are costly or painful to change. For the same reason that we are cautious in changing taxes that are capitalized or that are embodied in contracts or that may have induced other economic behavior, we should hesitate before we modify transfers on the expectation of which people may have based behavior that is costly or impossible to reverse. That does not mean that benefits once given should never be withdrawn. But it does mean that one should be modest about claiming fairness and that one is obliged to describe how one proposes to achieve an objective, however self-evident its fairness may appear.

In summary, the methods that this paper applies are familiar but subject to important challenge, the results confirm previous findings, and their applicability to public policy is yet to be established.

Notes

1. This fact arises from the higher mortality rates of blacks before age 65. Mortality rates of blacks and whites after age 65 are virtually identical.
2. Even if in some data heaven one might hope to get information sufficient for such calculations, one would not be able to get them from a survey like the Retirement History Survey.
3. This result appears inconsistent with the findings of Frieden et al. (1976) based on actual social security earnings and benefit records. The exclusion of two-earner families in Frieden et al. may resolve this apparent inconsistency.
4. These comments are more mea culpa than criticism, as they apply with just as much force to work I have done as they do to this paper.
5. The other rare but useful scientific contribution is the test of a set of conclusions for robustness, based on slight variations in specification using the same body of data.

References

Aaron, H. J. 1977. Demographic effects of social security benefits. In *The economics of public services*, ed. M. S. Feldstein and R. P. Inman. New York: Macmillan.

Boskin, M.; Avrin, M.; and Cone, K. 1983. Modeling alternative solutions to the long-run social security funding problem. In *Behavioral simulation methods in tax policy analysis*, ed. M. S. Feldstein. Chicago: University of Chicago Press.

Burkhauser, R. V., and Warlick, J. L. 1981. Disentangling the annuity from the redistributive aspects of social security in the United States. *Review of Income and Wealth* 27:401–21.

Feldstein, M. S. 1976. On the theory of tax reform. *Journal of Public Economics*, pp. 77–104.

Frieden, A., et al. 1976. *Internal rates of return to retired worker-only beneficiaries under social security, 1967–1970.* Studies in Income Redistribution no. 5. Washington, D.C.: Department of Health, Education, and Welfare.

Leimer, D. R., and Petri, P. A. 1981. Cohort specific effects of social security policy. *National Tax Journal* 34:9–28.

8 The Structure of Uncertainty and the Use of Nontransferable Pensions as a Mobility-Reduction Device

W. Kip Viscusi

8.1 Pensions as a Labor Compensation Instrument

Although pensions are an undeniably important component of most workers' compensation packages, whether or not their role is unique is more problematic. In terms of the structure of compensation, pensions have the following effects. By shifting compensation from one's working years to the period of retirement, they tilt the life-cycle earnings path upward. During the initial periods of employment, workers typically make contributions to the pension but acquire no earned rights to the benefits, thus effectively reducing their wage rate and imposing a transactions cost on job changes. As their experience increases, these contributions are coupled with at least partial earned benefit rights.

The extent to which market processes will lead to the use of nontransferable pension benefits is greater than might be concluded from current pension plan characteristics since the 1974 Employee Retirement Income Security Act (ERISA) imposes minimal vesting requirements. Before the advent of ERISA, the majority of workers (70% from 1950 to 1970) who left their jobs for voluntary or involuntary reasons forfeited their pension benefits (see U.S. Senate 1971).

ERISA now requires full pension vesting after 10 years of service, but for the high-turnover group of inexperienced workers a primary implication of pensions is that they impose a fixed cost on job changes. The ERISA requirements have led to "cliff vesting" for almost three-fourths of all workers covered by private pensions.[1] Under these provisions,

W. Kip Viscusi is director of the Center for the Study of Business Regulation at the Fuqua School of Business at Duke University and a research associate at the National Bureau of Economic Research.

Research support for this chapter was provided by the NBER pension project and by the Center for the Study of Business Regulation, Fuqua School of Business, Duke University.

workers with fewer than 10 years of experience forfeit all pension benefits if they leave the firm. These fixed costs will reduce worker turnover, an effect that has strong empirical support.[2]

The economic rationale for this transactions cost component of compensation has been discussed in a number of contexts. The forfeitable portion of the pension benefits can be viewed as the worker's compensation to the employer for its training investment in the worker.[3] Such a role for pensions has been formalized for both models of external job search (Mortenson 1978) and models of on-the-job experimentation by workers and firms.[4] Pensions further reduce turnover costs in that they serve as a self-selection device by attracting more stable employees to the firm (Viscusi 1980). Finally, pensions can also induce efficient turnover in situations in which there is the potential for worker shirking.[5]

These constructive functions are by no means unique to pensions. Other forms of upward tilting in the temporal wage structure can produce similar effects. If, however, it is difficult to vary wages on a period-by-period basis, pensions can increase the flexibility of the compensation system. Firms may attempt to link wages on the job to job-specific experience to provide a sense of equity for all those working at the position. Pensions permit firms to make a link between wages and total periods worked at the firm, as well as to past job performance (as reflected in past wages). If there is an enterprise-specific component to worker productivity or the firm's hiring and training investment (or in stochastic models to the information workers possess), it will be desirable to have such wage flexibility.

Even apart from such wage structure rigidities, pensions may be a more attractive compensation mechanism for promoting the aforementioned labor market functions. In addition to their very favorable tax status, pensions can be distinguished from a simple wage payment in that they serve to promote savings for old age and insurance against postretirement declines in income. By avoiding problems of adverse selection through mandatory pension coverage, reducing the fixed costs associated with annuity purchases, and promoting forced savings,[6] pensions may offer advantages that individually purchased annuities do not offer. There is, however, a trade-off since provision for increased resources in one's postretirement years reduces one's preretirement income, which might also have served an insurance function to the extent that it promoted stability in the preretirement earnings path.

In this paper I will not be concerned with such factors that might give pensions a unique role to play, but rather I will address the role of pensions as a form of deferred compensation that is contingent on remaining at the firm. The transferable pension benefit rights do not affect mobility decisions and will not be the focus of my analysis.

The two mobility-related functions of pensions to be considered are interrelated. First, the deferred compensation structure of pensions will re-

225 Nontransferable Pensions as a Mobility-Reduction Device

duce labor turnover by leading more stable employees to self-select into the firm. Second, once at the firm, workers' incentive to switch employers will be reduced by the transactions cost aspect of pension benefits.

This reduced mobility represents a beneficial labor market function from the standpoint of hiring and training costs, but if a worker is trapped in a job he would like to leave the implications may be quite different, particularly if he did not have accurate perceptions of all of the uncertainties he faced. These effects are reminiscent of the types of concerns that led to the passage of ERISA. The principal issue to be considered here is whether this immobility is optimal and, if so, when.

Uncertainty plays a critical role in this analysis, both in terms of providing workers an incentive to change jobs and through its effect on the welfare implications of nontransferable pensions. Because of the long lags before individuals acquire full benefit rights, the nature of the uncertainties may be quite different from that in the standard one-period compensating wage differential model in which workers encounter a single lottery. Learning is likely to play an important role, as will the possibility that individuals may face a sequence of interrelated risks over time.

Section 8.2 of the paper begins with a relatively conventional compensating differential model, and sections 8.3 and 8.4 consider learning and other structures of uncertainty. Although pensions have no essential role to play in a single-period lottery model, once the uncertainty assumes a dynamic character they do serve an important mobility-reducing function.

8.2 The Optimal Wage Structure under Uncertainty: The Standard Case

The most prevalent uncertainty assumption, which is the foundation of the classic compensating differential analysis, is that the worker faces lotteries that are independent and identically distributed over time. In the case of job risks, there is assumed to be an invariant stochastic process governing the chance that a worker will be injured. If the worker has a reservation wage w_0 and the prospective alternative job poses a chance p of suffering a loss $-\theta$ in each period and a probability $1 - p$ of no loss, to attract the worker to this uncertain job the employer must offer a wage w_1 equal to $w_0 + p\theta$ in each period.[7] This wage will not only attract the worker initially, it will always keep him at the firm if there are no time-related changes in his employment choice problem.

Instead of offering a uniform wage rate, the firm could offer wages on a period-by-period basis. Any upward tilting of the wage structure that offers the same present value as the compensating differential wage package will suffice. Downward tilting with the same present value will attract the worker initially but will not retain him once the expected net wage (including the loss $p\theta$ in each period) drops below w_0. The firm will not only incur mobility-related costs in this instance, its wage bill per period of employment will rise as well.

One form of upward tilting in the wage structure is the use of pensions. I will treat pensions as giving the worker a payment of z during his final year of employment, where z represents the discounted present value of his annuity. To the extent workers acquire at least a partial earned right to pensions during the earlier part of their careers, some of this value may be spread over a larger number of periods.

Although making the number of periods to the worker's choice problem arbitrarily large poses no conceptual problem, it is simplest to focus on the two-period case.[8] The worker selects his job based on its expected present value. Let r denote the worker's discount rate, which is the inverse of one plus the interest rate. The implicit assumption is that workers are free to borrow and lend at this rate. Workers would, for example, be indifferent to receiving their entire lifetime income through a pension or having this income spread more evenly over their lifetime. A principal reason we do not observe extreme outcomes such as this is that individuals' discretion over their work effort creates an adverse incentives problem when making loans based on anticipated lifetime income.

Any acceptable wage package consisting of a base wage w and a pension z must compensate the worker for the loss θ in each period and for the opportunity cost w_0 of employment, so that the compensation package must satisfy

$$(1) \qquad (w_0 + p\theta) \sum_{i=0}^{1} \beta^i = w \left(\sum_{i=0}^{1} \beta^i\right) + \beta z.$$

Any positive value of z will lead to tilting in the wage structure, as compared with the flat wage case. The maximum tilting occurs when the worker takes all of his wage in the form of pension payments or he sets w equal to zero.

A final possible wage structure is ex post compensation for the adverse job outcome. The firm can attract workers by offering a base wage w_0 and paying an additional premium of θ to each worker who suffers an adverse outcome. This approach will have the same cost to the employer as the pension and flat wage. The informational requirements for ex post compensation are, however, much greater since the firm must be able to monitor the adverse outcome. Although this task is not difficult for readily visible job injuries, for other job attributes such as those relating to job satisfaction it is not as straightforward. If a worker will be paid a bonus if he dislikes a co-worker or if he finds his job strenuous or boring, there will be an obvious incentive to misrepresent the job's attractiveness.[9]

The principal advantage of ex post compensation is that it eliminates any variance in the worker's net rewards in each period, which will always be w_0. This stabilization both across and within periods irrespective of the lottery outcome will be attractive if workers are risk averse. Under a flat wage policy there will be a possible within-period wage gap of θ. The pension package leads to a comparable within-period spread but a lower base wage. If the insurance value of the pension is not taken into account, so that z is treated as comparable to a bonus in the final period of work, risk-averse workers will value pay packages with pensions less than a flat wage, with ex post compensation valued highest.

8.2.1   Heterogeneous Workers

There will also be differences in the attractiveness of the wage structure arising from variations in individuals' probability assessments.[10] Suppose that a fraction f of the potential work force assesses the probability of incurring a loss θ in each period as $\hat{p}$, while a fraction $1 - f$ assess this probability as p, where $\hat{p} < p$. This heterogeneity will lead the wage structures to have different relative costs and different welfare implications, depending on the source of the heterogeneity.

Consider first the situation in which these probability assessments derive from actual differences in the lotteries. Some workers may be more accident prone or more likely to be productive. The wage costs to the employer will be least if the employer can design the wage structure to screen out the high-risk workers and to attract only low-risk workers. With a uniform wage over time of $w_0 + \hat{p}\theta$, the flat wage structure will serve as a perfect self-selection device as workers with assessed failure probabilities p will not find the job attractive. Pensions serve an identical self-selection function and will impose the same discounted expected cost, where the form of the pension continues to satisfy equation (1) (after replacing p by $\hat{p}$). Ex post compensation will not screen out any high-risk workers, as the per period wage bill per worker will be $w_0 + f\hat{p} + (1 - f)p$. Workers will be allocated inefficiently, and the firm's wage bill will be higher than for the other wage structures.

If the differences in probability assessment arise from misassessments of the risk, the relative costs to the employer remain the same, but the efficiency implications are altered. For concreteness, suppose that p is the true probability of failure for all workers but that a fraction f underestimate this p to be $\hat{p}$. The value of p will be assumed to be constant over time, or there is assumed to be no learning. For workers who misassess the risk, the actual expected utility of the uncertain job under either the flat wage or pensions will be $[w_0 + (\hat{p} - p)\theta] \sum_{i=0}^{1} \beta^i$, which is below the value of the alternative job; individuals who correctly assess the probability will be screened out. Ex post compensation prevents any such welfare losses and will attract a broad mix of workers. The wage costs will, however, be higher (i.e., $w_0 + p\theta$ per period, as before) so that there is no incentive for employers to utilize this wage mechanism.

If all workers systematically overestimate the risk, employers can limit their wage costs to $w_0 + p\theta$ by offering ex post compensation. Through judicious choice of the wage structure, the employer can always limit the per period employment costs to $w_0 + p\theta$. If some workers have a lower risk assessment, the wage costs can be lowered further through a self-selecting wage mechanism. Biased assessments consequently can never hurt the employer, but they can enable him to make money from systematic underassessments of the risk.

Under a situation of time- invariant lotteries, pensions have no essential role to play. Flat wages, pensions, and all intermediate forms of wage structure tilting impose the same wage costs, provide workers with the same level of welfare, and have the same self-selection properties. (There are, however, some differences for risk-averse workers involving a trade-off between expected utility before and after retirement if money is not transferable across periods on an actuarially fair basis.) Ex post compensation protects misinformed workers from welfare losses but sacrifices the self-selection properties of the other wage structures. Moreover, it is never in the employer's financial interest to utilize this mechanism when there is any heterogeneity in risk perceptions except in the bias case in which all workers overestimate the risk.

8.3 Lotteries with Worker Learning

8.3.1 Problem Structure

A variant on the standard lottery structure is to introduce the potential for worker learning. When workers do not possess perfect information regarding the job lotteries they face, it will be desirable to revise these perceptions as additional information is acquired. In the earlier misperception discussion, for example, it was perhaps unrealistic to assume that workers who underestimate the job risks would never revise these judgments in the face of repeated lottery outcomes. In the case of income uncertainties, there are a variety of sources of information that can be used to form these judgments. The ease of the job, the performance of one's co-workers, the reactions of the boss, and one's current productivity can all contribute to these assessments. Uncertainty regarding nonmonetary rewards can be treated similarly.

For concreteness, I will continue to assume that a loss of θ is generated by an underlying stochastic process that is independent and identically distributed over time. The difference is that the worker does not know the value of the probability p in these Bernoulli trials. I will assume that he has a prior assessment p of the chance of an adverse outcome but that he updates this prior in Bayesian fashion based on his on-the-job experiences. I will denote by q the true probability that θ will prevail, which is assumed to be known to the employer. I will often assume that the prior be characterized by a beta distribution, so that the posterior probability $p/p(m, n)$ of θ after observing m unsuccessful outcomes and n successful outcomes is

$$p(m, n) = \frac{\gamma p + m}{\gamma + m + n},$$

where γ represents the precision of the prior.

To investigate the role of pensions, it is instructive to focus on the two-period case.[11] The principal implications of the model will hinge on whether or not there is any chance that the worker may find it desirable to leave his job, which are principles with broad applicability. Two situations may occur. Either the worker chooses to leave the uncertain job after an unsuccessful outcome or he remains with it. A third possibility, that the worker may depart after a successful job experience, can be ruled out if the life-cycle wage structure is not downward sloping.[12]

The choice for the firm will be whether or not it chooses to retain the worker following an unfavorable outcome. Let W_a represent the per period wage costs if the worker is always induced to remain with the firm, and let W_b represent the per period wage costs if the worker leaves after an unsuccessful outcome. For the wage structures considered below, $W_a > W_b$, or it is always more expensive to retain the worker irrespective of the job outcome. Let h represent the hiring and training costs per worker.

In a two-period model, the discounted period of employment is $1 + \beta$ if the worker never leaves the job and $1 + \beta(1 - q)$ if there is a chance q of an unfavorable first-period outcome that will lead him to quit. It will be desirable to keep the worker irrespective of the job outcome if the per period employment costs are lower, or

$$\frac{h}{1 + \beta} + W_a < \frac{h}{1 + \beta(1 - q)} + W_b,$$

which reduces to the requirement

(2) $$h > \frac{[1 + \beta(1 - q)](1 + \beta)}{\beta q} (W_a - W_b) > 0.$$

If the turnover costs are sufficiently large, it will be desirable to always keep the worker. Rather than analyze the implications of turnover costs for each wage structure, I will focus on the wage mechanisms that yield the lowest values of W_a and W_b. One could then employ equation (2) to ascertain if it is worthwhile to prevent turnover.

8.3.2   Wage Structures That Prevent Turnover

To ensure that workers never leave the uncertain job, the wage in period 2 must be sufficiently large to retain them after an adverse job experience in period 1. Since the worker's maximum expected loss in period 2 will be $p(1, 0)\theta$, the flat wage will have an associated discounted cost C_f equal to $C_f = [w_0 + p(1, 0)\theta](1 + \beta)$. Unlike the results for time-invariant lotteries, the flat wage clearly can never be optimal from the firm's standpoint since workers are being overpaid in period 1 when their expected loss is $p\theta$. Since no flat wage below $w_0 + p(1, 0)\theta$ can retain workers in period 2, this wage structure is necessarily dominated by other, more flexible alternatives.

Ex post compensation will cost the employer $w_0 + q\theta$ in each period, where q is the employer's assessed probability of an adverse outcome. If the employer and worker assessments are identical and q equals p, the discounted cost C_x of this form of compensation will be $C_x = (w_0 + q\theta)(1 + \beta) = (w_0 + p\theta)(1 + \beta)$. It is noteworthy that C_x is independent of all characteristics of the worker's probability assessments except the value of his prior probability of an adverse outcome. The precision does not enter. This property is true more generally in situations possessing this two-armed bandit structure whenever there is no chance of leaving the uncertain job.

The final alternative is to vary wages on a period-by-period basis or, equivalently, to offer the worker a pension z in the second period if he remains with the job. The minimal tilting of the wage structure that will always keep the worker on the job occurs when

$$(3) \qquad\qquad w + z - p(1, 0)\theta = w_0,$$

or

$$z = w_0 - w + p(1, 0)\theta.$$

One must then ascertain the minimal base wage, which will satisfy the following condition:

$$w - p\theta + \beta p[w + z - \mathrm{p}(1, 0)\theta]$$
$$+ \beta(1 - p)[w_0 + z - p(0, 1)\theta] = w_0 + \beta w_0,$$

or

$$(4) \qquad \begin{aligned} w + \beta(w + z) &= w_0(1 + \beta) + p\theta + \beta p[p(1, 0)\theta] \\ &+ \beta(1 - p)p(0,1)\theta = (w_0 + p\theta)(1 + \beta). \end{aligned}$$

The expression on the left-hand side of equation (4) is the discounted wage cost C_p to the firm of the pension, which is equal to C_x above. Imposing the requirement in equation (3) on $w + z$, one can calculate the wage structure components, which are

(5) $$w = w_0 + p\theta + \beta[p - p(1, 0)]\theta$$

and

(6) $$z = (1 + \beta)[p(1, 0) - p]\theta > 0.$$

The value of z represents the minimal upward tilting of the wage structure that will induce the worker to remain on the job. The minimal tilting required decreases with the precision of the prior since $\delta p(1, 0)/\delta \gamma < 0$.

Alternatively, since the firm can always postpone wage payment arbitrarily so long as the discounted value to the worker is unchanged, it can give the worker all of his compensation in terms of a pension. I will denote this upper limit on pension payments that impose the same cost as the wage structure in equation (4) by $\bar{z}$, where

(7) $$\beta\bar{z} = (1 + \beta)(w_0 + p\theta) = C_p.$$

The discounted pension is simply the present value of the minimal wage structure cost under uncertainty. The value of C_p equals C_x for ex post compensation so that pensions and ex post compensation are the cheapest turnover- reduction mechanisms. If there are costs to monitoring the outcome of the job lottery, wage structure tilting will be dominant.

8.3.3   Heterogeneous Perceptions

If there is heterogeneity in workers' risk perceptions, wage structure tilting will be the least costly alternative except in one instance. If all workers have biased assessments and overestimate the risk, the firm can limit its wage costs to C_x by offering ex post compensation. This form of wage structure can never induce worker self-selection.

Pensions will, however, induce self-selection. Assuming that they are set so as to prevent worker turnover, the only relevant parameter of the prior distribution is its mean. Workers with lower mean values of the prior will be self- selected, and the cost of the firm's wage structure will be given by equation (4), where p corresponds to the assessed initial risk for the low-risk group. Although for this group there will be no turnover, there is no assurance that all turnover will be eliminated. Some workers with higher values of p but with very imprecise initial judgments may be attracted to the job and may then quit if the first-period outcome is unsuccessful.

Consider two groups of workers, which I will designate type 1 and type 2, where the respective prior probabilities of an adverse outcome are p_1 and p_2, where $p_1 < p_2$. For prior probability assessments from the beta family, if the precision $\gamma_1 \leq \gamma_2$, even pensions with minimal tilting (eqs. [5] and [6]) will screen out higher-risk group 2 workers. If however, $\gamma_2 < \gamma_1$, it may be that the group with the higher probability p_i of an adverse outcome may find it desirable to start the job, quit after an unfavorable outcome, and collect the pension with a favorable outcome.

To show that this is the case, it suffices to construct a numerical example. Let $\gamma_1 = 100$ and $p = .5$, and substitute these values into equations (5) and (6), yielding terms I will designate w_α and z_α. Worker 2 has beliefs characterized by $\gamma_2 = 1$ and $p_2 = .51$. Let the discount factor β be one. Whereas a $w + z$ value equal to $w_0 + .51\theta$ is sufficient to prevent turnover of worker 1 in period 2 after an adverse outcome, this value must be at least $w_0 + .75\theta$ to prevent worker 2 from quitting since his looser prior is updated more after the adverse initial job experience. Below I will assume that the pension tilting is set at the minimal level needed to retain worker 1, which in turn will lead worker 2 to quit after an unfavorable period 1 outcome.

Worker 2 will, however, find the job attractive in the initial period if

$$w_\alpha - p_2\theta + p_2w_0 + (1 - p_2)[w_\alpha + z_\alpha - p_2(0, 1)\theta] > 2w_0.$$

Since the terms on the left-hand side of the equation simplify to $2w_0 + .1\theta$, he will accept the uncertain job and will not be screened out.

Pensions $\overline{z}$ that involve maximum upward tilting (i.e., all wages are paid in period 2) are more likely to serve as a complete self-selection device since any worker who leaves after an adverse outcome will have a chance $1 - p_2$ of receiving no wage payment. Moreover, concentrating the entire wage in the second period makes it more likely that the worker will stay in period 2 following an adverse outcome, in which case only the mean p_i of the prior is relevant.

Letting $\overline{z}$ denote the maximum wage structure tilting package that is required to attract and retain the low-risk type 1 worker, we have the result that the type 2 worker will remain on the job after an adverse outcome if $\overline{z} - p_2(1, 0)\theta \geq w_0$, or, on substitution for z from equation (7) and rearranging terms, $w_0 \geq \theta[\beta p_2(1, 0) - p_1]$. The maximum pension always prevents turnover if w_0 exceeds the terms on the right-hand side of this inequality. Unless $p_2(1, 0)$ exceeds p_1, and either this gap is very large or θ is sufficiently large, pensions can always prevent turnover. Once this condition is met, the type 2 worker will necessarily be screened out since the attractiveness of a wage structure involving no turnover hinges solely on the initial risk assessment, and $p_2 > p_1$. Although pensions do not always act as perfect self-selection devices, increasing the upward tilt of the wage structure enhances their effectiveness as a self-selection mechanism.

When there are legitimate differences in worker riskiness, this risk-selection property is attractive because it reduces wage costs by matching low-risk workers to the job. With biased perceptions, there will be cost savings for the firm but less favorable implications for worker welfare. As in section 8.2, the cost of ex post compensation will be based on the average riskiness of workers attracted and will be more expensive than wage structures for a self-selected, low- risk group.

8.3.4   Wage Structures That Permit Turnover

If the wage structure permits worker turnover to occur, the choice is narrowed to flat wages and period-by-period wage payments. Ex post compensation never enters since any time- invariant compensation system of this type will necessarily prevent turnover in both periods unless the employer fires all workers with adverse initial job experiences.

Unlike the case in which the wage structure must always prevent turnover, the flat wage structure will be successful in attracting workers and keeping them following a success but not after a failure in the first period. Since workers with favorable job experiences update their priors to $p(0, 1)$ $< p$, any flat wage that attracts the worker to the firm initially will overpay him in later periods.

The minimal flat wage w_f that will attract the worker to the firm must meet the condition that

$$w_f - p\theta + \beta p w_0 + \beta(1 - p)[w_f - p(0, 1)\theta] = w_0 + \beta w_0,$$

or, solving for w_f,

$$w_f = w_0 + \theta \frac{[p + \beta(1 - p)p(0, 1)]}{1 + \beta(1 - p)} < w_0 + p\theta,$$

since $p(0, 1) < p$. With learning, the firm lowers its wage costs per period worked by only retaining those workers with favorable experiences. One can also show that $\delta w_f/\delta\gamma > 0$, or the value of this wage increases with the precision of the prior.

The pension option must meet three requirements. First, the pension must not retain the worker in period 2 after an adverse outcome, or $w + z - p(1, 0)\theta < w_0$; otherwise the wage structure reduces to a situation treated in section 8.3.2. Second, the wage structure must retain the worker following a favorable outcome, or $w + z - p(0, 1) \geq w_0$. And, finally, the worker must accept the job initially, or

$$w - p\theta + \beta p w_0 + \beta(1 - p)[w + z - p(0, 1)] = w_0 + \beta w_0.$$

The minimal pension z can be negative since it is easier to retain the worker after a success than to attract him initially.

A fundamental concern is how individuals' probability assessments relate to the properties of the wage structure. In particular, for what combinations of precision γ and initial risk assessments p will the worker never start the job, accept the job and quit after an adverse experience, or never leave the position? I will present these requirements for pensions which, depending on the degree of tilting, will include all possible temporal wage structures.

The requirement that the worker just be indifferent between remaining on the job after an adverse outcome or quitting can be written as

$$G = w + z - p(1, 0)\theta - w_0 = 0.$$

The combination of acceptable (γ, p) values that satisfy this requirement is positively related since

$$\frac{\partial \gamma}{\partial p} = \frac{-G_p}{G_\gamma} = \frac{-\gamma(\gamma + 1)^2}{p - 1} > 0,$$

or the highest γ value that is acceptable is positively related to the initial risk p. Similarly, the worker will be indifferent to starting the job initially if

$$H = w - p\theta + \beta p w_0 + \beta(1 - p)[w + z - \frac{\gamma p \theta}{\gamma + 1}] - w_0 - \beta w_0 = 0,$$

where one can show that

$$\frac{\partial \gamma}{\partial p} = \frac{-H_p}{H_\gamma} < 0.$$

As the assessed initial risk rises, the worker requires that his prior be less precise if he is to accept the job initially.

Figure 8.1 sketches the three possibilities.[12] For very high risks, the worker never starts the job. Tighter probabilities lower the value of the highest acceptable initial risk since the worker updates tight priors less, thus reducing the potential value of the job after a success. The precision of the prior has the opposite effect for preventing workers from ever leaving. Higher values of p will be accepted for tighter priors since these priors

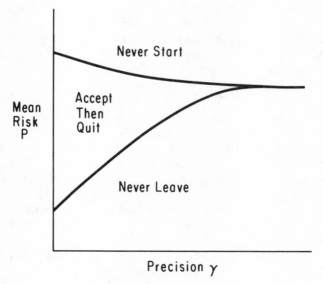

Fig. 8.1   Turnover decisions and prior beliefs.

are not updated as much after an adverse outcome, making it easier to retain the worker. In the intermediate (γ, p) range, the worker accepts the job initially and quits after an adverse outcome. The probability range satisfying this condition is greatest for low values of γ. In the limiting case, as $\gamma \to \infty$, this middle range disappears; the worker simply has a cutoff probability above which he will not start the job and below which he will never leave it.

This diagram can also be applied to the issue of self-selection. Although pensions that attract workers but do not keep them may screen out some high-risk workers, pensions will not always serve as a perfect self-selection device. As the top curve in figure 8.1 suggests, workers with higher assessed risks may find the job acceptable if the precision γ of their priors is sufficiently low. For workers with very high values of p, however, tilting the wage structure will screen them out.

The role of the precision of workers' priors is closely related to that of the variability of the risk, although the implications are quite different. If a worker were in a job situation that he would never leave, the only matter of consequence would be the mean risk. It would not matter, for example, if he faced a chance .5 of an adverse outcome or an equal probability that the underlying lottery poses a risk .4 or a risk .6. Even though he risks incurring an unfavorable lottery with p equal to .4 for every period of his work career, so long as there is no worker turnover the situations are identical.

For situations involving turnover, the variability is of substantial consequence. Workers prefer loose priors because they create possible employment paths on which they can quit if the information is unfavorable and remain if the information is favorable. Since the compensation package makes the worker indifferent between the uncertain job and alternative employment, variations in p have no effect overall on expected utility. A related issue that does have nontrivial implications is whether *for a given compensation structure and for particular employment paths,* variability in p raises or lowers the worker's expected utility.

The worker's expected utility in a situation where he finds the job acceptable but quits after an adverse outcome is given by

$$EU = w - p\theta + \beta p w_0 + \beta(1 - p)[w + z - \frac{\gamma p}{\gamma + 1}\theta].$$

Raising the assessed risk lowers worker welfare, as expected, since

$$\frac{\partial EU}{\partial p} = -\theta - \beta[w + z - \frac{\gamma p}{\gamma + 1}\theta - w_0] - \beta(1 - p)\frac{\gamma}{\gamma + 1}\theta < 0,$$

with the loss in utility decreasing in p, or

$$\frac{\partial^2 EU}{\partial p^2} = 2\frac{\beta\gamma\theta}{\gamma + 1} > 0.$$

These results imply that the worker's expected utility for this employment path is convex in p and takes the form sketched in figure 8.2. The EU curve lies below the dotted line representing linear combinations of the expected utility when there is no chance of an accident (the vertical intercept) and the expected utility when an accident is certain. From Jensen's inequality we have the result that the worker would prefer a lottery on the extreme certainty situations (with a chance p of the unfavorable outcome) to a situation in which he faces the same lottery in each period with the risk p of an adverse outcome.

It would be preferable from the worker's point of view to have an equal chance of facing a risk .4 or .6 for both periods, as opposed to a lottery with a risk of .5. The attractiveness of this lottery on extremes increases as one increases the probability spread, where the highest-ranking situation is that in which there is a 50:50 chance of suffering a loss or being free of this loss throughout the employment path. For given employment paths and wage structures, workers prefer greater risk in the sense of a mean preserving spread on the job lottery probabilities.[13] The preferability of such a lottery on extreme certain situations parallels the earlier result in which workers display a preference for uncertain situations (i.e., low γ values, since as $\gamma \to 0$ the mass of the probability density functions is concentrated around the values zero and one).

For the situation in which turnover may occur, it is instructive to ascertain whether the employer will be indifferent to the degree of wage struc-

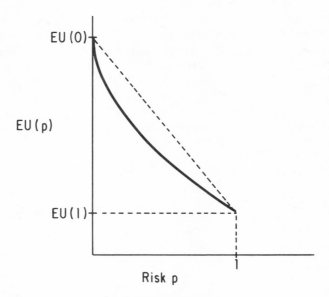

Fig. 8.2   The convex shape of expected utility.

ture tilting. The range of $w + z$ values consistent with keeping the worker in period 2 only after a success must satisfy

(8) $$w + z - p(1, 0)\theta < w_0 \leq w + z - p(0, 1)\theta.$$

For concreteness, let

(9) $$w + z = w_0 + p(0, 1)\theta + s,$$

where the parameter s will be successively increased to assess the desirability of affecting the steepness of the earnings profile through greater reliance on pensions. The base period wage w required to attract the worker will be

(10) $$w = w_0 + p\theta - \beta(1 - p)s.$$

Suppose the firm's assessment of the risk of an adverse outcome is q. With this wage structure, it estimates that the discounted expected wage costs over the employment path C_p will be

$$C_p = w + \beta(1 - q)[w_0 + p(0, 1)\theta + s],$$

which on substitution for w simplifies to

$$C_p = w_0 + p\theta + \beta(1 - q)[w_0 + p(0, 1)\theta] + \beta(p - q)s.$$

The fundamental concern is how the firm's costs are affected by the degree of tilting. If workers overestimate the risk (i.e., $p > q$), C_p is minimized by setting s equal to zero; the earnings profile will be downward sloping or the pension z is negative. Moreover, if the degree of overestimation is sufficiently great, the employer can limit the per period wage costs to $w_0 + q\theta$ by offering ex post compensation. If p equals q, the firm is indifferent to the degree of tilting in the experience-earnings profile. Finally, if workers underassess the risk, the firm will set the value of s at its maximum value consistent with the requirements of equations (9) and (10), thus placing great reliance on pensions as a compensation investment.

The role of pensions in the presence of misperceptions is consequently to enable employers to reduce their wage costs by exploiting underestimates of the risk. Since workers with low values of p (and low γ) will tend to be self-selected into the job, there will be a tendency to attract such workers to the job. If workers underassess the risk and $p < q$, the optimal second-period wage for the case permitting turnover will be $w_0 + p(1, 0)\theta - \epsilon$, where ϵ is some arbitrarily small amount.

The issue then becomes whether the employer should raise the second-period wage by ϵ and prevent turnover altogether. This will generally not be the case since one can show that the condition that per period wage costs are lower with turnover,

$$\frac{w + \beta q(w + z - \epsilon)}{1 + \beta q} < \frac{w + \beta(w + z)}{1 + \beta},$$

reduces to the requirement $q \leq 1$. In the presence of pensions and misperceptions, the per period wage bill is always reduced by attracting workers who underestimate the risk and then permitting them to leave.

In effect, the firm is engaging in an unfair bet against the worker. The worker is shifting resources from period 1 to period 2 in the hopes that he will have a favorable job outcome and collect the pension. The firm makes money from these bets because workers do not collect the pension with as high a probability as they assessed; or, viewed somewhat differently, they shift their earnings forward in time on an actuarially unfair basis.

8.3.5   Streaks, Misperceptions, and Worker Welfare

If the worker is engaged not in a two-period problem but in a multi-period problem, the difficulties caused by misperceptions will be enhanced. In the extreme case, the worker must have a string of n favorable outcomes in n periods in order to collect his pension (e.g., the risk of death). In this situation, the discounted expected pension benefit is $\beta^{n-1} z E(1 - p)^n$. Since biases in the assessed risk have a multiplicative effect, there may be severe losses in worker welfare and, as before, there will be an incentive for the employer to exploit these biases.

This outcome is of policy concern for several reasons. First, workers are gambling with resources for a heavily subsidized portion of their life cycle. If the pension system is not effective, the burden on publicly funded programs will be increased. Second, workers may be matched inefficiently to jobs. Third, ex post, workers will be unhappy with the outcome. This dissatisfaction by itself is not compelling since workers will always be unhappy after an unfavorable lottery outcome unless there is full contingent compensation. What distinguishes this situation is that ex ante the lottery might not have been attractive based on the true risks.

Finally, employers' discretion over the wage structure enables them to exploit these misperceptions. If ex post compensation is feasible, any losses arising from all workers systematically overestimating the risk can be prevented. If at least some workers underestimate the risk, any such losses can be prevented (irrespective of γ) by designing a self-selecting wage structure to exploit the misperceptions.

8.4   Alternative Lottery Structures

Even with the introduction of worker learning, the format in which individuals face uncertainties generated by a Bernoulli process does not reflect the nature of all job lotteries. For example, an individual may discover whether or not he will be successful in a particular line of work during the initial period. If he incurs an initial lottery on θ and will suffer whatever loss (possibly zero) he experiences in the first period throughout his work career, this situation can be handled in the two-period case using the model in section 8.3 once we let $\gamma \rightarrow 0$. If, however, there is no such initial loss but the worker learns about his future prospects, the structure of the model is somewhat different. This situation is the focus of section 8.4.2.

Some outcomes, such as the arrival of an outside job offer or the chance of promotion, may occur with some probability p in each period, but once they have occurred they affect the rewards structure in all subsequent periods. A variation on this structure allows for the possibility that the size of the reward may vary as, for example, the attractiveness of the job may continually deteriorate or the worker may be promoted to increasingly higher positions. These situations will be addressed in sections 8.4.2 and 8.4.3.

Although this group of lottery structures is not exhaustive, it does span a rather broad spectrum of labor market possibilities. A principal purpose of this comprehensive coverage is to ascertain whether the desirability of upward-tilting wage structures, such as those induced by pensions, is a specific characteristic of situations with learning or whether, to take the opposite extreme, the optimality of flat wages pertains only to a very special type of uncertainty.

8.4.1 A Single Lottery

Suppose that the worker faces a single lottery in the initial period that will affect his rewards at the firm in all subsequent periods. He may discover whether or not he will like a particular line of work or be successful at it. There is some probability p that he will suffer a loss $-\theta$ in all subsequent periods and a chance $1 - p$ of no such loss. The lottery does not affect rewards in the initial period. To distinguish the payoff structure of pensions from that of ex post compensation, I will assume that there are three periods to the choice problem.

If the firm wished to retain only the low-cost workers with favorable experiences, the solution would be simple; it would simply offer a flat wage w_0. To give other wage structures a possible role, I will assume that turnover costs are sufficiently high that the firm wishes to keep workers with unfavorable experiences as well. It will, however, wish to hold down its wage costs by attracting workers with a lower risk p, a point I will return to below when heterogeneity is introduced.

The firm can offer a flat wage $w_0 + \theta$, with a present value C_f of

$$C_f = (w_0 + \theta) \sum_{i=0}^{2} \beta^i,$$

but it is clearly not in the firm's interest to do so. The worker experiences no loss in the initial period and is consequently overpaid by θ. In periods 2 and 3 there is a chance $1 - p$ that he will be overpaid by θ under this wage structure.

Ex post compensation,if feasible, can reduce these wage costs to

$$C_x = (\beta + \beta^2)p\theta + w_0 \sum_{i=0}^{2} \beta^i.$$

Workers' expected and realized utility is always w_0 in each period, just matching the value of the alternative job.

With accurate worker perceptions, pensions clearly cannot offer any improvement on this outcome, but they can offer firms the same wage costs without the requirement to monitor the lottery outcome. There is considerable leeway in the degree to which wages can be shifted forward in time, on an actuarially fair basis, into a pension. In the extreme case, all wages received could be in terms of a pension. The minimal value of the pension z plus the base wage must be high enough to retain workers who have had unfavorable experiences.

Rather than pursue all possible wage structures in which the wage can vary for each of the three periods, I will focus on the case where the firm pays a base wage w in all periods and augments this wage with a pension z in period 3. The present value of the wage package C_p is given by

$$(11) \qquad C_p = \beta^2 z + w\sum_{i=0}^{2} \beta^i = (\beta + \beta^2)p\theta + w_0\sum_{i=0}^{2} \beta^i.$$

The value of C_p is the same as C_x so that pensions are as costly as ex post compensation.

Not all wage structures satisfying equation (11) are viable since this condition only ensures that the worker accepts the job. The temporal structure of the payments must be tilted toward the latter periods or else the worker will quit after an unfavorable outcome after having been overpaid initially. To prevent turnover in the final period,

$$(12) \qquad w + z \geq w_0 + \theta,$$

and to prevent turnover after the first period when the lottery outcome becomes known the wage structure must satisfy

$$(13) \qquad w + \beta(w + z) \geq (w_0 + \theta)(1 + \beta).$$

On dividing by $1 + \beta$, this condition is

$$(14) \qquad w + \frac{\beta z}{1 + \beta} \geq w_0 + \theta.$$

Since $\beta/(1 + \beta)$ is less than one, the second-period constraint in equation (14) is more stringent than the third-period requirement. Viewed somewhat differently, a firm cannot seek to retain workers with adverse experiences during period 2 and let them quit in period 3 because any wage structure that will retain them in the earlier period will do so in the final period as well.

In effect, the firm must pay a wage package in the final two periods with a discounted per period value of $w_0 + \theta$ or else turnover will result. Since the expected loss in each of these periods is only $p\theta$ at the time the job is accepted, workers are overpaid on an expected basis in the final periods and consequently can be underpaid initially. Rearranging equation (14) gives the form for the minimal pension as

$$z = \frac{1 + \beta}{\beta}(w_0 + \theta - w).$$

Substituting this value for z into equation (10) and solving for w produces the result that $w = w_0 + (\beta + \beta^2)\theta(p - 1)$. The worker takes a wage cut below his reservation wage in the first two periods and is compensated through his pension for both his expected loss and his initial underpayment. The worker must be overcompensated when viewed from the ex ante situation since his turnover choice is based on the actual lottery outcome, while his initial job acceptance decision is based on his expected prospects. The optimal wage structure is increasing over the worker's tenure with the firm. Finally, with only a single lottery, the worker is indifferent to the variations in the risk for any given mean initial risk level.

Unlike ex post compensation, pensions will serve as a perfect self-selection device. Even if workers' probability assessments p are subjective and potentially affected by learning, since there is only a single lottery being incurred, only the initial risk assessment is relevant. With a wage structure satisfying equation (11), those with risk assessments not exceeding p will find the job acceptable, while those with higher risk assessments will avoid the job. If the differences in risk perceptions arise from underlying heterogeneity in the risk, the efficiency of labor market matches will be enhanced by pensions, whereas with biased perceptions pensions serve primarily as a profit-making device. Since the situation being considered is that in which all workers remain at the firm, the gain from offering the pension does not arise because workers do not collect it. Moreover, the minimal wage outlays in periods 2 and 3 are unaffected by the assessed risk because the wage package must keep all workers after the lottery has been resolved. The financial gains for the firm arise from being able to lower the base wage as the worker's assessment of the chance of an unfavorable outcome declines.

When there is heterogeneity or misperception, there also will be an advantage to offering pensions even when turnover is permitted. Although paying a flat wage w_0 will only retain workers with favorable experiences, the proportion of workers with unfavorable outcomes will be higher if the firm does not offer a wage structure that self-selects only the low-risk workers. By shifting more of the compensation toward the latter periods, pensions will screen out workers who have a higher perceived chance of an unfavorable lottery outcome.

If the wage-pension package permits turnover, then the worker who has an assessed risk will prefer to leave after an unfavorable outcome, or

$$w - \theta + \beta(w + z - \theta) < w_0 + \beta w_0.$$

To simplify the subsequent analysis I will assume that θ is so large that even if all compensation is through the pension (i.e., $w = 0$) the worker will leave after an unsuccessful outcome. As before, one can show that the most desirable z will be its maximum value consistent with turnover whenever workers underestimate p and consequently overestimate the chance of collecting the pension.

To attract a worker with risk assessment $\hat{p}$ to the job, z must satisfy

$$(\beta + \beta^2)\hat{p}w_0 + \beta^2(1 - \hat{p})z \geq w_0 \sum_{i=0}^{2} \beta^i.$$

The least costly pension is consequently

$$z = \frac{w_0[1 + (\beta + \beta^2)(1 - \hat{p})]}{\beta^2(1 - \hat{p})}.$$

If p represents the true risk faced by the worker, which is assumed to be known by the firm, the discounted expected wage costs are

$$\beta^2(1 - p)z = \frac{(1 - p)}{(1 - \hat{p})} w_0[1 + (\beta + \beta^2)(1 - \hat{p})]$$

$$= w_0[\frac{1 - p}{1 - \hat{p}} + (\beta + \beta^2)(1 - p)].$$

Dividing by the discounted expected periods worked, the wage bill per period is

$$\frac{\beta^2(1 - p)z}{1 + (\beta + \beta^2)(1 - p)} = \frac{w_0[\frac{1 - p}{1 - \hat{p}} + (\beta + \beta^2)(1 - p)]}{1 + (\beta + \beta^2)(1 - p)} < w_0.$$

If there are misperceptions in which workers underestimate the risk, or $\hat{p} < p$, the wage-pension combination with turnover can lower the per period wage cost below w_0 by engaging workers in pension bets at unfavorable odds. Without misperception, $p = \hat{p}$, and there is no wage gain, but there is a reduction in the proportion of workers who quit because of adverse lottery outcomes.

8.4.2 Binary Failure Processes

A somewhat more complicated lottery structure is a binary failure process in which for all workers who have not yet experienced an adverse outcome there is a chance p of a loss $-\theta$ in each period. As in the model in section 8.4.1, once this loss is incurred, the worker will suffer it in each of the remaining periods as well should he decide to remain with the firm. These assumptions best characterize situations in which a worker discovers that his job will be unpleasant, or he will be unproductive and consequently never promoted. Since θ also can be treated as altering the relative rewards of the job, one can view this situation as one in which the worker gets a permanent outside job offer. Instead of having a reservation wage w_0, he has a required wage $w_0 + \theta$ for the remainder of his work career.

For job lotteries of this type, it suffices to consider the implications in a two-period model. The flat wage option continues to impose as low costs as any alternative approach if worker turnover is permitted and if all workers assess the risk as p. The per period wage bill of w_0 is the same as the expected per period cost with pensions as well. Under pensions, however, the firm can potentially attract the low-turnover workers if there is heterogeneity in the risk assessments. With either legitimate risk differences or misperceptions, when some groups of workers have a risk assessment $\hat{p} < p$ pensions will impose the least costs.

As a means for preventing worker turnover, the flat wage is dominated since the wage must be $w_0 + \theta$ to achieve this result, leading to overpayment of all workers who, in each period, do not have adverse job experiences. Contingent wage payments offer a lower-cost method of preventing turnover in situations in which the lottery outcome can be monitored. The present value of the ex post compensation package is

$$C_x = w_0 + p\theta + \beta p(w_0 + \theta) + \beta(1 - p)[w_0 + p\theta]$$

or

$$C_x = w_0(1 + \beta) + \theta\{p + \beta[1 - (1 - p)^2]\}.$$

The contingent payment just compensates the worker for his reservation wage plus his on-the-job losses. With homogeneous risk assessments and accurate perceptions, this approach imposes the same costs as pensions; if all workers overassess the risk, ex post compensation continues to be less expensive.

Any viable pension package (w, z) offered by the firm must satisfy

(15) $$\begin{aligned} w_0(1 + \beta) = w - p\theta + \beta p \max[w_0, w + z - \theta] \\ + \beta(1 - p)\max[w_0, w + z - p\theta] = EU. \end{aligned}$$

Any wage structure with a nonnegative pension that attracts workers initially will retain them after a favorable first-period outcome, or

(16) $$w + z - p\theta \geq w_0.$$

If pensions retain workers with an adverse initial job outcome,

(17) $$w + z - \theta \geq w_0,$$

whereas if this condition is not met, turnover occurs for all workers with adverse initial job experiences.

In each turnover case, pensions meeting the conditions above will induce the self-selection of all workers with risk assessments below p. Biases in risk perception will, as before, make it desirable to shift income forward in time, particularly when workers overestimate the chance that they will collect the pension. Finally, the wage structure induced by pensions will always be upward sloping if pensions are designed to prevent turnover. Otherwise the firm in effect is operating within the context of section 8.2's compensating differential model except that all workers with unfavorable experiences in period 1 drop out of the sample.

The principal difference with the results in section 8.4.1 is the effect of variability in the risk p. If the compensation package is always adjusted to ensure that equation (15) holds, workers would be indifferent to such fluctuations. I will focus instead on workers on particular employment paths that will not be altered by minor variations in p, where the wage structure is viewed as exogenous. In this instance, the variability of p may be consequential.

Consider first the situation in which turnover is permitted, that is, equation (15) holds but equation (17) does not. The effect of altering p is given by

$$\frac{\partial EU}{\partial p} = -\theta + \beta w_0 + \beta(1 - p)(-\theta) - \beta(w + z - p\theta) < 0$$

and

$$\frac{\partial^2 EU}{\partial p^2} = 2\beta\theta > 0.$$

As in the learning case, workers' expected utility is convex in p.

Similarly, when no turnover occurs under the pension (i.e., eq. [17] holds), one obtains

$$\frac{\partial EU}{\partial p} = -\theta + 2\beta\theta(p - 1) < 0,$$

and

$$\frac{\partial^2 EU}{\partial p^2} = 2\beta\theta > 0.$$

In each case workers' expected utility is convex in p, as illustrated in figure 8.2. A lottery on the extreme certainty situations will, for any given employment path, be preferred to lotteries with intermediate probabilities.

Unlike the model in section 8.3, no learning was included in this analysis. The result pertaining to the effect on variability hinges not on changes in the assessed risk but on the creation of an asymmetric lottery structure over time. In the learning case, there was no such asymmetry when no turnover occurred and $\partial^2 EU/\partial p^2$ equaled zero. Similarly, for the replicated identical lotteries in section 8.2 and the single lottery of section 8.4.1, the fact that whatever lottery was incurred never changed produced the result that workers were indifferent among all lotteries with the same initial risk level.

8.4.3   Deterioration Processes

These results must be altered somewhat if the job lotteries do not pose simply a chance of losing θ but a more general risk in which the attractiveness of the job may steadily deteriorate. Either the attractiveness of the job itself may steadily decline or the job alternative may become increasingly attractive. If the worker receives outside offers with the option of recall, his reservation wage may rise to $w_0 + \theta$, then to $w_0 + \theta'$, where $\theta' > \theta$. For concreteness, I will treat the lottery in terms of a loss θ on one's present job, where this loss occurs with probability p. Once the initial loss θ has been incurred, the worker faces a chance p' that the loss will rise to θ'. Although p' need not equal p, this posibility is not ruled out.

Many of the results for this lottery structure follow a familiar pattern. In the two-period case, the flat wage that prevents turnover costs $C_f = (1 + \beta)(w_0 + \theta')$, which overpays all workers over the course of employment since it matches their highest reservation wage. Contingent compensation continues to be the least costly solution when risk perceptions are accurate, where

$$C_x = w_0(1 + \beta) + p\theta + \beta p p' \theta' + \beta p(1 - p')\theta + \beta(1 - p)p\theta.$$

Pensions can attract and retain workers at the same cost and, if there is heterogeneity in workers' risk assessments, they will serve as a self-selection device, whereas contingent compensation will not. Moreover, with heterogeneity or biased perceptions in which the risk is underestimated, pensions continue to impose fewer costs.

The role of the variability of the risk is somewhat different, however. Consider first the situation in which pensions prevent worker turnover. The present value of the pension pay package is

$$C_p = w + \beta(w + z)$$
$$= w_0(1 + \beta) + p\theta + \beta p[p'\theta' + (1 - p')\theta] + \beta(1 - p)p\theta,$$

and the worker's expected utility is

$$EU = w - p\theta + \beta p[w + z - p'\theta' - p(1 - p')\theta] + \beta(1 - p)(w + z - p\theta).$$

If p and p' are different,

$$\frac{\delta EU}{\delta p} = -\theta + \beta[w + z - p'\theta' - p(1 - p')\theta]$$

$$- \beta p(1 - p')\theta - \beta(w + z - p\theta) - \beta(1 - p)\theta < 0,$$

and

$$\frac{\delta^2 EU}{\delta p^2} = 2\beta\theta p' > 0.$$

Expected utility is convex in p, and the worker prefers a mixture of extreme lotteries to the lotteries with intermediate probabilities (see fig. 8.2). If, however, $p = p'$,

$$\frac{\delta EU}{\delta p} = -\theta + \beta[w + z - p\theta' - p(1 - p)\theta] + \beta p(-\theta' - \theta + 2p\theta)$$

$$- \beta(w + z - p\theta) + \beta(1 - p)(-\theta) < 0,$$

and

$$\frac{\delta^2 EU}{\delta p^2} = -2\beta\theta' + 6\beta p\theta.$$

Expected utility is convex in p if θ' is sufficiently small relative to θ, or, more specifically, if $3p\theta > \theta'$. For every large θ' the EU function is bowed outward, and the worker prefers an intermediate lottery to a mixture on extremes with the same expected initial risk. The reason for this reversal is that with extreme p values the worker has a greater chance of incurring the successive losses θ and θ'.

For very large θ' the firm will not find it attractive to retain the worker unless turnover costs are very high. In instances in which turnover occurs, the discounted expected pension cost is

$$C_p = w + \beta(1 - p)(w + z) = w_0 + p\theta + \beta(1 - p)(w_0 + p\theta).$$

The worker's expected utility is given by

$$EU = w - p\theta + \beta p w_0 + \beta(1 - p)(w + z - p\theta),$$

which is the same as in the binary failure case in section 8.4.2. In this situation EU is convex in p.

8.5 Conclusion

The only job lottery situation in which pensions do not play a useful role is the standard compensating differential model in which workers face an identical sequence of lotteries over time and never leave the job after starting it. In all other situations, pensions and other forms of rising earnings profiles can achieve the same desired turnover properties for risk-neutral workers as does ex post compensation. Moreover, unlike contingent compensation, there is no need to monitor the lottery outcome.

If workers have heterogeneous risk perceptions, pensions offer an additional advantage even in situations in which turnover is not a matter of concern. By self-selecting the workers with low risk assessments and, in the biased perceptions case, by enabling the firm to make unfair bets with workers, pensions reduce firms' wage costs.

The welfare implications and the efficiency of the job matches will, however, be quite different depending on the source of the heterogeneity. If some workers underestimate the risk, pensions will create incentives that will lead to the self-selection of workers into the job. Workers may then be trapped inefficiently based on the true risks, and those workers who leave will forfeit their pension benefits.

The fact that pensions trap some workers in jobs they would like to leave does not in itself suggest that workers entered jobs with biased perceptions. Even with accurate perceptions, ex post workers who have experienced unfavorable lottery outcomes may be on jobs they wish to leave, but to which their forfeitable pensions tie them. The existence of a negative pension-turnover relationship and dissatisfaction among immobile workers does not necessarily provide a rationale for mandatory vesting requirements.

The variability of the risks faced by workers also plays a critical role. Except in the case of single or replicated identical lotteries and one instance of the deterioration process, workers' expected utility is convex in p. A lottery on extreme, more stable employment paths is preferred to the situation in which workers face an intermediate risk each period. In the presence of learning, jobs associated with less precise priors are perferred. Since less precise priors make possible a wider divergence of posterior-assessed risks, the underlying principle involved is quite similar.

A recurring theme in these results is that the design of the compensation structure in situations of uncertainty is quite sensitive to the structure of the uncertainty the worker encounters. Although pensions serve no productive function in the presence of lottery structures such as those considered in the compensating differential literature, the other forms of uncertainty considered suggest that pensions have a legitimate role to play as a compensation instrument. Situations of learning are one such stochastic structure, but learning is by no means required for pensions to serve a useful function.

In the presence of uncertainty and turnover costs, nontransferable pensions can be important in self-selecting more stable employees and reducing the turnover of workers attracted to the firm. Unfortunately, if workers have biased perceptions, pensions will be offered by employers even in situations in which there would be no cost reductions from pensions if workers were fully informed. The possibility of such abuses may create a potential rationale for collective action.

Notes

1. For further description of the turnover-related benefit provisions see Ellwood (in this volume) and Kotlikoff and Smith (1983).

2. Three representative studies are Viscusi (1979), in which I focus on dummy variables for whether or not the worker was covered by a pension; Schiller and Weiss (1979), who analyze a series of variables related to pension characteristics; and Mitchell (1982), who uses pension dummy variable and a survey that was the sequel to the data set I examined.

3. This point was first made by Becker (1964).

4. See Viscusi (1983) for the results presented in terms of time-varying wage rates. Analogous findings are presented for pensions in a preliminary form of the paper, "Specific Information, General Information, and Employment Matches under Uncertainty," NBER Working Paper no. 394 (1979).

5. This analysis is presented in Lazear (1984).

6. The forced savings argument presupposes that the worker wishes to be tied to a "Christmas club"–type plan for old age. It may be that forced savings lead to an inefficiently large deferral of savings for old age.

7. The loss need not be financial, but I will assume that it can be converted into a nonmonetary equivalent. The uncertainty could be with regard to worker productivity, which in turn affects output. This case, which I consider in Viscusi (1983), yields similar results but is a bit more complicated to analyze.

8. The results in this section generalize to n periods by simply changing the range of the summation in the equation below and by letting the discount factor multiplying pensions z be β^{n-1}.

9. Ex post compensation also may eliminate lotteries that serve a productive function. If the worker is assured of making his piecework quota or if he is guaranteed a promotion, there will be less incentive for him to work hard. These concerns arise in situations in which employers may pay workers according to relative performance because of the difficulty in monitoring performance. See, e.g., Lazear and Rosen (1981), and O'Keeffe, et al. (1984).

10. For treatments of self-selection in somewhat different contexts, see Salop and Salop (1976) and Viscusi (1979).

11. In the n-period case, the analysis becomes quite complicated. Although the worker will always remain on the job after a favorable outcome on the previous trial, how soon he chooses to switch jobs cannot in general be ascertained. Since the value of $p(m, n)$ is continually changing, the problem is not amenable to closed-form solutions such as one encounters in the job search literature. The most that can be determined is that there is a quite broad range of turnover possibilities.

12. Moreover, so long as the downward tilt is not too great the worker will not leave after a success. Although the relative shapes generally hold, the various curves may intersect the horizontal axis rather than the vertical axis. In the extreme case, one might never leave the job for any (p, γ) combination, or one might never be willing to start the job. In these situations, the wage structure can be redesigned to provide the desired turnover properties.

13. This definition of increasing risk is adopted by Rothschild and Stiglitz (1970).

Comment   Sherwin Rosen

This paper discusses how nonvested pensions affect labor mobility (quit) decisions of workers who are only imperfectly informed of some job attribute and who become better informed of it through on-the-job

Sherwin Rosen is Edwin A. and Betty L. Bergman Professor in the Department of Economics at the University of Chicago and a research associate at the National Bureau of Economic Research.

experience. We know from previous work that the use of deferred pay biases self-selection toward more stable workers. Unstable workers find these jobs less attractive because they have a larger chance of losing much of their pay by quitting before the pension is received. Viscusi extends this argument in a subtle and sophisticated way to incorporate worker uncertainty on how the job matches to workers' prior perceptions.

In a world where long-term contracts are not binding on workers, the option of quitting increases the value of greater initial uncertainty about job outcomes. The reason is similar to why a stock-market option has greater value when risk increases: quitting truncates the lower tail of the distribution and induces new workers to gamble that a favorable outcome will be realized, since losses are limited. This has two effects: First, workers who are initially misinformed about conditions take the job at low wages in the hope that conditions turn out to be favorable. In that case the pension is received. If the outcome is unfavorable, they quit and forgo their pension. The firm makes money on this and takes advantage of quitters in calculating the optimal life-cycle wage policy. Second, given the subset of workers who do not leave because of insufficiently unfavorable realizations, nonvested pensions make it more costly to quit: some workers invariably are trapped into jobs they do not like.

The paper concentrates on self-selection constraints. These are the supply conditions confronting the firm, given the distribution of worker prior perceptions and their optimal stopping rules based on experience. This is an interesting exercise because so little has been written on how perceptions and misperceptions affect choices. Nonetheless, one wonders why the next logical step was not taken. Why not specify and analyze the maximum problem for the firm subject to the constraints that have been so thoroughly discussed?

Such a problem would clarify the advantages to the firm of reducing turnover, which play very little role in the formal analysis. It would also introduce other interesting factors, including incentives for the firm to affect the loss and the probability of the adverse outcome, as well as workers' prior perceptions of them. As the paper stands, firms are totally passive. They merely adopt a wage policy, and the onus of staying or leaving is put entirely on the worker. Yet as I recall the testimony surrounding the passage of ERISA, it was not only the complaints of the workers locked into large pensions or those who voluntarily quit their jobs that led to pension reforms. The horror stories of workers who were involuntarily terminated prior to vesting were also important considerations.

The incentives for a firm to engage in such behavior are clear enough. Any backloaded pension-wage contract involves an element of bonding by the worker. The worker effectively lends money to the firm, because the first-period wage is less than the opportunity cost. The worker gets the bond back, plus interest, only if he stays long enough to collect it. The firm gains, myopically to be sure, by reneging in the second period and terminating the worker prior to receipt of the pension, similar to default on a loan. No doubt cheating of this sort is limited by longer-run considerations, such as loss of reputation. Nonetheless, marginal analysis suggests that a little cheating will persist in equilibrium. For example, in those cases involving close calls about probable cause of termination, the probability of the firm's committing type II error in discharges is increased. One wonders how a more complete treatment of this problem would change the positive and normative nature of the results and suggest alternative reforms.

One hopes in subsequent work that more attention will be paid to the empirical predictions of the model. What does the model say about the circumstances under which nonvested pensions will be an important consideration? When will they be observed? In fact, as it stands, wage variations in a multiperiod model could easily perform the same self-selection role as pensions do. It is the wage gradient that is important to the model, not pensions per se, because there are no end period unraveling conundrums in this problem. Be that as it may, the interest of the work would be considerably enhanced if it were related to some conceivable data. Perhaps a good place to start thinking about these problems concretely is in the military, where nonvesting is complete up to 20 years of service. In this instance, pensions not only save resources by avoiding retraining through retention of skilled personnel, they also assist in solving an important principal-agent problem. The threat of getting cashiered and losing one's pension makes enlistees better soldiers. Surely considerations such as these are relevant to all organizations.

Finally, the paper restricts self-selection schemes to virtually one parameter, namely, the gap between the first- and second-period wage. Yet selection occurs over two parameters: the prior probability and its precision. One suspects that two instruments—the gap plus something else—would be necessary to sort people in a more efficient manner. This is complicated by the fact that initially homogeneous workers become heterogeneous through differential experience. I have not been creative enough to identify precisely what that second instrument might be, though the risk-is-good argument suggests that randomization schemes and lotteries might be useful candidates to consider.

References

Becker, G. 1964. *Human capital.* New York: National Bureau of Economic Research.
Ellwood, D. 1985. Pensions and the labor market: A starting point. In this volume.

Kotlikoff, L. J., and Smith, D. E. 1983. *Pensions in the American economy.* Chicago: University of Chicago Press (for NBER).

Lazear, E. P. 1984. Pensions as severance pay. In *Financial aspects of the United States pension system,* edited by Z. Bodie and J. Shoven. Chicago: University of Chicago Press (for NBER).

Lazear, E. P., and Rosen, S. 1981 Rank-order tournaments as optimum labor contracts. *Journal of Political Economy* 89:841–64.

Mitchell, O. 1982. Fringe benefits and labor mobility. *Journal of Human Resources* 27:286–98.

Mortenson, D. 1978. Specific capital and turnover. *Bell Journal of Economics* 9:572–86.

O'Keeffe, M.; Viscusi, W. K.; and Zeckhauser, R. J. 1983. Economic contests: Comparative reward schemes. *Journal of Labor Economics* 2:27–56.

Rothschild, M., and Stiglitz, J. 1970. Increasing risk: A definition. *Journal of Economic Theory* 2:225–43.

Salop, J., and Salop, S. 1976. Self-selection and turnover in the labor market. *Quarterly Journal of Economics* 90:619–27.

Schiller, B., and Weiss, R. 1979. The impact of private pensions on firm attachment. *Review of Economics and Statistics* 61:369–80.

United States. Senate. Committee on Labor and Public Welfare. Subcommittee on Labor. 1971. *Private welfare and pension plan study.* Washington, D.C.: Government Printing Office.

Viscusi, W. K. 1979. *Employment hazards: An investigation of market performance.* Cambridge: Harvard University Press.

———. 1983. Employment matches with joint employer and worker experimentation. *International Economic Review* 24:301–10.

———. 1980. Self-selection, learning-induced quits, and the optimal wage structure. *International Economic Review* 21:529–46.

9   Incentive Effects of Pensions

Edward P. Lazear

Private pensions have grown rapidly during the past 30 years. Although there are elements of pensions that many plans share, there are also large differences across plans. The most obvious differences relate to the basic structure of the pension benefit formula: the plan may be of the defined contribution or of the defined benefit type. In the latter category the flat or pattern plan can be distinguished from the formula or conventional plan.

Economists often refer casually to the effects that changes in the benefit formulas have on worker behavior. Most frequently, these comments relate to the effects of vesting on worker turnover. But as far as I am aware, no systematic attempt has been made to analyze the ways in which various provisions of the pension benefit formulas influence worker behavior.[1] This essay attempts to do just that. Specifically, it examines the effects of pension benefit provisions on worker turnover, labor supply, investment in human capital, and worker effort. Existing benefit formulas are compared with formulas that produce first-best results and an attempt is made to determine if and understand why provisions may deviate from those that produce efficient outcomes. In so doing, it is hoped that the understanding of the existence of private pensions will be furthered.

The paper examines a number of different pension institutions. It analyzes how worker productivity (as affected by turnover, investment in human capital, and effort) is influenced by a change from defined benefit to defined contribution plans and why pattern plans and conventional plans induce very different behavior. It also examines the effects of minimum

Edward P. Lazear is professor of industrial relations at the University of Chicago and a research associate at the National Bureau of Economic Research.

Helpful comments by Jerry Hausman, Herman Leonard, Barry Nalebuff, and Sherwin Rosen are gratefully acknowledged.

and maximum years of service requirements, industrywide versus companywide plans, the relationship between hours-of-work constraints and pensions, why pensions are often related to final salary, and a number of other issues. For most of the analysis, the pension rule is taken to be exogenous so that the incentive effects of that rule per se can be described. This is a less ambitious task than understanding why those rules exist and what other factors are involved. Occasionally some conjectures on the reasons for particular rules are presented, but that is not the primary purpose of the essay. The most important findings are summarized below.

Pension benefit formulas cannot affect worker behavior or cause deviations from efficiency if each worker's wage is directly and appropriately related to his own pension level. Without explicit offsets, the following results obtain:

- Defined benefit pattern plans induce an efficient allocation of resources.
- Defined benefit conventional plans induce too little turnover, too much work, too much effort, and too much human capital investment relative to the efficient outcome.
- Defined contribution plans always induce an efficient allocation of resources.
- Complete and immediate vesting is a necessary condition for fully efficient pension plans. Incomplete vesting tends to result in too little work by some and too much by others. The standard intuition that pensions create longer job tenure on average is not necessarily correct. The apparent inefficiency, but widespread existence, of imperfectly vested pension plans suggests that the sorting or retention of workers may be an important problem.
- Minimum years of service constraints create inefficiency in pattern plans, whereas such constraints may actually reduce the inefficiency of conventional plans. Further, maximum years of service constraints tend to offset the inefficiency introduced by minimum years of service constraints.
- The inefficiencies introduced by defined benefit conventional plans can be undone by specifying required effort levels. Thus, piece-rate workers, who choose their own effort levels, should not have defined benefit conventional plans.

9.1   A Model

The essence of the relationship between benefit formulas and worker behavior can be analyzed in the context of a one-period model. Workers are paid some wage, W, and are entitled to a pension, P, which may depend on years of service, salary, and a number of other rules having to do with minimum and maximum age and years of service. In this one-period context, "years of service" is thought of simply as the number of years or hours, H, worked during the period so that a benefit formula that depends on years of service is one that has H as an argument.

Workers can control two variables: The amount of time worked, H, is the labor supply variable and is affected by the worker's alternative use of time function, $L(H)$. This reflects either the value of leisure or the wage on an alternative job, whichever is highest. In this way, we can analyze worker turnover in this simple framework since there need be no formal distinction between retirement and quitting to take another job (although the pension flow may differ depending on what the worker does with his time).

Both effort and investment in human capital are captured by the worker's control over K, which affects worker productivity and potentially the wage. No distinction is made in this model between effort and human capital, although some differences may be relevant.[2] There is some cost associated with increasing K, given by the total cost function $C(K)$. This carries either the interpretation of costs of investment in human capital, in the form of formal schooling or on-the-job training that occurs before the current period, or the disutility value associated with additional effort.

The reason H and K must be distinguished is that effort or investment in human capital affects pensions differently than years of service. All defined benefit plans depend on years of service, but only some depend on salary as well. Effort and human capital investment are likely to affect salary directly, years of service only indirectly.

The approach does not build in any explicit reason for the existence of pensions, although a number have been given in the literature.[3] Instead, the reverse strategy is adopted. The effects of various provisions are analyzed in hope of obtaining clues to the reasons for their existence.

Given the two choice variables, it is trivial to write down the efficiency conditions for labor supply, H, and effort or human capital, K. The value of K in increasing output is normalized to be \$1 and the worker's productivity at $K = 0$ is V per unit of time. Thus, the worker's output is $(V + K)H$ and the efficiency criterion is derived by maximization of social benefit minus social cost or, under separability, by

(1) $$\max_{H,K} (V + K)H - C(K) - L(H).$$

The first-order conditions for efficiency are

(1i) $$H = C'(K)$$

and

(1ii) $$V + K = L'(H).$$

Whether the worker behaves in such a way as to insure efficiency depends on his own utility maximization. Additionally, since firms wish to maximize profits, it is necessary to look to the interaction between the two in order to derive implications for changes in the pension plan.

For generality, allow that the worker's choice of K and H can affect both W and P. Then the worker's problem is

(2)
$$\max_{H,K} W(K, H)H + P(K, H) - C(K) - L(H),$$

which yields, as first-order conditions,

(2i) $\partial/\partial K = (\partial W/\partial K)H + \partial P/\partial K - C'(K) = 0$

and

(2ii) $\partial/\partial H = (\partial W/\partial H)H + W + \partial P/\partial H - L'(H) = 0.$

What makes the issue less than straightforward is the fact that payments that take the form of a pension must be offset by a decrease in the wage rate. This is the result of the firm's zero profit constraint, which is

(3) $(V + K)H = WH + P ,$

or $W = V + K - P/H$

Equation (3) says that total payments to the worker must equal total output by the worker.

The way in which the worker perceives that his wage is affected by his pension is important. Although it is true that (3) must hold for all workers, it is not necessary that the worker's wage respond directly to his own pension level. For example, a wage could be "fixed" and the worker could be allowed to choose his pension by altering H, but these actions would not affect W as he perceives it. Although it is true that for all workers (3) must hold, any one worker's effect on W may be regarded as trivial or zero.

First consider the opposite situation, where the worker recognizes that any increase in P that is not accompanied by a corresponding increase in productivity must result in a lower wage. (This would be true in a one-worker firm.) The result is that the provisions of the pension plan cannot affect behavior. There is never a deviation from first-best efficiency. The reason is that the worker internalizes the full extent of his actions, no matter how inefficient the pension formula may appear. This is trivial to show formally:

If the worker recognizes that (3) holds, then his maximization problem from (2) becomes

(4)
$$\max_{H,K} (V + K - P/H)H + P - C(K) - L(H)$$

or

$$\max_{H,K} (V + K)H - C(K) - L(H),$$

which is the same as (1). The first-order condition must be the same, namely,

(4i) $$\frac{\partial}{\partial K} = H - \frac{\partial P}{\partial K} + \frac{\partial P}{\partial K} - C'(K) = 0,$$

or

$$H = C'(K), \text{ and}$$

(4ii) $$\frac{\partial}{\partial H} = V + K - \frac{\partial P}{\partial H} + \frac{\partial P}{\partial H} - L'(H) = 0,$$

or

$$V + K = L'(H).$$

Equations (4i)–(4ii) are identical to (1i)–(1ii), so the worker chooses (H, K) so as to guarantee first-best efficiency, irrespective of the pension benefit formula. Any action the worker takes that affects his pension also affects his wage in the opposite direction and by a corresponding amount. If the worker is fully aware of this, then all pension changes are offset and internalized, no matter how bizarre the pension formula. It is the worker's recognition that things must add up on the firm side of the problem that forces him to behave efficiently.

There is another way to state the same proposition: Distortions caused by the pension can always be undone by a judiciously chosen wage function. As long as

$$W(K, H) \equiv V + K - P(K, H)/H,$$

for all K, H, the worker's behavior cannot be affected by the pension. Whatever effect K and H have to increase P is exactly offset by a reduction in $W(\ )$. As long as the worker understands this relationship, pension effects wash out.

Then how can pension formulas affect behavior? In a multiworker firm, it may well be that the individual's wage is not a direct function of his own pension benefits, even though all must add up across workers. This has nothing to do with worker heterogeneity but is the result of an externality that is produced by separating the wage determination process from the pension determination process at the level of the individual worker. Two points are worth noting: First, there is no obvious reason the firm does not make the worker explicitly aware of the true relationship between P and W. This is explored below. Second, a difference between the defined benefit and defined contribution plans may be that the latter makes explicit the relationship between P and W whereas the former does not. This too is discussed below.

Those points aside, consider the worker's problem when $\overline{P/H}$ is set so that in equilibrium $\overline{P/H} = V + K - P(H^*, K^*)/H^*$ where H^*, K^* are the result of the worker's maximization problem, which takes $\overline{P/H}$ as constant. This insures zero profits, but the worker does not take that condition into account in choosing H, K. For most of what follows, it is useful to recognize that pension benefit formulas rarely depend on K directly,[4] but instead depend on K indirectly through W. Therefore let $P = P(W, H)$ for the remainder. Further, suppose for simplicity that W is independent of H. If workers take $\overline{P/H}$ as given, then the worker's maximization problem is

(5)
$$\max_{H, K} W(K)H + P(W, H) - L(H) - C(K),$$

where[5]

$$W(K) = V + K - \overline{P/H}.$$

The first-order conditions are

(5i)
$$\frac{\partial}{\partial K} = H + \frac{\partial P}{\partial W} - C'(K) = 0$$

(5ii)
$$\frac{\partial}{\partial H} = V + K - (\overline{P/H}) + \frac{\partial P}{\partial H} - L'(H) = 0.$$

The difference between (5i)–(5ii) and (4i)–(4ii) is that in (4) the individual recognizes that increases in P are offset by decreases in W. In (5) W is unaffected, as far as the individual worker is concerned, by changes in P.

Even if the worker does not take into account the effect of pension on wage, it is not necessarily the case that pensions result in an inefficient allocation of effort, human capital, turnover, and leisure. This is easily seen by examining the maximization problem in (2). In order for efficient outcomes to result, it is sufficient that (2i) reduce to (1i) and (2ii) to (1ii). The first condition is met if and only if

(6a)
$$\frac{\partial P}{\partial K} = H \left(1 - \frac{\partial W}{\partial K} \right)$$

and the second condition is met if and only if

(6b)
$$\frac{\partial P}{\partial H} = V + K - W - H\frac{\partial W}{\partial H}.$$

Any pension-wage relationship that the worker perceives as satisfying (6a) and (6b) induces an efficient allocation of resources.

When the worker internalizes the firm's side of the problem, he knows that (3) holds or that

$$P = (V + K - W)H.$$

Differentiating (3) yields

$$\frac{\partial P}{\partial K} = H\left(1 - \frac{\partial W}{\partial K}\right)$$

so that (6a) is satisfied and

$$\frac{\partial P}{\partial H} = V + K - W - H\frac{\partial W}{\partial H}$$

so that (6b) holds. Thus, internalization of (3) results in full efficiency.

9.2 Some Implications

9.2.1 Pattern Plans

Although complete internalization is sufficient for efficiency, it is not necessary. The standard defined benefit pattern plan, where the pension depends only on years of service and not salary, induces an efficient allocation of resources. That pension takes the form

$$P = \beta H,$$

where β is a fixed dollar amount and H is chosen by the worker. Under those circumstances, and retaining the assumption that $W = V + K - \overline{P/H}$, $\partial W/\partial K = 1$ and $\partial P/\partial K = 0$ so that (2i) becomes

(7i) $$H - C'(K) = 0.$$

Also, $\partial W/\partial H = 0$ and $\partial P/\partial H = \beta$ so (2ii) becomes

(7ii) $$W + \beta - L'(H) = 0$$

or

$$V + K - L'(H) = 0$$

since

$$W = V + K - \overline{P/H}$$
$$= V + K - \beta.$$

Thus, (7i) and (7ii) are identical to (1i)–(1ii), so efficiency is achieved.

Stated alternatively, since $\partial P/\partial K = 0$ and $\partial W/\partial K = 1$, (6a) holds. Also, since $\partial P/\partial H = \beta$, $\partial W/\partial H = 0$, and $W = V + K - \beta$, (6b) reduces to $\beta = \beta$ and holds as well.

This yields the conclusion that all standard pattern plans are efficient. The reason is that even though the worker does not explicitly take into account that his wage is reduced by an amount corresponding to pension size, he does implicitly. Since the increase in pension value is a function only of time worked, as is earnings, all is implicitly internalized. The worker's "true" annual wage is $W + \partial P/\partial H$. When the pension formula is βH, his true wage

$$= W + \beta$$
$$= V + K - \overline{P/H} - \beta$$
$$= V + K - \beta\overline{H}/\overline{H} - \beta$$
$$= V + K,$$

so the worker's true wage, as he sees it, is equal to his value to the firm. Thus, all is efficient.

9.2.2 Conventional Plans

The conventional defined benefit plan, where the pension benefit depends on some salary average times a factor times years worked does not result in an efficient allocation of resources if the worker does not take (3) into account explicitly. This can easily be shown:

The conventional plan has the form

$$P = \gamma HW$$

so that

$$\frac{\partial P}{\partial H} = \gamma \left(W + H\frac{\partial W}{\partial H} \right)$$

and

$$\frac{\partial P}{\partial K} = \frac{\partial P}{\partial W} \cdot \frac{\partial W}{\partial K} = \gamma H$$

since

$$W = V + K - \overline{P/H}.$$

(The worker takes P/H as given at $\overline{P/H}$ and W is independent of H.) Thus, $\partial P/\partial K = \gamma H$, but $\partial W/\partial K = 1$ so $\gamma H \neq H(1 - \partial W/\partial K)$ unless $\gamma = 0$ and (6a) is violated. However, $\partial P/\partial H = \gamma W$ and $V + K - W - H(\partial W/\partial H) = \gamma W$ since $\partial W/\partial H = 0$ and $W = (V + K)/(1 + \gamma)$ because $P/H = \gamma W$. Thus, (6b) holds.

Thus, (2i) does not become (1i) even though (2ii) does become (1ii) for conventional plans. Explicitly, for the conventional plan, first-order conditions are

(8i) $H(1 + \gamma) - C'(K) = 0$

or

$$H = C'(K)/(1 + \gamma)$$

(8ii) $$V + K - \gamma W + \gamma W - L'(H) = 0$$

or

$$K = L'(H) - V.$$

If the conventional plan results in inefficient effort and labor supply, which way do the effects go? The answer can be easily seen in figure 9.1. First-order conditions (1i) and (1ii) are shown by the solid lines, and (8i) is shown by the dotted line. (Recall that [8ii] is identical to [1ii].) Point Q is the solution to (1i)–(1ii) and also to (7i)–(7ii) corresponding to the pattern plan since pattern plans are efficient. Point R is the solution to (8i)–(8ii). Since $\gamma > 0$, the line corresponding to (8i) must lie below that to (1i) which implies that $H_C > H^*$ and that $K_C > K^*$. There is too much investment in human capital and effort and too much labor supply with too little turnover.

Thus, the simplest form of pattern plan provides incentives for an efficient allocation of resources, whereas the standard conventional plan does not. This suggests that conventional plans will also carry other provisions that seek to undo the inefficiencies inherent in these plans. Hours constraints, maximum and minimum numbers of years of service, and other restrictions can be imposed to restore some of the lost efficiency, and these are explored in a later section.

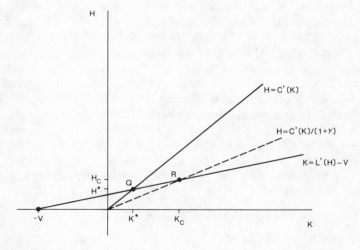

Fig. 9.1

It is interesting to perform some comparative statics to predict when inefficiencies will be most pronounced.

The most obvious relationship is that inefficiency is increased the larger is γ. Since the current specification of the conventional plan is a one-parameter one, this simply says that the inefficiency is increased the larger is the pension for any given number of hours worked and wage level. This is hardly surprising since if γ were zero, there would be no pension and no inefficiency. Given the shapes of the functions, however, an increase in γ causes more inefficiency increase in K than it does in H.[6]

The inefficiency is greater when the value of raw labor, V, is large. Mechanically, this is because the $K = L'(H) - V$ function shifts to the northwest. Intuitively, it is because the higher is V, the larger is the number of hours worked, even when all is efficient. Thus, the absolute size of the inefficiency increases with V. This is more than a neutral change in units, however, because the $C(K)$ function is not permitted to change simultaneously.

Contrast this with the effect of a steepening of the cost function described by an increase in $C'(K)$ at every K. This has the interpretation of an increase in the disutility of effort or an increase in the cost of improving skills. The effect is similar to a decrease in γ. It reduces the size of the inefficiency, and does so to a greater extent for K (effort and human capital) than for H. The intuition here seems straightforward. Steepening the cost function dampens the inefficiency effect because it makes it more costly to behave in an opportunistic fashion.

The story is analogous for the disutility of hours worked function. An increase in $L'(H)$ for all H flattens the K function and results in a reduction in both K and H. The reduction, however, is proportional so that only the absolute size of the inefficiency decreases.

An obvious question is, Why are conventional plans widespread if they introduce inefficiency? There are a few possible answers.

First, everything said has been in terms of real wages rather than nominal ones. A conventional plan that bases the pension on the final few years' salary indexes benefits to inflation. But even in an inflationary environment, the same potential for distortion of too large H and K exists. Further, pattern plans are often indexed to inflation, although usually on an ad hoc basis. All that is necessary is that β, the dollar amount per year of service, be adjusted to the CPI or another easily obtainable index.

There are other possibilities. It has been assumed throughout that the wage takes the form

$$W = V + K - \overline{P/H}.$$

As mentioned at the outset, it is always possible to undo the distortion introduced by the pension by changing the wage function in a corresponding fashion. But in this case the way by which the wage function changes to restore optimality is of particular interest because it implies a direct relationship among wages, human capital, and the pension formula.

It turns out that the efficient wage function that also guarantees zero profit is

$$W = \left(\frac{1}{1 + \gamma} \right) (V + K) .$$

That efficiency is guaranteed is easily seen. Equation (6a) becomes

$$\gamma \left(\frac{1}{1 + \gamma} \right) H = H \left(1 - \frac{1}{1 + \gamma} \right)$$

or

$$\frac{\gamma}{1 + \gamma} = \frac{\gamma}{1 + \gamma}$$

and (6b) becomes

$$\gamma W = V + K - W$$
$$W(1 + \gamma) = V + K$$
$$W = \left(\frac{1}{1 + \gamma} \right) (V + K) .$$

Since both (6a) and (6b) are true, efficiency is guaranteed. Further, since

$$W + P/H = W(1 + \gamma)$$

and since $W = \left[1/1 + \gamma \right] (V + K)$, $W + P/H = V + K$ so zero profits are guaranteed.

Thus, $W = \left[1/1 + \gamma \right] (V + K)$ is the efficiency-inducing wage to couple with conventional defined benefit plans. This is a specific example of the earlier statement that setting

$$W \equiv V + K - P(W, H)/H$$

always insures efficiency. In this case, that identity holds when $W \equiv (1/1 + \gamma) (V + K)$.

This produces an implication. The efficient wage function for a pattern plan is

$$W = V + K - \beta$$

and

$$W = \left(\frac{1}{1 + \gamma} \right) (V + K)$$

for a conventional plan so that, other things equal, wages should rise more rapidly with K for pattern plan workers than for conventional plan workers. As a corollary, conventional plans with large values of γ should reward effort and human capital less well.

These implications are somewhat difficult to test because K is not easily observed. However, since K reflects human capital investment as well as effort, one possibility is to examine the effect of schooling and experience on wages. If wages and pensions are set to induce efficiency, then workers on jobs with conventional plans with high γ's should have the lowest effect of schooling and experience on earnings. This will be tested in subsequent work.

Again, no rationale for setting up conventional, as opposed to pattern, plans is built into the analysis. The obvious explanation is that making the pension a function of salary allows one formula to be used for many different worker types. But most companies distinguish between worker types anyway, assigning conventional plans to white-collar workers and pattern plans to blue-collar workers. Many make finer distinctions. Tying pension to wage in order to conserve on paper seems to be a weak explanation.

The argument that pensions are linked to wages for incentive reasons is not correct. There are two related reasons. First, the wage itself is sufficient to provide the appropriate incentives. Second, *too much* incentive is generated by tying pension to wage. That was the first result of this section. More subtle explanations are required.

9.2.3 Defined Contribution Plans

What has been shown so far is that conventional defined benefit plans result in inefficiencies when the worker's wage is not adjusted to his own pension receipt. With defined contribution plans, what the worker receives is equal (in an actuarial sense) to what he contributes. Thus, defined contribution plans cannot introduce inefficiencies, irrespective of their provisions. This is simply a trivial restatement of the proposition that if the worker takes into account that his wage offsets any pension benefits received, he will always internalize the full effects of the pension and behave efficiently. Writing this down rigorously, note that with the defined contribution pension plan, the contribution per period of time, $G(W, H)$, times the length of working life, H, must equal the received pension benefit, $P(W, H)$.

In the absence of pensions, the wage must be set equal to $V + K$ in order to achieve efficiency. This follows directly from necessary condition (6b) because in the absence of a pension, $\partial P/\partial H = 0$.

Thus, start by setting $W = V + K$ and then introduce a defined contribution plan that taxes $G(W, H)$ per H worked. The worker's problem is then

(9) $$\max_{H,K} H[W - G(W, H)] + P(W, H) - C(K) - L(H).$$

But since the rules of the plan imply that $P(W, H) = HG(W, H)$, (9) becomes

$$\max_{H,K} WH - C(K) - L(H)$$

or

$$\max_{H,K} (V + K)H - C(K) - L(H).$$

This is identical to (1) so that efficiency is guaranteed. The first-order conditions are

(9i)
$$\frac{\partial}{\partial K} = \frac{\partial W}{\partial K} H - C'(K) = 0$$

(9ii)
$$\frac{\partial}{\partial H} = W - L'(H) = 0 \, .$$

Since $\partial W/\partial K = 1$, (9i) reduces to (1i). Further since $P = [G(W, H)]H$, $W = V + K$ from (3). Since $\overline{P/H} = G$, (9ii) reduces to (1ii).

Thus, defined contribution plans are always efficient without any required additional constraints. This suggests that defined contribution plans should be more prevalent in situations where the inefficiencies associated with the conventional defined contribution plan are most pronounced. Using the comparative statics results generated above, defined contribution plans should be used over conventional plans when pensions are relatively large (γ causes greater inefficiency), when investment in human capital is high—$C(K)$ function is flat—and when hours worked are large—$L(H)$ function is flat. This suggests the use of defined contribution plans for high-wage, highly skilled workers.[7]

9.3 Vesting

In order to consider the effects of vesting, it is necessary to allow for some workers to leave before the vesting date and others to stay beyond that date. The easiest way to do this is to allow for two types of individuals: the first type has alternative use of time function $L(H)$ and the second has alternative use of time function $\tilde{L}(H)$ such that $\tilde{L}(H) > L(H)$ for all H. Let λ of the population be of the first type and $(1 - \lambda)$ be of the second type.

A full and immediate vesting pension of the pattern plan type is always efficient. This simply requires duplication of the analysis in section 9.2.1 above for the two types of workers because implicit in that analysis was the assumption that pensions vest immediately. The first-order conditions of the worker's maximization problem are

$$H = C'(K)$$

$$V + K - \beta + \beta = L'(H)$$

for the first type and

$$\tilde{H} = C'(K)$$

$$V + K - \beta + \beta = \tilde{L}'(\tilde{H})$$

for the second type.

Now consider the same pattern plans without vesting. The simplest form of nonvesting is to assume that $\beta = 0$ if $H < \overline{H}$. There are three cases: First, $H < \overline{H}$ and $\tilde{H} < \overline{H}$. This is the same as no pension since $\overline{P}/\overline{H} = 0$, and so there is full efficiency. Second, $H > \overline{H}$ and $\tilde{H} > \overline{H}$. This is the case just analyzed as fully vested pension benefits, and it yields efficiency as well. The only interesting case arises when $H < \overline{H}$, $\tilde{H} \geq \overline{H}$ or when $H \geq \overline{H}$, $\tilde{H} < \overline{H}$.

The important feature is that there is subsidization of the stayers by the leavers and this causes a distortion. The wage paid to workers must be sufficiently low to cover the pension costs to λ of the population who are stayers. Thus, the zero profit condition is

(3') $\lambda(WH + \beta H) + (1 - \lambda)W\tilde{H} = (V + K)[\lambda H + (1 - \lambda)\tilde{H}]$

or

$$W = V + K - \frac{\lambda\beta}{\lambda + (1 - \lambda)\dfrac{\tilde{H}}{H}} \,.$$

Now, the maximization problem for the stayers is

(10') $\displaystyle \max_{K,H} H \left\{ V + K - \left[\frac{\lambda\beta}{\lambda + (1 - \lambda)\dfrac{\tilde{H}^*}{H^*}} \right] \right\}$

$$+ \beta H - C(K) - L(H)$$

where asterisks denote equilibrium values. The first-order conditions are

(10'i) $\displaystyle \frac{\partial}{\partial K} = H - C'(K) = 0$

and

(10'ii) $\displaystyle \frac{\partial}{\partial H} = V + K + \frac{(1 - \lambda)\beta}{\lambda + (1 - \lambda)\dfrac{\tilde{H}^*}{H^*}} - L'(H) = 0 \,.$

Similarly, for leavers,

(10̃') $\displaystyle \max_{\tilde{K},\tilde{H}} \tilde{H} \left[V + \tilde{K} - \left(\frac{\lambda\beta}{\lambda + (1 - \lambda)\dfrac{\tilde{H}^*}{H^*}} \right) \right] - C(\tilde{K}) - \tilde{L}(\tilde{H}),$

since $\tilde{H} < \overline{H}$ so pension $= 0$. The first-order conditions are

(1õ'i) $$\frac{\partial}{\partial \tilde{K}} = \tilde{H} - C'(\tilde{K}) = 0$$

and

(10'ii) $$\frac{\partial}{\partial \tilde{H}} = V + \tilde{K} - \frac{\lambda\beta}{\lambda + (1 - \lambda)\dfrac{\tilde{H}^*}{H^*}} - \tilde{L}'(\tilde{H}) = 0.$$

The situation is shown in figure 9.2.

Points Q and $\tilde{Q}$ are the efficient points for movers and stayers, respectively, and are obtained in the absence of a pension. Note that $H > \tilde{H}$ and $K > \tilde{K}$ because $L'(H) > \tilde{L}'(H)$ for all H.

In the presence of the pension that does not vest immediately, (10'i) and (1õ'i) are identical to (1i), but (10'ii) and (1õ'ii) shift as shown in figure 9.2. Thus, the new equilibrium points are R and $\tilde{R}$ for movers and stayers.

The most important result is that both H and K deviate from the efficient levels. Stayers spend too much time on the job and invest in too much human capital and effort because the marginal return to a year worked,

$$V + K + \frac{\beta(1 - \lambda)}{\lambda + (1 - \lambda)\dfrac{\tilde{H}^*}{H^*}},$$

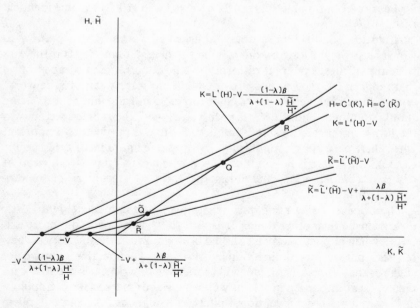

Fig. 9.2

exceeds the true value of work, $V + K$. Similarly, leavers leave too early and do not invest in enough human capital and effort because the marginal return to a year worked,

$$V + \tilde{K} - \frac{\lambda\beta}{\lambda + (1 - \lambda)\dfrac{\tilde{H}*}{H*}},$$

is less than the true value of work, $V + \tilde{K}$.

A few additional points are in order. First, average tenure in the economy may rise or fall with the addition of an imperfect vesting provision. Although average tenure rises for those who eventually receive a pension, average tenure falls for those who do not. The effect on the average for the economy as a whole depends on the proportion of people in each group and on the increase and decrease for the respective groups, which depends in turn on the slopes of $L(H)$ and $\tilde{L}(H)$. But it is indeed quite possible that average tenure falls as the result of vesting.

Second, although it has not been my approach in this analysis to determine why or whether particular provisions exist in long-run equilibrium, ignoring those issues is especially bothersome here. In particular, since leavers subsidize stayers, one would expect some firms to cater only to leavers, offering no pension and paying wage $W = V + K$. This type of self-sorting, akin to Salop and Salop (1976), causes the non–fully vested pension equilibrium to become efficient. The reason is that firms that offer pensions obtain only stayers: Thus $\lambda = 1$ and (10′ii) become identical with (1ii).[8]

A sorting equilibrium is not established if workers do not know to which class they belong before joining the firm. Of course, as is the case with any of these apparent distortions, a firm that offered compensation that induced efficiency could provide higher average wealth to the workers and should attract the entire labor force. So full and immediate vesting should dominate. But if $L(H)$ is positively sloped, then some specificity to the firm-worker relationship is implied. Sorting is particularly important when there exist substantial hiring costs or large amounts of firm-specific capital. Still, there is no obvious reason why a pension is used instead of deferred compensation that takes the form of steeply rising tenure-earnings profiles.

These deeper issues aside, plans that do not vest immediately introduce distortions. Thus, other things constant, fully vested plans are more efficient, which implies that plans should be organized at the industry or, better, national level to eliminate such distortions. The fact that they are not suggests that some other issue, and the sorting of workers is a logical candidate, raises important problems with which labor markets must grapple.

The analysis for conventional plans is similar, has the same implications, and is not repeated here.

9.4 Minimum Benefit Levels

A number of plans have minimum benefit levels below which pension payments are not permitted to fall. These provisions are almost exclusively a characteristic of conventional defined benefit plans. It might be thought that this lump sum feature of the plan is a way by which the inefficiency associated with conventional plans is eliminated. This is not the case.

A conventional plan with a minimum level of benefits takes the form $P = \gamma WH$, for $P > \underline{P}$, $P = \underline{P}$ otherwise . Efficiency requires that (6a) and (6b) hold. When $P < \underline{P}$, then (6a) holds because $\partial P/\partial K = 0$. But (6b) is violated because $\partial P/\partial H = 0$, and $\underline{P} > 0$ implies that $W < V + K$.

If the equilibrium were such that $P > \underline{P}$, then (6a) implies that

$$\gamma H = H(1 - 1)$$
$$= 0 .$$

This can only hold if $\gamma = 0$, that is, if there is no pension so efficiency is not achieved here either. Therefore, the addition of a minimum benefit level cannot restore efficiency.

9.5 Minimum and Maximum Years of Service for Pension Accrual

Some plans have minimum service requirements. Pension benefits do not accrue for years worked less than, say, five so that a typical pattern plan formula is $P = \beta(H - \underline{H})$, for $H > \underline{H}$, $P = 0$ otherwise. Others have maximum years of service allowances so that the pension formula is $P = \beta H$, for $H < \overline{H}$, $P = \beta\overline{H}$ otherwise. Some plans have both. This section examines the effects of these constraints on behavior. The generalized pattern plan takes the form $P = 0$, for $H < \underline{H}$, $P = \beta(H - \underline{H})$, for $\underline{H} < H < \overline{H}$, $P = \beta(\overline{H} - \underline{H})$, for $H > \underline{H}$. The generalized conventional plan is $P = \gamma(H - \underline{H})W$, for $\underline{H} < H < \overline{H}$, $P = \gamma(\overline{H} - \underline{H})W$, for $H > \overline{H}$, $P = 0$ for $H < \underline{H}$.

The result is that if the equilibrium level of hours, H, exceeds $\overline{H}$ then there is too little K and H relative to the efficient amount. If $\underline{H} < H < \overline{H}$, then there is too much K, H. If $H < \underline{H}$, then all is efficient.

The analysis is most straightforward for pattern or flat benefit plans. Here, (2i) remains as in the efficient case (1i), $H - C'(K) = 0$, but (2ii) becomes

(2iia) $$K = L'(H) - V, H < \underline{H};$$

(2iib) $$K = L'(H) - V - \frac{\beta H}{H}, \underline{H} < H < \overline{H};$$

(2iic) $$K = L'(H) - V + \frac{\beta(\overline{H} - \underline{H})}{H}, H > \overline{H}.$$

Again a graph helps to understand the solution. Q denotes the efficient point in figure 9.3.

If $H < \underline{H}$, then the constraint is binding for all workers and no one receives pensions. The marginal value of hours in the creation of pension benefits and the average cost of pension benefits is zero, so this reverts to the no pension case and all is efficient.

If the relationships are such that the equilibrium has $\underline{H} < H < \overline{H}$, then the relevant function is $K = L'(H) - V - \beta\underline{H}/H$ and the equilibrium is at F_1. Here, $K_1 > K^*$ and $H_1 > H^*$, so there is too much effort, human capital, and labor supplied. The reason is that when $\overline{H} > H > \underline{H}$, the marginal return to an additional year worked in increasing the pension is β. But the cost of the pension earned for only $H - \underline{H}$ years is spread over all years H so that wage is reduced by less than the marginal value of pension benefits. Thus, the net value of an additional hour worked is positive so workers overachieve, and overachievement depends directly on the level of $\underline{H}$. The larger is $\underline{H}$, subject to $H > \underline{H}$, the larger is the inefficiency.

The reverse is true when $H > \overline{H}$. Then the marginal pension value of an additional year of work is zero, but the cost of previous accruals is spread over all years so that W is reduced without an offsetting marginal benefit. Thus, workers underachieve. This is shown at F_2 with $H_2 < H^*$ and $K_2 < K^*$.

The analysis for conventional plans is similar but slightly more complicated. Here, (2i) is altered as well, depending on the regime, since $\partial P/\partial W$ is not generally equal to zero. Instead,

(2ia') $H = C'(K), H < \underline{H};$

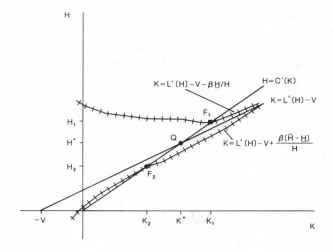

Fig. 9.3

(2ib') $H = [C'(K) + \gamma \underline{H}]/(1 + \gamma), \underline{H} < H < \overline{H};$

(2ic') $H = C'(K), H > \overline{H}.$

Similarly, (2ii) becomes

(2iia') $K = L'(H) - V, H < \underline{H};$

(2iib') $K = L'(H) - V - \dfrac{\gamma \underline{H} W}{H}, \underline{H} < H < \overline{H};$

(2iic') $K = L'(H) - V + \dfrac{\gamma(\overline{H} - H)W}{H}, H > \overline{H}.$

Figures 9.4 and 9.5 graph the possibilities.

Figure 9.4 illustrates the cases where $H < \underline{H}$ and $\underline{H} < H < \overline{H}$. Efficiency is shown at Q. If $\underline{H}_0$ is sufficiently high so that $H < \underline{H}_0$, then Q is the equilibrium and all is efficient. No one works long enough to receive a pension so it drops out completely and all is efficient.

If H_1 is sufficiently low so that $\underline{H}_1 < H < \overline{H}$ in equilibrium, then the relevant conditions are (2ib') and (2iib'). Equation (2ib') is shown. But since W is a function of H, the exact shape of (2iib') is unknown. Still, it is clear that (2iib') lies to the northwest of $K = L'(H) - V$. Point C denotes

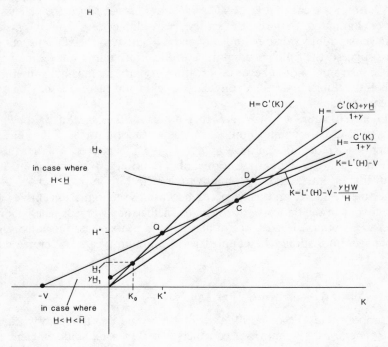

Fig. 9.4

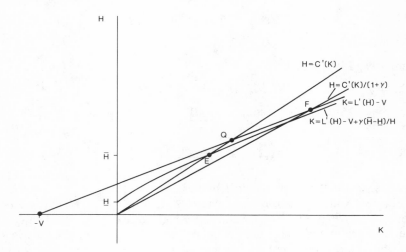

Fig. 9.5

the solution to the standard conventional plan with $H > H^*$, $K > K^*$. The solution with $\underline{H} > 0$ occurs at D. D can lie almost anywhere with respect to Q and C, so nothing can be said about the efficiency of D relative to C. But it is clear that at D, $H > H^*$ and $K > K^*$ so the inefficiency is never eliminated. In the case of pattern plans, larger deviations of $\underline{H}$ from zero make things worse for both H and K relative to the efficient values. This suggests the following empirical proposition: minimum years of service constraints should never be a feature of pattern plans but sometimes will make things better in a conventional plan and therefore may be part of conventional plans.

Finally, in figure 9.5, if $H > \overline{H}$ then it must be the case that $H < H^*$, $K < K^*$ because the equilibrium, E, must lie to the southwest of the efficient point (since [2iic′] lies below $K = L'(H) - V$). However, whether this is an improvement on the conventional plan solution at F is ambiguous. It is clear that it reduces K and H, but by too much. This implies that too little investment, effort, and work occur because the marginal incentives are too low as in the flat case. Further, the inefficiency worsens, the larger is $\overline{H} - \underline{H}$, so that the existence of a maximum years of service constraint, when binding, should be coupled with minimum years of service constraints.

9.6 Constraints on Work Time and Effort

Suppose that "all-or-nothing" contracts could be offered to workers. The general rule is that these contracts can always be made efficient because they remove all chance of opportunistic behavior by the worker. In this context, this would amount to a contract that specified $H = H^*$, $K = K^*$ and some lump sum payment. Ignoring costs of monitoring and enforcement, it is useful to ask whether, when, and what kind of constraints are desirable. In particular, it is interesting to consider when fixing H or K alone is sufficient to bring about efficiency.

A general statement follows from examination of (2). Equation (2i) reduces to (1i) (efficiency) if and only if (6a) holds. So when (6a) holds, even if (6b) is violated, fixing $H = H^*$ will result in full efficiency. The reason is that then the worker maximizes only with respect to K and the solution to (2i), given $H = H^*$, is $K = K^*$. The reverse is true if (6b) holds and (6a) does not. Then setting $K = K^*$ eliminates (2i) as a first-order condition and the solution to (2ii), given $K = K^*$, is H^*.

Equations (6a) and (6b) always hold for pattern plans. Therefore, there should be no constraints on years of service or investment and effort with pattern plans. One might then argue that mandatory retirement should be less prevalent for workers with pattern plans than for conventional plans. This is not a direct implication, however, because mandatory retirement refers to age rather than to years of service.

Conventional plans satisfy (6b) but violate (6a). This implies that only constraints on K (and not H) are required to bring about efficiency. Thus skill and effort levels are to be precisely specified for conventional plan workers. As the result, piece-rate workers who are allowed to select their effort levels should not have defined benefit conventional plans.

9.7   Extensions of the Model and Additional Issues

9.7.1   Multiple Wage Rates

So far, wages have been constant over the lifetime. One question is, How does generalization to multiperiods with different wage rates in each affect the results? Specifically, in a two-period context, the pension can be paid for out of the wages from either period or from some combination of the two. The result is that no matter how it is done, as long as the worker recognizes that his wages depend on the pension through the zero profit constraint, or is forced to recognize it by an appropriate shift in the wage function, all is internalized and no inefficiency results. Tilting the age-earnings profile has no effect on behavior. This is easily seen. The worker's problem is now

(11)
$$\max_{K, H_1, H_2} \quad W_1 H_1 + W_2 H_2 + P(H_1, H_2, W_1, W_2) - C(K) - L(H_1, H_2)$$

subject to

(3')
$$W_1 H_1 + W_2 H_2 + P = (V + K)(H_1 + H_2)$$

and

$$W_1 = V + K - \theta P/H_1, \quad W_2 = V + K - (1 - \theta)P/H_2, \quad 0 \le \theta \le 1.$$

First-order conditions are

(11i)
$$\frac{\partial}{\partial K} = H_1 - \theta\frac{\partial P}{\partial K} + H_2 - (1 - \theta)\frac{\partial P}{\partial K} + \frac{\partial P}{\partial K} - C'(K) = 0$$
$$= H_1 + H_2 - C'(K) = 0;$$

(11ii)
$$\frac{\partial}{\partial H_1} = V + K - \theta\frac{\partial P}{\partial H_1} - (1 - \theta)\frac{\partial P}{\partial H_1} + \frac{\partial P}{\partial H_1} - \frac{\partial L}{\partial H_1} = 0$$
$$= V + K - \frac{\partial L}{\partial H_1} = 0;$$

(11iii)
$$\frac{\partial}{\partial H_2} = V + K - \theta\frac{\partial P}{\partial H_2} - (1 - \theta)\frac{\partial P}{\partial H_2} + \frac{\partial P}{\partial H_2} - \frac{\partial L}{\partial H_2} = 0$$
$$= V + K - \frac{\partial L}{\partial H_2} = 0.$$

Equations (11i), (11ii), and (11iii) are the two-period analogue of (1i) and bring about efficiency. Thus, independent of the division of pension costs, that is, for any θ, as long as the worker is aware of the competitive firm's response to his pension increase, all is internalized and efficient.

This does not imply that pensions never distort incentives. If the worker's own wage does not adjust to his own pension, but rather to the average pension on which he has only a trivial effect, then inefficiencies can result as they do in the one-period case. More fundamentally, if the "true" wage, including the value of pension accrual and other perks, does not equal marginal product, and if the worker is allowed to choose his hours, then inefficiencies result. But this point, which is analyzed in more detail in Lazear (1981), is quite independent of pensions and holds even when all compensation takes the form of a direct money wage.

9.7.2   Corner Solutions

It is useful to consider some special cases. First, consider the case where the H function, (2i), and the K function, (2ii), do not intersect in the positive quadrant. This can happen either because the $L'(H)$ function is too flat, reflecting a very low utility loss associated with forgone additional hours of leisure, or because the $C'(K)$ function is too flat, reflecting a very low marginal cost of effort or investment. Under such circumstances, time worked, effort, and human capital investment are infinite. It is clear that such a situation cannot occur if for no other reason than that the $L(H)$ function becomes vertical (horizontal in the diagrams) when time worked reaches length of life.

Second, it is possible that the $L(H)$ function is perfectly inelastic at $H = 0$. This means that the worker views work at this firm as so distasteful that he is unwilling to supply even one hour at any price. Then the intersection is at the origin, yielding the corner solution that $H = 0$ and $K = 0$.

Third, the worker may view all jobs as identical, in which case the $L(H)$ function is perfectly elastic at $L(H)$ equal to the market wage. This makes the K function a vertical line at (market wage $- V$). If this lies in the positive quadrant, then equilibrium is at the interior intersection, because the worker's value to this firm is sufficient to bid him away from rivals. In the case where that vertical line lies to the left of the vertical axis, no work occurs, because the worker's marginal product, V, at this firm is insufficient to warrant employment given the market price of his services. If that line is coincident with the vertical axis, then all are indifferent because his marginal product here is identical to the market wage so neither the worker nor firm has a preference over his work location.

Finally, if $C'(K)$ is positive for $K = 0$, then a corner solution exists if $L'(H)$ is sufficiently steep (flat K function in the diagram) to avoid an intersection in the positive quadrant. The interpretation is that the fixed cost of effort or investment is sufficiently high to discourage any work at this job. The solution is $H = 0, K = 0$.

Incidentally, when comparing the solution, K has the interpretation of effort or human capital *specific* to this firm. Obviously, if a corner solution is reached because, say, V is too low relative to the market wage, investment in human capital and effort at the other firm is still possible.

9.7.3 Maximum Age Restrictions

A number of plans have a maximum age of starting employment such that workers who start after that age are not entitled to enrollment in the pension plan. This is quite aside from any issues of vesting which depend on years of service independent of age. Although no solid explanation of this phenomenon is presented, it is useful to consider the issues.

The fact that firms do not want to put old workers of a given tenure together with young workers of given tenure suggests that old workers cost more in terms of pension payouts even holding years of service constant. The most obvious reason this is the case is that a worker who starts at age 59 is likely to retire with fewer years of service than a worker who starts at, say, age 45. If defined benefit plans were set up in a way that subsidized retirees with fewer years of service, then it would be more costly to enroll older workers in a pension plan than younger workers. Elsewhere (Lazear 1982, 1984) I have argued that it is efficient to set up pension plans the actuarial value of which declines with increased years of service because of incentive and turnover effects. I also find empirical support for this proposition. This story seems to provide an explanation for age restrictions, but there remains the question, Why aren't plans made dependent on age as well as experience? Such a provision would probably be illegal under the Age Discrimination in Employment Act, but this is a relatively recent constraint and it is not clear why it does not apply to the provision that denies pensions to older new hires.

9.7.4   Individualized Wage-Pension Combinations

The basic result, that pensions cannot affect behavior if the corresponding wage adjustments are accounted for by the worker, leads to an obvious question: Is the wage set independent of the pension, and if so, why? Why doesn't the firm call out a wage-pension combination such that $W = V + K - P(H, K)/H$, so that the worker is forced to internalize everything and to behave efficiently?

The obvious answer is almost definitional. To do so makes the pension identical to wage payments and the pension might as well be eliminated altogether. The fact that wages and pensions are somewhat independent provides some clue as to why there are pensions in the first place.

If pensions are part of an optimal compensation scheme that attempts to deal with problems of incentives and turnover (as argued in Lazear [1982]), then a pension that is independent of the wage for the individual worker provides the extra degree of freedom necessary to restore efficiency. Merely offering a higher wage does not provide the appropriate incentives because of the contingent nature of pensions on performance. Pension "buyouts" of relatively less productive workers are part of the optimal compensation scheme.

The same is true if the pension functions as an insurance device, paying more to workers who live longer (or who live to the same age but retire earlier). Reducing the pension while at the same time increasing the wage defeats the usefulness of the pension as an insurance device. Allowing the worker to choose his wage-pension allocation results in the standard adverse selection problem and separating equilibrium issues discussed by Akerlov (1970) and Rothschild and Stiglitz (1976).

The exception to this is the rationalization of pensions as a tax-free savings account.[9] If it were performing only this function, then allowing the worker to choose the combination of wage with pension would in no way negate the tax saving effects of a pension and would allow the individual to tailor the compensation to his individual situation. As the result, no rationalization of independent wage-pension provisions is provided by the tax argument. Further, if taxes were the issue, a defined contribution plan would win on almost every count. Yet defined benefit plans are prevalent.

9.7.5   Plans That Are Not Actuarially Fair

All of the analysis is conducted under the simplifying assumption that $P(H, K)$ is some fixed payment rather than some annual flow, which more closely describes most pensions. If risk neutrality is assumed, the fact that some workers may receive less than P while others receive more than P is not essential. What is essential is that the interpretation of a pattern plan as one that has P depend on years of service in a linear fashion and a conventional plan as one that depends on some salary average and years of service in a linear fashion is not accurate. Aside from explicit nonlinearities built into the benefit formulas, there are implicit nonlinearities that have to do with when the worker retires.

For example, in the pattern plan, it is the annual flow of pension benefits, not the expected present value of those benefits that increases at constant rate per year of service. For this to cause the present value of pension benefits to increase at a constant rate per year of service, additional restrictions having to do with life expectancy, discount factors, and rate of accrual are required. In reality, I have shown that the contrary is generally the case (Lazear 1982, 1984). Beyond a certain number of years of service, the present value of pension benefits actually declines with years of service. The same is true for conventional plans of the defined benefit type.

In fact, in the case of conventional plans, the reduction in present value with years of service beyond a certain point may help to restore the efficiency that is lost when workers fail to account appropriately for the relationship between wages and pensions. Since, in the absence of a decline, workers tend to overinvest in human capital, to work too hard, and to put in too many hours and years of service, this decline may actually move the situation toward the first-best solution.

Finally, it has been assumed throughout that the wage never exceeds the worker's marginal product. If it does, then, as I have suggested elsewhere, seemingly inefficient pensions may actually bring about efficiency.

9.8 Conclusion

This paper creates as many questions as answers. The goal is to identify the incentive effects of different pension provisions. In doing so, puzzles arise because many provisions appear to have adverse incentive effects. Although few of the puzzles are solved, some directions for empirical investigation are suggested. In particular, the link between the wage relationship and productivity variables bears a special correspondence to the pension plan. For example, one implication is that pattern plans should be coupled with wage functions that reward increased effort more generously than those coupled with conventional plans. Further, the incidence of maximum and minimum hours restrictions in pension plans is predicted, as well as the pattern of hours and effort requirements.

Perhaps more important than the empirical implications of the model is the clarification of the effects induced by various pension provisions. Many of the effects are subtle in mechanism, although not necessarily in size. Few have been considered in the past, and this essay takes a first step toward the understanding of these institutions that often seem either innocuous or arbitrary to the casual observer.

Notes

1. Blinder, Gordon and Wise (1978), Burkhauser and Quinn (1981), and Fields and Mitchell (1981) examine the effects on retirement behavior. Stiglitz (1975) considers vesting effects as well.

2. For example, investment in human capital may be more easily observed than changes in the level of effort, because the former may require the use of the firm's resources (e.g., other employees as teachers, etc.).

3. For example, some emphasize tax breaks enjoyed (Black 1980; Tepper 1981; Merton 1982; Sharpe 1976; Bulow 1979, 1981), while others emphasize incentive and mobility effects (Miller and Scholes 1979; Lazear 1979, 1982, 1983).

4. The exception is the split in benefit formula between white- and blue-collar workers.

5. This is a special case because $W(K) = V + K - \overline{P/H}$ implies that $W'(K) = 1$. Additional distortions and offsets can be introduced by choosing other $W(K)$ functions. But unless the general condition that $W(K, H) \equiv V + K - P(K, H)/H$ holds, the deviation from first best remains. Only then can the firm break even and have conditions (2i) and (2ii) reduce to (1i) and (1ii).

6. In order to achieve an interior solution, it must be the case that the K function is flatter than the H function or that the disutility of labor hours (i.e., the value of leisure) rises more rapidly than the cost of additional human capital or effort. Suppose it did not. Then the solution would be to continue to invest in K and keep working more and more hours. Eventually, H approaches maximum feasible hours, so $L'(H)$ must become infinite, guaranteeing an interior solution.

7. This ignores differences that result from consideration of the reasons for pensions in the first place. This set of predictions is most consistent with the view that a pension serves as a tax-free savings account but neglects any explanation for pensions having to do with incentives or separation efficiency.

8. Asch (1983) explores this mechanism both at the theoretical level and empirically.

9. See Miller and Scholes (1979), Bulow (1979, 1981), Black (1980), Tepper (1981), Sharpe (1976), Merton (1982) for discussions.

Comment   Roger H. Gordon

In "Incentive Effects of Pensions," Lazear examines the incentive effects of various types of pension plans on labor supply and human capital investment. The analysis is clear and straightforward, and Lazear is careful to point out the testable implications of the theory. However, it is hard to know how much faith to put in the conclusions. In order to assess their plausibility, let me start by examining several of the key assumptions underlying the model.

One basic assumption is that all decisions would be made efficiently without pensions, so that any change in incentives caused by pensions creates an efficiency loss. For example, when firms have a conventional pension plan, which Lazear argues creates inefficiencies, he then forecasts that such firms would be likely to introduce modifications to their pension plans to lessen the resulting efficiency loss.

Roger H. Gordon is associate professor of economics at the University of Michigan and a research associate at the National Bureau of Economic Research.

I find this basic approach surprising. My presumption would have been that there is likely to be something omitted from our models that leads firms to rationally behave as they do. The strategy of the paper would then be that an analysis of the incentives created by existing pension plans, and an examination of which firms adopt which style of pension, ought to suggest what these omitted factors are. Any omitted factors that lead firms to adopt "inefficient" plans might also lead them to introduce further seemingly inefficient characteristics into their pension plans, for example, delayed vesting. It seems premature to forecast that detailed characteristics of a plan would be designed to lessen an inefficiency whose very existence we cannot yet rationalize. This complaint is mostly about the tone of the paper and the conclusions drawn, rather than about the analysis itself.

One further note about interpretation: within this paper, Lazear examines the incentive effects of pensions per se. The implication again is that if pensions were eliminated, the inefficiency would be eliminated as well. Yet if the firm intends to have the net compensation of a worker deviate from his marginal product in any period, then the deviation is not caused by the pension per se and presumably would not disappear if the pension were eliminated. Pensions may facilitate certain forms of deviations, but other institutions may accomplish almost the same purpose.

Another key modeling decision that Lazear had to make early in the paper was how to handle the fact that if the individual's wage adjusts to fully offset any characteristics of the pension, then the pension plan will have no effects on behavior, and so is fully "efficient," regardless of how peculiar it may appear. Lazear plausibly assumes that the wage-setting procedure is sufficiently separated from the pension plan that any one individual's wage will not necessarily fully reflect the value of his pension accruals each period, even if on average it does (as required by competition). In particular, he assumes that the individual expects his wage to satisfy

$$(1) \qquad\qquad W = V + K - \overline{P/H},$$

where $\overline{P/H} = P(H^*, K^*)/H^*$ is assumed by the individual to remain constant even when he changes his behavior.

It is not clear from the discussion what motivates this particular specification. Is it a description of individual expectations, which may often prove to be incorrect? Or is it an accurate description of how any one individual's wage responds to his own behavior? Given the strong presumption in the profession in favor of rational expectations, I will presume that the motivation is the latter. But why should we presume that the firm chooses this particular time pattern of compensation? No empirical evidence supporting it is provided.

I presume the intended justification for equation (1) is administrative expedience. However, in general the process of setting wages in response to behavior seems quite flexible. Many of the more highly trained individuals participating in pension plans would have individually determined wages. Taking into account clearly specified time patterns of pension accruals seems much easier than taking into account many of the other relevant factors. Even when wages are set for a group as a whole, the variation in wage rates necessary to offset the effects of pensions is quite simple. For the conventional plan described in the paper, all that is needed is to set wages so that $W = (V + K)/(1 + \gamma)$. Perhaps there is a reluctance to change wages sharply in response to such factors as vesting or minimum service requirements, though why is unclear. But this does not prevent wages from responding smoothly to other factors entering the pension formula, such as years of service. That the manager setting wages is distant from the pension plan is not a convincing response, as the general guidelines used for setting wages can reflect most of the effects of pension plans quite easily. Of course, wages may respond more easily to some effects of pensions than to others, and the firm may desire that wages offset only certain of the effects created by the pension plan. The nature of the remaining "inefficiencies," however, may not be very similar to those found by Lazear when he assumes wage rates do not respond at all to the effects of pensions.

An additional uncomfortable implication of equation (1) is that it is inconsistent with each individual receiving in compensation over his time with the firm the total value of his marginal product. For if the individual always breaks even over his career, his wages must necessarily adjust at some point to changes in the value of his pension—$\overline{P/H}$ cannot remain constant. As long as individuals are heterogeneous, equation (1) implies interpersonal transfers—some receive on average more than their marginal product and others receive less. If these transfers become significant, then competitive pressures ought to undermine the situation.

Finally, if administrative expedience is the justification for equation (1), why do firms adopt conventional pension plans, which generally are much more complicated to administer than the alternatives? Handling vesting questions, mandatory retirement, the detailed definitions of factors entering the pension formula, and inflationary readjustments in the formula itself, all seem to create far more administrative problems than running a plan like TIAA-CREF. It would appear that factors other than administrative expedience are at issue in determining the design of pension plans.

Lazear does not consistently accept equation (1), however. In modeling defined contribution plans, Lazear assumes that the wage rate reflects pension contributions at each date, regardless of how peculiar the time pattern of contributions. I find this puzzling. If the justification for equation (1) is administrative expedience, is it that much easier to adjust wage rates for an explicit contribution than for an implicit contribution? Actuarial calculations are done anyway for ERISA, and rules of thumb would be expected to develop approximating the correct offset when the contribution is implicit. The distinction in the paper between conventional plans and defined contribution plans seems much too sharply drawn.

So far I have confined my comments to the plausibility of the basic assumptions underlying the model. Let me comment briefly on the specific conclusions reached by the analysis:

1. *Firms with efficient conventional plans should have wage structures that reward schooling and experience less well than elsewhere, and least so among those with the largest pensions.* This forecast is unassailable given the model. However, if as in Lazear (1981) pensions are used to delay compensation so as to lessen agency problems, then it may well be that the wage structure would be designed to delay compensation as well, rather than to offset the delay built into the pension formula. Also, in implementing any test empirically, many complications would have to be faced, such as the endogeneity of the characteristics of pension plans and the variety of time patterns of pension accruals.

2. *Defined contribution plans ought to be relatively more common for high-wage, highly skilled workers.* Given the model, all that really follows is that conventional plans ought to be less likely in this setting, assuming that the first conclusion is false. (If the first conclusion is satisfied empirically, then all the plans would be "efficient.") Pattern plans, defined contribution plans, or no pension plan, are each efficient within the model. I have also argued above that it could as easily have followed within the framework of the model that defined contribution plans are "inefficient." This forecast is not persuasive.

3. *Only conventional plans ought to place restrictions on human capital or years of service.* This conclusion assumes both that the first conclusion is false, so that conventional plans are "inefficient," and that there are no efficiency reasons to create a divergence between the time patterns of compensation and marginal products. If there are such omitted factors, they could affect the design of all types of pension plans. One basic question, though, is why firms which choose an inefficient form of pension when efficient forms are available, then act to minimize the resulting efficiency loss when designing detailed characteristics of the pension.

What, then, do we learn from the paper? The prime conclusion seems to be that in assessing the incentive effects of pensions, it is critical to examine how wage rates adjust in response to pension provisions. This paper analyzes the effects of pensions when wage rates reflect only the average pension accrual for the group covered by the plan, and not its time pattern. Many other assumptions could have been made, with very different implications. The most fruitful direction of research would seem to be to examine empirically the nature of compensation schemes. Measuring the time pattern of marginal products, for comparison with the time pattern of compensation, will not be easy, however.

References

Akerlov, G. 1970. The market for "lemons": Quality uncertainty and the market mechanism. *Quarterly Journal of Economics* 84 (August): 488–500.

Asch, B. 1983. Pensions and self selection. Mimeographed. University of Chicago.

Black, F. 1980. The tax consequences of long-run pension policy. *Financial Analysts Journal* (July–August): 3–10.

Blinder, A.; Gordon, R.; and Wise, D. 1978. Market wages, reservation wages and retirement decisions. Princeton University.

Bulow, J. 1979. Analysis of pension funding under ERISA. NBER Working Paper 402.

————. 1981. What are corporate pension liabilities? Stanford University Working Paper.

Burkhauser, R., and Quinn, J. 1981. The effect of pension plans on the pattern of life cycle consumption.

Fields, G., and Mitchell, O. 1981. Pensions and optimal retirement behavior. NYSSILR WP 27 (March).

Lazear, E. P. 1979. Why is there mandatory retirement? *Journal of Political Economy* 87:1261–64.

————. 1981. Agency, earnings profiles, productivity and hours restrictions. *American Economic Review* 71:606–20.

————. 1982. Severance pay, pensions, and efficient mobility. NBER Working Paper 854.

————. 1983. Pensions as severance pay. In *Financial aspects of the United States pension system*, ed. Z. Bodie and J. Shoven. Chicago: University of Chicago Press (for NBER).

Miller, M., and Scholes, M. 1979. Executive compensation, taxes and incentives. University of Chicago, October.

Merton, R. C. 1982. On consumption-indexed public pension plans. NBER Working Paper 910.

Rothschild, M., and Stiglitz, J. E. 1976. Equilibrium in competitive insurance markets: An essay on the economics of imperfect information. *Quarterly Journal of Economics* 90:629–49.

Salop, J., and Salop, S. 1976. Self-selection and turnover in the labor market. *Quarterly Journal of Economics* 90:619–27.

Sharpe, W. 1976. Corporate pension funding policy. *Journal of Financial Economics* 3 (June): 183–93.

Stiglitz, G. 1975. An economic analysis of labor turnover. Economic Working Paper 53. Stanford, Calif.: Stanford University, Institute for Mathematical Studies in the Social Sciences.

Tepper, I. 1981. Taxation and corporate pension policy. *Journal of Finance* 36 (March): 1–13.

10 Pensions and the Retirement Decision

Barry Nalebuff
Richard J. Zeckhauser

10.1 Introduction

Pensions facilitate labor contracting. They provide an additional instrument beyond wages for attracting, sorting, and motivating workers. The key difference from other forms of labor compensation is that pensions are paid during the last years of one's life, usually as a contingent claim with payments continuing as long as one lives. The late-payment feature has the advantage of allowing an individual's reward to depend not only on the present period but also on future experiences. Its disadvantage is that it may hinder a worker's lifetime allocation of income unless he can trade on well-functioning capital markets.

The contingent claims feature has obvious risk-spreading advantages. However, contingent claims markets are often flawed in that they change incentives for individuals to engage in various types of behavior and induce them to "purchase" inappropriate claims. The problem of moral hazard is not severe here. Individuals have quite adequate incentives, apart from the pensions they will receive, to increase their survival. Similarly, problems of adverse selection may be limited, because pensions tend to be universal in a workplace, and pension considerations are unlikely to be the critical factor in job choices. Moreover, individuals are not likely to have substantial information about their life expectancy early in life, at the time pension benefits start to be accrued.

Barry Nalebuff is a junior fellow of the Society of Fellows of Harvard University. Richard J. Zeckhauser is professor of political economy at Harvard University's John F. Kennedy School of Government and a research associate of the National Bureau of Economic Research.

We received great insight and support from Andrew Nevin. Brian Sullivan provided excellent research assistance. John Dunlop, Jerry Hausman, Larry Summers, and seminar participants at Princeton, UCSD, and NBER provided stimulating comments. Cathy Lydon worked magic with the word processor, Nancy Jackson with the red pencil.

283

Given their contingent claims nature, and the fact that they are paid at the end of one's life, the most direct labor market effect of pensions may be on individuals' retirement decisions. In most pension plans, the per period benefits and expected payouts that a worker receives depend significantly on the age at which he retires. The central purpose of this analysis is to explore the effects of pensions on retirement decisions and to discuss the implications of those effects for policy choice.

A roadmap to our paper may be of assistance. Section 10.1.1 provides a brief description of our major results. Section 10.1.2 explores seven factors influencing individuals' retirement decisions, the factors that motivate our subsequent formulations. We then provide a capsule overview of the historical reasons leading to the introduction of pensions. The section concludes with a summary of the labor market effects apart from retirement decisions.

Sections 10.2, 10.3, and 10.4 present our substantive results. Each part is self-contained. All results are motivated by intuition. When proofs seem complicated, look for the intuitive arguments nuzzling with the mathematics.

Section 10.2 examines the effects of pensions on retirement. Pensions are first viewed as forced savings. As such, pensions encourage retirement; indeed, that is one of their primary purposes. Since it is difficult to monitor a worker's true disutility or work or to make contracts in which the worker commits himself to retire, pensions are used to help induce appropriate retirement behavior. How does the value of "pension savings" vary with age? Section 10.2.3 begins this inquiry, taking typical defined benefit pension plans—as revealed in a survey described in the appendix—and examining the relationship they produce between retirement age and expected benefits. Since individuals who choose to retire at different ages may have different (possibly unobservable) characteristics (e.g., how long they expect to live), we emphasize the distinction between the actuarial treatment of individuals and the actuarial treatment of retirement cohorts.

Section 10.3 focuses on populations that are heterogeneous with respect to such factors as preferences or life expectancy. It explores the design of optimal pensions (e.g., the way annual benefits should vary with retirement age), given heterogeneity. If there are asymmetries of information, a second-best outcome in which allocative efficiency tugs against full risk spreading must be expected. Again, confusion reigns on the issue of actuarial fairness. We hope to dethrone it just a bit.

Section 10.4 examines the effects of requiring pension offers to be the same among workers with dissimilar preferences, life expectancies, and productivity profiles. Social security programs and numerous regulations now in effect in the United States encourage or require common structures. We show how all workers may lose from such commonality, no matter what plan is adopted.

Section 10.5 presents the conclusions.

285   Pensions and the Retirement Decision

10.1.1   Summary of Results

Our paper includes several models. We list here some of the major results, grouped under three headings.

Appropriate Retirement (10.2.2)

1. It is a stylized fact that wages frequently exceed productivity in the later periods of work life. Because workers are unable to commit themselves to retire under appropriate circumstances (i.e., when disutility exceeds productivity, not wages), they will choose to work too long. Pensions can be used to force workers to save more than they want to save. Since these excess savings are accessible only on retirement, workers choose to retire earlier. In the new equilibrium, firms can pay higher wages, raising the worker's lifetime expected utility.

Optimal Pensions with Unmonitorable Information (10.2.3, 10.3.1, 10.3.2)

2. *Actuarial treatment of cohorts.* Most defined benefit pension plans appear to be actuarially unfair to late retirees. However, when workers can estimate their life span, those who expect to live longer choose to retire later and the pattern of actuarial benefit may be reversed.

3. *Actuarial treatment of individuals.* The structure of optimal pension plans, that is, those that maximize ex ante expected utility, must make it actuarially unfavorable for an individual to retire later.

4. *Disutility unmonitorable.* The optimal pension plan when disutility of work is unmonitorable offers a benefit that rises with retirement age up to a point and is then level. This point, in effect, is the maximum retirement age.

The rising portion of the pension curve sacrifices risk spreading to discourage workers from retiring too early. Under the optimal plan, assuming that death dates do not correlate with disutility, cohorts that retire later receive lower expected pension benefits.

Common Pension Plan for Heterogeneous Populations (10.4)

5. Consider the optimal pension plans for each group of workers with different characteristics. If, as required and encouraged by law, these plans are merged, then problems of adverse selection and moral hazard may make *all* groups worse off. Indeed there may be no common pension plan that is superior for any group of workers to what they each received when treated separately.

10.1.2   Why People Retire

The purpose of this analysis is to identify the role of pensions in affecting individuals' retirement decisions. At the outset, it is important to identify why retirement occurs; seven factors play a role in our models. They are (1) decreasing productivity; (2) increasing disutility of labor; (3) outside employment opportunities; (4) entitlements for retiring, such as pensions; (5) information about health and longevity; (6) indivisibility of labor; and (7) declining marginal utility of consumption. The first five factors are obviously related to the passage of time. Were they constant over time, and were labor perfectly divisible, there would be no reason to retire. Individuals would work the same amount each period. Full divisibility of labor would lead to scaled-down participation in the labor force rather than retirement. Obviously, in many instances labor is divisible at a price. One can work part time, but at a less than proportional salary. The analysis is simplified by assuming complete indivisibility of labor.

Given indivisibility of labor, individuals might still choose to work throughout their lives unless marginal utility from consumption declines. Thus, as is standard, individuals are assumed to have a concave period utility of consumption (though in some instances, to facilitate exposition, marginal utility may be constant). With decreasing productivity or increasing disutility of labor as one ages, it will be reasonable for individuals to consider retirement toward the end of their lives. If outside employment opportunities decline over time, the date of retirement from a given company will be advanced. Retirement patterns from the public employment sector illustrate this point; many individuals leave military or civil service at a time when they can still get a good outside job offer.

Entitlements may also be a function of age. Both social security and private pensions are age related. Presumably, individuals make some rough calculation of the value to them of the entitlements streams for different retirement dates and choose accordingly. A matter of central concern in this analysis is the structure of returns that an individual can expect from retirement, the effect that this will have on individual decisions, and ultimately the structure of the pension plans that will be supportable in a competitive marketplace.

In valuing the entitlements to be received on retirement, a key consideration is how long the individual expects to live. If working one more year yields a 10% increase in the per period benefit, the additional year may be a worthwhile sacrifice for a person with a life expectancy of 25 years, but not for one with an eight-year life expectancy.

Though two factors—indivisibility of labor and declining marginal utility of consumption—are in themselves sufficient to explain why individuals would take periods of leisure in their lives, they do not explain why these periods should be at the end of one's life. This phenomenon is better explained by age's adverse effects on productivity and disutility of work, in conjunction with the important role of uncertainty. The disutility of labor at later ages is something workers cannot predict accurately at an early age. They also learn more about their longevity as they age. This suggests that if the discount rates for the disutility of work and consumption are the same, it is best to work at the beginning of life and to make decisions on when to retire later when more information is available.

10.1.3   Historical Origins of Private Pensions

In 1875, the American Express Company established the first formal private pension. Only permanently disabled workers who were over 60 and had worked at least 25 years in the firm were eligible. As a large holder of railroad companies, American Express employed workers in dangerous jobs. Many of them, once injured, had no means of supporting themselves; guaranteeing workers an income if disabled made them more likely to accept dangerous jobs. By 1905, the railroads had created 12 formal plans covering 488,000 workers, or 35% of all railroad employees. By 1929, over 80% of all railroad workers were covered by some sort of retirement plan (Greenough and King 1976).

Other industries, not all in hazardous fields, also began pension plans, and by 1920 almost 400 existed. Companies began to realize the benevolent and economic consequences of retirement plans. Before long, this mostly discretionary and nonlegally binding form of retirement compensation was seen as a moral obligation of the employer. Corporations welcomed this interpretation, but to become a permanent institution in the private sector, pensions had to produce some tangible economic benefits to the employer. The employee's gold watch represented an investment, not just a gift.

Most significantly, pensions enabled the employer to retire older and incapacitated workers. Previously, employers were forced to adopt such inefficient alternatives as retaining employees on the payroll at reduced pay, reassigning them to less demanding jobs, or offering occasional relief packages to particularly needy retirees. By establishing a formal pension plan, the employer could remove these workers in an orderly and employee-approved fashion without fear of adverse public reaction. When the maximum retirement age was fixed, retirement became ingrained as part of working life. Pensions allowed the employer to retire less productive workers while retaining an air of equity and appreciation for a job well done. Replacement of these older workers with younger, more agile ones would increase labor productivity through the increased efficiency of a younger work force. Pension plans thus became an instrument for fostering the retirement of older workers with a minimum of employee resistance.

While the employers emphasized the reward aspect of a pension for those actually retiring, the emphasis for the active workers was on earning the reward; it encouraged them to give the kind of service that was of greatest value to the company. By basing pensions on continuity of employment, business organizations thought they had found a means not only of preventing strikes but also of promoting long, loyal, and uninterrupted service. Presumably long and continuous service records would mean reduced labor turnover and lower training costs. Thus, pensions not only provided a means of replacing older workers with more efficient younger ones, they made younger employees more reluctant to quit and increased their efficiency; from the employers' standpoint, the economic cost of a pension could be more than offset by the improvement of labor productivity.

Pensions strengthened the worker's allegiance to the firm at the expense of his loyalty to his union. Employers understood the unions' dislike of these plans and became determined to maintain control over pensions. Over 95% of the workers covered by pension plans paid nothing into the scheme. By not requiring worker contributions and making the benefits discretionary, management could bar unions from involvement in retirement policy and set the requirements themselves. As a result, employers gained considerable leverage over employees' work decisions. The effect, it was hoped, would be a reduction in strikes and a weakening of union appeal.[1]

10.1.4 Pensions and Labor Market Performance

Many economic factors contributed to the historical development of pensions. Feldstein (1982, p. 1) identifies the myopia argument for forcing workers to protect themselves for old age when their productivity will be lower. Moreover, since pensions can be a means of backloading compensation, they may be an important factor in rewarding, motivating, and tying workers to firms. By delaying rewards, the firm can better deal with uncertainty that is resolved over time. As information on worker's effort level or productivity accumulates, the firm discovers how much to pay him. Many of the standard adverse selection and moral hazard problems disappear as the time span becomes sufficiently long (assuming that there is no efficiency cost to withholding earlier rewards).

Pensions have considerable advantages as a delayed reward mechanism. In contrast to wages that rise faster than productivity, pensions reallocate resources to a time period to which the individual himself wishes to reallocate resources. There is, of course, a limit on the amount that can be efficiently reallocated to the retirement period. Until this constraint becomes binding, pensions need not entail any efficiency loss. In this respect, they differ from other common means of withholding or backloading rewards, such as wage streams that rise faster than productivity or big prizes in contests (promotion lotteries). The function of pensions as a reward and motivational mechanism is widely cited in relation to retention of workers. But pensions may also come to play a significant role in sorting workers by quality and motivating them.

Many market imperfections may be mitigated through the use of pensions. For example, the firm may be able to invest at a greater rate of return than the worker can, whether because of tax wedges or transactions costs in raising funds. If some funds are left for the firm to invest through pensions, both parties gain. In general, this analysis looks at the benefits that go to the worker and firm together. The predominant prediction is that possible efficiencies will be pursued.

Pensions have a straightforward tax benefit as a form of compensation. They are not taxed at the time they are earned, and returns to these investments are not taxed along the way. In any single instance, it is a complex problem to figure out the precise trade-off between a dollar of pension and a dollar of compensation. But virtually all analyses agree that under current tax provisions it is desirable to use some element of pensions as part of the wage package (see Woodbury 1983).

Why should the government be promoting the use of pensions in this way? In the 1980s, some might say that the problem for our economy is insufficient capital formation. Government favoritism for pensions stretches back to periods when it was thought that insufficient consumption in the economy was the predominant problem. One possible explanation is that pensions tend to protect the government, much as flood insurance and health insurance—both subsidized—protect it. If people reach old age without a visible means of support, the government will be forced to support them.[2]

10.2   Pensions and Retirement

We have argued that pensions serve several functions distinct from their effects on retirement. This suggests that pension plans will remain part of our economy, inevitably affecting retirement, conceivably in an adverse fashion. As we observe pension plans in operation, it may be difficult to determine their intended consequences for retirement, since they serve multiple purposes. Moreover, we may not be able to tell whether their design is optimal. At some junctures, we will discuss the form of optimal pension plans given retirement objectives, stripping away other concerns. We shall also make predictions about the consequences of pensions that have traditional structures on workers' retirement decisions.

Why should pensions be used to affect retirement? A variety of reasons are identified in the models below. They center on problems stemming from an inability to make enforceable contracts. Firms typically do not reduce a worker's wages as he grows older, even though his productivity declines. If productivity could be predicted as a function of age, then in the first-best contract, the worker would agree in advance to retire at a particular age and the firm would offer a level wage over his lifetime. Even in this simplified world, where critical uncertainties about the evolution of productivity have been eliminated, present regulatory structures would make such contracting impossible. Congress recently raised the mandatory retirement age to 70. In March 1983, such "protection" was accorded as well to state and local workers. There is some speculation that prohibitions on mandatory retirement will be further relaxed.

Many firms have discovered that the best way to guard against having to keep low-productivity workers on the payroll is to offer them pension inducements to depart. Such inducements are also in the interest of workers, who would otherwise not be in a position to "promise" to retire.

Pensions play a second major role vis-a-vis retirement by spreading risks in heterogeneous populations. Suppose productivity and earnings were constant, but individuals come to differ over time in their disutility for work. The critical policy issue is how to induce those with low disutility to continue working while providing adequately for those who, say for reasons of ill health, are unable to continue productive endeavors or could do so only at unacceptable cost.

The analysis here focuses on these two concerns: inducing appropriate retirement and spreading risks associated with factors affecting retirement. In past discussion of these issues, much has been made of the question of the actuarial fairness of pension plans. Such fairness is likely to turn out to be a legal issue as well as an economic one. We believe that actuarial fairness is an elusive concept, and we discuss several different potential definitions. No single concept of actuarial fairness does a good job of capturing what we should expect from pension plans across a variety of situations.

10.2.1   The Retirement Decision

As a worker ages, several factors become important in influencing his decision to retire. Savings and pension entitlements grow with work tenure; this raises the level of sustainable consumption during retirement. This increase in consumption is further enhanced by the fact that additional work shortens the retirement period. The disutility from work also rises as the worker ages and his health deteriorates. Eventually, productivity and outside opportunities decline, although real wages may not fall to reflect this fact. Near retirement, workers have a more accurate idea of their life expectancy. They are better able to compare the trade-off between working and retirement. Other issues, such as the presumed improvement in the quality of life and increased longevity from retirement, are also important when making the retirement decision.

The incentives to retire increase with age. The main factors influencing retirement are shown in figure 10.1. Here $\bar{L}(R)$ = disutility of work at age R; $W(R)$ = wage at R; $C_2(R)$ = retirement consumption given retirement at age R; $F(R)$ = productivity at age R.

The individual should continue working until the utility of working plus the higher retirement consumption it affords falls short of the utility of retirement.

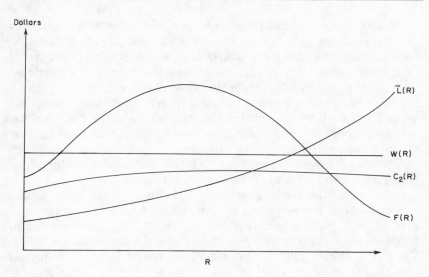

Fig. 10.1

10.2.2   Savings and Appropriate Retirement

The decision to retire is based largely on a worker's postretirement income and his perceived health and life expectancy. Workers with sufficient foresight can save for themselves. Alternatively, their employer can provide forced savings as part of the total compensation package. In the second-best world of labor contracting, it is not always advantageous for workers to have the option of choosing their level of savings. When a worker cannot commit himself to retire at the optimal age, pensions can induce him to retire earlier. By forcing a worker to save too much, pensions offset the externality created by the fact that wages do not fall during an older employee's less productive years.

Firms base wages on the expected productivity of a worker over his lifetime with the firm. The wage schedule is decided in advance and is based on a worker's expected retirement age. Given the schedule, the worker is then free to choose when to retire. But, his actions must be consistent with what the firm expected him to do.

Because wages stay constant over a worker's lifetime, he will not have sufficient incentives to retire when productivity is declining. Laws against mandatory retirement prohibit contractual agreements to retire at a prespecified age, and firms realize that, without a binding commitment, workers will delay their retirement. Accordingly, they reduce lifetime wages to compensate for the period of high wages and low productivity before retirement.

Pensions help solve this problem by providing economic incentives to retire at an earlier age.[3] Pensions put aside higher savings than the worker would choose and make them accessible only on retirement. They provide the counterbalance that speeds up retirement that otherwise would be sub-optimally delayed by wages higher than productivity.

Under any given wage schedule, an employee would be better off if he could select both his savings and his retirement age. But the same wage schedules are then not feasible. Workers who feel that they are being forced to save too much are not attracted by contracts without pensions because the freedom to save is more than offset by the resulting lower wages (due to employer's inability to induce retirement).

We illustrate this use of pensions in a simple model in which workers care only about consumption and leisure. They start with a firm at age Y_0 and stay with the firm until they retire at age R. Wages are constant and equal to expected productivity. A worker of age Y has productivity $F(Y)$. The risk-neutral employer, if he is to attract any workers in a competitive equilibrium, must maximize his workers' expected utilities subject to the zero profit constraint. Initially, we assume that the discount rate is zero for both workers and firms,[4] and that everyone knows his exact life span. The results can be extended to include positive discounting and uncertain life expectancy under the assumption that perfect annuity markets exist.

The worker's period utility is represented by $U(C, L)$,

(1) $\partial U(C, L)/\partial C > 0; \quad \partial^2 U(C, L)/\partial C^2 < 0; \quad \partial U(C, L)/\partial L < 0,$

where C is consumption and L is labor supply. Institutional requirements force the labor supply to be either $\bar{L}$ or 0. The age-productivity profile is assumed first to rise as the worker gains experience and eventually to fall if the worker stays past a sufficiently old age.

It is optimal for consumption levels to be constant, given the labor supply, as there is declining marginal utility from consumption. The worker chooses his consumption while employed, C_1, and his consumption when retired, C_2. Since both wages and consumption (while working) are constant, savings will also be a constant fraction, α, of salary. The retirement decision, R, is constrained by the condition that savings must be sufficient to meet the cost of the expected retirement consumption. Total lifetime utility is given by

(2) $(R - Y_0)U(C_1, \bar{L}) + (T - R)U(C_2, 0)$

Consumption is financed out of earnings and savings. The budget constraint for a worker earning wage W can be separated into two parts, work life and retirement. When working, his consumption is by definition equal to his salary net of savings,

(3) $C_1 = W(1 - \alpha).$

The retirement age and postretirement consumption are jointly determined. Given a desired level of postretirement consumption, a worker retires when his accumulated savings are sufficient to finance his consumption. For a worker who knows that his life span is exactly T years, this implies:

$$(4) \qquad W\alpha(R - Y_0) = (T - R)C_2.$$

A worker's lifetime wage is based on his expected productivity,

$$(5) \qquad W = \left[\int_{Y_0}^{R} F(Y)dY \right] / (R - Y_0).$$

Assuming competitive conditions, a firm knowing a worker's R would offer him the wage defined by (5). If the worker could commit himself to retire at a prespecified time, he would select R to maximize his utility, taking into account the effect on his wages of postponing retirement. (If there were uncertainties to unfold in the future, he would make contingent retirement commitments contingent on his condition.)

Unfortunately, a worker cannot commit himself to retire at a prespecified age. His wages must be determined in advance, and independently from his actual retirement decision. Moreover, if productivity declines later in life, as is commonly the case, wages are likely to exceed productivity. A worker deciding on retirement will equate marginal disutility with wage, whereas efficiency requires that it be equated with productivity. This constellation of factors creates an inefficient situation. Workers, unable to commit themselves in advance to a retirement date, will choose to retire "too late."

The firm meets its zero profit constraint by choosing wages based on when it expects its employees to retire. These assumptions must be consistent with the optimal retirement age given the chosen wages. Given a fixed wage W, a worker chooses C_1 and C_2 to maximize his lifetime utility subject to (3) and (4). The Lagrangian may be written as

$$(6) \qquad \max_{C_1, C_2, \alpha, R} \mathcal{L} = U(C_1, \bar{L})(R - Y_0) + U(C_2, 0)(T - R)$$

$$+ \lambda[W(1 - \alpha) - C_1] + \mu[W\alpha(R - Y_0) - C_2(T - R)].$$

The constrained optimal choice of C_1, C_2, α, and R yields

$$(7) \qquad C_1: \; U_1(C_1, \bar{L})(R - Y_0) - \lambda = 0$$

$$(8) \qquad C_2: \; U_2(C_2, 0)(T - R) - \mu(T - R) = 0$$

$$(9) \qquad \alpha: \; -\lambda W + \mu W(R - Y_0) = 0$$

$$(10) \qquad R: \; [U(C_1, \bar{L}) - U(C_2, 0)] + \mu(W\alpha + C_2) = 0,$$

where $U_1(C, L) = \partial U(C, L)/\partial C$.

The equations may be combined to provide two first-order conditions that are more intuitive:

$$(11) \qquad U_1(C_1, \bar{L}) = U_1(C_2, 0),$$

$$(12) \qquad U_1(C_2, 0) = \frac{U(C_2, 0) - U(C_1, \bar{L})}{W\alpha + C_2}$$

Because there are perfect capital markets, resources will be transferred from the work period to the retirement period until the marginal utilities of consumption are equalized. Working longer brings an extra $W\alpha + C_2$ in savings. This must be balanced by the loss in utility from delaying retirement.

The optimal solution is determined by jointly solving equations (3), (4), (10), (11), and (5); this yields C_1^*, C_2^*, α^*, R^*, and the resulting W. If, at the retirement age, wages are more than productivity, $F(R^*) > W$, then workers will have incentives to work for an inefficiently long time. The firm can partially correct this problem by forcing workers to save more.[5] In theorem 1, forced saving is shown to induce earlier retirement, and this results in higher wages.

Since C_1, C_2, α, and R are all chosen optimally, small changes in their values will not directly affect expected utility. The only way to improve expected utility is to be able to support higher wages,

$$(13) \qquad \frac{dEU}{dW} = \frac{\partial EU}{\partial C_1}\frac{dC_1}{dW} + \frac{\partial EU}{\partial C_2}\frac{dC_2}{dW} +$$

$$\frac{\partial EU}{\partial \alpha}\frac{d\alpha}{dW} + \frac{\partial EU}{\partial R}\frac{dR}{dW} + \frac{\partial EU}{\partial W}$$

$$= \lambda(1 - \alpha) + \mu\alpha(R - Y_0)$$

$$= U_1(C_1, \bar{L})(R - Y_0) > 0.$$

In equilibrium, as determined by equation (5), the wage rate is a function of the retirement age and productivity,

$$(14) \qquad \frac{dW}{dR} = \frac{F(R) - W}{R - Y_0}.$$

Theorem 1: Under the assumption that $F(R) < W$, increasing the savings rate, α, above α^* improves expected utility, $(dEU/d\alpha|\alpha^*) > 0$.

Proof: From the assumptions of the theorem, earlier retirement raises wages, $(dW/dR) < 0$. Higher wages improve expected utility (eq. [13]). Thus, it only needs to be demonstrated that raising α hastens retirement. This part of the proof is longer and more complicated. Differentiating the budget constraints (3) and (4) shows

$$(15) \qquad \frac{dC_1}{d\alpha} - (1 - \alpha)\frac{dW}{d\alpha} + W = 0,$$

(16)

$$\frac{dC_2}{d\alpha}(T - R) - (W\alpha + C_2)\frac{dR}{d\alpha} - \alpha(R - Y_0)\frac{dW}{d\alpha} - W(R - Y_0) = 0.$$

As W is affected by α only through R, we use equation (14) to substitute

(17) $$-\alpha[R - Y_0]\frac{dW}{d\alpha} = \alpha[W - F(R)]\frac{dR}{d\alpha}$$

into equation (16).Collecting terms, rewrite equation (16) as

(16') $$\frac{dR}{d\alpha}[\alpha F(R) + C_2] = \frac{dC_2}{d\alpha}(T - R) - W(R - Y_0).$$

To determine $dC_2/d\alpha$, differentiate equation (12),

(18) $$\frac{dC_2}{d\alpha}[U_{11}(C_2, 0)] = -\frac{[U_1(C_1, \bar{L})\frac{dC_1}{d\alpha} + U_1(C_2, 0)(W + \alpha\frac{dW}{d\alpha})]}{[W\alpha + C_2]}$$

Note from equation (11) that $U_1(C_1, \bar{L}) = U_1(C_2, 0)$. Thus, substitute the value of $dC_1/d\alpha$ from (15) and collect terms,

(19) $$\frac{dC_2}{d\alpha} = \frac{\frac{dW}{d\alpha}}{(W\alpha + C_2)A} = \frac{[F(R) - W]\frac{dR}{d\alpha}}{(R - Y_0)(W\alpha + C_2)A},$$

where $A = -U_{11}(C_2,0)/ U_1(C_2, 0)$ is the measure of absolute risk aversion. It is now possible to sign $dR/d\alpha$ using (16'), (19) and (4),

(20) $$\frac{dR}{d\alpha} = \frac{-W(R - Y_0)}{\alpha F(R) + C_2 + W\alpha[W - F(R)]/[C_2(W\alpha + C_2)A]} < 0.$$

Changes in α affect expected utility only through changes in W. The argument above demonstrates that when savings are "too high," retirement takes place earlier, wages are higher, and workers are better off. Essentially, when choosing α^* and R^*, workers neglect the impact on their wages. This externality is reduced if the firm chooses $\alpha > \alpha^*$; the worker is induced to retire earlier and expected utility increases.

If firms are providing pensions that are larger than workers' desired savings, then why do we observe any private savings taking place? Savings in the form of pensions is not a perfect substitute for other types of savings. In particular, since pensions are accessible only on retirement after the age of 55, they cannot provide capital needed for large purchases (such as a house) or insurance against preretirement events such as illness or unemployment. Some forms of savings outside of pensions—notably investment in home ownership—are encouraged and subsidized by the government. The value of their house, net of mortgage, forms the largest part of most families' savings.

10.2.3   Life Expectancy and Retirement—Who Gains, Who Loses

A major role of pensions is to induce workers to retire. This role will become even more important if the current movement against mandatory retirement succeeds. Pensions may provide economic incentives to retire in two significant ways: (1) pensions provide savings that can be accessed only during retirement; (2) pensions may not be actuarially fair to workers who retire after normal retirement age. The forced savings role of pensions is discussed in the previous section. This section concentrates on the actuarial value of the pension as a function of the retirement date.

Workers in their later years earn wages greater than their productivity and thus have incentives to work after their first-best retirement date. Lazear (in this vol.) argues that it is possible to correct for this externality by reducing the actuarial value of pensions to workers who postpone retirement. Changing the compensation through pensions is a graceful way to lower the "effective" wage (salary plus pension value) and restore incentives to retire early.

A first look at the data seems to confirm this observation (see the appendix). Most defined benefit plans reduce benefits only by 4%–6% for each year of early retirement (before age 65). For workers retiring after 65, pensions are generally not increased (except to take account of extra years of service). If all workers had identically distributed life spans, then, as illustrated in the model below, an actuarially fair benefit reduction for early retirement would be close to 9.5% and benefits would be similarly increased for late retirement.[6] This significantly larger factor reflects the fact that early retirement gives an extra year of benefits now; the costs occur over a discounted and uncertain future and are proportionally less important.

Consider a worker with pension P per year that is reduced (increased) by fraction b for each year of early (late) retirement. Workers know only the probability distribution of their death date. The real discount rate is 3%.[7] No retirement is allowed before age 55. At age 55, a worker's chance of living until age $55 + r$ is $G(r)$. With a uniform distribution of life spans between 55 and 90, $G(r) = 1 - r/35$. The equality defining an actuarially fair adjustment for retirement at age $55 + r - 1$ is

$$(21) \quad [1 - b(r)]P \int_{r-1}^{35} e^{-.03t}(1 - t/35)dt = P \int_{r}^{35} e^{-.03t}(1 - t/35)dt$$

This implies

$$(22) \qquad b(r) \int_{r-1}^{35} e^{-.03t}(35 - t)dt = \int_{r-1}^{35} e^{-.03t}(35 - t)dt.$$

At age 65, $r = 10$ and the appropriate penalty for early retirement is

$$(23) \quad b(r) = [(33.3t - 55.5)e^{-.03t}|_9^{10}]/[(33.3t - 55.5)e^{-.03t}|_9^{35}] \approx .095.$$

Results above suggest that with most penalties smaller than 6% per year of early retirement (and no bonus for late retirement), workers who retire late receive relatively less in pension benefits than those who retire early.

Appearances may be deceiving. When workers have different life spans and know these differences, then the decision about when to retire is highly correlated with age. Workers who know that they have relatively longer life spans work later into their life. The literature of gerontology suggests that workers who retire early have shorter life spans. For example, the work of Haynes et al. (1979) demonstrates that the mortality rate of early retirees is higher than would be expected if no self-selection were occurring.

The fact that pensions do not seem to rise very fast with retirement age may reflect the different life expectancies for the different retiring age groups. Indeed, given the structure and parameters of most defined benefit plans, workers who postpone retirement receive relatively more benefits than those who retire earlier. Otherwise there would be a severe problem of adverse selection. If workers who retire early were given larger benefits to compensate them for their shorter life expectancy, then workers with long life expectancies would also retire early.[8] The pension plan could not afford to pay pensions based on short life expectancies to workers with long life spans who retire early.[9] The model presented below shows that workers who retire early are actuarially penalized in a typical defined benefit pension plan. This may be necessary to give workers with longer life expectancies sufficient incentives to remain in the labor force.

The typical defined benefit pension plan has payments proportional to a function of wages[10] multiplied by years of service with a multiplicative linear penalty for early retirement. A worker entering at age Y_0 and retiring at R receives an annual pension

$$(24) \qquad P(R) = \begin{cases} \tilde{\alpha}F(W)[R - Y_0][1 + (R - \bar{R})\beta], & Y \le \bar{R}, \\ \tilde{\alpha}F(W)[R - Y_0], & Y > \bar{R}. \end{cases}$$

When a firm can choose the fraction of wages, $\tilde{\alpha}$, normal retirement date, $\bar{R}$, and the early retirement penalty, β, then the pension payment for retirement before age $\bar{R}$ can be written as a general quadratic function of R,

$$(25) \qquad\qquad P(R) = A(R^2 + BR + C)$$

where $A = -\tilde{\alpha}F(W)\beta$; $B = [1 - \beta(\bar{R} + Y_0)]/\beta$; $C = Y_0(\bar{R}\beta - 1)/\beta$.

The pension payment for retirement after age R is a linear function of $\bar{R}$ as seen in equation (24). There is some loss in generality when wages are not also a function of retirement age and seniority. However, at least for pattern plans, $F(W)$ is a constant and this effect is unimportant. At present, we are concerned with demonstrating the effect of life span on retirement decisions and the actuarial value of pensions, and hence assume that wages and productivity are constant over the life span. Wages are not affected by the retirement date. The discount rate is zero and conditional on the labor supply, the marginal utility of consumption is constant. Thus, retirement decisions will be based solely on expected longevity.

A worker who knows that his life span will be exactly T years and who faces a pension schedule, $P(R)$, chooses his retirement age R to maximize his expected lifetime utility.

$$(26) \qquad EU = U[(1 - \alpha)W, \overline{L}](R - Y_0) + U[P(R), 0](T - R).$$

The first-order condition determining the optimal retirement date is

$$(27) \quad P'(R)(T - R)U_1[P(R), 0] = U[P(R), 0] - U[(1 - \alpha)W, \overline{L}].$$

For retirement prior to age $\overline{R}$ this equation can be solved explicitly for R as a function of T under the earlier assumption of a quadratic pension plan and constant marginal utility of consumption,

$$(28) \qquad (2AR + AB)(T - R)U_1(0, 0) = A(R^2 + BR + C)U_1(0, 0)$$
$$- (1 - \alpha)WU_1(0, \overline{L}) + U(0, 0) - U(0, \overline{L}).$$

Let γ equal the ratio of the marginal utility of consumption when retired to when employed, $\gamma = U_1(0, 0)/U_1(0, \overline{L})$. Define $\tilde{L}$ as the disutility from work measured in wage units, $[U(0, 0) - U(0, \overline{L})]/U_1(0, 0)$. Then, (28) can be reduced to

$$(29)$$
$$R(T) = \frac{1}{3}\left(T - B + \sqrt{T^2 + B^2 + TB - 3\{C + [\tilde{L} - (1 - \alpha)W\gamma]/A\}}\right)$$

For retirement after age $\overline{R}$, pension benefits rise linearly with age. The optimal retirement date as a function of life span is

$$(30) \qquad R(T) = \frac{1}{2}\{T + Y_0 + [(1 - \alpha)\gamma - \tilde{L}]/[\tilde{\alpha}F(W)]\}.$$

Usually, there will be some overlap among these solutions; during this period all workers choose to retire at age $\overline{R}$. A small difference in the marginal incentives for retirement before versus after $\overline{R}$ may induce a large segment of the work force to retire at $\overline{R}$.

To illustrate an example of the optimal retirement decisions, let pension benefits be 1.5% of net wages for each year of service with a 5% reduction for each year of early retirement before age 65: $\tilde{\alpha} = .015$, $\beta = .05$, $F(W) = (1 - \alpha)W$, and $\overline{R} = 65$. The disutility from work is $.57W$. Saving 14% of wages balances the budget when population life spans are triangularly distributed between ages 59 and 88. The solution to the optimal retirement decision is graphed below in figure 10.2.

Who wins and who loses? The value of a pension to a worker with life span T is

$$(31) \qquad V(T) = P[R(T)][T - R(T)] - \alpha W[R(T) - Y_0].$$

Living longer changes this value by

$$(32) \qquad V'(T) = P[RC(T)] - R'(T)(W - \tilde{L}),$$

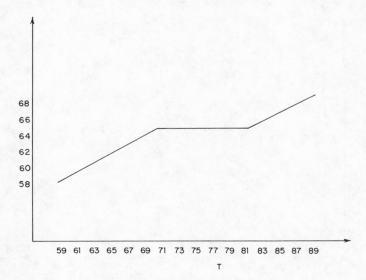

Fig. 10.2   Retirement age as a function of life span.

where $P'(R)$ was substituted in from equation (27). Workers who live longer have greater pension benefits provided that their replacement ratio, P/W, exceeds their incremental time in the labor force, R', times the net dollar value of working, $1 - \tilde{L}/W$. In the example presented above, pension value strictly increases with life span (and hence retirement age) as illustrated in figure 10.3.

10.3   Optimal Pensions with Heterogeneous Populations

What are the consequences of offering a single pension plan to a heterogeneous population? Models in various areas, ranging from insurance markets to health coverage to labor contracting, have shown that important problems arise when a single policy is applied to a heterogeneous population. Pensions in some sense combine elements of all of these models.

Heterogeneity would pose no difficulty if it could be readily diagnosed and if different policies could be offered to workers with different characteristics. Such screening is impossible in practice for a variety of reasons. The differences among workers may be imperceptible to the employer. Moreover, the pension contract is generally drawn up long before many of the differentiating characteristics manifest themselves to anyone, including the worker. It would be a violation of the earlier contract to exclude any worker from a pension option.[11] Legal restrictions and general labor practices make it exceedingly difficult to afford different treatment to workers who, despite differences in some present characteristics, have the same employment histories. Unless pensions are negotiated through col-

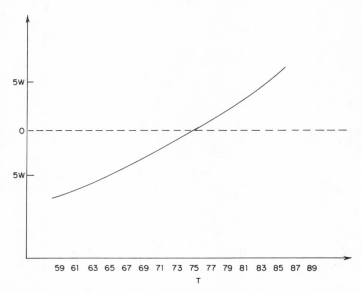

Fig. 10.3   Net actuarial value as a function of death date.

lective bargaining, corporations are prohibited from offering different pensions to different classes of workers. Thus, a corporation is not permitted to have different pension plans for white-collar and blue-collar workers.

10.3.1   The Order of Retirement

The decision to retire is determined by many factors; the following models focus on the role of life expectancy and disutility from work. All other things equal, workers who live longer or who enjoy work more will choose to retire later. This result is true for any pension plan whose annual payments do not decrease with retirement age.

Consider workers of type $i = (A,B)$ who enter the labor force at age Y_i and retire at age R_i with pension $P(R_i)$ and life expectancy T_i. Utility when employed is $U(C_i, i)$ and when retired is $U[P(R_i),0]$. Assume that it is optimal for A to retire before $B, R_A < R_B$. Because A retires earlier, his annual pension payment is smaller, $P(R_A) < P(R_B)$.

Theorem 2: Under the assumptions stated above, worker B, who retires later, must have either a longer life expectancy, a greater utility when employed, or both.

Proof: The fact that each worker prefers his retirement date implies

$$
(33) \qquad
\begin{aligned}
&U[P(R_A), 0](T_A - R_A) + U(C_A, A)(R_A - Y_A) \\
&\geq U[P(R_B), 0](T_A - R_B) + U(C_A, A)(R_B - Y_A),
\end{aligned}
$$

(34)
$$U[P(R_B), 0](T_B - R_B) + U(C_B, B)(R_B - Y_B)$$
$$\geq U[P(R_B), 0](T_B - R_A) + U(C_B, B)(R_A - Y_B).$$

Adding these inequalities together yields

(35)
$$(R_A - R_B)[U(C_B, B) - U(C_A, A)]$$
$$\geq \{U[P(R_B), 0] - U[P(R_A), 0]\}(T_A - T_B).$$

Any contradiction to the theorem would require the worker who retires earlier to have both a longer expected life span and greater utility from work, $T_A > T_B$ and $U(C_A, A) > U(C_B, B)$. However, this must violate equation (35).

10.3.2   The Costs of Postponing Retirement under Optimal Pensions

If two groups differ in terms of either length of life or utility from work, one group will always retire before the other. This no-switching property results more generally when the indifference curves of different groups have a single crossing point (SCP).[12] This seems to be an especially reasonable assumption in the context of retirement decisions. We further assume that all workers have the same utility function when retired. There is neither reemployment nor outside income once retired. Moreover, given that retirement is preferable to working, the schedule of annual pension payments must be increasing with age, otherwise workers would retire earlier. The higher annual pension payments to workers who retire later imply that they have a lower marginal utility of consumption.

Here we shall seek the optimal pension scheme; it is the benefit schedule that maximizes the sum of the individuals' utilities subject to a budget constraint. A salient feature of the optimal pension schedule is that it is actuarially unfavorable for a specified individual to retire later. The logic supporting this result parallels that in the optimal taxation literature: it is desirable to tax those with lower marginal utilities of income (penalize late retirees in this instance) to redistribute income to those with higher marginal utility of income (early retirees). At least initially, efficiency loss associated with inappropriately influencing work or retirement are outweighed by the utility gains from the income transfer. This result is formalized in theorem 3.

Theorem 3: The SCP property is sufficient to imply that with the optimal pension scheme, the value of pensions plus wages net of productivity must be actuarially larger for a worker who chooses to retire earlier; that is, any particular worker who retires earlier will receive pensions plus total wages (net of productivity) with a higher actuarial value.

Comment: It is still possible that the type of workers who choose to retire earlier may be the ones with lower pensions; indeed, as seen in section 10.2.3, current pension plans actuarially favor later retirees. Thus, in the subsequent discussion it is important to distinguish between the differences in the actuarial value of a particular worker's pension based on his decision when to retire (individual fairness) and the differences between the actuarial value of a pension for different types of workers (cohort fairness). It is also important to maintain the assumption that reemployment once retired is not permitted; otherwise, workers would retire if their pension value began to decline and then seek reemployment.

Proof: In the proof, we take productivity and wages as given; pensions are adjusted to achieve the result. The firm offers the worker a choice between various retirement dates and their associated pension benefit, $[R, P(R)]$. The first part of the proof demonstrates that each worker must be indifferent between his retirement date and the one preceding his. Given indifference, earlier retirement is shown to cost the firm more. Intuitively the optimal pension scheme will distribute the largest feasible benefits to workers retiring early since they receive the lowest payment and thus have the highest marginal utility of income. Because early retirees' pensions are maximized, late retirees will be pushed to the point of indifference between their chosen retirement date and retiring earlier. However, if the late retirement benefit had a higher actuarial value, the pension plan could improve welfare by eliminating the expensive option; the late retiree is indifferent to retiring earlier so that his utility is the same but the total cost to the firm is smaller.

Consider the first worker to retire who strictly prefers his retirement date to the one preceding his. This is the case with worker C illustrated in figure 10.4. Lower his pension and raise the benefits for worker B. Since C strictly preferred retiring at R_C rather than R_B, it is possible to raise $P(R_B)$ and lower $P(R_C)$ without inducing C to retire earlier. Raising $P(R_B)$ does not result in A's retiring later because A must strictly prefer retiring at R_A to R_B. This strict preference follows from the single crossing property and the fact that B is indifferent between retiring at R_A and R_B (as C was the first worker to strictly prefer his retirement date over the preceding one). By transferring money from worker C to B, social welfare is improved; worker B has a smaller pension and thus a higher marginal utility of income. An optimal pension scheme must make workers indifferent between their retirement date and the preceding retirement date.

Since workers are indifferent between their chosen retirement date and the preceding one, it directly follows that the later (and chosen) retirement date must have a lower total cost to the firm. If not, simply eliminate the later retirement date. The worker then takes the earlier retirement; he is indifferent. His utility remains constant, but the total cost to the pension fund is smaller. The excess profits can be redistributed to make everyone better off.

This result holds for a broad range of problems. Workers may have varying life spans, differing disutilities from work, and unequal productivities. However, in all these problems the marginal utility of income is a

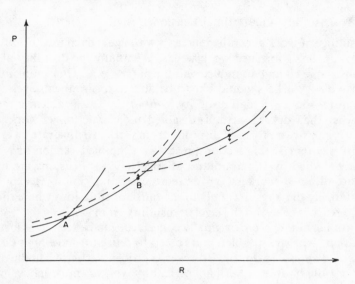

Fig. 10.4

decreasing function of retirement age; workers who retire later receive larger pension payments and thus have smaller marginal utilities of income. The theorem would be reversed if the marginal utility of income rose as a function of retirement age; then, the value of pension payments plus wages net of productivity would be more than actuarially fair for workers who delayed their retirement. This situation might occur if the primary difference among individuals is outside income. If those who retire early are the ones with high outside income and thus low marginal utility of income, then the optimal pension scheme (plus wages net of productivity) must be actuarially advantageous to a worker who chooses to retire later. Theorem 3 has a simple generalization.

Theorem 3': The SCP property is sufficient to imply that with the optimal pension scheme, the value of pensions plus wages net of productivity must be actuarially larger for a worker who chooses to retire earlier (later) if marginal utility of consumption decreases (increases) with retirement age.

The proof for theorem 3' needs only one small modification to incorporate the generalization that the marginal utility of consumption may increase with retirement age. In this case, workers will all be indifferent between their retirement date and the following one. The earlier retirement date cannot be more expensive as otherwise it will be eliminated.

An illustration of theorem 3, that is, when marginal utility of income declines with retirement age, is presented in the following section.

10.3.3   Disutility and Optimal Pension Design

Disutility of work generally increases with age. Given institutional constraints against shortened work weeks, eventually the disutility of labor becomes large enough to induce retirement (see, e.g., Hausman and Wise in this vol.). Workers would like to be able to insure themselves against prematurely having a high disutility from work. This problem is most severe when the worker is actually disabled and can no longer work. A disability is an extreme form of disutility from work. To illustrate an application of theorem 3, this section presents a simplified version of a model initially studied by Diamond and Mirrlees (1978). Pensions are used to support disabled workers, an extreme case that simplifies exposition. Qualitatively these results apply to the range of situations where the decision to retire is based on the level of disutility from work.

Pensions, as they were originally conceived, can be viewed as insurance to workers who are disabled and forced to retire (or have high disutility and would choose to do so). However, a problem arises when the disability is not observable or verifiable. Healthy workers must have sufficient incentives to continue working. Consequently, less insurance is provided than in the first-best solution when the disability is observable. Insurance can still be provided to workers who can prove that they are disabled— witness the separate provisions for early retirement with certain restricted and verifiable disabilities.

To highlight the insurance feature of pensions, let the disability affect neither the utility of consumption nor the worker's life expectancy.[13] There may be some exogenous utility loss but, effectively, the disability simply forces the worker to retire. It is easiest to imagine that the disutility from labor is initially zero and becomes infinite if the worker remains in the labor force after he is disabled.

In a first-best contract, pensions are conditional on the worker becoming disabled and there is no problem of adverse selection. Disabilities occur stochastically. Pensions should be constant, independent of the retirement date. This is demonstrated below.

Let utility from income Y be $U(Y)$, whether working or not. The discount rate is zero. The disability takes place at age R with probability distribution $h(R)$ and is verifiable. Workers all have a life expectancy of exactly T years. The savings and contributions to pensions have previously taken place; there is a fixed amount of savings, S, available to fund the pension scheme (and no other private savings are allowed). While working, employees are given their constant marginal product, W. The optimal pension payment, $P^*(R)$, is constant and independent of the retirement date. There is, however, a maximum retirement date, $\hat{R}$. Even workers who are healthy should retire by $\hat{R}$ in order to receive some benefit from the pension savings. A worker's utility is maximized subject to the constraint that the expected pension payout equal the pension savings,

$$\frac{Max}{\hat{R}, P(R)} \; \mathcal{L} = \int_{Y_0}^{\hat{R}} \{U(W)(R - Y_0) + U[P(R)](T - R)\}h(R)dR$$

(36)
$$+ \{U(W)(\hat{R} - Y_0) + U[P(\hat{R})](T - \hat{R})\}[1 - H(\hat{R})]$$

$$+ \lambda \left\{ S - \int_{Y_0}^{\hat{R}} P(R)(T - R)h(R)dR - P(\hat{R})(T - \hat{R})[1 - H(\hat{R})] \right\}$$

The first-order conditions are

(37)
$$U'[P(R)](T - R)h(R) - \lambda(T - R)h(R) = 0$$
$$\rightarrow \quad U'[P(R)] = \lambda,$$

(38) $\{U(W) - U[P(\hat{R})]\}[1 - H(\hat{R})] + \lambda P(\hat{R})[1 - H(\hat{R})] = 0.$

Together they imply that the pension is constant and

(39) $U[P(\hat{R})] - U(W) = U'[P(\hat{R})]P(\hat{R}).$

Depending on the level of savings, S, there are three possible solutions to the first-order conditions. The maximum retirement date is chosen to make the constant pension, $P(\hat{R})$, affordable. If this is possible, the level of pensions does not depend on the amount of pension savings. As the savings become larger, the maximum retirement date is simply shifted forward. It is conceivable that the savings are sufficiently small that $P(\hat{R})$ is never affordable; then, there is no maximum retirement date ($\hat{R} = T$) and the pension payments are just large enough to exhaust the budget, $P = S/(T - \bar{R})$ where $\bar{R}$ is the expectation of the disability date. At the other less realistic extreme, when savings are larger than needed to finance $P(\hat{R})$, everyone retires immediately and the savings are equally distributed, $P = S/(T - Y_0)$.

It is impossible to provide the same constant pension scheme when disabilities are not verifiable. All workers would choose to retire at the earliest possible age. The problem is then to give high pensions to workers who are disabled at a young age without inducing other healthy workers to retire. The optimal second-best solution is obtained when the feasible pension for the youngest disabled worker is maximized. As seen in the first-best solution, the ideal pension is equal for all workers. When pension payments are unequal, welfare can be improved by transferring pension wealth from workers who receive high payments to workers who receive lower payments. The problem of adverse selection results in workers who are disabled young receiving the lowest pension. To the extent that it is feasible (in terms of both the budget constraint and the self-selection constraint) to raise the payments to young disabled workers, welfare is improved.

In the constrained optimal solution, a healthy worker must be indifferent between retiring and working (as proven in Diamond and Mirrlees [1978]). This holds if pension benefits satisfy the relationship,

(40) $U(W) - U[P(R)] + U'[P(R)]P'(R)(T - R) = 0.$

This differential equation determines the minimum increase in pensions with retirement age necessary to prevent healthy workers from pretending that they are disabled. Under this formulation, a worker's retirement age is a matter of indifference, and a worker is assumed to continue working until he becomes disabled. Because of the indifference to retirement date, utility at the time of retirement when disabled is identical to the utility at the minimum retirement date,[14] R_0, with pension $P(R_0)$,

$$
(41) \quad
\begin{aligned}
& U(W)(R - Y_0) + U[P(R)](T - R) \\
&\equiv U(W)(R_0 - Y_0) + U[P(R_0)](T - R_0).
\end{aligned}
$$

Since the utility is identical for all workers, expected utility is also equal to this representative utility. As can be seen from equation (41), expected utility increases with $P(R_0)$.

The pension payments are chosen to rise just fast enough to keep workers from retiring until they are disabled. There is also a maximum retirement age, R^*. Because pensions are constant from R^* onward, at age R^*, all remaining workers will choose to retire, disabled or not. The budget constraint requires that the cost of the pensions, $B[P(R_0),R^*]$, must equal the pension savings, S, where

$$
(42) \quad
\begin{aligned}
B[P(R_0), R^*] = {}& H(R_0)P(R_0)(T - R_0) \\
& + \int_{R_0}^{R^*} P(R)(T - R)h(R)dR \\
& + [1 - H(R^*)]P(R^*)(T - R^*).
\end{aligned}
$$

The choice of R^* leads to an R_0, which in turn determines expected utility. Recall that $P(R)$ is determined by the initial conditions and equation (40).

$$
(43) \quad
P(R) =
\begin{cases}
P(R_0) + \int_{R_0}^{R} \{U[P(x)] - U(W)\}/\{U'[P(x)](T - x)\}dx, \\
\qquad\qquad R_0 \le R \le R^* \\
P(R^*) \qquad\qquad R > R^*
\end{cases}
$$

Increasing $P(R_0)$ raises $P(R)$ for R between R_0 and R^*. Hence, the cost of an increase in $P(R_0)$ is unambiguously positive.

$$
(44) \quad \partial B[P(R_0), R^*]/\partial P(R_0) > 0.
$$

It is possible to increase $P(R_0)$ and satisfy the budget constraint only so long as $\partial B[P(R_0), R^*]/\partial R^* < 0$, where

$$
(45) \quad \frac{\partial B[P(R_0), R^*]}{\partial R^*} = [1 - H(R^*)][P'(R^*)(T - R^*) - P(R^*)]
$$

$$
(46) \quad = \frac{[1 - H(R^*)]\{U[P(R^*)] - U(W) - P(R^*)U'[P(R^*)]\}}{U'[P(R^*)]} .
$$

To maximize $P(R_0)$, the optimal choice of R^* occurs at the unique solution[15] to $\partial B/\partial R^* = 0$,

$$(47) \qquad U[P(R^*)] - U(W) - P(R^*)U'[P(R^*)] = 0.$$

Because pensions rise with retirement age, workers receive less than perfect insurance. Workers who are disabled later benefit at the expense of those who must retire early. On the other hand, theorem 3 still applies; pensions rise more slowly than is actuarially fair.

Right at the maximum retirement age, R^*, there is no longer any adverse selection and pensions rise exactly at the actuarially fair rate. From equation (46), $P'(R^*) = P(R^*)/(T - R^*)$. A comparison of second derivatives[16] shows that the actuarially fair curve is steeper than $P(R)$ for retirement before R^*. Second-best pensions must be as illustrated in figure 10.5.

As an example of the second-best solution, consider workers who arrive at age 60 each with 60 units of pension savings. Life span is known to be exactly 20 years. The probability of disability is uniform between ages 60 and 80. While the individual works, his wages are 2. Utility is logarithmic and there is no disutility from work until disabled. The first-best pension plan (when disabilities are verifiable) offers an annual benefit of 5.4 to disabled workers and permits everyone to retire after 13.67 years. When disabilities are unobservable, the constrained optimal pension offers an annual benefit of 3.3 for retirement at age 60 and rises exponentially to a maximal payment of 5.4 for retirement at age 70. Between ages 60 and 70, only disabled workers retire; at age 70, all remaining workers retire.

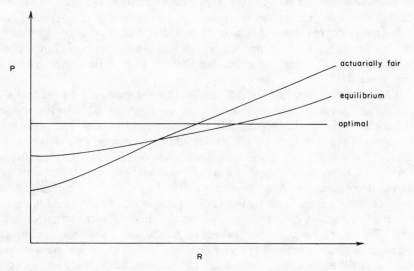

Fig. 10.5   Pensions as a function of retirement age.

The problem becomes more complicated if, as might be expected, dis-utility (perhaps due to illness) is negatively correlated with life expectancy. The expected cost of offering a pension plan will be greater than in the case where retirement decisions and life expectancy are unrelated. This phenomenon is referred to as adverse correlation. The effect of adverse correlation may be of actuarial advantage to late-retiring cohorts.

An interesting area of speculation concerns the role played by the distri-bution of disability dates. In an optimal plan, the relative rewards to indi-viduals retiring at ages 65 and 70 may depend on the sizes of those two groups. Yet the sizes of the two groups could hardly have anything to do with actuarial fairness. Workers who are disabled early may have relative-ly lower pensions to counter the problem of adverse selection. If these ear-ly retirees received an actuarially fair pension, large numbers of relatively healthy workers might prefer early retirement, an outcome which is not feasible. The distortion away from the first-best solution is greater for young retirees than for old retirees; favorable early retirement options create moral hazard problems for a relatively large number of workers while favorable late retirement options have little adverse effect on work-ers who had to retire early.

10.4 Merged Pensions and Strict Pareto Inferiority

A major theme of informational economics is that inefficiencies are generated when individuals with differing characteristics are treated alike. The equal treatment may result from a regulatory requirement or an in-ability to distinguish between workers' characteristics. Despite the overall inefficiency, one group usually benefits at the expense of the other. High-risk drivers benefit when they are lumped in the pool with low-risk driv-ers. Under ERISA, all companies are charged the same premium for in-surance; this helps the poorly funded pension plan at the expense of the well funded.

The effects of pooling are of considerable importance in retirement plans. The government is becoming increasingly involved in legislation in this area. Raising the permissible mandatory retirement age creates a problem of separating populations that did not previously need to be sep-arated. Presently, there is serious discussion about eliminating all manda-tory retirement ages. Legislation that requires pensions to be constant across a firm becomes more significant with the growth of conglomerates. When two disparate firms merge, there is a tendency to integrate towards the more generous pension plan, in part because of contractual obliga-tion. The issue is perhaps most salient with regard to discussion of altering pension programs, which at present frequently differ by sex.[17] As workers have very different needs, desires, and life expectancies, there is no single neat solution to the social security problem. There will be an inevitable tug-of-war between the white-collar workers who want to work into their later years and the blue-collar workers who want to retire as soon as possible. Interestingly, both groups might be better off if each were able to have a plan of its own.

What is the cost of combining two pension plans? This question cannot be answered in general, for it depends on how the workers vary. To simplify, consider a company with two groups of workers, A and B. One Pareto optimal outcome will have the preferred pension for group A; call it $P^*(A)$, and likewise for B and $P^*(B)$. The constraint is that each of these contracts must be chosen from among those that break even. Assume for further simplification that there is no variability within groups.

There is no loss in combining the plans if the A's prefer $P^*(A)$ to $P^*(B)$ and the B's prefer $P^*(B)$. Our experience with insurance models suggests that this may not be the case. If, as U.S. law requires, the two groups are merged under a common pension offering both plans, the A's might choose $P^*(B)$. This leads to a problem since $P^*(B)$ is not achievable when used by both A and B type workers. The general solution under such circumstances is to alter $P^*(B)$, making it less attractive to the A's until they just choose their own plan (see Nichols and Zeckhauser 1982). At the same time, the plan for the A's need not be self-supporting; there can be a cross-subsidy to the plan intended to attract the A's. If so, we may get a pair made up of a somewhat distorted $P^*(B)$ that makes money and a subsidized $P^*(A)$.[18]

The pension problem is considerably more complex than the standard area of application of information economics. It leads to qualitatively new phenomena. It is quite possible that the optimal plan for A's in isolation will be chosen by the B's and that the preferred plan for the B's in isolation will be chosen by A's. If so, both groups may suffer losses from the merger of their pension funds. This is demonstrated below.

Two companies with different type of employees have each worked out their own optimal pension plan. All contributions have already been made and the per capita funds in the two plans are equal at 3/2 per worker. There are two periods remaining. The employees of the two firms have the common expected utility function

(48) $$EU = U(C_1) + p_s U(C_2) - D^i(L),$$

where C_i = consumption in periods i, $i = (1, 2)$, p_s = the probability of survival in the second period, L = the first-period labor supply, either 0 if retired or 1 if working, $D^i(L)$ = the disutility of work, $D^i(0) = 0$, $i = (1, 2)$. The functional form of the utility function is the same for all employees. It is concave, hence risk averse, and is illustrated in figure 10.6.

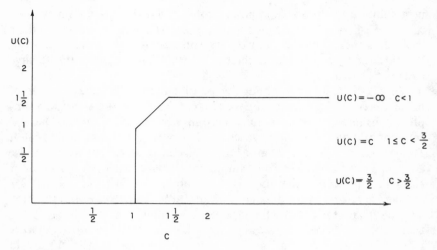

Fig. 10.6

$$U(C) = -\infty, \; C < 1,$$

(49)
$$U(C) = C, \;\; 1 \le C < \frac{3}{2}$$

$$U(C) = \frac{3}{2} \, C > \frac{3}{2} \; .$$

The employees of company A have the following characteristics

(50)
$$p_s = \frac{1}{2} \; ; D^A(1) = 3/5; \;\; \textit{marginal product} = 0.$$

Since their marginal product is zero, it is optimal for them to retire immediately. With their accumulated pension savings of $1\frac{1}{2}$ units per capita, the optimal plan yields

(51)
$$C_1^A = 1; \;\; C_2^A = 1$$

(52)
$$EU^A = U(1) + \frac{1}{2} \, U(1) - D(0) = 1\frac{1}{2} \; .$$

Note that this is also actuarially feasible, since the expected total pension $= C_1^A + p_s C_2^A = 1\frac{1}{2}$, which is the original accumulated pension savings.

The employees of company B have the characteristics

(53) $$p_s = 1; \;\; D^B(1) = 5/4; \;\; \textit{marginal product} = 3/2.$$

Here, the optimal strategy for a B employee is to work in the first period, retire in the second. He receives

(54)
$$C_1^B = 3/2; \;\; C_2^B = 3/2$$

(55) $$EU^B = U(3/2) + U(3/2) - D^B(1) = 1\frac{3}{4}.$$

This consumption pattern is also actuarially supportable, since expected total consumption $= C_1^B + p_s C_2^B = 3 =$ total pension savings + marginal product.

Now assume that the two pension plans are merged. Who will benefit and who will lose? First, notice that if offered the opportunity, any A would prefer B's pension plan to his own. That is, he would work in the first period if by doing so he could earn a consumption stream of 3/2, 3/2. This yields

(56) $$EU^A = U(3/2) + \frac{1}{2} U(3/2) - D^A(1) = 1\frac{13}{20}.$$

And, somewhat surprisingly, B would prefer A's plan. B would retire in the first period with a consumption stream of 1,1.

(57) $$EU^B = U(1) + U(1) = 2.$$

The comparisons are as follows:

	Expected Utility	
	A	B
A's plan	$1\frac{1}{2}$	2
B's plan	$1\frac{13}{20}$	$1\frac{3}{4}$

This paradoxical situation arises only when A's pension program is not supportable if B's comprise the population, and B's is not supportable if A's comprise the population. The difficulty is that any program that gets the productive B's to work will also induce the nonproductive A's to work; if the low life expectancy A's retire, the B's will also retire.

The choice for the merged pension plan is to have both groups retire or to have both groups work in the first period. Given this constraint, there exists no pension plan that breaks even and offers either group a situation as favorable as the one with which it started.

Let there be equal numbers of A's and B's, normalized to one for each group. Assume that both retire early. There is a total of three units of pension savings. Given that $U(C) = -\infty$ for $C < 1$, we must have $C_1 = C_2 = 1$. But this consumption program will take 1½ units of consumption for A and 2 for B. It is infeasible. Any plan that induces both individuals to retire in the first period must offer each of them a lower expected utility than he had with his initial plan.

Consider now plans that induce both A and B to work for one period. The total resources available will be 3 of pension savings plus 1½ from B's production, which equals 4½. The first-best outcome for B is to receive a consumption stream of 3/2, 3/2, since additional consumption offers no utility. But this consumption stream is not supportable for the combined groups, because A would require 3/2 in the first period and his probability of survival, 1/2, times 3/2 in the second, totaling 2¼. Adding to B's requirement of 3, the required resources are 5¼, but only 4½ is available.

The best supportable consumption stream for A is 3/2, 1. (Both A and B get 3/2 in the first period. A gets an expectation of 1/2 in the second period while B gets 1). But since A's disutility of work is 3/5, he too must lose from a merged pension plan where both work.

The conclusion is that all pension plans for the merged group leave both parties strictly worse off than they were in isolation. This demonstration was facilitated by having a utility function with vertical and horizontal segments, but the possibility for a counterexample is general and could be created for a utility function with continuous curvature.

A policy conclusion emerges from this demonstration. Considerations of risk spreading and equity have been used as arguments for homogenizing pension programs across different types of workers and firms. Sometimes the restrictions are specific: the pension plans must be the same. Other times regulatory impositions, such as some of those associated with ERISA, encourage conformity. This example shows that it is important to ask whether the imposition of "equal treatment" in retirement programs may hurt many or most if not all.[19]

10.5 Conclusions

Labor markets are quite different from the markets studied in introductory textbooks. The products sold are heterogeneous, substantial uncertainties are compounded by asymmetric information flow, and interdependencies in "sales" may extend across several periods because of such matters as training and proprietary information. Given such complexities, secure contracting possibilities and flexible reward schedules (i.e., prices that depend on outcome,) would be particularly desirable. However, rules and standards against indenturing limit possibilities in the first area. The second is constrained by a variety of institutions that limit wage flexibility, and by quite considerable risk aversion on the part of sellers in the market (i.e., the workers).

Pensions are a powerful instrument for compensating labor. They may be able to facilitate labor market operations. They offer several significant advantages: awarded late in life, pensions can be based on extensive performance; they are granted in periods to which workers might wish to reallocate resources on their own; and they offer many degrees of freedom in a reward structure that can depend on such factors as salary, age, and years of service.

The purpose of this analysis was to provide a framework for examining the effects of pensions on retirement decisions. At least since the 1920s, the advantages of pensions as a mechanism for securing the retirement of workers whose productivity is falling have been understood and applied. This feature is likely to become more important with the passage of time for at least three reasons: (1) individuals are living longer; (2) as the workplace becomes more technologically sophisticated, the dangers of technological obsolescence of older workers become more pronounced; and (3) both overtly, as through legislation, and implicitly, society is increasing its "protection" of workers who might not choose to retire. The recent congressional decision to raise the mandatory retirement age of private sector workers to 70 has now been extended to state and local government employees. Age discrimination suits associated with layoffs and dismissals have become relatively commonplace. There is talk, indeed, about abolishing mandatory retirement provisions altogether.

We have begun by focusing on the factors that induce individuals to retire. The first model incorporates the qualitative features of most defined benefit pension plans in the United States and inquires how such plans can be employed to induce optimal retirement decisions. Pensions are viewed as a form of forced saving whose purpose is to enable the worker to "commit himself" by making it in his own self-interest to retire at an appropriate age.

The remaining models examine the use of pensions in populations that are heterogeneous with respect to such features as disutility of work or expected life span. Given heterogeneity, a major policy concern is whether pensions are actuarially fair to different groups, retirement cohorts, and so on. An optimal pension plan cannot be actuarially "more than fair," in the sense that someone who retires later must impose a smaller cost on the pension pool than he would if he retired earlier. However, people who retire later are likely on average to live longer. Under most common pension plans, late retirees impose a greater cost on the pension fund than those retiring earlier.

In a first-best world, a separate pension plan would be designed for each group of workers. (Conceivably there would be lump-sum transfers among plans. They need only break even as a whole.) However, government-mandated retirement programs, legislation regulating private pension programs, and the forced common form of pension programs within single firms are powerful forces for homogenization. Such homogenization is shown to work to the possible detriment of workers as a whole.

Pensions are a workhorse compensation mechanism, meeting a variety of objectives in labor market operations and dealing with a range of imperfections and contracting difficulties. This analysis has focused on the ideal use of pensions to facilitate appropriate retirement decisions. The challenge both for conceptual work and for policy is to design pensions that blend the objectives of attracting, sorting, motivating, and retaining workers with the need to induce reasonable retirement choices.

Appendix
Pension Benefits and Retirement Age

A survey of noncontributory pension plans from 75 United States companies revealed several patterns about the general structure of private pensions in this country. These companies, which had businesses ranging from communications and insurance to manufacturing and mining, all had prescribed minimum requirements at least for the age of retirement and often for the years of service as well. Benefits were calculated on a monthly basis in each case, the most common formulas multiplying the years of service by a set dollar figure or by a percentage of salary. While most companies utilized the standard retirement age of 65 as the minimum requirement, several allowed retirement at 62 or even 60. Often the workers were given an option of retiring, for instance, at 65 with 10 years of service or at 60 with 30 years of service. It thus becomes difficult to classify the retirement ages encouraged by pensions.

The benefit formulas ranged from the exceedingly simple to the bewilderingly complex. Many companies offer the employees the option of choosing among several formulas that take into account, among other things, years of service, average monthly pay over the last five years, and future social security benefits. Others simply multiplied the years of service the worker had put in with the firm times a set dollar amount. Most of them, whether simple or complex, incorporate either a set dollar amount or a percentage of salary, multiplied times the years of service. A typical plan might offer the worker a monthly benefit of his years of service multiplied times either $15 or 1.5% of final monthly earnings. Extra percentages were offered by a few companies to workers with 30 or more years of service. The number of variables in the benefits formula make it difficult to directly compare benefit payments across companies.

All of the pension plans incorporate an early retirement option that allows the workers to retire before the prescribed minimum age, while imposing a penalty if they want payment before they reach the normal retirement age. These penalties usually deduct a set percentage of the pension for each year that the employee retired early. Many companies take into account other factors such as years of service; the early retirement penalty thus varies across workers. Forty-six of the companies surveyed utilized a uniform percentage reduction system. These penalties ranged from 3% to 7% for every year under the prescribed age; most were between 4% and 5%. If an employee retired at age 60 when the minimum retirement age was 65 and a 5% per year penalty was imposed, that worker would receive 75% of the benefit he would normally receive. In a few cases, the penalties are scaled down when early retirement occurs within three years of the normal retirement age.

Notes

1. The union attempted to counter these employer-sponsored plans by instituting independent pension plans of their own. While the firms concentrated on providing future old age benefits, the unions initially offered only general benefit programs; immediate benefits for sickness, disability, death, and strikes appealed more to the younger workers they were trying to attract. They gradually expanded the scope of program benefits and soon focused primarily on old age payments. By 1928, about 40% of union members belonged to national unions offering one form or another of old age benefits. These pensions were funded by assessments on union members, and they became increasingly burdensome as the number of older workers increased. Raising union dues became more difficult, especially with the advent of the Depression. Other demands on the unions' treasuries, combined with the nation's financial chaos, resulted in the almost complete collapse of all union welfare plans by the early 1930s. After social security was adopted in 1935 only a handful of union plans survived, and it was not until the Second World War that union interest in pensions revived.

2. At present, this is done through the Supplemental Security Income program.

3. Pensions can also provide an effective wage adjustment if they are actuarially unfair to workers who postpone retirement (Lazear, in this vol.). However, as discussed later, pensions that appear unfair may only be a reflection of the heterogeneous life spans in the population.

4. As discussed earlier, there are tax advantages for savings in pensions. These deferred taxes result, all other things equal, in an effectively lower discount rate for savings held by the firm. This provides an additional argument for pensions.

5. Larger pensions increase workers' forced savings. To raise savings in equilibrium, we must assume that workers cannot fully counter this effect by borrowing against their pension to restore current consumption. We assume that there is no borrowing act of this sort.

6. Bulow (1981) demonstrates that workers who retire early should take advantage of the early retirement option rather than wait until the normal retirement age before collecting benefits.

7. If inflation were recognized in the design of the pension plan, and if it were constant, all calculations using real dollars would pertain. Given that most pension plans deal in minimal dollars, variable inflation rates impose risk costs on the worker unless inflation indexation is perfect and immediate.

8. One theoretical solution to this problem would be to stop paying pensions after 20 years of retirement. Indeed, some plans allow the workers to take the pension's actuarial value in a lump sum payment. If this were required rather than an option, workers with longer life spans would have less incentive to take advantage of early retirement provisions.

9. This problem is complicated if, as is common, the pension plan gives a surviving spouse a substantial fraction of the worker's benefits. The problem will be mitigated if variability in expected benefits is less once spouse's benefits are included. We do not consider survivors' benefit in this analysis, leaving for the future such interesting questions as the correlation among life expectancies of worker and his spouse (i.e., do young women seek as husbands older workers with high pensions offering survivor clauses?) or the extent to which workers take into account when making retirement decisions the welfare of their spouse after their own death.

10. In conventional plans this may be some average of final-year wages. In pattern plans, the function would be a constant.

11. In theory, the corporation could make a contract for the way it treats the work force as a whole. For example, it could commit itself to have no more than 25% early retirements. An alternative means of allowing for differential treatment, yet providing adherence to earlier contracts, is to offer to pay someone (not necessarily the worker) an amount that depends on

the action that is taken relative to the worker. This latter case simply creates a mechanism to make the contract self-enforcing.

12. Cooper (1983) nicely categorizes some general properties of the optimal second-best solutions in problems with adverse selection or moral hazard when the agents' preferences obey SCP.

13. Disabilities do shorten life spans. Models of pensions with heterogeneous life expectancies are considered in the previous section.

14. Workers who are disabled before the minimum retirement date stop working but do not start collecting pensions until age R_0.

15. For small values of R, $\partial B/\partial R$ is negative. To see that there is a unique solution to $\partial B/\partial R^* = 0$, observe from eq. (45$'$) that at any solution to $\partial B/\partial R = 0$, the second derivative $\partial^2 B/\partial R^{*2} = -U''[P(R^*)]P'(R^*)(T-R)/U'[P(R)]^2$, which is positive.

16. The second derivative of the actuarially fair curve is $P'' = 2P'/(T-R)$ while the curve that keeps workers indifferent about retirement age has a larger second derivative, $P'' = 2P'/(T-R) - U''P^{12}/U'$. Since the curves are tangent at R^*, the actuarially fair curve must lie below the indifference curve for $R < R^*$.

17. In 1983, the Supreme Court in *Arizona Governing Committee v. Norris* held that for tax-deferred compensation plans, the monthly retirement benefits cannot be lower to women who made the same contributions as men.

18. Such a subsidy is not possible in a competitive market in which the A's and B's can be distinguished. A firm could make positive profits by offering only the $P^*(B)$ plan and not hiring A type workers.

19. Negative outcomes of this type are particularly likely if other aspects of the labor packages get adjusted to take account of retirement packages. If so, there might be a presumption that any attempt to eliminate distinctions in retirement programs that promote inefficiency would work to the detriment of all.

References

Bulow, J. I. 1981. Early retirement pension benefits. NBER Working Paper 654.

Cooper, R. 1983. Towards a solution to the general problem of self-selection. Yale University Working Paper.

Diamond, P., and Mirrlees, J. 1978. A model of social insurance with variable retirement. *Journal of Public Economics* (December).

Feldstein, M. 1982. The optimal level of social security benefits. NBER Working Paper 970.

Greenough, W. C., and King, F. P. 1976. *Pension plans and public policy.* New York: Columbia University Press.

Hausman, J., and Wise, D. 1985. Retirement and subsequent work. In this volume.

Haynes, S., McMichael, A.; and Hyroler, H. 1979. Survival after early and normal retirement. *Journal of Gerontology.*

Lazear, E. P. 1985. Pension benefit formulas and worker productivity. In this volume.

Nichols, A., and Zeckhauser, R. 1982. Targeting transfers through restrictions on recipients. *American Economic Review* (May).

Woodbury, S. A. 1983. Substitution between wage and nonwage benefits. *American Economic Review* 73 (March): 166–82.

11   Insurance Aspects of Pensions

Peter A. Diamond
James A. Mirrlees

11.1   Deferred Wage Payments

If the State does not provide an adequate system of pensions, it is to be expected that employers will provide their workers with pensions, and some do. In a world of full information and perfect markets, private pensions could be individual contracts by workers with independent insurance companies. We shall not comment on all the reasons why that does not happen. Instead, we consider the forms of private pensions that are likely to arise when the employer provides the pension. We do this as an alternative to analyzing optimal pension policy by a benign State and comparing it with features of what currently exists. It should be possible to identify ways of regulating or supplementing private pensions that are likely to increase welfare.

The first task is to capture the important features of company pensions in a model that is easy to think about. To identify some of these features, we begin by asking why pensions exist, which is to say, why some part of what might have been paid as an immediate wage may be converted into future pension rights. (This should throw some light on the reasons the employer does it for the worker, rather than leaving it to the worker's independent arrangements.) Then we ask what might be expected to limit the extent of deferred payments. We are led to formulate a simple three-period model, which is used in sections 11.2–11.4 to see how the limitations referred to affect pensions in the model. In section 11.5 we ask how well private pensions in the model would provide for early retirement. The remaining sections discuss informally some issues the simple model does

Peter A. Diamond is professor of economics at Massachusetts Institute of Technology. James A. Mirrlees is professor of economics at Oxford University.

not illuminate: the consequences of inflation, the form of pension plans, and the effects of repeated wage and pension negotiations.

Why, then, might some part of the wage be deferred? In the first place, it might be done to provide saving. In the past there have often been tax advantages to saving channeled through an employer's pension plan. In any case, a higher return on capital might be available to the larger investments handled by the employer, particularly since marketing costs are low in this context. A further possibility is that deductions from the wage provide a particularly effective commitment to save that could be attractive to workers and their representatives who are apprehensive of future weakness of will. We do not propose to model any of these considerations here, since their bearing on pensions is easy to understand and their existence is unlikely to affect the desirable form of a pension plan, given that some plan is desirable.

There is a second class of reasons for deferring part of the wage, namely, to provide various kinds of insurance. We assume workers to be rational, an assumption we shall make throughout the paper; thus they would like to have insurance against many work-related contingencies. The first and most obvious is disability. More generally, there is substantial uncertainty for any worker about his future productivity. We want to distinguish between uncertainty about his productivity generally and uncertainty about his productivity in the current employment relative to his productivity elsewhere in the economy. This distinction will later turn out to be quite significant. These uncertainties relate to what might be directly observed in due course, wages to be earned in the future. There are also important uncertainties about the desirability of changing employment for reasons other than wage differences, because of, say, changing relationships within the firm, with people elsewhere. Indeed there is always uncertainty about the relative intertemporal value of consumption, quite apart from desires to change employment. Being related, often, to events that are hard to verify, these uncertainties cannot be directly the object of insurance.

A worker would therefore like to put some part of his current full wage into providing income in contingencies when it will be more important to have. Provision of a pension on final retirement may be a convenient way of getting his insurance, if he can expect to make a small contribution to the retirement and disability pensions when he has a lower full wage. It is not impossible that, at some stage in his working life, he would want to reduce his guaranteed retirement pension and consume more than his full wage currently: depending on the wage history, he might want a negative pension or to borrow against pension rights.

This last consideration suggests that the level of pension contributions should vary, perhaps greatly, with the worker's individual experience. Why then should we observe that workers in employment generally have their pension plan arranged by the employer rather than by an independent insurance company? The obvious answer, and probably the right one, is that it pays insurance companies to arrange insurance with groups of workers rather than with individual workers, both because it saves marketing costs (which are remarkably high for individual insurance) and because it limits the impact of adverse selection. It is hard to see how these advantages can be obtained other than by pension plans universal within a company, an occupation, or large categories within a nation.

Since the providers of pension plans have done so much to eliminate the adverse selection problem, we shall take advantage of that to confine our attention (other than some remarks in section 11.5) to the two other issues that reduce the extent of insurance: unobservability of events that ideal insurance contracts would relate to, and the inability of workers to commit themselves to future payments. The reason that leads a worker to resign or retire may be unobservable: ideal insurance would pay more to a worker who becomes unable to work than to a worker who could work but chooses not to, and it would similarly avoid the problem of inducing workers to leave for pleasanter jobs elsewhere by making pensions conditional on the reasons for mobility. It turns out that the problem of observability interacts with the problem of commitment. The issue of commitment arises with all future contracts and is controlled by law and by reputation. Even when the law allows enforcement of promises to pay, it may be costly to ensure compliance: the cost in reputation of breaking a promise is therefore always important. There are also other observable costs, such as social disapproval—more important within some groups and classes of commitments than in others—which we shall ignore.

Considerations of reputation suggest that believable and effective commitments are easier for firms to make than for workers. We discuss this issue further in section 11.8 at the end of the paper. It might be possible for the State to provide cheaply an effective mechanism to ensure compliance with commitments made by individual workers, for example by introducing voluntary commitments to taxes or social insurance contributions. But, on the whole, the appropriate assumption for a realistic model is that workers are unable to commit themselves to make future payments to employers, whereas employers are able to commit themselves to make future payments to workers. We shall assume, for example, that a worker cannot enter into arrangements that ensure he does not benefit from accepting a higher wage offer from a competing employer, although he might have preferred to use the proceeds from such an agreeable contingency in less satisfactory states of nature.

These considerations suggest that we model the labor market as follows. There are three periods for the worker. In the first period, a wage contract is agreed between the worker and the firm employing him. That contract specifies the payment to be made in the first period and payments to be made by that firm in subsequent periods, contingent on various possibilities, such as whether the worker remains with the initial employer and whether he works in the second period. The payments specified refer to both of the remaining periods. In the third period, the worker is retired. Our economy is competitive: workers and firms compete for one another. But workers may have different productivities in different firms—this is an issue in the second period. In the first period, we shall suppose, neither worker nor firm knows what the worker's productivity or alternative wage opportunities will be in the second period. For the second period, we shall consider explicitly a number of the possible patterns of knowledge and observation: the worker may or may not know his marginal productivity to the firm he was with in the first period, and the firm may or may not be able to rely on observation of the wages available to the worker in alternative employments. An interesting hybrid case is where the wage in alternative employment is observable for determining the level of a transferable pension but not for determining the wage should the worker remain with his first-period employer.

Whatever our assumption about observability, we find it helpful to distinguish three mobility possibilities. The first is that, in equilibrium, workers never in fact change employment because their productivity is the same whichever firm they work for, although they might have moved, and equilibriuim contracts take account of that possibility. This situation has been studied by Harris and Holmstrom (1982) in a model with many time periods: we call it the case of *mobility threats*. Their model is the starting place of our analysis. The second case is that of *exogenous mobility*, where, for reasons not subject to objective verification, workers may wish to move to other employments (or to none). In this case, employment contracts are drawn up with full awareness that insurance for such an eventuality might encourage mobility also when the unobservable reasons do not apply. The remaining case is called *endogenous mobility,* where workers may find that better wages are available from other firms and the first employer may, because they have greater productivity elsewhere, be willing to allow them to move. In this case, it may or may not be possible for the first employer to observe the alternative wage offers. If it is not possible, there is still this distinction between endogenous and exogenous mobility, that a rational worker wants to insure against the latter happening and against the former not happening. Necessary early retirement because of disability is the extreme case of exogenous mobility.

11.2 Mobility Threats

We first set up the model and show it working in the case of mobility threats. It is our policy to simplify wherever possible in order to make results more vivid. This leads us to specify the same utility of consumption in each period, $u(c)$, with the disutility of labor, of alternative employers, or of disability being subtracted from the utility of consumption as appropriate. We assume that u is increasing, concave, and differentiable with u' tending to $+ \infty$ and zero as consumption goes to zero and $+ \infty$. We also assume a zero real interest rate. In a world ideally well informed, consumption would then be the same in all periods and all states of nature. We focus on deviations from this ideal constancy.

The marginal productivity of labor with the first employer is denoted by m_1 and m_2 in the two periods when there is work. When we come to consider alternative employers, we shall denote marginal productivity there by m_2'. Wages actually paid are w_1, w_2, and w_2', respectively. Workers have no access to a capital market (an extreme assumption made because we are emphasizing insurance aspects, and the presence of savings complicates matters in some ways, without significantly changing anything that matters.[1]) Firms can freely borrow and lend at a zero real interest rate (an obvious simplification so long as we are not going to look at the effect of interest rate changes). Since no problems of observability or commitment attach to the distribution of payments to workers between the second and third periods, with workers all receiving payments in the third period, and all known to be retired in that period, we may as well aggregate the total payment received in these two periods. Whatever it is, it will in fact be divided equally between the two periods.[2] We therefore write b, b' for the contribution to pension arising from first-period employment, indicating that it may be different if the worker moves to a new occupation in the second period. Total worker income, from wage and pension, in the second and third periods is $w_2 + b$ or $w_2' + b'$, depending on whether he remains with his first employer or not. We write $W = w_2 + b$, $W' = w_2' + b'$, $U(W) = 2u(W/2)$.

Firms are taken to be risk neutral. Then in equilibrium, expected payments to a worker, including deferred payments, equal his expected marginal product. In competing for workers, firms must devise contracts that maximize the expected utility of workers, always having regard to mobility possibilities.

In the case of mobility threats, $m_2 = m_2'$. If a worker moved in the second period, he could obtain from his new employer income equal to m_2'. If his initial labor contract made that worthwhile, it must pay the first employer to change the contract without disadvantage to the worker. Thus the equilibrium contract is given by

(1)
$$\max_{w_1, W(\cdot)} \quad u(w_1) + EU[W(m_2)]$$

subject to
$$w_1 - m_1 + E[W(m_2) - m_2]. = 0$$
$$W(m_2) \geq m_2$$

Notice that m_2 is a random variable, to which the expectation operator applies.

If m_2 is such that $W(m_2) > m_2$, the second constraint does not apply and marginal utilities are equated: $W = 2w_1$. Otherwise the constraint determines the wage. Therefore the solution is

$$(2) \qquad W(m_2) = 2w_1, \quad m_2 \leq 2w_1,$$
$$= m_2, \quad m_2 \geq 2w_1,$$

with the first constraint in (1) determining the level of w_1. This is just the Harris-Holmstrom result, modified by the presence of a retirement period. The Harris-Holmstrom result was that wages do not fall but may rise if marginal product increases enough. If we had a two-period model, with $U(W) = u(W)$, we would get the result that the second-period wage is higher than the first-period wage if the second-period marginal product is higher than the first-period wage. The existence of a retirement period allows the first employer to pay a pension only if the worker has remained with him. Therefore the worker's current income can remain constant with greater probability, increasing for the second and third periods only if $m_2 > 2w_1$.

Using nontransferable pension rights becomes less attractive when mobility may be desirable.

11.3   Exogenous Mobility

We introduce exogenous mobility by specifying a positive probability p of leaving the first employer by "necessity." We maintain the assumption that a worker who is not under the necessity of moving would have the same marginal product in alternative employments as with the first firm. It is then a constraint on the contract that such a worker should not be induced to move. Denoting the marginal product (elsewhere) of a worker who has to move by m', we see that the equilibrium contract is defined by

$$(3) \qquad \max_{w_1, W(\cdot), b'} \quad u(w_1) + (1 - p)EU[W(m_2)] + pEU(m' + b')$$

subject to $w_1 - m_1 + (1-p)E[W(m_2) - m_2] + pb' = 0$

$$W(m_2 \geq m_2 + b', b' \geq 0.$$

Notice that we allow for a transferable pension component, b', which however is independent of m': that is, the new wage is supposed to be unobservable. The third constraint, that $b' \geq 0$, expresses the inability of workers to commit themselves to making future payments. The main questions to be addressed are whether in equilibrium $b' > 0$, and if so, how large it is.

For the same reasons as in the previous section, W should be set equal to $2w_1$ unless that would violate the constraint on W; in which case the second-period wage is just enough to prevent mobility of workers who do not need to move. Explicitly,

(4) $$W(m_2) = 2w_1, \qquad m_2 \leq 2w_1 - b',$$
$$= m_2 + b', m_2 \geq 2w_1 - b'.$$

Granted (4), the derivative of expected utility with respect to b' is

$$(1 - p) \int_{2w_1 - b'}^{\infty} U'(m + b')dF(m) + pEU'(m' + b'),$$

where F is the distribution function for m_2. The derivative of the first constraint in (3) (i.e., minus profit per man) with respect to b' is

$$(1 - p)[1 - F(2w_1 - b')] + p = 1 - (1 - p)F(2w_1 - b').$$

Since the value of the constraint is $u'(w_1)$ (by variation of w_1), the first-order condition for b' is that

(5) $$(1 - p) \int_{2w_1 - b'}^{\infty} U'(m + b')dF(m) + pEU'(m' + b')$$

$$- [1 - (1 - p)F(2w_1 - b')]u'(w_1) = 0,$$

with $b' > 0$; or that, alternatively, $b' = 0$ and the left-hand side of (5) is nonpositive. When $b' > 0$, first-period marginal utility equals second-period expected marginal utility.

Using (4), we also have the zero profit condition:

(6) $$w_1 - m_1 + (1 - p) \int_{0}^{2w_1 - b'} (2w_1 - b' - m)dF(m) + b' = 0.$$

That is, first-period wages are below the first-period marginal product to finance a second-period unconditional transfer of b' and an increase in the second-period wage when (observed) marginal product is low. When can (5) and (6) be satisfied simultaneously with $b' > 0$? One case is where the endogenous mobility threat would not be effective with $b' = 0$ ($m_2 < 2w_1$ for all m_2).[3]

Proposition 1: Suppose that m_2 is known never to take a value greater than

(7) $$M = \frac{m_1 + (1 - p)E(m_2)}{\frac{3}{2} - p}$$

and that

(8) $$U'(M) < EU'(m').$$

Then the optimal b' is positive.

Proof: We show that, under the stated assumptions, when b' is set to zero in (6), the left-hand side of (5) is positive. It is therefore impossible that $b' = 0$, and the desired conclusion follows. With $b' = 0$, it is readily seen that the solution of (6) is

$$w_1 = M/2,$$

for in that case $F(2w_1) = 1$ and the integral is $M - E(m_2)$. That is, with zero transferable pension it is feasible to equalize pay in both periods.

Turning to the left-hand side of (5) with this value of w_1, we see that the integral vanishes, and the expression in square brackets becomes p. We get

$$pEU'(m') - pu'(M/2) = p[EU'(m') - u'(M)],$$

which is positive by assumption (8). Q.E.D.

It will be noticed that, when U' is convex, a sufficient condition for (8) is that $M > E(m')$. Granted the first assumption, this is eminently plausible, as indeed is (8) for any utility function. The significance of the result is that $b' = 0$ only if the distribution of m_2 is highly dispersed or departure under "necessity" tends to lower the marginal utility of consumption. The upper bound M is quite restrictive: with $m_1 = E(m_2)$ and $p = 1/2$, $M = (3/2)E(m_2)$; but the conditions of the proposition are quite strongly sufficient. We may safely conclude that often $b' > 0$, recognizing that necessity is likely to raise the marginal utility of consumption.

It is not so easy to see just how large b' is likely to be. The greater it is, the more commonly will second-period wages and the final pension be greater than first-period wages. Some insurance for exogenous mobility is available, but at the expense of reduced insurance against low second-period productivity when mobility is unnecessary.

The case where m' is always zero is that of disability, and in that case b' is positive whether or not m_2 is bounded above by M. We have studied this case (with m_2 nonrandom) in a previous paper from the point of view of the social optimum. We shall return to the many-period disability case below in section 11.5 where we address the commitment issue in more detail.

11.4 Endogenous Mobility

We now study a version of the model in which workers may have different values to different employers, the values not being known in the first period. Because workers cannot bind themselves in advance to remain with their first employer in the second period, contracts must be negotiated on the assumption that a worker will move if it pays him to do so.[4] It will pay him to do so if a wage offer from some other employer (net of costs of moving) plus any transferable pension rights exceed the wage (plus pension) available if he stays with his first employer. To emphasize the contrast with the case of exogenous mobility, we suppose that there is no utility or disutility attached to moving, other than what can be allowed for in the alternative wage offer; and indeed we assume, in the first instance, that this net wage offer is observable. This observability assumption is unduly strong for some cases. We also consider two other alternatives: that the wage offer is not at all observable and that the wage offer is observable for the transferable pension (which is not paid until period 3), but not observable at the time of wage offer from the first-period employer. As in the implicit contract literature (see Hart [1983] for a survey) productivity with the first employer in the second period may not be observable. We deal with that by considering two cases, depending on whether m_2 is or is not observable. Thus we have six cases to analyze, of which we look at five. We do not consider more realistic, less extreme cases where outside offers are sometimes observable and marginal product is imperfectly observable.

Marginal productivities with the original firm and elsewhere (identified with the observable wage offer) m_2 and m_2' are jointly distributed without atoms, the distribution being given by a density function,[5] $f(m_2, m_2')$. Thus, we assume that the distribution of m_2' is independent of the wage contract. With both variables observable, W and b' are functions of both m_2 and m_2'. The commitment constraint is that b' be nonnegative, and movement is determined by which of W and $m_2' + b'$ is the greater. Equilibrium is given by

(9)
$$\max_{w_1, W, b'} \quad u(w_1) + EU[\max(W, m_2' + b')]$$

subject to

$$w_1 - m_1 + \iint_{W \geq m_2' + b'} (W - m_2) f dm_2 dm_2' + \iint_{W < m_2' + b'} b' f dm_2 dm_2' = 0,$$

$$b' \geq 0.$$

As before, the shadow price of the constraint is $u'(w_1)$. For each m_2 and m_2', W and b' have to be chosen optimally, that is, so that the function

(10)
$$V(W, b') = \begin{cases} U(W) - u'(w_1)(W - m_2), & W \geq m_2' + b', \\ U(m_2' + b') - u'(w_1)b', & W < m_2' + b', \end{cases}$$

is maximized subject to $b' \geq 0$. When $m_2 > m_2'$, the first of these expressions is larger than the second when we set $W = m_2' + b'$. Therefore we maximize the first expression subject to the constraint $W \geq m_2'$ (which follows from $b' \geq 0$). This is achieved by setting W equal to the larger of $2w_1$ and m_2'. In that case, b' can be anything between zero and max $(2w_1 - m_2', 0)$, since it will not be collected. When $m_2 < m_2'$, a similar argument shows that the worker will be induced to move. Then b' is set equal to $\max(2w_1 - m_2', 0)$, and W takes any value less than $\max(2w_1, m_2')$ since it will not be collected.

Summarizing, we have

Proposition 2: With endogenous mobility, observability of wage offers and marginal products, and no precommitment by workers, workers go where their productivity is greatest in the second period. If productivity is greatest with the original employer, income in the second and third periods is w_1 or $m_2'/2$, whichever is the greater. If the best alternative wage offer is greater than productivity with the original employer, the transferable pension is just sufficient to increase total income in the second and third periods to w_1, if that is greater than $m_2'/2$, and the transferable pension is zero otherwise. The proposition is illustrated in figure 11.1.

With m_2 not observable by the worker, the firm guarantees minimal levels of W and b' and preserves the option of raising either variable when m_2 is observed by the firm, if that is in the interest of the firm. We denote the guaranteed levels by $W_0(m_2')$ and $b_0'(m_2')$. The worker is assumed to know the distribution of payments the firm will actually make. Thus the equilibrium contract remains the solution to (9) with the additional control variables W_0,b_0' and the additional constraints

$$(11) \qquad W,b' \max V^*(W,b') = \begin{cases} m_2 - W, & W \geq m_2' + b', \\ -b', & W \leq m_2' + b', \end{cases}$$

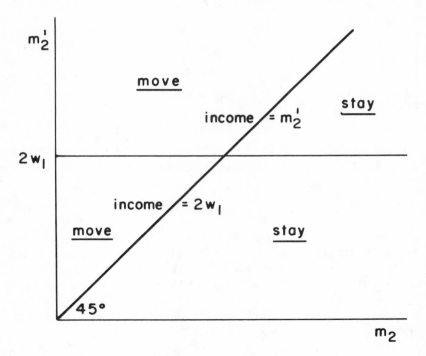

Fig. 11.1   Propositions 2 and 3.

subject to
$$W(m_2, m_2') \geq W_0(m_2')$$
$$b'(m_2, m_2') \geq b_0'(m_2').$$

The firm can precisely duplicate the optimal contract when m_2 is observable by setting W_0 equal to $2w_1$ and $b_0'(m_2')$ equal to $\max[(0, W_0 - m_2')]$ and choosing W and b' to induce mobility if and only if $m_2' > m_2$. Since the contract in this case satisfies a maximization problem without the additional constraints, the optimum with observability is the optimum without observability. Thus we have

Proposition 3: With outside wage offers observable, the optimal allocation is the same whether marginal productivity at the original firm is observable or not.

The outcome is rather like the Harris-Holmstrom case, with the "wage," or income, remaining constant unless the alternative employment opportunity makes an increase in income necessary. It is not the unpredictable increase in the worker's marginal productivity to the economy that brings about an (undesirable) increase in his income, but the unpredictable increase in his marginal productivity to the rest of the economy. Thus an economy with fewer but larger firms should have an equilibrium closer to the ideal case, since there are fewer possibilities outside the firm, implying that the wage then increases in fewer states of nature and a higher initial wage results in equilibrium.

If workers leave one employment in search of a higher income, or have incentive to show a low wage ($w_1 > m_2/2$, $m_2' > m_2$), or are—less realistically—unable to prove that alternative wage offers are genuine, W cannot be made to depend on m_2', although, perhaps with the help of the State, b' might still depend on m_2'. We examine next the case where b' is a function of m_2' but W is not. We also make the simplifying assumption (ignoring the search case) that the worker knows m_2' when he decides whether to move or not, although m_2' is not verifiable by the employer.

If m_2 is observable, W depends only on m_2 but b' can depend on both m_2 and m_2', then, considering a particular m_2, W, and b', maximize

(12)
$$\int V(W, b') f \, dm_2',$$

with V defined (as in [10]) by

$$V(W, b') = \begin{cases} U(W) - u'(w_1)(W - m_2), & W \geq m_2' + b', \\ U(m_2' + b') - u'(w_1)b', & W < m_2' + b'. \end{cases}$$

We should note straight away that, in this case, W is never less than $2w_1$, for if it were we could increase V by increasing W and simultaneously increasing b' if necessary to keep the division between the two cases in the definition of V unchanged.

Now consider the choice of b', keeping W fixed for the moment. b' is constrained to be nonnegative. Therefore $m_2' > W$ implies $W < m_2' + b'$, and, bearing in mind that $W \geq 2w_1$, b' should be made as small as possible:

$$(13) \qquad\qquad b' = 0, m_2' > W.$$

Suppose now that $m_2' \leq W$. If $m_2 \geq m_2'$, the worker should be induced to stay, for $U(W) - u'(w_1)W \geq U(m_2' + b') - u'(w_1)(m_2' + b')$ when $W > m_2' + b'$. Thus

$$(14) \qquad\qquad b' < W - m_2', m_2' \leq m_2, W.$$

If $m_2 < m_2'$, the worker should be induced to move, with wage plus pension as close to W as possible. This can be done by setting

$$(15) \qquad\qquad b' = W - m_2' + \epsilon, m_2 < m_2' \leq W,$$

where ϵ is a small positive number. ϵ should be "infinitesimally" small.

With these choices of b', we have

$$V(W, b') = \begin{cases} U(W) - u'(w_1)(W - m_2), & m_2 \geq m_2' \leq W, \\ U(W) - u'(w_1)(W - m_2'), & m_2 < m_2' \leq W, \\ U(m_2') & m_2' > W. \end{cases}$$

Here, since we have taken account of the mobility decision induced by b', we can set $\epsilon = 0$. When $m_2 \leq 2w_1$, W should be set equal to $2w_1$, since it maximizes

$$\int_0^W [U(W) - u'(w_1)W] f\, dm_2' + \int_W^\infty [U(m_2') - u'(w_1)m_2'] f\, dm_2'.$$

When $m_2 > 2w_1$, W should be less than m_2; for when $W > m_2$, the integral of V is

$$\int_0^W [U(W) - u'(w_1)(W - m_2')] f\, dm_2' + \int_W^\infty U'(m_2') f\, dm_2'$$
$$+ u'(w_1) \int_0^{m_2} (m_2 - m_2') f\, dm_2',$$

which is increased by reducing $W > 2w_1$. Therefore in fact W maximizes

$$\int_0^W [U(W) - u'(w_1)(W - m_2)] f\, dm_2' + \int_W^\infty u(m_2') f\, dm_2'.$$

The first-order condition is

$$(16) \qquad [U'(W) - u'(w_1)] \int_0^W f\, dm_2' = u'(w_1)(W - m_2)f(m_2, W)$$

We have proved

Proposition 4: With endogenous mobility, observability of marginal products with the original firm, but observability of wage offers only for the determination of transferable pensions, a worker whose second-period productivity in all firms is less than twice his first-period wage has the same income in all periods of life, and works where his productivity is greatest; while one whose second-period productivity is greater than that in some employment has no transferable pension if he moves, and if he does not move has a wage plus pension less than his productivity, given by (16).

This situation is illustrated in the figure 11.2.

Equation (16) does not tell us much about W without further assumptions. When m_2 and m_2' are independently distributed, $f(m_2, m_2') = g(m_2)g'(m_2')$, and we have

$$(17) \qquad m_2 = W + \left[1 - \frac{U'(W)}{u'(w_1)} \right] \frac{\int_0^W g'\, dm_2'}{g'(W)}$$

If, as is reasonable, $\int_0^W g'\, dm_2'/g'(W)$ is an increasing function of W for W

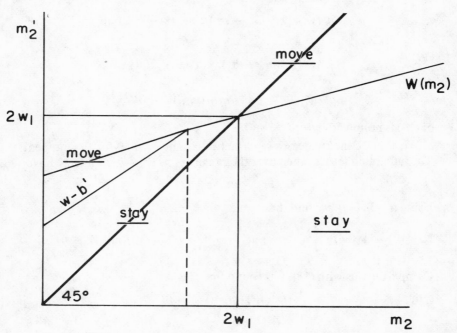

Fig. 11.2   Proposition 4.

$\geq 2w_1$, the right-hand side is an increasing function, with gradient greater than one. It follows that W is an increasing function of m with gradient less than one.

If employment contracts do not condition b' on m_2, but do condition it on m_2', the results are a little less neat, and we do not explore them here.

With m_2 observable, equilibrium is given by the same maximization, (9), except that W and b' are now constrained to be independent of m_2'. Before turning to the first-order conditions, let us note that W and b' are set to induce some mobility provided there is a positive probability that m_2' exceeds m_2. There is no mobility if $W - b'$ exceeds the maximal possible m_2'. In this case, consider raising b' to any level not exceeding $W - m_2'$. Doing this makes those who move better off and saves revenue for the firm, since each mover represents a loss in productivity that is no greater than the savings in compensation from mobility. Of course, this argument does not imply that the optimal b' equals $W - m_2$. Thus we have $W - b' \leq \max m_2'$. The usual envelope argument implies that this inequality is strict for the optimal b'. This being so, the first-order conditions are

(18)
$$[U'(W) - u'(w_1)] \int_0^{W-b'} f dm_2'$$
$$- u'(w_1)(W - b' - m_2)f(m_2, W - b') = 0$$

(19)
$$\int_{W-b'}^{\infty} [U'(m_2' + b') - u'(w_1)] f dm_2'$$
$$+ u'(w_1)(W - b' - m_2)f(m_2, W - b') = 0$$

or (19) is nonpositive with $b' = 0$.

We analyze the two cases separately. Assume $b' > 0$ for the moment. The integral in (19) is taken over the range $m_2' > W - b'$. Thus we have

$$U'(m_2' + b') < U'(W).$$

Using this in (19), we find that

$$[U'(W) - u'(w_1)] \int_{W-b'}^{\infty} f dm_2' + u'(w_1)(W - b' - m_2)f(m_2, W - b') > 0.$$

Comparing this with (18), it is found that

(20)
$$U'(W) - u'(w_1) > 0$$
$$W - b' - m_2 > 0.$$

From (20) we have

(21)
$$2w_1 > W > m_2 + b' > m_2.$$

Thus b' is necessarily zero for $m_2 \geq 2w_1$. The latter condition in (20) represents an implicit tax on moving (workers who stay have net compensation more than their marginal products).

Now assume $b' = 0$. Then, (18) becomes

$$[U'(W) - u'(w_1)] \int_0^W f \, dm_2' = u'(w_1)(W - m_2)f(m_2, W).$$

Thus we have

$$\text{sign}(W - 2w_1) = \text{sign}(m_2 - W).$$

Thus W lies between $2w_1$ and m_2 for values of m_2 for which b' is set equal to zero. We can conclude that workers with high marginal products are paid less than their marginal products.

Summarizing these results, we have

Proposition 5: With endogenous mobility, observability of marginal products with the original firm but no observability of wage offers, and no precommitment by workers, income is lower in the second and third periods than in the first for any worker who remains with the original employer and has marginal product below the first-period wage. For workers with positive transferable pensions, the pension is les than $W - m_2$. For any worker who remains with the original employer and has marginal product above the first-period wage, there is no transferable pension, and income is higher in the later period than in the first period but less than the marginal product. The question of which values of m_2 have b' positive appears to be difficult in general, depending on the properties of f. The proposition is illustrated in figure 11.3.

One case remains to be analyzed, that where neither m_2 nor m_2' is observable. In this case, the firm chooses w_1, W_0, b_0', $W(m_2)$, and $b'(m_2)$ to maximize (9) subject to the constraints of self-interest in the second period:

(22) $\qquad W,b' \max \int_0^{W-b'} (m_2 - W)f \, dm_2' + \int_{W-b'}^\infty -b' f \, dm_2'$

subject to $\qquad W \geq W_0$
$\qquad\qquad\quad b' \geq b_0'$

Thus we have the first-order conditions

$$(m_2 - W + b')f(m_2, W - b') - \int_0^{W-b'} f \, dm_2' \leq 0$$

(23)

$$-(m_2 - W + b')f(m_2, W - b') - \int_{W-b'}^\infty f \, dm_2' \leq 0$$

with equality if $W > W_0$ and $b' > b_0'$ respectively. From the signs of the different terms, we have either $W = W_0$ or $b' = b_0'$, or possibly both.

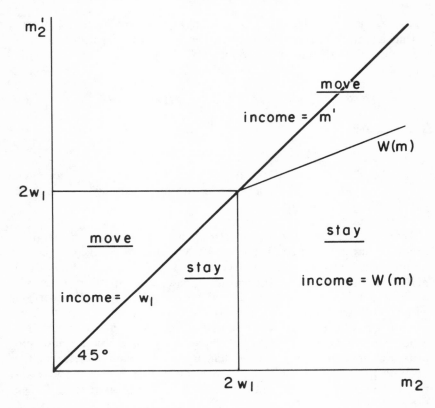

Fig. 11.3   Proposition 5.

Moreover, $b' = b_0'$ for $m_2 > W_0 - b_0'$ and $W = W_0$ for $m_2 < W_0 - b_0'$. In addition, where $W > W_0$, $W < m_2 + b_0'$. Where $b' > b_0'$, $b' < W_0 - m_2$.

To analyze W_0 and b_0' we would need to consider the first-order conditions from (9). This is a messy calculation since W depends on b_0' when $W > W_0$ and b' depends on W_0 when $b' > b_0'$, and we leave analysis of this problem for the future.

11.5   Early Retirement

In the models analyzed above, everyone worked in the first two periods and no one worked in the third. This approach ignores the wide spread in the distribution of retirement ages that is currently observed. Indeed, many pension plans allow a choice of retirement age and relate the size of pension to the age at which it is first claimed as well as wage history and job tenure.

Our earlier analyses of public retirement systems concentrated on the relationship between optimal benefit size and age at retirement. In that work, there is naturally no constraint corresponding to the nonnegativity of transferable pension rights. We recall the ideas of that analysis briefly and relate it to the issues in the current paper by checking when the non-negatively constraint on worker debt to the firm needed for private pensions is binding.

Assume that both the productivity of workers and the fact of working are observable but the ability to work (taken to be a zero-one variable) is not. Then, ignoring those unable to work their entire lives, one can implement a system of lump sum redistributions based on productivity and have actuarially fair pensions. Actuarially fair pensions imply that the ex post lifetime budget constraint varies with the length of working career in the same way as output produced. Length of working career depends on both choice and random factors affecting productivity. (This is a short-hand for factors that affect the disutility of work and the availability of jobs as well as productivity.) There are two reasons for believing that one may be able to improve on the choice of actuarially fair pensions for a public redistribution and retirement system—income redistribution and insurance provision.

To isolate the income redistribution motive, let us temporarily ignore the uncertainty about work ability. If individuals differ in (unobservable) labor disutility as well as productivity, then lump sum redistribution based solely on productivity still leaves room for further redistribution based on disutility of labor. Normally, those retiring earlier will have a higher social marginal utility of consumption. It is therefore worthwhile to distort the retirement decision to redistribute further toward early retirees, who have lower ex post budget constraints. (Essentially the same argument holds when we consider the insurance argument below.) This argument is strengthened once we recognize that redistribution for productivity differences is done by a distorting annual income tax rather than a lump sum tax. Income redistribution is then limited by work incentive problems on hours worked. Rather than an actuarially fair pension system (with fairness defined in terms of the government's total budget), it is likely to be appropriate also to redistribute in a way that discourages longer working lives, once we recognize the positive correlation between productivity and length of working life (which reflects a negative correlation between productivity and disutility of labor as well as higher compensation).

Under conventional economic assumptions redistribution plays no role in private pension design (although unions may be concerned). Indeed, adverse selection problems imply that the attempt to provide insurance against early loss of earnings ability will have a cost. We ignore both redistribution and adverse selection in the rest of this section.

With all individuals ex ante identical in productivity, preferences, and disability risk, actuarially favorable early retirement provisions provide insurance against an early loss of earnings ability and are a natural part of the optimal labor contract. In our earlier papers, we derived equations for the optimal wage and retirement benefit plans under the alternative assumptions that workers do, or do not, save on their own. If we now make the same commitment assumptions as in the first part of the present paper and assume identical opportunities elsewhere, the socially optimal contracts remain privately feasible as long as expected future compensation is not less than expected future productivity. We now examine when this condition is satisfied.

In both of our earlier papers we related lifetime consumption under the optimal plan to length of working life for the case of constant marginal product. Lifetime consumption was an increasing function of working life, but increasing more slowly than lifetime production (until the planned retirement date, when the rates of increase are equal). Put differently, the optimal plan has an implicit tax on work throughout the working life up to the planned retirement age, when the tax is zero. This is the natural way to provide insurance against the adverse event of early retirement. Under the simple institution of a wage paid that is either consumed or saved, the optimal plan is thus not sustainable under mobility since the taxes on work are used to finance a lump sum transfer at the start of working life.

Pensions, however, represent a different institutional setting from simple annual wage payments, with pension benefits at a future date depending on the date of retirement. In actual pensions, benefits are paid conditional on stopping work at one's own firm. In a world of uniform marginal products and costless mobility this condition has no bite, and pensions do not offer any greater insurance possibilities than simple wages. If pensions are conditional on full retirement, then there is the possibility of insurance. The private equilibrium can support the social optimum if there is implicit taxation of early work, but not if there is implicit subsidization of early work. To examine the feasibility of privately imitating the social optimum we consider the following institution. Work at age t results in a wage of $c(t)$ which is fully consumed. Retirement at age t results in a benefit $b(t)$ for all later periods of life. Mobility at age t results in a lump sum transfer of resources $R(t)$ which is taken to an alternative firm to help finance retirement. The socially optimal system is privately supportable if the optimal $b(t)$ and $c(t)$ imply a net surplus of output over expected payments, which is nonnegative.

A worker who moves at age t must bring to his new employer an amount sufficient to cover the expected value of future payments to him, net of his product in the firm, in case he stays with a new employer until retirement. If this is so when he stays, it is also the case when he moves again, provided that the new transfer sum is similarly just sufficient to cover the expected net loss from employing him. We express this formally, using the notation of our previous papers, where $F(t)$ is the probability that a worker is still able to work at age t; r is the age at which a healthy person retires; T is the length of life; and m is the constant marginal product. It is convenient to write the equation in terms of the expected values of transfer, and of payments subsequent to t, with the expectation taken as of time O. The same result of course follows if we use conditional probabilities. The required level of $R(t)$ satisfies

(24)
$$R(t)[1 - F(t)] = \int_t^r [c(s) - m][1 - F(s)]ds$$
$$+ \int_t^r b(s)(T - s)f(s)ds + b(r)(T - r)[1 - F(r)].$$

R would be zero at $t = 0$ by the budget balance constraint for the social optimum. R is evidently positive at $t = r$. If the right-hand side should be first a nondecreasing function of t, then nonincreasing, it would follow that $R \geq 0$ for all t. Differentiating, we see that this is true when there exists $s \leq r$ such that

(25)
$$\leq m \text{ for } t \leq s$$
$$c(t) + b(t)(T - t)\frac{f(t)}{1 - F(t)}$$
$$\geq m \text{ for } s \leq t \leq r.$$

Since, as we showed in the papers referred to, b and c are increasing functions of t, a sufficient condition for $R \geq 0$ is that

(26)
$$\frac{(T - t)f}{1 - F}$$

is a nondecreasing function of t.
This holds in particular for the uniform distribution, and more generally when

(27)
$$f(t) = \frac{ae^{at}}{e^{aT} - 1} \quad a > 0.$$

Since (26) is very strongly sufficient for (25), we conclude that it is none too easy to find simple cases where the social optimum should not, in theory, be privately implementable. Yet again, we find that a system of transferable pension rights is, besides being evidently desirable, consistent with private rationality. Even if the socially optimal R were sometimes negative, it would still be true that a constrained optimum would have R positive for ages of mobility.

11.6 Inflation

The analysis above made no mention of inflation. If inflation were fully neutral, the analysis above would stand and imply labor contracts in real terms. However, inflation often occurs at times when other factors are changing too. To analyze inflation in the setting used above, one would want to know how the joint distribution of marginal products with and without mobility tends to change as inflation rises. Also one would want to incorporate changes in real interest rates. We have not pursued such an analysis.

It is natural, also, to ask how existing pension structures are affected by inflation. This requires consideration of the full labor contract. With a defined contribution pension plan, workers bear the real interest rate risk associated with inflation assuming that the response of wages to inflation is independent of the size of existing pension fund. While this is a plausible assumption, there is nothing to prevent actual or implicit contracts from relating current wages to pension fund performance. Analysis of optimal sharing of real interest risk would require a description of the full portfolio positions of workers and shareholders. Under a defined contribution plan, workers who have left a firm bear the full risk.

With defined benefit plans, we should again distinguish between departed and present workers. For departed workers, the presence of a promise to pay future sums stated in nominal terms is a plan to make workers worse off, and firms better off, the greater the inflation rate. Decreases in the real rate of return would lessen the advantage accruing to firms. Only when a rise in inflation decreases the nominal rate of return does it move the utility of firms and workers in the same direction. Thus defined benefit plans appear, at first examination, not to be part of an optimal contract.

For workers staying with a firm, the sharing of inflation risk depends on the relationship of final wages to inflation. In some cases it is clear that workers are protected as part of the long-term contract (in contrast to the lack of protection under spot contracts, as analyzed by Bulow [1982]). For example, if wages depend on job done and on age, and the allocation of workers to jobs depends on ability, and perhaps seniority (with the usual effect of seniority), pension obligations are in real terms to the extent that labor contracts will be independent of past pension obligations. This independence will generally depend on the proportions of workers of different ages and is very likely to be true where near retirees are a small fraction of the labor force.

11.7 Pension Plans

The analysis so far has considered a single worker. In effect, it applies to pension arrangements for a body of workers who are ex ante identical.

Even if workers differ in some dimension but behave identically in supplying labor to the firm, the analysis applies. We can consider the discovery by workers of their true productivity distributions as one of the risks being insured by the labor contract. The only problem for the firm is having the correct productivity distribution for doing the expected present discounted value calculation.

If workers are aware of their differences (or merely have labor supply responses to contractual terms that are correlated with productivities), then there is an adverse selection problem along with the moral hazard problem of mobility. (We continue to ignore other moral hazard problems associated with effort.) We do not model this formally, but simply ask what kind of worker is particularly attracted to the equilibrium contract for a given level of expected productivity. We suppose that alternative employments offer wages equal to marginal products each period.

When there is no equilibrium mobility, and wages are downwardly rigid, the convexity of the second-period wage schedule in terms of productivity (eq. [2]) makes the contract particularly attractive to high-risk workers, as well as to risk-averse workers. In the case of endogenous mobility, workers with lower anticipated outside offers are particularly attracted. These workers are most likely to collect on the insurance premium implicitly paid in the first period. In the case of exogenous mobility, the answer depends on the division of insurance benefits between unfortunate moves and low productivity in continued employment. In the mixed case, the latter seems likely to predominate empirically.

Once we consider heterogeneity of the labor force, two of our simplifying assumptions—no worker savings and risk neutrality of the firm—appear much less satisfactory. Without savings by workers, there is considerable symmetry between oversaving and undersaving for a particular worker's ex post (and so ex ante) position, as can be seen by considering movements along an intertemporal budget line away from the optimal allocation. With worker savings we introduce a further moral hazard problem (as has been discussed in our earlier papers). In addition, any asymmetries in market opportunities for savings and dissavings would imply that workers find it easy to save to offset undersaving but hard to borrow to offset oversaving. This asymmetry translates into an asymmetry in the evaluation of pension plans that oversave for some and undersave for others. Presumably, that is a case for smaller plans than the analysis above would suggest, but we have not undertaken formal analysis.

Risk neutrality of firms was a very handy simplifying assumption. But bankruptcy means that firms are not risk neutral either about outcomes or about paying promised benefits in all states of nature. We do not pursue this. We have also ignored the complications that come from firm-specific risks and decreasing returns, which have been central to much of the implicit contract literature.

11.8 Repeated Negotiations

The models analyzed above can be used for normative purposes; for example, one can evaluate the degree of success of existing arrangements in achieving a constrained optimal allocation for the models. With the additional assumption of optimal contracting, the model becomes a positive model of equilibrium. As a positive model, some of its assumptions may be too inaccurate empirically to serve as an adequate model. One such assumption is that of objective probabilities. There is little reason to believe that subjective probabilities about events affecting the value of the lifetime labor contract are either similar between worker and firm or correct for workers. Firms have a direct financial experience to draw on in revising beliefs. Workers experience retirement a small number of times. Insofar as subjective beliefs of workers and firms are different, labor contracts will, in part, be bets on the events for which the parties have different beliefs. Thus, inaccuracy of the assumption of identical beliefs is likely to have sizable implications for the equilibrium allocation of resources.

A second source of potential shortcoming is the assumption of a lifetime contract that is binding on the firm. Mostly, we see labor contracts that are at-will contracts (no set termination, with freedom to terminate at any time or after notice which is short relative to a working lifetime) or contracts for a relatively short time, one to three years. The short contracts, however, are associated with considerably longer relationships, on average.[6] Since circumstances generally change over time, there is little reason to think that a series of equilibrium short-term contracts (under some bargaining theory) would produce the same allocation as a single long-term contract (under the same bargaining theory). However, this may not be the right comparison if a model of short contract equilibrium is not an accurate picture of the economic environment. We mention three reasons for doubting that account. First, some agents behave as if they were legally bound even when they are not. Second, firm reputation may affect both current worker efficiency and the ability to attract additional workers, making it optimal for a firm to carry out implicit contracts. We return to a reputation model below. Third, government rules affecting the labor market (both legislated and common law) affect the validity of the assumptions of the classical short-term contract equilibrium model (i.e., imply some ability to commit beyond the length of contract). We will discuss these mechanisms in the process of discussing the short-term model introduced by Bulow and coauthors (Bulow 1982; Bulow and Scholes 1984; Bulow et al. 1984).

In the classical competitive model the wage equals the marginal product of labor. If part of the wage is paid currently and part in deferred compensation, total compensation in equilibrium equals the marginal product. Presumably, the fact that equilibrium is defined in terms of a relationship between total compensation and marginal product would generalize to a matching model where the next best alternatives for both firm and worker were strictly inferior to their current match.[7] Then total compensation would continue to be determined independently of the pension structure. Under this interpretation (and a finite horizon), one cannot have a perfect equilibrium where firms carry out implicit contracts that imply total compensation in excess of marginal product late in life. Presumably, in reaching the short-term contract equilibrium, some further mechanism (such as transaction costs) is involved to rule out explicit longer-term contracts that provide insurance.

For both of these models (classical and matching), we can examine the robustness with respect to legal and institutional considerations of the result that the absence of explicit long-term contracts implies a short-term contract equilibrium in terms of total compensation. The Age Discrimination Act prohibits discrimination on the basis of age. Generally, nondiscrimination legislation has been interpreted in terms of wages, not total compensation, making it illegal to pay lower wages to an otherwise identical worker for whom fringe benefits are more expensive. Presumably this would hold for defined benefit pensions, where the cost of the pension varies with both age and seniority. Thus in the presence of this act, we cannot have an equilibrium with both defined benefit plans and age uniform total compensation.

Even without the Age Discrimination Act, common law requires good faith exercise of discretion in completion of a contract (see Burton 1980). Good faith can be seen as a preservation of expectations. Thus, if everyone understands that equilibrium is in terms of total compensation, it is not bad faith to carry it out. If workers believe that wages are independent of pension promises in "normal" times and pension plans will not be terminated in "normal" times, then firing of workers, plan terminations, and low wage offers solely to preserve a relation between total compensation and marginal product would probably be held to be bad faith actions and result in liability for compensatory damages.[8] Thus, legal restrictions can enforce and make credible some implicit contracts much as they do explicit contracts.

Thus, it appears that legal interpretations of employment relations and pension provisions would sustain an equilibrium with some degree of insurance for workers even in an economy where explicit intertemporal labor contracts did not exist. In addition to this mechanism, it may be possible to construct a perfect equilibrium with implicit contracts once one recognizes that firms have (potentially) infinite horizons.

Although it seems to be a promising line of inquiry, we have not developed a formal model of equilibrium (perfect or otherwise) with reputation effects. Nevertheless, we shall sketch briefly how such a model might look and what it might imply.

To start, assume no uncertainty for a firm but uncertainty for individuals plus a desire to save by way of pensions. Assume that the supply of new workers depends on current treatment of older workers as a basis for forecasting how new workers will be treated in the future. (This overlapping generations model seems simpler than the probably more important effect of reputation on efficiency of existing workers.) In some circumstances, it becomes worthwhile for firms to overpay (at least some) current older workers relative to their marginal products and alternative jobs. In a steady state, with naive expectations and an interest rate equal to the growth rate, the equilibrium contract will probably be similar to the ones analyzed in sections 11.2–11.4 above. The critical condition is that the profitability of continuing to fulfill these contracts exceeds that from exploitation of current older workers and an end to implicit contracting.[9] Critical to this possibility is the assumption of noninsurable, nondiversifiable risk, which makes a risk-averse worker value the asset of future benefits more highly than the firm values the liability of providing those benefits. In this equilibrium, one will have inflation protection for workers who have pension benefits keyed to final wages or pension benefits regularly adjusted in step with general wages. One may also have an effect on capital accumulation similar to that of unfunded social insurance.

The use of reputation rather than contracts for this mechanism affects the outcomes in a major way once one recognizes the importance of uncertainty for firms. First, events may occur that decrease the value of maintaining reputation, for example, bankruptcy or a corporate takeover permitting a repudiation of the previous management's implicit contracts. Then, the optimal contract must consider not only the problem of worker mobility but also the need to maintain the value of preserving reputation. This fact probably limits the extent to which insurance can be offered to workers and brings in a major role for funding rules in determining sustainable benefit packages. Second, a model with firm risk probably implies the sharing of profitability risk by workers, a phenomenon that appears to be present in the United States.[10] Pension rules then affect the distribution of wage risks among workers of different ages. There is an a priori suspicion that final wage defined benefit plans put too much risk on near retirees because of the leverage of wage changes on future pension benefits. The same conclusion would hold for a flat or service-related plan that sustained a constant ratio of pension benefit parameter to wages. Third, the implicit contract sustained by reputation effects is likely to be a very complicated contract, suggesting all the concerns normally associated with consumer protection in the presence of complicated contracts.[11]

11.9 Summary

Using a variety of competitive three-period models, this paper analyzes equilibrium labor contracts. It is assumed that risk-neutral firms save for workers and try to provide insurance against poor levels of second-period productivity. The first period has known productivity, while the third has retirement. With no restrictions on observability or commitment (and zero interest, for convenience), the optimal contract would yield constant consumption over the three periods, equal to one-third of the expected value of the sum of productivities in the two working periods. In the second period, the worker would move to another firm if and only if the offered wage exceeded his marginal product with his first-period employer. The worker would receive a payment from the first-period employer if his second-period wage were less than the contracted consumption level over his two remaining periods, and the worker would make a payment to his first-period employer if his second-period wage exceeded the contracted consumption level over his two remaining periods. The starting place of our analysis is that this contract is not attainable. Throughout the paper, we assume that the worker cannot commit himself either to staying with his first-period employer in the second period or to paying compensation to his first-period employer should he leave the firm. We assume that the firm can commit itself to a three-period contract, limited only by observability restrictions. (We also speculate on how the analysis would change if firm reputation replaced commitment.)

If it is known that the worker's productivity with his first-period employer is the same as his best alternative wage offer, there is a threat of mobility limiting the contract, but no reason for the worker to leave the firm that helps the design of the optimal contract. The optimal contract has nondecreasing consumption over time and increasing consumption if second-period productivity is large enough. In order to limit the extent to which the mobility threat curtails the provision of insurance, the optimal contract has no further payment to any worker who leaves his first-period employer. When there is no social reason for mobility, it is natural for the contract to discourage mobility as much as possible—by having no transferable pension, in this case.

The central focus of the paper is the examination of circumstances where this conclusion does not hold. That is, we identify circumstances where the optimal contract contains deferred payments to workers who switch employers.

First we note that workers sometimes leave firms for reasons other than higher wages elsewhere. These reasons include health and interpersonal relations which limit the ability to continue performing the work (or raise its disutility) and a variety of reasons for geographic mobility that may preclude continued employment in the same job. If there is sufficiently low expected marginal utility of consumption conditional on such a move, a positive transferable pension is called for, even though this decreases the insurance available against low productivity with the first-period employer.

Second, we examine the case where individuals only leave an employer for a better offer. Once we recognize that wages elsewhere can exceed marginal productivity with the first-period employer at the same time that both wage and productivity are low, there is a reason for the optimal contract to contain a pension payment for a worker who leaves his first-period employer. The extent of these payments depends on the observability of both productivity with the first-period employer and the wage offer elsewhere. With both of these observable, the optimal contract implies that the worker moves if and only if his wage elsewhere exceeds his marginal productivity with the original firm. The transferable pension is positive when the wage elsewhere is sufficiently low. This same outcome is achievable with suitable counteroffers by the firm when the wage elsewhere is observable but productivity with the first-period employer is not observable.

The analysis becomes more complicated when there are limits on the observability of the outside wage offer. For reasons of tractability, we only consider cases where productivity with the first-period employer is observable. Two cases are analyzed—where the outside offer is never observable by the firm and where it is not observable in time to make a counteroffer but becomes observable in time to condition the transferable pension on earnings elsewhere.

When the transferable pension can depend on earnings elsewhere, low earnings and low productivity result in constant consumption over time, a positive transferable pension, and mobility if and only if wages elsewhere exceed productivity with the first-period employer. With low productivity and a high outside offer, there is mobility and no transferable pension. With high productivity, there is no transferable pension and a wage offer from the first-period employer below productivity. Mobility depends on the comparison of wage offers. Thus, workers sometimes move when wages elsewhere are below productivity with the first-period firm.

When the outside offer is totally unobservable, both types of inefficiency become possible. When productivity is high, the worker will sometimes move to a wage below his productivity. When productivity is low, the worker sometimes will stay with his first-period employer even though the wage exceeds productivity. There will be a positive transferable pension for some of his productivities.

Notes

1. To see the effects of private savings on optimal social insurance, contrast our papers (1978) and (1982).

2. This is not quite right if deferred payments are made only in period 3, but there is no reason in the model for such a restriction.

3. We are indebted to Robert Merton for pointing out this aspect of this example.

4. For analyses of mobility with alternative contractual assumptions, see Mortenson (1978), Diamond and Maskin (1979), Hall and Lazear (1981), Moore (1982), Deere (1983), and Spinnewyn (1982).

5. We also assume that f has a sufficiently large support to allow all the cases we consider below. In particular, we assume that $m\frac{1}{2}$ might be larger or smaller than m_2 for all values of m_2 and m_2 might be larger or smaller than $2w_1$ for the equilibrium value of w_1.

6. Hall (1982) has estimated that approximately half of current jobs will have lasted for at least 20 years by their termination. From his numbers, one can also infer the obverse, that approximately half of workers will never hold any single job for as long as 20 years.

7. Bulow and Scholes (1984) consider a model where implicit contracts between firm and worker are replaced by implicit contracts among workers. Because of the complications of union institutional structure and politics we confine our discussion to nonunion plans. However, it is tempting to speculate on the large differences between single-employer and multi-employer plans.

8. Firing a salesman to prevent his collecting commissions on a previously negotiated deal did lead to damages in Fortune v. National Cash Register Co., Supreme Judicial Court of Massachusetts 1977, 373 Mass. 96, 364 N.E. 2d 1851. We are indebted to Melvin Eisenberg for this reference.

9. For models of reputation for consumer good quality with a similar character, see Dybvig and Spatt (1980), Klein and Leffler (1981), and Shapiro (1981).

10. This appearance is clearest in the use of profit sharing for defined contribution plans.

11. The ERISA rules to limit backloading are an example of such consumer protection. It is curious that the rules assume no wage growth.

Comment   Robert C. Merton

1. Introduction

In a world of full information and perfect markets, where all assets (including human capital) are freely tradable, private pensions provide nothing more than another way for individuals to save.[1] With a full complement of risk-sharing securities available, the worker can fully offset or modify any particular form of payouts prescribed by the pension plan. Hence, the type of pension plan offered would be a matter of indifference to workers. Like the Modigliani-Miller theorem for corporate liabilities, the optimal choice of pension plan would at most be a function of the tax laws and perhaps certain kinds of transactions costs. In such an environment and in the absence of explicit contracts to the contrary, the spot-market view of total employee compensation would obtain where this period's wages plus incremental vested retirement benefits are equal to the worker's current marginal product.[2] For pension plans to have a greater functional significance than that of "just one more security," there must

Robert C. Merton is J. C. Penney Professor of Management at the Sloan School of Management, Massachusetts Institute of Technology, and research associate, National Bureau of Economic Research.

1. The saving component is obvious for a defined contribution plan. It also takes place for a defined benefit plan whether or not the firm funds the plan with a pension fund since the (pension) liability issued to the worker in lieu of other cash compensation provides resources to the firm for financing investment just like the issuing of any other liability.

2. This assumes that firms are competitors in the labor market. For a development of the spot market theory with respect to pension liabilities, see Bulow (1982).

be important market imperfections, and the most likely place for these imperfections to occur is in the labor market.[3]

There are, of course, severe impediments to the trading of human capital. The two most prominent explanations for this nontradability are (1) the moral hazard or incentive problem that having once sold off the rights to their earnings, workers will no longer have the incentive to work, and (2) the broad social and legal prohibition of (indentured) slavery whether voluntary or otherwise. The well-known effects of this nontradability are to "force" workers to save more than they might otherwise choose and to cause them to bear much of the risk (both systematic and nonsystematic)[4] of their human capital. In addition to distorting the consumption-saving choice, the nonoptimal risk bearing of the risks of human capital may cause inefficient investment of resources in developing human capital.[5]

In "Insurance Aspects of Pensions," Diamond and Mirrlees explore the possible role of private pensions in insuring the worker against some of the risk associated with his nonmarketable human capital.[6] Their analysis leans heavily on the Harris and Holmstrom (1982) theory of implicit contracts in the labor market. By assuming away the incentive problems associated with the effective sale of human capital, Diamond and Mirrlees focus on contracts that taken into account the limitations on workers to bind themselves now to work in the future for less than they could otherwise earn in the absence of such contracts.

As Diamond and Mirrlees themselves note, their model uses a number of assumptions that are wholly unrealistic even by the standards of casual empiricism. Many of these assumptions are constructive in that they merely simplify the analysis without severely distorting the validity of their central conclusions. Others, however, are crucial in reaching their results, and it is on these that I focus this discussion.

As will be shown, the structure of the labor contracts derived by Diamond and Mirrlees (and, for that matter, by Harris and Holmstrom) are isomorphic to various put and call option contracts. Reformulating

3. If the state is paternalistic and wants to avoid the free rider problem, it may choose to provide tax incentives to induce saving through pensions together with nonassignment of the pension and penalties for early withdrawal to enforce the availability of adequate unencumbered assets for the individual to fund his retirement. Even with no labor market imperfections, these distortions could lead to optimal characteristics for pension plans that minimize the effects of the distortions.

4. Nonsystematic risk is risk that can be eliminated through diversification when there are available adequate risk-sharing financial instruments. Systematic risk is risk that cannot be eliminated by these means and hence is a risk that must be borne by the economy even with perfect insurance markets.

5. Thus, a worker may spend real resources to reduce the risk of his human capital by pursuing training that makes him able to undertake a wider variety of jobs. Such diversification of the worker's human capital would not be an optimal allocation if it simply reduces nonsystematic risk.

6. See Nalebuff and Zeckhauser (1981), especially App. 1, for a similar analysis.

their findings in this context will help to shed light on the sensitivity of their conclusions to certain of their assumptions. Moreover, the extensive literature on the evaluation of options permits the derivation of comparative statics results that might otherwise not be apparent.[7] The options analogy is developed first in section 2 within the context of the "mobility-threat" model where the equilibrium contract leads to no actual changes in employer by the worker. In section 3, the analogy is extended to the more complex cases of exogenous and endogenous mobility where workers will change employers under the appropriate equilibrium conditions. Section 4 provides a brief summary and overview of the Diamond-Mirrlees model.

2.   Optimal Labor Contracts Viewed as Options: Mobility Threats

The model presented in section 11.2 of the Diamond-Mirrlees paper assumes a three-period life for each worker (two work periods and a retirement period) and that workers are risk averse with an additive separable and symmetric utility function for lifetime consumption. It is assumed that firms have full access to a well-functioning capital market and that all securities are priced to yield the same expected return. This "common" expected return is assumed to be zero in real terms, and all contracts (explicit or implicit) are expressed in real terms. In sharp contrast, workers are assumed to have no access to the capital market and own no assets other than their human capital. Thus, workers cannot borrow, and they can only save if the firm (acting as an intermediary) does it for them. In this version of the model it is assumed that a worker's marginal product in period t ($t = 1, 2$) is the same for all firms (i.e., $m_t = m_t'$). (This assumption is relaxed in later sections.) Firms (other than perhaps the worker's current employer) are always willing to pay the worker his marginal product (to them), m_t', if the employee is willing to move.

To locate and understand the model, consider first the case where there are no restrictions on contracts between the worker and the firm. In this case, the only constraint on the contract is that its present value, PV, satisfy

$$(1) \qquad\qquad PV = m_1 + E(m_2),$$

which is the value to the firm at time 1 of receiving the labor of the worker throughout his work life. Because there is no risk premium paid for risk bearing and workers are risk averse, the optimal (worker utility maximizing) contract provides for the worker to bear no risk. By the assumptions of symmetric utility and a zero interest rate, the optimal contract would pay the worker a first-period wage, $w_1 = PV/3$; a guaranteed second-period wage, $w_2 = PV/3$; and a pension benefit payment, $b = PV/3$. In return, the worker would agree to work for his original employer for his

7. See Smith (1976) and Mason and Merton (1984) for surveys of the option literature including its application in the evaluation of nonfinancial market options.

entire work life, independently of what his (currently unknown) marginal product, m_2, turns out to be in period 2. If the worker were permitted to enter into such a binding agreement with his employer, then this unrestricted optimal contract is feasible.

The worker cannot, however, bind himself to work for his current employer in the second period. The employer must, therefore, take into account that the worker will leave in the event that the total compensation offered by a competing firm in the second period plus any transferable component of his pension from his original employer, $m_2' + b'$, exceeds the total compensation $2PV/3$ provided by the contract with his original employer. Thus, unless the probability that $m_2' + b' > 2PV/3$ is zero, the unrestricted optimal contract is not feasible and the worker must bear some risk.

Given this constraint and the condition that $b' \geq 0$, Diamond and Mirrlees (eq. [2]) show that the optimal contract calls for a (combined retirement and) second-period compensation given by

$$(2) \qquad W(m_2) = \max(2w_1, m_2)$$

and a transferable pension $b' = 0$.

A call option on a security (or payment) gives its owner the right to buy the security at a specified price I (the "exercise price") as of a given date. The right to buy also implies the right *not* to buy. If the owner chooses not to buy, the call option expires, worthless. Thus, the payoff to a call option on its expiration date is given by $\max(0, X - I)$, where X is the price of the security on that date. Rewriting (4) as

$$(2') \qquad W(m_2) = 2w_1 + \max(0, m_2 - 2w_1),$$

we have that the optimal contract provides for a guaranteed payment of $2w_1$ plus a call option on the worker's second-period marginal product with an exercise price of $2w_1$. If $C(X, I)$ denotes the market value of a call option on a security with current value X and exercise price I,[8] then the budget constraint (1) requires that the value of what the worker receives— first-period wage, w_1, plus second-period guaranteed payment, $2w_1$, plus the call option $C[E(m_2), 2w_1]$—equals the present value of his human capital. That is,

$$(3) \qquad 3w_1 + C[E(m_2), 2w_1] = PV = m_1 + E(m_2).$$

Because the payoff to a call option is nonnegative, $C[E(m_2), 2w_1] \geq 0$ with equality holding if and only if $\mathrm{pr}\{m_2 > 2w_1\} = 0$. It follows, therefore, that $w_1 < PV/3$ unless $\mathrm{pr}\{m_2 > 2[m_1 + E(m_2)]/3\} = 0$.

---

8. In the special case assumed by Diamond and Mirrlees of risk-neutral security pricing and a zero interest rate, $X = E(\tilde{X})$ where $\tilde{X}$ is the random variable value of the security at the expiration date of the option and $C(X, I) = E[\max(0, \tilde{X} - I)]$.

Armed with this description, the following comparative statics results follow directly from budget constraint (3): If we hold fixed the distribution of $m_2 - E(m_2)$, then by the implicit function theorem, we have that

(4)
$$\frac{dw_1}{dE(m_2)} = \left[1 - \frac{\partial C}{\partial X} \right] / \left[3 + 2\frac{\partial C}{\partial I} \right].$$

As is well known for call option valuations, $0 \leq \partial C/\partial X \leq 1$ and $0 \geq \partial C/\partial I \geq -1$. Hence, $dw_1/dE(m_2) \geq 0$ with strict equality holding only if $\mathrm{pr}\{m_2 < 2w_1\} = 0$. Thus, ceteris paribus, a higher expected second-period marginal product leads to a higher current wage and a higher second-period "guaranteed" wage floor.

Consider instead a "mean-preserving" spread on m_2, where $E(m_2)$ is held fixed and the uncertainty about the second-period wage, σ, increases. From (3),

(5)
$$\frac{dw_1}{d\sigma} = -\frac{\partial C}{\partial \sigma} / \left(3 + 2\frac{\partial C}{\partial I} \right).$$

Again a well-known result for call options is that $\partial C/\partial \sigma \geq 0$ with strict equality holding only if $\mathrm{pr}\{m_2 > 2w_1\} = 1$ or 0. Thus, the greater the uncertainty about the worker's second-period marginal product, the smaller is the current wage and the lower is the second-period wage floor. It follows immediately that the amount of risk borne by the worker increases the greater the uncertainty about his future marginal product.

Although pursued no further here, the known relations for option prices can be used to derive other comparative statics results. It should be noted that the applied properties for option prices do not depend on the assumptions of risk-neutral pricing of securities in the capital markets or a zero interest rate. Hence, relaxing these assumptions will not affect the basic comparative statics results, although the existence of a positive risk-return trade-off may alter somewhat the structure of the optimal contract.

A put option gives its owner the right to sell a security at a specified exercise price on a specified date. The payoff to a put option on its expiration date is given by $\max(0, I - X)$, where I is the exercise price and X is the price of the security on that date. The standard functional description of a put option is that of insurance because the purchase of a put protects the owner of the underlying security against losses (in value) below the specified floor I. To see this insurance feature of the optimal contract, I rewrite (2) as

(2″)
$$W(m_2) = m_2 + \max(0, 2w_1 - m_2).$$

Hence, the optimal contract provides the worker with a put option or insurance on the future wage he would otherwise earn if the labor market were simply a spot market. Of course, the worker pays for this insurance out of his current wage. That is, the budget constraint (1) can be written as

(6) $w_1 = m_1 - P[E(m_2), 2w_1]$,

where $P(X, I)$ is the value of a put option with an exercise price of I on a security with current value X. Although (6) follows directly from (3) by the parity theorem for option prices,[9] expressing the budget constraint in the form of (6) makes more apparent the result that the first-period wage w_1 must always be less than the first-period marginal product m_1.

This result underscores how binding the assumed constraint of no borrowing by workers (embedded in the model by requiring $b' \geq 0$) can be in the determination of the optimal feasible contract. Thus, at the extreme where the worker's current marginal product $m_1 = 0$, the worker's current wage $w_1 = 0$, and moreover he can obtain no insurance for his future earnings. This is so no matter how large is the worker's future expected productivity $E(m_2)$. In a richer model where the worker can influence his current and future marginal products through training or choice of career path, it is readily apparent that the no-borrowing constraint (which is central to the model here) will cause severe distortions of the optimal labor force configuration. That is, with this constraint, workers achieve substantial benefits in terms of both the level of early life consumption *and* the reduction of risk surrounding later life consumption by choosing a job pattern with relatively high early life marginal product m_1 even at the expense of a large reduction in expected future marginal product, $E(m_2)$.

3.   Optimal Labor Contracts Viewed as Options: Exogenous and Endogenous Mobility

In the Harris-Holmstrom type model where the worker's marginal product is the same for all firms, the worker will never change employers in equilibrium and transferable pensions play no role in intermediating the risk of human capital. However, if the worker must change employers for exogenous reasons, or if the worker can have different marginal products at different firms, then the worker may move in equilibrium. Although Diamond and Mirrlees discuss the cases of exogenous and endogenous mobility separately, the discussion here combines these cases in a single model.

As with the mobility-threat analysis, Diamond and Mirrlees derive the optimal contract under the condition that the firm can offer a transferable pension b' if the employee moves and a total compensation floor if the employee stays. If the worker is forced to move ("exogenous mobility"), then he receives $m' + b'$. The probability of such a move, p, is given exogenously. Otherwise, the worker will move only if his total compensation at the new firm, $m_2' + b'$, exceeds that offered by his original employer.

---

9. See Smith (1976) or Mason and Merton (1984) for proof of the theorem by arbitrage. In the special case of a zero interest rate, the theorem requires that $C(X, I) = X - I + P(X, I)$.

Although not stated explicitly, Diamond and Mirrlees make an important assumption about the structure of the labor market. In the initial period, all firms compete equally to hire the services of the (unattached) worker. In the second-period compensation negotiations, Diamond and Mirrlees assume an asymmetry between the worker's current employer and all other potential employers which gives the worker's current employer an advantage. They postulate those firms which attempt to hire a worker away from his original firm must pay a wage equal to his full marginal product m_2' whereas the current employer need only match the total compensation provided to the worker for moving, $m_2' + b'$, to induce the worker to stay. Since the transferable pension (if any) b' is a "sunk" cost which the firm will have to pay if the employee moves, the current employer derives a benefit from this monopsony power equal to $(m_2 - m_2')$, which is nonnegative whenever it is optimal for the worker to remain with his original employer.

As in the discussion of the mobility threat case in the previous section, I begin with an analysis of the worker's situation when there are no restrictions on contracts. In the absence of monopsony power, the present value of the worker's human capital is given by

$$(7) \qquad W_1 = m' + pE(m') + (1 - p)E[\max (m_2, m_2')].$$

As before, the unrestricted optimal contract is riskless to the worker with $w_1 = W_1/3$, $w_2 = W_1/3$, and $b = b' = W_1/3$; and in return the original employer receives the worker's marginal product whether he moves or not. Introduction of the Diamond-Mirrlees asymmetry assumption might seem to lower the present value of the worker's human capital to equal $m_1 + pE(m') + (1 - p)E(m_2')$. However, because firms are competitive in the initial period, they must pay for this right to "exploit" the worker in the second period. That is, they will pay the worker a "signing bonus" given by

$$(8) \quad (1 - p)E[\max (m_2, m_2') - m_2'] = (1 - p)E[\max(0, m_2 - m_2')].$$

By inspection of (8), max $(0, m_2 - m_2')$ is the payoff to a call option on a payment of $m_2 - m_2'$ with a zero exercise price, and we denote its price by $C[E(m_2 - m_2'), 0]$. (Note: Unlike the "usual case" of a call option on a limited liability instrument, $C[E(m_2 - m_2'), 0] > \max [0, E(m_2 - m_2')]$ if the $\mathrm{pr}\{m_2 > m_2'\} > 0$. Hence, even if the expected future marginal product of the worker with his current employer, $E(m_2)$, is less than or equal to his expected future marginal product elsewhere, $E(m_2')$, the signing bonus will be positive.) In the Harris-Holmstrom case, where $m_2 = m_2'$, there is no value to the firm of obtaining this second-period monopsony power, and hence its assumption has no influence on the analysis of the mobility threat case.

As Diamond and Mirrlees show, when the worker's second-period earnings, y (whether with the current employer or not), can be observed ex post at the end of the second period, the optimal labor contract calls for a transferable pension given by $b'(y) = \max(0, 2w_1 - y)$ if the worker moves and a compensation package equal to $\max(2w_1, m_2)$ if the worker stays with his original employer. If the worker is not forced to move, then this contract leads to the worker's staying with his current employer if and only if $m_2 \geq m'_2$.

The worker's second- (and retirement) period compensation is given by

$$(9) \qquad W(y) = y + \max(0, 2w_1 - y),$$

which in terms of structure is the same as the Harris-Holmstrom case $(2'')$. However, in (9), $y = m'$ if the worker is forced to move and $y = m'_2$ otherwise. From (9), it would appear that, from the worker's perspective, his second-period compensation does not depend on his second-period marginal product with his original employer, m_2. This is true in the ex post sense of the uncertainties surrounding y, given the wage floor, $2w_1$. However, the ex ante distributional characteristics of m_2 do affect $W(y)$ because they affect the first-period wage and hence the second-period wage floor.

To determine the first-period wage w_1, equate the value that the firm receives in return for the contract (i.e., the worker's first-period marginal product plus the right to exploit the worker in the second period) to the cost of the contract (i.e., the worker's first-period wage plus the insurance provided by the transferable pension and the wage floor). Expressed in terms of the option value equivalent of the contract, we have that

$$
\begin{aligned}
(10) \qquad w_1 = {} & m_1 + (1 - p)C[E(m_2 - m'_2), 0] \\
& - pP[E(m'), 2w_1] - (1 - p)P[E(m'_2), 2w_1].
\end{aligned}
$$

By inspection, the distributional characteristics of m_2 (and not just its expected value) affect the first-period wage through their influence on the call option price, which reflects the value of the signing bonus.

Comparative statics results along the lines of the previous section can be computed from (10). I do so here only with respect to the effect of a change in p as the means of providing a few comments on the Diamond-Mirrlees exogenous mobility model presented in their section 11.3. From (10), we have that

$$
\begin{aligned}
(11) \qquad \operatorname{sign}\left(\frac{dw_1}{dp}\right) = {} & \operatorname{sign}\{P[E(m'_2), 2w_1] \\
& - P[E(m'), 2w_1] - C[E(m_2 - m'_2), 0]\}.
\end{aligned}
$$

In the case of exogenous mobility alone (i.e., $m_2 = m'_2$), the sign of dw_1/dp depends on the value of a put option on the worker's marginal product when he is forced to move, m', relative to the value of a put option of identical terms on the worker's marginal product when he can either stay or move, m_2'. Although it is, of course, conceivable for m' to have a more favorable distribution than m_2 or m_2', it would appear to be a rather strained definition of a forced or exogenous move if the worker receives a wage m' in excess of what he would have earned otherwise. This belief is further reinforced by the model's assumption that among all the firms that might offer the worker a job in the nonforced case, the best offer will be a wage equal to the one available from the worker's current employer. Moreover, if, as Diamond and Mirrlees at one point assume, the exogenous move is the result of a disability, then the case for $m' < m_2$ would seem especially compelling.

If one postulates that $m' < m_2'$, then, the value of the put option insurance on m' is greater than the value of the corresponding insurance on m_2'. From (11), we have unambiguously that $dw_1/dp < 0$. That is, if the probability of ending up in the disadvantaged state of being forced to leave your current employer increases, then the worker must (and is willing to) pay more to insure against the lost income in this state by accepting both a lower first-period wage and a lower floor on guaranteed compensation.

Making this incremental assumption also provides some insight into Diamond and Mirrlees's proposition 1, which provides sufficient conditions for the optimal transferable pension, b', to be positive. By assuming that $m_2 < [m_1 + (1 - p)E(m_2)]/3/2 - p)$ for all m_2, they ensure that $m_2 < 2w_1$, the equilibrium wage floor. Hence, in the event of no forced move, the put option on m_2 will always be exercised and the worker receives a guaranteed second-period wage with no uncertainty. If the transferable pension is restricted to be a constant, then the budget constraint is

$$(12) \qquad w_1 = m_1 - pb' - (1 - p)[2w_1 - E(m_2)]$$

because $P[E(m_2), 2w_1] = 2w_1 - E(m_2)$ in this case. From (12), if $b' = 0$, then $2w_1 = [m_1 + (1 - p)E(m_2)]/[3/2 - p]$, which, by hypothesis, strictly exceeds the maximum possible marginal product to be earned in period 2. Thus, it pays to transfer at least the residual value to a transferable pension, which reduces the risk of lost income when forced to move.

By dispensing with the requirement that $b' > 0$ be a constant and positive for all possible m' and assuming that $m' < m_2$, the role for a transferable pension is established without the extreme conditions of proposition 1.

Although Diamond and Mirrlees examine a variety of other cases where various marginal products are or are not observable, I have focused exclusively on the case where the transferable pension can be made a function of the ex post second-period earnings of the worker and the wage floor provided to the worker, if he stays, is a constant. This choice was not arbitrary. This case surely establishes a nontrivial role for private pensions as a means of reducing risk to workers. The derived rules for the transferable pension and wage floor are simple and yet appear to be reasonably robust.

Thus, while the level of the floor and maximum transferable pension depend on the symmetry of the worker's utility function to be a true optimum, they do not depend on the specific form of the worker's utility function, which some of their other derived rules do. Having the transferable pension benefit depend on ex post earnings seems to be a practical possibility. By inspection of income tax returns, the pension-paying firm could verify the later year earnings for computing pension benefits. Although there is in principle an incentive for the worker to cheat by hiding his income, this possibility would not appear to be serious because it is difficult for workers to avoid declaring wages or benefits reported on W-2 forms. Moreover, to do so would require that the worker cheat on his federal income taxes and thereby expose himself to those penalties as well. The derived plan has the further virtue of not requiring the pension-paying firm to distinguish between involuntary moves (e.g., disability) and voluntary moves.

4. Summary and Conclusion

The Diamond and Mirrlees analysis should stimulate much-needed additional research into the role of pensions when there are significant labor market imperfections. Although their model is almost too simple, many of their assumptions can be relaxed without seriously affecting their basic conclusions. I applaud their attempt to bring institutional and legal constraints into the discussion of feasible contracts for their model.

Perhaps with a bit of irony, such real world legal constraints may rule out their assumption that the firm can "exploit" its current employees by paying them $m' + b'$ when $m_2 > m_2'$. If, for example, $m_2 > m_2' > 2w_1$, then it is likely that the firm will be hiring new workers in addition to their current labor force. Since by their other assumption firms must pay new workers their full marginal product, it is not clear that it would stand a legal test for the firm to pay "new" workers (who are otherwise the same) more than "old" workers. The sensitivity of their contract schemes to this issue warrants further study.

Diamond and Mirrlees raise the important issue of the firm's defaulting on its labor contracts. The manifest impact of such a default is that the workers may not be paid the transferable pension and "wage floor" benefits promised in both the explicit and implicit parts of the labor contract. If workers fully recognize this possibility ex ante, when the contract is negotiated, they will receive compensation for this risk in the form of either a higher first-period wage or larger promised future benefits. Even in this case, however, it is straightforward to show that the workers' expected utility will fall relative to the case where such defaults are ruled out. If, as would seem reasonable, the fortunes of the firm and the future marginal product of its workers are strongly positively correlated, it is more likely that default will occur in precisely those states where the worker most needs the promised benefits. Thus, the utility loss from the possibility of default could be substantial.

There is another—perhaps latent—impact of default that may significantly limit the magnitude and duration of the future promised benefits component of labor contracts. Bankruptcy is, of course, bad for the firm—but it is less bad than if the owners (shareholders) were required to contribute additional sums to the firm in order that it could fulfill its obligation and avoid bankruptcy. As has been shown in the finance literature, it is not the shareholders who lose in a bankruptcy, but the other liability-holders who are not paid what they are promised. From this follows the well-known result that if the riskiness of the firm's assets increases, then there will be a transfer of value from the current nonequity liability-holders to the stockholders, and this occurs even if such an increase has no effect on the overall market value of the firm. Thus, the managers of limited liability firms have an incentive to increase the riskiness of their assets (even if there is no compensating higher expected return on the assets).[10] In the Diamond-Mirrlees context, the workers are explicit non-equity liabilityholders of the firm with respect to their vested pension benefits and implicit liabilityholders with respect to the firm's promise of a floor on future wages. Hence, they face a potential moral hazard problem with respect to the firm not unlike the one that rules out or severely limits the sale of their own human capital.

Since the potential for gain to the stockholders from such a "liability-induced" shift in the risk of the firm's assets is an increasing function of both the size and the maturity of the nonequity liabilities, the moral hazard problem can be reduced by limiting the magnitude of the liabilities and making them of relatively short duration. For explicit corporate liabilities, the problem is further reduced by the introduction of indenture restrictions that limit the types of investments the firm can make without the liabilityholders' approval. A relevant example is a corporate pension plan that requires that a specified portion of the firm's assets be segregated in a pension fund; gives the pension liabilityholders first claim on these assets; and sets guidelines for the types of assets held in the fund. Thus, with the possibility of default, optimal labor contracts will have a smaller proportion of total compensation in the form of promised future benefits than would be predicted by the Diamond-Mirrlees analysis. Moreover, the relative proportion of explicit to implicit contract benefits will also be larger, which suggests that vested and transferable pensions may have an even more important role in improving the risk-bearing opportunities for workers.

---

10. Thus, even if all securities and assets are priced in a risk-neutral fashion, the presence of bankruptcy possibililties may induce what appears to be "risk-loving-like" behavior on the part of managers in their selection of the firm's assets.

If the moral hazard problem surrounding default by the firm can be neglected, then the manifest impact of bankruptcy can be formally integrated into the current Diamond-Mirrlees model by recognizing that the workers, as part of the implicit labor contract, grant a put option to the firm with an exercise price equal to the total promised second-period benefits.

In the case of default on pension benefits, which are a legal liability of the firm, the firm would face actual bankruptcy and the underlying security for the put option would be the firm's assets. In the (perhaps more interesting) case of default on implicitly contracted wage floors, there would be no formal bankruptcy. While it is not always clear what the underlying security for the put is in this case, I would agree with Diamond and Mirrlees that it is probably the value of the intangible asset called "reputation" lost by the firm when it does not meet its implicit contract obligations. Such an analysis might also explain why some firms when facing hard times choose to employ all their long-term workers part time instead of firing some workers and keeping others full time. In effect, like bondholders in a single debt issue, partial employment permits all workers with defaulted implicit claims to share what amount is available, whereas full employment of some and no employment for others would be the equivalent in a regular bankruptcy of randomly paying some bondholders full face value and others nothing at all. Using the established results from option pricing, one could perhaps identify the type of firms (e.g., by risk characteristics) in which implicit labor contracts with floors are likely to be important.

Finally, I would note that the derived payoff structure to the transferable pension benefit, $b' = \max(0, 2w_1 - y)$, looks remarkably similar to the structure of a defined benefit private pension plan that is integrated with social security.[11] In effect, the Diamond-Mirrlees pension benefit is equivalent to a defined benefit plan integrated with other private plans instead of social security. Since they derive this structure as the solution of an optimal plan, it may be possible to derive similar normative properties, heretofore unrecognized, for integrated pension plans.

References

Bulow, J. I. 1982. What are corporate pension liabilities? *Quarterly Journal of Economics* 97:435–52.
Bulow, J. I., and Scholes, M. S. 1984. Who owns the assets in a defined benefit pension plan? In *Financial aspects of the United States pension*

11. See Merton et al. (1984) for a discussion of the insurance aspects of integrated pension plans and their isomorphic relation to put options.

system, ed. Z. Bodie and J. B. Shoven. Chicago: University of Chicago Press (for NBER).

Bulow, J. I.; Scholes, M. S.; and Menell, P. 1984. Economic implications of ERISA. In *Financial aspects of the United States pension system,* ed. Z. Bodie and J. B. Shoven. Chicago: University of Chicago Press (for NBER).

Burton, S. 1980. Breach of contract and the common law duty to perform in good faith. *Harvard Law Review* 94:369–405.

Deere, D. 1983. Labor market distortions, labor turnover, and the role of unemployment insurance. Ph.D. dissertation, Massachusetts Institute of Technology.

Diamond, P. and Maskin, E. 1979. An equilibrium analysis of search and breach of contract. *Bell Journal of Economics* 10:212–316.

Diamond, P., and Mirrlees, J. 1978. Social insurance with variable retirement. *Journal of Public Economics.*

———. 1982. Social insurance with variable retirement and private savings. MIT Working Paper.

Dybvig, P., and Spatt, C. 1980. Does it pay to maintain a reputation? Unpublished.

Hall, R. 1982. The importance of lifetime jobs in the U.S. economy. *American Economic Review* 72:716–24.

Hall, R., and Lazear, E. 1984. The excess sensitivity of layoffs and quits to demand. *Journal of Labor Economics* 2:000–000.

Harris, M., and Holmstrom, B. 1982. A theory of wage dynamics. *Review of Economic Studies* 49:315–33.

Hart, O. 1983. Optimal labour contracts under asymmetric information: An introduction. *Review of Economic Studies* 50:3–35.

Klein, B., and Leffler, K. 1981. The role of market forces in assuming contractual performance. *Journal of Political Economy* 89:615–41.

Mason, S., and Merton, R. C. 1984. The role of contingent claims analysis in corporate finance. Harvard Business School Working Paper (February).

Merton, R. C.; Bodie, Z.; and Marcus, A. J. 1984. Pension plan integration as insurance against social security risk. NBER Working Paper 1370.

Mirrlees, J. 1982. Migration and optimal income taxes. *Journal of Public Economics* 18:319–41.

Moore, J. 1982. Optimal labor contracts when workers have a variety of privately observed reservation wages. Birkbeck College Discussion Paper.

Mortenson, D. 1978. Specific capital and labor turnover. *Bell Journal of Economics* 9:572–86.

Nalebuff, B., and Zeckhauser, R. 1981. Involuntary unemployment reconsidered: Second-best contracting with heterogenous firms and workers. Mimeographed. Cambridge: Harvard University, Department of Economics, October.

Shapiro, C. 1983. Premiums for high quality products as rents to reputation. *Quarterly Journal of Economics* 97:659–79.

Smith, C. W. 1976. Option pricing, a review. *Journal of Financial Economics* 3:3–51.

Spinnewyn, F. 1983. Long-term labor contracts viewed as saving workers within the firm: A dual approach. CORE Discussion Paper 8308.

12   The Riskiness of Private Pensions

Jerry R. Green

12.1   Introduction

Private pensions represent the contract between workers and their employers. The future benefits of the pensions are an asset for the workers who hold them. The contractual obligations of the plan to the worker are quite complex. Benefits are due in a variety of circumstances, in each of which a complicated formula may be employed to determine the amount to be paid. Plans differ both in the description in these circumstances and in the nature of these formulas.

It is important to recognize that the pension does not represent a claim to a perfectly certain stream of resources. Plans with differing provisions will differ both in the mean payoff and in its variability. Moreover, when computing the mean and the variability of pension benefits the age of the worker and his length of job tenure should be considered. Different plans may favor different sets of workers.

The object of this paper is to discover how the alternative forms of the pension contract affect these means and variabilities for workers of different circumstances. Specifically, I aim to provide some information relevant to the following questions. How should workers evaluate respective benefit packages offered to them by different plans? How does this assessment depend on the workers' expectations of economic risks such as fluctuations in wages, interest rates, and inflation? How does it depend on their beliefs about longevity, disability, retirement, and their propensity toward mobility in employment? Will the evaluation of different plans differ markedly for workers of different ages and job tenure?

Jerry R. Green is professor of economics at Harvard University and a research associate at the National Bureau of Economic Research.

I gratefully acknowledge excellent research assistance by Arturo Estrella and helpful comments from Alan Auerbach, Peter Diamond, and Herman Leonard.

357

It may be useful at the outset to reflect on the sources of risk faced by a worker enrolled in a pension plan. Some risks, such as fluctuations in the price level or interest rate, are common to all workers living at the same time. Others, like the future wage of a worker on which a pension may be based, are correlated across workers covered in the same plan. They are also positively correlated for workers in different plans or different industries. Finally, individual-specific risks such as death and disability are unlikely to be strongly correlated even among workers in the same plan.

In addition, we must consider risk factors that are not exogenous to the individual. For a worker with vested benefits, his decision to leave the firm would cause a reduction in the benefits he would receive from his pension plan on retirement. Moreover, for those plans with an early retirement provision, such a decision would change the value of accrued benefits. Workers who are not fully vested face even more of a loss when they voluntarily terminate employment.

The complexity of pension plans and the multifaceted nature of the risks mentioned above make it impossible to conduct a purely theoretical analysis of the questions in which we are interested. Therefore, the methodology of this paper will be to use simulation analysis. I compare four different forms of a pension contract. I simulate the economically relevant events during the worker's lifetime, both macroeconomic events and the individual-specific events mentioned above, as they evolve during his lifetime. To the extent possible I have used current actuarial projections.

The analysis in this paper has importance for studying the impact of private pensions in the national economy. Most studies to date have regarded the pension asset as a claim to a perfectly certain stream of consumption for the worker. It is clear that this is far from the case. In studying saving behavior, for example, it is important to distinguish between individuals' holdings of financial assets in their own name and the amount of their private pension wealth. The two are far from perfect substitutes.

Similar considerations apply for the issuers of pensions. Firms have an implicit liability to their pension holders. The riskiness of this liability has not as yet been treated. Because pensions cover a large number of workers, the law of large numbers mitigates those components of the risk that are due to individual-specific events. However, macroeconomic risks do affect the realized present value of aggregate plan liabilities. Therefore, even if pensions were recognized by both sides of the "pension market" as a form of contractual arrangement that should be incorporated into their respective wealth calculations, the net effect on national savings might very well be nonzero because the relevant risks cannot be perfectly insured. The certainty equivalent value of a pension for workers in the plan is probably much less than the value of the liability that it represents to the stockholder in the firm. Therefore, distributional considerations aside, pensions decrease the value of other forms of saving by workers by less than they increase the required saving by stockholders necessary to offset their indirect pension liabilities.

By providing information about the risks inherent in pension contracts this paper will be a useful and important ingredient in the analysis of the role of private pensions in the economy. In addition, by comparing different plans with respect to their riskiness, insight might be gained into the problem of designing new plans and into the selection of benefit changes in existing plans that would be most beneficial to their members.

12.2   Description of Plans to Be Compared

I compare four hypothetical forms of pension plans. These plans differ both in the way that they compute benefit levels for retired workers and in the circumstances other than retirement under which benefits are paid. There are three types of these payments: early retirement, disability, and death benefits. Some of the plans provide benefits to a surviving spouse in the event of preretirement death. None provides postretirement death benefits.

The four plans studied also differ slightly in the vesting formulas used. Basically, they provide for 10-year vesting, but two of them gradually increase the vesting level from 50% at the tenth year to 100% at the fifteenth year of service.

The most important difference among the plans is in the way the benefits are computed.

In Plan 0, a "conventional" plan, benefits are proportional to the average of the highest 10 annual compensations. The proportion is increasing linearly with years of service. In Plan 1, a "pattern" plan, the benefit is a fixed dollar sum per year of service. Plans 2 and 3 are more complex. Plan 2 is a "career average" plan. The benefit is a fixed proportion of each year's compensation. This plan is favorable to workers with long tenure in the firm. Plan 3, a "final salary basis" plan, is a mixture of a proportion of the individual's highest salary plus a bonus for workers with very long tenure. In addition, Plan 3 uses the worker's best four years as a base for the computations, whereas Plan 2 bases benefits on the compensation received in all years.

Table 12.1 summarizes these provisions.

12.3   Description of the Simulation of Benefits Received

12.3.1   General Description

Two sets of simulations were conducted. The first takes the plans precisely as specified above. The second suppresses all pension benefits except the retirement benefit. This enables us to focus more clearly on the

Table 12.1   **Plans**

Plan	Vesting	Early Retirement	Disability	Death Benefit (Preretirement)	Benefit
0 Conventional	10 years	—	—	—	1½% per year of service times average of highest 10 annual compensation
1 Pattern	10 years	a)Age 55 Pension minus 3% for each year under 65 (or if less, by 3% for 85 − age + service) b)Age 62 Full pension if 10 years' service	10 years' service Full pension	Age 55 or more Spouse receives 50% of early retirement benefit for life	$144 per year for each year of service
2 Career average	10 years: 50% + 10% for each additional year. 5 years if age + service ≥ 45: 50% + 10% for each additional year. Age 60: 100%	Age 55 and 10 years' service. Reduce pension by 2.2% per year for first 3 years below 65; 4.8% per year thereafter	Age 55, 10 years' service. Reduce pension by 2.2% per year for first 3 years below 65; 4.8% per year thereafter	None	½% of 1973 compensation times years of service prior to 1975 + ¾% of each subsequent year's compensation
3 Final salary	10 years: 50% + 10% for each additional year. 5 years if age + service ≥ 45: 50% + 10% for each additional year. Age 60: 100%	Age 50 and 15 years' service. Pension reduced by 6⅔% for each year age if less than 65	None	Age 50 and 15 years Spouse receives 50% of early benefit	55% of annual compensation in highest 4 consecutive years + ½% extra for each year of service over 30, up to maximum of 65% of average annual compensation in 4 highest consecutive years

differences in the retirement benefit formulas. I shall now describe how the common components of these two simulations were set up. These include the macroeconomic risks, the worker's wage process, and the individual risks to which each worker is exposed.

The simulation of benefits is based on the presumption that the structure of the plan will remain fixed. The plans' basic provisions for computing benefits determine their risk characteristics. In order to calculate benefits for Plans 0, 2, and 3, we need to know the worker's wage history. Plan 1 does not require a wage history because it is a flat benefit per year of service. The wage process, therefore, is the first essential piece of information that must be simulated.

Although we assume that the structure of plans is fixed, we do not assume that the precise provisions are immutable. Quite to the contrary, we presume that the level of benefits specified in the pattern plan, Plan 1, will be updated so as to reflect the rise in real wages of the average worker, over time. It is important to note, therefore, that it is the average worker's wage that affects Plan 1 payoffs, whereas it is the individual worker's wage that is an input into the other calculations.

The risk characteristics of Plan 1 are different from the other plans for this reason. Workers in Plan 1 are at risk for fluctuations in the difference between the adjusted dollar benefit level and actual inflation. But they are not at risk for the difference between their own personal compensations and the average over all workers in the plan.

The demographic factors are the second major ingredient in the simulations: job leaving, disability, death, and death of a spouse where this is relevant.

My procedure is as follows. The age and years of experience of an individual are fixed. For example, assume that the individual is now 30 years old and has already been in the plan for five years at the time when the simulation is performed. It is assumed that the worker receives compensation in the current year. Thereafter, annually, I simulate the wage of all workers, his wage, and his demographic status. If he or his surviving spouse is due benefits under any plan, I keep track of them. Thus, at the end of each individual's lifetime I have a record of the stream of benefits received and the circumstances under which they were paid. From this series one can compute, retrospectively, its present value and its present values conditional on the occurrence of various events.

For every age/experience situation, and each plan, I run a sample of 900 individuals through the simulated lifetime described above. Experimentation has indicated that this size is enough to eliminate most of the sampling variance and to provide fairly accurate evidence on the risks due to the random factors driving the simulation.

In the next two subsections I provide the details of the simulation methods for the wage rates and the demographic factors, respectively.

12.3.2 Simulation of Wage Process

The initial wage in all cases was taken to be $20,000. Because I am primarily interested in the risks faced by workers relative to their total wages or total compensations, one can regard this merely as a normalization.

The growth rate of average wages from t to $t + 1$ is denoted $\bar{w}_t$. For the individual worker it is w_t. Suppose that

$$w_t = \bar{w}_t + \eta_t,$$

where η_t is a normal random variable, independently and identically distributed over time. The parameter η is assumed to have a mean of zero and a standard deviation of .005.

As the individual ages, shocks via η_t are cumulative. It is the idiosyncratic component of rate of growth of his wages that evolves independently.

The stochastic structure of $\bar{w}_t$ is autoregressive: $\bar{w}_t = \epsilon_t$, where $\epsilon_t = \rho\epsilon_{t-1} + u_t$.

The parameter ρ is taken to be .9 and the mean and standard deviation of u_t are assumed to be .001 and .002179, respectively. Thus the mean of $\bar{w}_t$ is .01, as is the mean of w_t.

For Plans 0, 2, and 3, the resulting individual wage for a worker with s years of service in the future is

$$w_s = 20,000\left[\underset{t=0}{\overset{s}{\pi}}(1 + w_t)\right], s = 1, 2, \ldots$$

The series $w_0, w_1, \ldots, w_s, \ldots$ forms the basis of compensation and the benefit package.

In Plan 1, a different computation for pension benefits is used, based on average wages rather than on the personal wage of the individual in question,

$$\bar{w}_s = 20,000\left[\underset{t=0}{\overset{s}{\pi}}(1 + \bar{w}_t)\right], s = 1, 2, \ldots$$

and the annual retirement benefit is simply

$$\$144 \times \frac{\bar{w}_T}{20,000} \times T,$$

where T is the number of years of service at retirement.

Because of the positive drift in real wages built into this process, virtually all workers will have a higher real wage on retirement than they do at the date when the simulation is undertaken. However, because of the cumulative effect of η_t, which represents promotions and other random variations due to the profitability or lack thereof in the firm or industry in question which may affect the wages of its workers, there will be a substantial variation across workers, and increasingly so as time passes.

I initiate the simulation for various ages of workers, in each case trying to assess the remaining risk in the plan benefits and their correlation with the worker's wage. The parameter specifications above determine the distribution of the worker's terminal wage, at age 65, and how its variance breaks down into the part due to aggregate real wage fluctuation and the idiosyncratic component. This breakdown is shown in the unnumbered table below.

Age	EW_{65} 20,000	Standard Deviation of EW_{65} 20,000	Fraction of Variance Due to Idiosyncratic Risk
25	1.43	.152	.13
30	1.45	.168	.11
35	1.35	.161	.08
40	1.31	.126	.11
45	1.21	.093	.13
50	1.15	.073	.11
55	1.09	.055	.23
60	1.05	.028	.37

12.3.3 Simulation of Events in Workers' Lifetimes

The possible states in which a worker or his beneficiary can be found within my simulation are shown in figure 12.1 below.

It can be seen that the passage through this flowchart is governed by the probabilities of transition from working to the three other states. In the first set of simulations, I assume that these are a function of age only, not

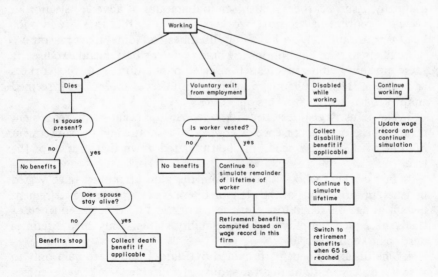

Fig. 12.1   One step in simulation of a worker's pension benefits.

of experience. In the second set of simulations, the probability of withdrawal from employment is allowed to depend on both age and experience. Table 12.2 gives the probabilities used.

For the simulation of spouses' lifetimes, I used the age-specific mortality for men shifted by eight years. Three years represents the average age differential of husband and wife, and the remaining five years is an attempt to capture the different mortality probabilities for men and women. It approximates standard actuarial practice.

Table 12.3 presents the assumed mortality table, up to age 110, where the simulation of lifetimes was always terminated.

The specific features of this flowchart embody the characteristics of the benefit packages studied and some other special features owing to the limitations on our actuarial knowledge.

1. No early retirement is provided for in this flowchart, even though Plans 1, 2, and 3 have early retirement provisions. The reason is that I do not have estimates of early retirement probabilities. Many "disabilities" are probably early retirements of a certain kind. To incorporate early retirements separately would require some reduction in the assumed disability probabilities, and the extent of this is beyond my knowledge.

Moreover, the early retirement benefits provided by these plans are arranged to approximate an actuarially fair payment of the accrued benefit. For example, if a worker age 55 retires in Plan 1, he receives 70% of the pension he would have received at age 62. If he were simply to withdraw, he would get these benefits in full beginning at age 62. Depending on his mortality, the value of that stream could be higher or lower than the early retirement benefits.

Finally, I suspect there is a substantial amount of adverse selection in the early retirement decision. Workers who know that they are in poor health or are unlikely to have long lifetimes for some other reason are more likely to take this option. It would therefore be a mistake to use the same mortality tables for this self-selected population as for the workers as a whole. Because the magnitude of this effect is unknown, it seemed simpler to leave these workers out entirely.

2. No plans pay spouse benefits except in the event of preretirement death. Therefore the presence or absence of a spouse and the subsequent lifetime of the spouse need only be simulated down that branch of the tree.

3. For workers who withdraw from the plan after they have vested benefits, no provisions of the plan are operative except for the retirement benefit at age 65. Therefore, for these workers I need not keep track of their subsequent employment or disability status. Only their lifetimes need to be simulated.

4. The disability benefits provided by Plans 1 and 2 are paid only to vested workers. Assume that the spouse of a disabled worker who subse-

Table 12.2   **Age-Specific Probabilities of Death, Withdrawal, and Disability as Assumed in the Simulation (Percentage of the Population at Risk in the Indicated Age Group)**

Age	Death	Withdrawal	Disability
20	.0044	24.30	.0263
21	.0463	22.44	.0266
22	.0488	20.70	0270
23	.0513	19.07	.0271
24	.0538	17.56	.0274
25	.0569	16.15	.0275
26	.0602	14.85	.0278
27	.0636	13.64	.0281
28	.0679	12.53	.0279
29	.0717	11.51	.0283
30	.0763	10.58	.0382
31	.0817	9.73	.0382
32	.0872	8.95	.0381
33	.0940	8.26	.0382
34	.1006	7.63	.0386
35	.1080	7.08	.0386
36	.1164	6.57	.0487
37	.1261	6.13	.0586
38	.1360	5.74	.0680
39	.1475	5.40	.0781
40	.1593	5.11	.0873
41	.1748	4.86	.0971
42	.1945	4.65	.1177
43	.2208	4.47	.1365
44	.2509	4.32	.1566
45	.2852	4.20	.1762
46	.3240	4.09	.1952
47	.3680	4.01	.2156
48	.4131	3.93	.2442
49	.4640	3.87	.2751
50	.5165	3.80	.3034
51	.5757	3.74	.3339
52	.6341	3.68	.3722
53	.6971	3.60	.4108
54	.7650	3.52	.4493
55	.8508	0	.4971
56	.9238	0	.5362
57	.9997	0	.5966
58	1.0859	0	.6762
59	1.1868	0	.7968
60	1.3042	0	.9721
61	1.4337	0	1.2319
62	1.5748	0	1.5857
63	1.7329	0	2.0619
64	1.8932	0	2.6739

Source: H. E. Winklevoss, *Pension Mathematics, with Numerical Illustrations* (Homewood, Ill.: R. D. Irwin, 1977).

Table 12.3   **1971 Male Group Annuity Mortality Rates**

Age	Mortality	Age	Mortality	Age	Mortality	Age	Mortality	Age	Mortality
20	.00050	40	.00163	60	.01312	80	.08743	100	.32983
21	.00052	41	.00179	61	.01444	81	.09545	101	.35245
22	.00054	42	.00200	62	.01586	82	.10369	102	.37722
23	.00057	43	.00226	63	.01741	83	.11230	103	.40621
24	.00059	44	.00257	64	.01919	84	.12112	104	.44150
25	.00062	45	.00292	65	.02126	85	.13010	105	.48518
26	.00065	46	.00332	66	.02364	86	.13931	106	.53934
27	.00068	47	.00375	67	.02632	87	.14871	107	.60609
28	.00072	48	.00423	68	.02919	88	.15849	108	.68747
29	.00076	49	.00474	69	.03244	89	.16871	109	.78543
30	.00081	50	.00528	70	.03611	90	.17945	110	1.00000
31	.00086	51	.00587	71	.04001	91	.19049		
32	.00092	52	.00648	72	.04383	92	.20168		
33	.00098	53	.00713	73	.04749	93	.21299		
34	.00105	54	.00781	74	.05122	94	.22653		
35	.00112	55	.00852	75	.05529	95	.24116		
36	.00120	56	.00926	76	.06007	96	.25620		
37	.00129	57	.01004	77	.06592	97	.27248		
38	.00140	58	.01089	78	.07260	98	.29016		
39	.00151	59	.01192	79	.07969	99	.30912		

Source: Winklevoss, *Pension Mathematics* (see table 12.2 n.).

quently dies receives nothing, although the specification of Plan 1 is arguably vague on that point (does "preretirement" death imply that the worker is actively working at that point in time?).

The result of this simulation is that workers end up in one of the four branches of the tree depicted in figure 12.1. The probabilities of each of these four terminal states, for workers of differing initial ages are shown in table 12.4.

12.4   Results of Simulations: First Set

The first set of simulations treats all the benefits from the four plans exactly as specified in section 12.2. Table 12.5 shows the expected present values in each of the plans from the point of view of workers at various ages and various levels of experience. In all circumstances, Plan 3 is the most generous and Plan 0 is second.

Interesting differences appear between Plan 1, the pattern plan, and Plan 2, the career average plan. The former is much better at the older and more experienced end of the spectrum and the latter is superior for younger and less experienced workers. Both age and experience are important determinants of the relative benefits. The 45-year-olds with only five years of experience clearly prefer the career average plan, while those with 20

Table 12.4 **Probability of a Worker's Ending the Simulation in Each State**

Age	Death	Withdraw from Plan	Disabled	Retires with Benefits at 65
20	.010	.960	.006	.024
25	.026	.877	.018	.079
30	.050	.748	.036	.167
35	.075	.601	.055	.269
40	.096	.456	.073	.375
45	.113	.316	.087	.484
50	.121	.167	.098	.613
55	.118	0	.103	.779
60	.075	0	.080	.846

Note: In the second set of simulations, a more complex simulation of the decision to withdraw voluntarily from the plan is made. This allows years of experience in the plan as well as age to affect the withdrawal probability. The probabilities of death and disability remain exclusively age dependent. This change results in only minor shifts in the cumulative withdrawal probabilites, predictably being lower for the more experienced workers within each age cohort.

Table 12.5 **Expected Present Values of Pension Benefits**

Plan Type	Plan 0: Conventional	Plan 1: Pattern	Plan 2: Career Average	Plan 3: Final Salary
0 experience				
Age 25	21666	8380	13456	32087
Age 40	40205	20264	33109	95554
5 years' experience				
Age 30	50826	20815	27071	73762
Age 45	57560	26435	34233	121497
10 years' experience				
Age 35	76947	34612	38475	114711
Age 50	75228	36365	38343	137765
20 years' experience				
Age 45	109853	51683	49751	138026
Age 60	89440	47704	39095	154902

Note: Flow of benefits over worker's and spouse's lifetime at 1% real discount rate.

years of experience have a preference for the pattern plan, risk considerations aside.

Table 12.6 shows the correlations between the present value of the wage stream remaining and the present value of benefits as specified in the plan. Quite naturally there is a substantial correlation in Plans 0, 2, and 3, where benefits are proportional to some sort of salary average, although the precise provisions vary from one to the other. But note also that Plan 1 displays a high correlation, indeed, the highest at the younger ends of the

Table 12.6   Correlations between Wages and Pension Benefits

	Plan 0: Conventional	Plan 1: Pattern	Plan 2: Career Average	Plan 3: Final Salary
0 experience				
Age 25	.78	.80	.78	.77
Age 40	.66	.76	.71	.66
5 years' experience				
Age 30	.76	.76	.77	.67
Age 45	.67	.68	.58	.42
10 years' experience				
Age 35	.66	.62	.65	.47
Age 50	.55	.48	.45	.30
20 years' experience				
Age 45	.52	.46	.48	.38
Age 60	.37	.19	.31	.12

spectrum. This is due to the simulation of the real wage process as highly autoregressive. The present value of an individual's wages is substantially influenced by the general level of wages in the economy in which he lives. Those with favorable experiences, in my simulation, enjoy the benefits of a high wage as individuals, on average, as well as a high level of pension benefits because these are proportional to the average wage. This effect is attenuated only for the oldest workers—those at 60 years old with 20 years of experience. The effective fluctuation in their benefits is sharply curtailed because the level of benefits for any one individual is assumed not to be adjusted after age 65. Subsequent variations in workers' real wages do not induce any dispersions in the benefits received by a cohort of retired workers. Moreover, having already lived to 60, the largest portion of the fluctuations in wages is already behind them, and the wages remaining vary only slightly within the final five working years.

Table 12.7 shows the risks inherent in the various plans for the total compensation of workers. Because the plans differ in the level of benefits provided, some adjustment had to be made to equate their average returns before a meaningful comparison of risks could be attempted. The procedure I used is as follows. The benefit levels of Plans 1, 2, and 3 were factored up by an amount such that their average payoff to all workers is equal to that in Plan 0. The age/experience distribution of the work force is assumed to be uniform over the eight classes. Then, the coefficient of variation of the present value of wages, pension benefits, and their sum was computed for each plan and each age/experience category. This procedure is justified by the idea that the expected costs of the benefit package, as viewed by the firm, are the relevant aspect of the bargaining agreement. Such a bargain, whether explicit or implicit, is struck collectively, covering all workers in the firm whatever the age and experience they happen to have at the time.

Table 12.7   **Ratios of Standard Deviations to Means: Wages, Pensions, and Total Compensation**

	Wages*	Plan 0: Conventional		Plan 1: Pattern		Plan 2: Career Average		Plan 3: Final Salary	
		Pension	Total	Pension	Total	Pension	Total	Pension	Total
0 experience									
Age 25	1.185	2.477	1.266	2.256	1.246	2.447	1.308	2.132	1.236
Age 40	.587	1.278	.632	1.124	.649	1.114	.667	.945	.624
5 years' experience									
Age 30	.874	1.433	.918	1.354	.897	1.458	.938	1.168	.871
Age 45	.534	1.036	.577	.923	.566	.890	.559	.683	.498
10 years' experience									
Age 35	.736	1.000	.736	.854	.707	.996	.738	.740	.671
Age 50	.427	.794	.450	.625	.420	.714	.437	.593	.391
20 years' experience									
Age 45	.521	.812	.531	.675	.492	.781	.520	.656	.478
Age 60	.182	.604	.340	.518	.308	.592	.337	.508	.289

*Wages are the same in every plan simulation.

The results are quite unambiguous. Plan 3, the final salary plan, is the safest at all ages and experience levels. This is somewhat surprising at first glance because the level of benefits depends heavily on events at the end of the working life. It might seem that Plan 3 is considerably more risky than plans, such as the career average plan, that allow a wider dependence on such stochastic phenomena and presumably more pooling of risk over the workers' lifetimes. The reason for the result, as can be seen in table 12.2, is the low correlation between these benefits and lifetime wages. A worker who wants a safe lifetime earnings package should prefer a plan whose benefits are not overly sensitive to his own lifetime wages. This is precisely why Plan 3 does well.

One might ask why the pattern plan (Plan 1) is not best in this regard, since its benefits are fixed and independent of the worker's wage. Indeed, Plan 1 ranks as the second safest at every age/experience class except the 45-year-olds with five years of experience, where the difference is very small. The reason might be that the pattern plan is based on terminal average wages, whereas the so-called final salary plan is based on an average of four years' salary, which allows an intertemporal pooling of wage risk. In addition, however, other types of benefits are included in the plans, and Plans 1 and 3 differ in these regards. Plan 1 provides a disability benefit and Plan 3 does not, and there is a slight difference in their preretirement health benefits. To sort out the components of these risks more carefully we present a set of conditional calculations below.

Economic theory and common sense tell us that the risks inherent in any asset cannot be assessed without reference to other random factors with which they may be correlated. The calculations above are based on a presumption that the worker cannot offset any of his wage or pension risk by other market actions. Thus far we have neglected the fact that many of the fluctuations in pension benefits are in direct response to events in the worker's lifetime.

The termination of benefits on the death of a retired worker represents an annuity aspect of the pension contract that may well be preferable to its equivalent in terms of expected present value, paid in cash. Similarly, the need for money in the event of disability or preretirement death is not the same as if the individual were continuing to work within the same firm.

At the most detailed level of generality the utility function should be conditioned on the "state" realized by the worker, the state being a full description of all relevant events in his or his family's life. As an approximation of this, I present some calculations of the riskiness of various plans conditional on certain categories of lifetime experience. Specifically, I look at those subsets of my 900 simulated individuals in each age/experience category that reach the states of disability, voluntary withdrawal, preretirement death, or retirement. I make no attempt to distinguish individuals according to the age at which the first three of these events take place. Needless to say, this approximation is a coarse one because the severity of the loss in future income, from the surviving family's point of view, is quite sensitive to their stage in the life cycle.

Tables 12.8, 12.9, 12.10, and 12.11 present these conditional calculations for four events. Individuals are grouped into disability, preretirement death, and withdrawal categories. In table 12.11 I group those who have withdrawn from the plan together with those who retire. These individuals are likely to have had similar experiences regarding health and lifetime work patterns. To this extent they are in the same state. But it

Table 12.8 **Ratios of Standard Deviations to Means: Conditional on Preretirement Death**

	Plan 0: Conventional	Plan 1: Pattern	Plan 2: Career Average	Plan 3: Final Salary
0 experience:				
Age 25	.440	.469	.440	.495
Age 40	.357	.441	.512	.478
5 years' experience:				
Age 30	.496	.536	.496	.521
Age 45	.417	.442	.417	.479
10 years' experience:				
Age 35	.440	.486	.440	.507
Age 50	.462	.495	.462	.535
20 years' experience:				
Age 45	.487	.544	.487	.553
Age 60	.458	.433	.458	.477

Table 12.9 **Ratios of Standard Deviation to Means: Total Compensation Conditional on Withdrawal**

	Plan 0: Conventional	Plan 1: Pattern	Plan 2: Career Average	Plan 3: Final Salary
0 experience:				
Age 25	1.082	1.074	1.135	1.091
Age 40	.698	.739	.769	.762
5 years' experience:				
Age 30	.833	.825	.856	.818
Age 45	.701	.710	.532	.491
10 years' experience:				
Age 35	.663	.629	.644	.583
Age 50	.418	.389	.362	.362
20 years' experience:				
Age 45	.488	.434	.402	.404
Age 60	—	—	—	—

Table 12.10   Ratios of Standard Deviations to Means: Total Compensation Conditional on Disability

	Plan 0: Conventional	Plan 1: Pattern	Plan 2: Career Average	Plan 3: Final Salary
0 experience:				
Age 25	.202	.149	.233	.182
Age 40	.395	.389	.407	.385
5 years' experience:				
Age 30	.336	.294	.369	.315
Age 45	.435	.404	.426	.379
10 years' experience:				
Age 35	.381	.293	.419	.353
Age 50	.475	.378	.454	.433
20 years' experience:				
Age 45	.349	.317	.352	.317
Age 60	.382	.305	.299	.355

Table 12.11   Ratios of Standard Deviations to Means: Total Compensation Conditional on Retire or Withdraw

	Plan 0: Conventional	Plan 1: Pattern	Plan 2: Career Average	Plan 3: Final Salary
0 experience:				
Age 25	1.274	1.249	1.312	1.235
Age 40	.633	.643	.649	.608
5 years' experience:				
Age 30	.936	.912	.953	.882
Age 45	.555	.550	.525	.463
10 years' experience:				
Age 35	.731	.700	.725	.652
Age 50	.379	.267	.359	.319
20 years' experience:				
Age 45	.457	.428	.441	.409
Age 60	.246	.266	.253	.252

must be recognized that those younger workers who withdraw from the firm will have other earnings and presumably other pension benefits. Thus the dispersion in total compensation induced by their withdrawal is likely to be highly negatively correlated with other earnings, and to that extent the figures presented in the table are an overestimate of the risks inherent in the plan. The comparison across plans, however, should be relevant. And for older workers the "retire or withdraw" category consists almost entirely of retirements.

Table 12.11 indicates a considerable degree of similarity between these conditional results and the unconditional results of table 12.3. Plan 3 is the safest for almost every age/experience category. Only the oldest group, 60-year-olds with 20 years of experience, find Plan 0 safer than Plan 3. And for this group the four plans are so similar that the discrepancy is probably within the sampling error of the simulation.

The other conditional tables 12.8, 12.9, and 12.10 display a wider divergence from the unconditional calculations shown in table 12.7. Preretirement death benefits are paid only in Plans 1 and 3. Therefore all of the variances in total compensation in Plans 0 and 2, conditional on preretirement death, arise from the distribution of wages and the dispersion in working intervals until the death occurs.

Disability benefits are most generous under Plan 1. Since disability results in a termination of wages, the variance of total compensation is reduced to the extent that benefits compensate for this loss in income. Thus Plan 3 does poorly because it incorporates no provision for disability. Plan 2 is safe for older, experienced workers because they receive fuller compensation, but it does poorly for those disabled early in their careers because their benefits are sharply curtailed.

12.5   Results of Simulations: Second Set

Taking the pension plans as written and simulating their ultimate benefits, as is done in section 12.4 has left us with some unresolved issues. The variance in total benefits depends very much on benefits other than those paid at retirement. In order to compare benefit formulas more directly, I shall redo the simulations, suppressing all benefits except those received at retirement.

The variability in payoff still depends on all the stochastic factors mentioned in sections 12.3 and 12.4. When these simulations were run, a more elaborate and realistic probability structure for withdrawal was incorporated. Voluntary withdrawal from employment depends on experience within the firm as well as on age.[1] This change produces slightly different frequencies in the terminal states reached by the 900 people whose lifetimes are simulated, but they are small relative to the sampling errors in this calculation.

This simulation allows a cleaner comparison of the four pension benefit formulas. I look first at the mean benefits. As in section 12.4, I adjust the level of payoffs so that the average mean payoff is equalized for a population equally distributed over the 10 age/experience groups. Then I compare the mean retirement benefit as it would be prospectively viewed by the representative worker in each group. The results are shown in figure 12.2.

---

1. I am grateful to Peter Diamond for references to the work of Yves Balcer that were very useful at this point.

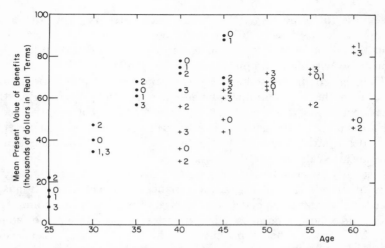

Each point shows the benefits received at retirement, on average, in the indicated plan. Points marked • are the benefits for the workers whose experience is 25 years less than their age. Points marked + are for workers with experience 40 years less than their age. The number indicates the plan. Benefit levels are adjusted so that the average overall ten age/experience groups is the same in each plan.

Fig. 12.2   Mean present value of benefits in the second set of simulations.

Younger workers find Plan 2, prospectively, the most favorable. Middle-aged, experienced workers rank Plan 0 highest. But their contemporaries with little experience rank it poorly. The final salary plan, Plan 3, does very badly for the younger workers and very well for the older ones.

It would be interesting to see whether the form of benefit calculation was systematically related to whether a well-defined subset of the workers had the predominant share of the negotiating power. Presumably this would vary across industries and across union versus nonunion firms. This must be left for future research.

The second use to which this simulation is put is a reassessment of the variability comparisons performed in section 12.4. The results are reported in tables 12.12 and 12.13. Because only retirement benefits are included, I report the conditional coefficient of dispersion of these benefits for retired persons only. These results in table 12.13 reveal the same general pattern as the comparable calculation in table 12.11. Plan 3, the final salary plan, is the safest throughout almost the entire age/experience spectrum. It is only for the 40-, 45-, and 50-year-olds with 0, 5, and 10 years of experience, respectively, that Plan 1, the pattern plan, seems slightly safer. Even these comparisons are probably within the sampling error.

On an overall, ex ante basis, table 12.12 indicates that Plan 3 is always the safest. These conditional calculations strongly confirm those reported in table 12.7.

Table 12.12   **Ratio of Standard Errors to Means: Second Set of Simulations Only Retirement Benefits Are Paid (All Workers).**

Experience	Age	Plan 0	Plan 1	Plan 2	Plan 3
0	25	1.2242	1.2068	1.2472	1.1888
	40	.7015	.6926	.7025	.6644
5	30	.9067	.8892	.9133	.8589
	40	.5607	.5494	.5376	.4919
10	35	.7194	.6768	.7011	.6241
	50	.4959	.4549	.4618	.4256
15	40	.6136	.5642	.5864	.5336
	55	.4412	.3862	.3840	.3796
20	45	.5545	.4993	.5194	.4823
	60	.3154	.3453	.2889	.3429

Table 12.13   **Ratio of Standard Errors to Means: Second Set of Simulations Only Retirement Benefits Are Paid: Only Retired Workers with Vested Benefits Included**

Experience	Age	Plan 0	Plan 1	Plan 2	Plan 3
0	25	.0828	.0657	.1006	.0594
	40	.0876	.0744	.1143	.0808
5	30	.0979	.0800	.1086	.0704
	45	.0986	.0872	.1114	.0908
10	35	.1044	.0879	.1056	.0721
	50	.1280	.1161	.1240	.1189
15	40	.1253	.1082	.1140	.0858
	55	.1698	.1587	.1381	.1584
20	45	.1410	.1257	.1146	.0982
	60	.1983	.2387	.1791	.2345

Comment   Alan J. Auerbach

This paper is in some ways easy to discuss but in other ways difficult. Jerry Careen has carefully laid out for us what he has done, so that we may pause at each stage for an evaluation. Ultimately, however, I find it hard to know what message about the riskiness of private pensions I should take away from the simulation results that are presented in the paper. For me, much of the difficulty lies in the concept of risk that Green uses, the different sources of risk in the pensions analyzed, and the many assumptions necessary to generate concrete numerical examples. All in all, the pa-

Alan J. Auerbach is associate professor of economics at the University of Pennsylvania and a research associate of the National Bureau of Economic Research.

per has helped clarify a number of issues that one must confront in assessing the risk inherent in private pension plans, and in the process has shown how difficult a task Green has set for himself. He should be commended for his efforts in exploring this extremely important but little researched question.

The numerical simulations in the paper consider the riskiness of four prototypical private pension plans, as measured by the coefficient of variation of the present value of pension benefits or total compensation, from the viewpoint of a representative worker at one of eight stages in his age and experience with a firm. Simulation is used because of the enormous complexity of the underlying random distribution of pension benefits.

Each worker, identical ex ante, faces four sources of uncertainty: (1) date of death; (2) the prospect of preretirement disability; (3) the prospect of preretirement withdrawal from the firm; and (4) the stochastic evolution of wages over time. All sources of risk are assumed to be exogenous from the individual's viewpoint, as well as independent. This rules out, for example, the withdrawal probability's being related to the individual's wage rate or the date of death's being hastened by early disability. These simplifications may be restrictive, but there is little alternative available, given the paucity of data and the great complexity already characterizing the problem.

The age-specific probabilities of death, disability, and withdrawal, presented in table 12.2, are based on actuarial data. The wage process is assumed to be one with an overall stochastic component, as well as individual-specific, or "idiosyncratic," risk. An individual's wage at date t, W_t, may be expressed in terms of his last year's wage by

$$W_t = W_{t-1}(1 + \overline{w}_t + \eta_t),$$

where $\overline{w}_t$ is the overall, or "market," disturbance, itself generated by a Markov process with an autocorrelation coefficient of .9, and η_t is an independent and identically distributed individual error. Both η_t and the white noise component underlying the process for $\overline{w}_t$ are normally distributed, the latter with a nonzero mean intended to capture secular wage growth at an expected rate of 1% per year. Without the term $\overline{w}_t$, this wage process would be a random walk in terms of the logarithm of the wage. With the highly autocorrelated market component, wherein the growth rate of overall wages is very close to a random walk, actual wage variation over time comes to consist more and more of the market component. Whether this outcome is appropriate is a question Green does not address, nor are we given any reason to have strong faith in the variances chosen for the two sources of risk that generate the wage process. Even if these assumptions come from the best "point estimate" available, a sensitivity analysis would be most enlightening.

The four pension plans considered vary with respect to the method of retirement benefit calculation and the extent to which they provide disability and survivor preretirement death benefits. They also differ with respect to the treatment of early retirement, but early retirement is ignored in the simulations. Vesting provisions are similar with full or partial vesting at 10 years of service with any remaining vesting occurring shortly afterward.

Retirement benefits under Plan 0 (conventional), 2 (career average), and 3 (final salary) are all based on some average over time of an individual's own wages, with the names of the plans reflecting fairly accurately the extent of averaging. Since there is no inflation in the model, one would expect that Plans 0 and 2, which are based on salaries from a certain number of the best years, would be more likely to include wages from early years; that is the case in reality. Plan 1, the pattern plan, provides for a fixed dollar amount multiplied by years of service, but Green interprets this, appropriately I think, as being implicitly indexed to overall wages in the year of retirement. One should note, of course, that this assumption ignores additional risks that would be associated with the presence of noise in the implicit indexing process.

The four plans also differ in their provision of death and disability benefits. Plan 0 provides neither, Plan 1 provides both, Plan 2 provides only for disability, Plan 3 only for death. The spanning of the set of possibilities is either quite fortunate or quite unfortunate, depending on where one's interest lies. I must vote for the latter, if what we seek is to understand the effects of various pension provisions on individual welfare rather than the impact of particular plans themselves. This is a problem that could be remedied by considering hypothetical plans that differed only with respect to benefit calculations or only with respect to auxillary provisions. At present, I suspect that the differences among the plans in the latter are what generate many of the differences in the results for the plans. This may be inferred from table 12.6, which presents the sample correlations between the present values of wages and benefits for individuals starting at each of the eight points analyzed in the paper. The lowest value, .12, occurs for individuals who are age 60, despite the fact that, for those who reach retirement at 65, pension benefits will be based on the four highest years of own wages, quite possibly four of the remaining five years. One would expect this to lead to a high correlation, but this ignores the fact that states in which death or disability intervene are included in the calculation. While such states have a relatively small chance of occurring, the change in benefits if they do is enormous.

This result foreshadows a problem in separating the effects of particular differences among plans but also brings out another difficulty with the analysis: the symmetric treatment of all states of nature. For example, a plan with a death benefit equal to half the nominal retirement amount might be just what would be required to insure completely per capita family consumption against a husband's death, yet this plan would be deemed riskier than one with full death benefits. Similar problems are associated with disability. There is a particular problem in the treatment of withdrawal, where all subsequent work experience and pension benefit accruals are ignored. Given the usual backloading of benefit accruals associated with pensions, a person withdrawing to take a better job would, by the current analysis, receive a low benefit relative to wages, even if vested. Finally, since the analysis considers only the risks associated with pensions and wages, we have no sense of which sources of risk are diversifiable and which are not. Even for those workers who are liquidity constrained, social security constitutes an important form of wealth that may offset some of the risks included in private pensions. Indeed, some of the pension provisions may have been designed to take the preexistence of social security into account.

With all of these difficulties in mind, I turn at last to the paper's simulation results. These results were generated for each of the eight cases by following 900 individuals through their working lives until some terminal event occurred. For example, no wage calculations were necessary for those already disabled. The same sample of 900 is used for each of the four pension plans in a given case, so that eight samples were generated overall. While Green argues that this sample size appeared large enough to eliminate most sampling error, this statement does not apply to subsamples as small as 11, conditioned on certain events such as disability.

Because I am unsure how to interpret the measured risk associated with withdrawal, disability, or death, I would find most meaningful calculations based on the condition of a worker actually reaching retirement. The closest Green comes to presenting such results is in table 12.11, which also includes those that withdraw. To focus on retirement, we can look at calculations for those of later ages for whom withdrawal is unlikely, and here there is a counterintuitive result: as in the full-sample calculations in table 12.7, the final salary plan is generally the safest. It is safer than the pattern plan in all but two of the eight cases in the table, even though the pattern plan is independent of the risks of individual wage variation. It is safer than the career average plan in all eight cases, and safer than the conventional plan in seven of eight, despite the fact that the latter two plans should permit more lifetime averaging of wage risks. I find the robustness of these results disturbing, because I can think of no convincing explanation for them. This demonstrates, perhaps, one of the weaknesses of simulation analysis of complicated problems: we cannot simply look at the formula for a derivative to see the origin of an outcome. However, sensitivity analysis is the best available alternative and would be a most helpful addition to the current study in light of the results presented.

13 The Relationship between Wages and Benefits

Jeremy Bulow
Wayne Landsman

13.1 Introduction

Benefits represent a growing fraction of total labor compensation.[1] In 1977–79 pension costs alone averaged 5.6% of payroll for large United States firms (Kotlikoff and Smith 1983, table 5.1.4). Because benefits are such an important part of compensation, employees and firm owners need to understand how to value benefits packages.

Unfortunately, benefit valuation may not be as simple as valuing a compensation package with only wages. For example, a faculty member at a university may receive a tuition subsidy from his school when his children attend college. Should the university treat this element of compensation differently from wages and spread the cost of this benefit over many years rather than simply expense the cost when incurred? Equivalently, when should the worker include this benefit as part of his income?

In this paper we explore the following questions: First, how should a firm choose the types of benefits it offers, and how will different benefits affect the firm's different worker constituencies? (These are important questions for a positive study of how different types of plans come to exist, as well as for normative analyses of optimal compensation package choice.) Second, what is the appropriate way of accounting for different types of benefits when making a financial appraisal of firm liabilities or workers' wealth? Third, what inferences can be made about firms that offer different sorts of benefits?

We suggest that the answers to these questions depend on one's model of the firm-employee relationship. In section 13.2 we describe three "eco-

Jeremy Bulow is associate professor of economics at Stanford University and a faculty research fellow at the National Bureau of Economic Research. Wayne Landsman teaches in the Graduate School of Business at Stanford University.

nomic" models of this relationship. A key implication of all of these models is that bargaining between firms and workers is over total compensation, not the components of compensation. Except in cases of asymmetrical information (where the firm and the worker have different information about the cost of providing a specific benefit), in these models it is optimal for the firm to offer workers all possible tax-free benefits and individually reduce salaries by the amount of benefits consumed by the worker.

In Section 13.3 we discuss some noneconomic models of the firm-worker relationship in which elements of compensation may have significance for the worker or the firm that is not strictly monetary or in which the firm's decision-making process may not be centralized or rational (in the classical sense). Specifically, we heuristically describe "equity" models in which workers with similar characteristics are paid identical wages even if they receive different benefits. We also consider "hierarchical" models in which the benefits office is distinct from the offices that determine salary, and information about the expense of providing a given worker's benefits is not internalized by those who set salaries. One implication of these models is that firms that offer specific types of benefits should expect to attract new workers who can particularly use those benefits—the school with large tuition benefits attracting professors planning large families. In this context the firm may find that the best benefits are those that are worth an equal amount to all workers.

Section 12.4 presents some empirical evidence on the relative applicability of economic and noneconomic models of firms and workers. We test whether or not Stanford University implicitly takes into account pension compensation in setting salaries. Our preliminary results are that the university does not take an individual's pension compensation into account when setting his wage, even if they do take into account overall pension compensation in setting the overall wage scale offered.

The crucial point of the noneconomic models is that we can only say a limited amount about the aggregate firm/worker implicit labor contract by looking at individuals' compensation profiles. For example, the fact that Stanford may not look at one's pension compensation in offering a salary does not mean that the university does not consider overall pension compensation in setting the overall level of salaries. Similarly, a firm may set a worker's salary without recognizing whether that worker is receiving a large amount of ancillary compensation through tuition benefits, housing subsidies, becoming vested in early retirement benefits, and so on. Nevertheless, the firm may still take into account aggregate benefits in setting the general level of salaries offered. The implication for defined benefit pension analysis is that individual workers may well be able to anticipate that at certain times they will receive especially high total compensation, but for the purposes of valuing the firm's aggregate pension liability at a given moment the accrued benefit method would still be correct.

13.2 "Economic" Models of the Labor Market

The questions we have asked about wages versus benefits must be answered in the context of specific models of worker-firm relations. In this section we consider three models that employ a traditional microeconomic approach. In each of these models it is assumed that workers value compensation only as a source of their own consumption; for example, the consumption of other workers does not enter into the individual employee's utility function. Workers choose compensation offers from firms which maximize their expected utility. Firms are profit maximizers, implying they are indifferent between alternative compensation packages that induce the same labor input and have the same total cost. In each model, experienced workers are assumed to accumulate firm-specific human capital (but no general skills).

In the first model we look at, individual workers offer their services each period on a spot market. Workers and firms both recognize that they will enter into a bilateral bargaining situation once that specific human capital is acquired, but no long-term bargain is struck.

The second model contains long-term contracts written between the firm and individual workers. The motivation for these contracts will be taken to be a desire for risk sharing, but other motivations (such as the prevention of shirking, as suggested by Lazear [1979]) lead to similar results.

Finally, the third model involves group-negotiated contracts of the sort described by Bulow and Scholes (1984). In this model, employees can be paid more than their individual marginal products, even without an implicit (or explicit) long-term contract, because of their leverage as part of a group.

While each of these models provide different valuations of firms with the same accounting statements, these differences turn out to be independent of the division of compensation between wages and benefits. Bargaining takes place over firm labor costs. The firm always ends up offering all tax-free benefits, the workers use these benefits up to the point where a dollar's worth of a benefit is as valuable as $1 - t$ dollars of income (where t is the tax rate on wage income), and the individual worker's salary is adjusted by the cost to the firm of providing that employee's benefits. These results are somewhat modified if information is asymmetrical, as we shall show.

For each model, the basic environment is the same. We use an overlapping generations framework: Each worker has a potential working life of two periods, followed by retirement. During each working period each worker supplies up to one unit of a homogeneous labor input. Workers get utility from the consumption goods they can buy with their wages; they have no disutility of labor. A constant number of new workers, L, enter the labor force each period.[2] The services of workers are bid for in each period by firms in a competitive industry with free entry and exit. Young workers are "inexperienced." Old workers who have remained with the same firm into their second period of life are "experienced"; however, old workers who switch firms in the second period are "inexperienced." (That is, specific human capital is accumulated in the first period.) Inexperienced workers, whether old or young, have the same current value in production.

Since in equilibrium it will turn out that all firms are identical, we may freely define notation with reference to the "representative" firm. Let

n_0 = number of inexperienced workers employed in a period,
n_1 = number of experienced workers employed,
F = fixed costs of production per period,
$q(n_0, n_1)$ = gross revenues per period,
r = constant real interest rate,
w_0 = per period wage paid to inexperienced workers,
w_1 = per period wage paid to experienced workers.

Each firm in the economy has the identical production function

(1) $$q(n_0, n_1) = n_0{}^a + en_1{}^a - F,$$

where e and a are parameters, with $a < 1$. To make computations easy, we assume

(2) $$e = 1/a > 1$$

and

(3) $$F = (1 + r + 1/a)(1 - a)/(1 + r).$$

In a competitive environment with zero disutility of labor, it is clear that the only sustainable equilibria are those in which all labor input is employed and the present value of industry gross revenues less fixed costs is at a maximum. Given the greater marginal productivity of experienced workers assumed in (1), it is also evident that in equilibrium workers will stay with their first-period firm through their working life; that is, for each firm, $n_0 = n_1$ in each period. The firm size $n_0 = n_1$ that maximizes the present value of industry gross revenues is easily found as the solution to

(4) $$\max_{n_0} (L/n_0)(1/r)[n_0{}^a(1 + r) + en_0{}^a - F(1 + r)],$$

where use has been made of the essential stationarity of the problem. Because of our judicious choice of values for e and F, the optimal firm size that emerges from (4) is

(5) $$n_0{}^* = n_1{}^* = 1.$$

This implies directly that the marginal product of an inexperienced worker in the current period will be a and that of an experienced worker will be 1;

equivalently, the expected lifetime value of a worker entering the labor force today is $a + 1/(1 + r)$.

In our first economic model, let us suppose that workers contract with employers each period on a spot labor market. This creates the usual ambiguity in the second period; namely, that because of the accumulation of specific human capital, worker and firm have quasi rents (equal to $1 - a$, where a is the value of an old worker at a new firm) to bargain over. Let us assume that some workers are "good bargainers" while others are "bad bargainers." Good bargainers capture all of the quasi rents from specific human capital in the second period, while bad bargainers capture no quasi rents. A fraction of workers b in each generation are good bargainers; but neither the firm nor the worker knows until the second period whether an individual worker will be a good or bad bargainer.[3]

Under these assumptions, a second-period worker obtains his or her full marginal product (equal to one) with probability b. With probability $1 - b$, he obtains only his opportunity cost a. Thus the expected value of second-period wages is $b + a(1 - b)$.

With free entry of firms into the industry, no worker will sign on with a firm unless he expects to capture his full lifetime marginal product $a + 1/(1 + r)$. Thus, under a spot labor market regime, all first-period workers are paid $w_0 = a + (1 - b)(1 - a)/(1 + r)$—their first-period marginal product plus the present value of the fraction of quasi rents that the firm can expect to capture in the second period.

An obvious problem with the spot labor market is that risk-averse workers may be forced to accept random second-period incomes owing to bargaining uncertainty. Firms and workers may choose to hedge the uncertainty generated by random bargaining abilities by entering into long-term contracts. The assumption that there is long-term contracting defines our second economic model. If two-period contracts that are binding on both parties can be negotiated, then the distribution of compensation over the two periods is indeterminate, so long as $w_0 + w_1/(1 + r) = a + 1/(1 + r)$. In the usual case of "one-way" contracts, where firms cannot back out of an agreement but employees can quit, w_0 must be less than or equal to a. If w_1 is set at less than 1 the worker still has the same threat as in the no-contract case, so a good bargainer should still be able to negotiate second period pay of 1.[4] Therefore, the only way to eliminate second-period uncertainty is to set w_1 greater than or equal to 1. If we also give firms the right to lay off workers, then the unique contract is $w_0 = a$ and $w_1 = 1$. Notice that workers' lifetime expected compensation is the same as in the spot labor market model; however, if workers are risk averse the contract model is Pareto superior ex ante.

Our third economic model is another bargaining model, only this time employees negotiate (either explicitly or implicitly) as a group. The old generation of workers can receive pay of a (their marginal product as "inexperienced" workers) if they quit the firm, as before. However, they realize that if they all left the average (per worker) cost in output to the firm would be $1/a$. Therefore, with group bargaining w_1 can be anywhere in the range from a to $1/a$. Let the expected wage bargain with a group of old workers be $w_1 = a + B(1/a - a)$, where B is a parameter that measures the bargaining skill of the group. Then $w_0 = a + (1 - a)/(1 + r) - B(1/a - a)/(1 + r)$. If B is greater than $(a - a^2)/(1 - a^2)$, then w_1 is greater than 1 and older workers are being paid more than marginal product in the second period. Of course, it is precisely when B is expected to have such a high value that w_0 will be less than a. Heuristically, we may think of the workers as investing in the firm's capital when young (by taking a low wage) and being repaid in the second period, when the new group of young workers assume the initial investment.

Now let us expand our analysis to include benefits. We may assume the use of benefits is motivated by a tax imposed on wages at rate t but not imposed on benefits. Firms offer workers packages of salary, s_0, and benefits, p_0, with $w_0 = s_0 + p_0$. The firm is indifferent to any combination of s and p with the same total cost. If the amount of benefits provided to any given worker is easily identified, then equilibrium will require that w_0 remain as before and each individual will choose to take benefits up to the point where a dollar's worth of benefits is worth $1 - t$ dollars of salary. The only exception to this rule is if workers' bargaining ability is correlated with their desire for benefits. In that case, the signaling problem adds to the risk-sharing motivation for long-term contracts.

In a contracts model, total compensation in each of the two periods is set at $w_0 = a$ and $w_1 = 1$. In this model and again in the "group" model the firm is indifferent to the distribution of compensation for young workers between s_0 and p_0 and for old workers between s_1 and p_1.

Note that if the benefit in question is deferred compensation (such as a pension), the amount of the benefit a young worker has received, p_0, is defined by his vested benefits. In any bargaining situation (and in the case of a contract written to avoid second-period bargaining problems), first-period compensation is determined by the "threat point" of the worker entering the second period. That threat point may be defined as the present value of lifetime income, including benefits, that the worker receives if no second-period agreement is reached. Therefore, if we are to treat pensions similarly to the way we treat salary and other benefits, we must use an accrued vested benefits approach to defined benefit pension accounting (see Bulow 1982). Similarly, a severance pay benefit is part of compensation in the year accrued. Severance clearly changes the "threat point" in negotiations and therefore the accumulation of severance rights may represent substantial compensation even if (perhaps because of the severance) there is little chance a worker will ever be laid off.[5]

We have presented three models of worker compensation determination that differ in the way firms negotiate with workers. In some sense these models are all the "same"—the allocations of labor and total expected worker compensation do not vary, though the time path of compensation may. However, for some real-world purposes there are important differences between these models.

For example, depending on the bargaining model chosen, firms with identical accounting balance sheets should be valued differently. First consider the simple "no-contract" model where $w_0 = a + (1 - b)(1 - a)/(1 + r)$ and $w_1 = a + b(1 - a)$. Because all investment in human capital is expensed, the firm will report a loss of $(1 - a)/a(1 + r) + (1 - b)(1 - a)/(1 + r)$ in its start-up period, when it has no experienced workers. However, this initial investment by the stockholders is returned by "profits" equal to r times the start-up loss in all subsequent periods. The market value of the firm always exceeds the book value by the amount of the start-up loss.

In the risk-sharing contract model $w_0 = a$ and $w_1 = 1$ so the start-up loss, and the difference between market and book value, is $(1 - a)/a(1 + r)$. Here the workers make a greater share of the investment in human capital. Consequently, reported start-up losses are lower, as are the subsequent positive cash flows reported as profits.

In the "group" model $w_0 = a + (1 - a)/(1 + r) - B(1/a - a)/(1 + r)$, and $w_1 = a + B(1/a - a)$. Here, in the extreme case where $B = 1$ so that the old workers are paid all the quasi rents from operating, the firm reports zero profits in all periods and market value equals book value.

An analyst trying to compare firms with identical book values would clearly benefit from understanding the nature of the firm's labor contract. The firm's compensation/tenure profile can provide information about the present value of future quasi rents that go to workers, and therefore about the value of stockholders' equity.

Does the *benefit*/tenure profile provide any useful information? That is, we know that if we only knew a firm's current total compensation costs then the compensation/tenure profile would provide us with extra information. If information about the compensation/tenure profile is not directly available, can information about the slope of the firm's benefit/tenure profile (e.g., whether it has a defined benefit pension plan or a defined contribution plan) be used as a proxy?

The question is an empirical one. Our models provide no logical reason why firms that have steep benefit/tenure profiles, or that provide substantial benefits, should have steep compensation/tenure profiles.

For example, unionized workers receive more benefits as a percentage of compensation than nonunionized workers in similar jobs. Many of these benefits, such as health and pension benefits, are most valuable for older workers. However, wage/tenure profiles may be less steep for union workers in these high-benefit firms, so that the total compensation/tenure profile is similar for firms with and without benefits.[6] In economic models the relative levels of employee benefits and salaries are determined by tastes and taxes. Whether there is a correlation between the chosen split between wages and benefits, and the share of future quasi rents on firm-specific human capital the work force can expect to negotiate, can only be determined empirically.[7] Only in the case of asymmetric information, where workers and firms have different knowledge about the cost of providing a benefit to a specific worker, will firms do anything other than offer all tax-advantaged benefits.[8] With asymmetric information, separating equilibria are possible where workers who most want a benefit will join firms that provide it.

As an example, assume that workers have perfectly inelastic demands for dental care, with individuals' demands uniformly distributed from zero to D. Assume further that firms are only allowed to offer full dental care or no benefits. Then two types of firms would develop, those providing and those not providing benefits. Workers would decide whether or not to join a firm that offered benefits depending on whether their demand was greater than or equal to $(1 - t)D/(1 + t)$. The average employee of a firm that offered benefits would use benefits costing $D/(1 + t)$, so salaries would be lower in benefit firms by that amount. The marginal employee would just break even by receiving the extra salary, paying taxes, and covering his own dental bills.

Therefore, with asymmetric information firms will attract a specific clientele if they offer a given benefit. If it were possible to obtain information ex post on such workers we would find that within the firm workers receiving benefits of different value would receive the same salary, but on a firmwide basis employees would not receive extra total compensation because a firm offered benefits.[9] With asymmetrical information, then, it is possible for workers to receive the same wage even if benefits are different, just as in the insurance-averse selection problem. Our noneconomic models of the next section will be similar to the asymmetric information case in terms of results, with the difference being that the information exists but for some reason is not used.

Summarizing, we have presented several economic models of labor contracting. Each model has different implications for the compensation/tenure profile and for issues of benefit valuation. With full information, the firm should offer workers all potential benefits, in any amount employees desire up to their full compensation, regardless of the model. There is no logical requirement that the benefit/tenure profile of firms be correlated with their compensation/tenure profile. The question of whether the benefit/tenure profile is correlated with labor's expected share of future quasi rents on firm-specific human capital (important for firm valuation) is strictly empirical.

With asymmetric information we would expect to see some firms offering and some not offering a given benefit. Workers would join firms that had the compensation package most valuable to them. Their salaries would be reduced based on the firm's expected cost of providing benefits, just as insurance premia are based on an insurer's expected cost of providing benefits in the face of asymmetric information.

13.3   Noneconomic Models

In this section we heuristically describe a set of noneconomic models in which workers' utility is a function not only of total compensation but of relative wages. Firms feel constrained to pay identical wages (rather than total compensation) to all workers of similar position and tenure, and may even feel constrained not to negotiate a lower wage bill if future benefit costs rise beyond expectations. In these models the distribution of benefits influences the distribution of total compensation.

Our two classes of noneconomic models are "equity" models and "hierarchical" models. In the equity models relative wages are set according to some equity formula, not taking into account the benefit expense associated with an individual worker. For example, relative wages may be used as a signal to workers about how well they are doing. Wages may provide a clearer signal than total compensation because wages are easier for workers to compare. It is also possible that antidiscrimination laws may make charging women more (and blacks less) for identical pension annuities difficult. While equity models may govern relative wages among workers, they may also cover the worker's *wage*/tenure profile. In this case, as we will emphasize below, a redistribution of a young worker's compensation between salary and benefits may affect the present value of future labor costs.[10]

In our hierarchical model the firm wishes to take benefit information into account in setting salaries; but, because of incentive problems caused by firm structure, the benefit information is mostly not transmitted into salaries.

We divide equity models into two categories. The first is a cross-sectional model. This turns out to be somewhat analogous to the group economic model. The wages and benefits of one cohort have nothing to do with those of another cohort. However, all workers of the same age must be paid the same wage, because of strong worker preferences for intragroup equity. The model produces results similar to those in the group model with asymmetric information. The firm's value is only affected by the total compensation deal it negotiates in a period. The breakdown of the young cohort's income into wages and benefits provides no information about what those workers expect to negotiate in total compensation in the subsequent period, any more than such a breakdown provides information in an economic model.

Alternatively, an equity model may have a time-series component to it, much as the long-term economic contract does. For example, workers and firms may feel that their contract is for a given wage/tenure profile plus a benefits package, and that alterations in the benefits package do not affect the wage/tenure profile. This is the kind of model required for projected benefit valuations of pension plans.

What are some of the implications of the time-series equity model? We can give some examples. First, if health care costs rose unexpectedly, a firm providing health benefits would decline in value by the increase in the present value of future health benefits to be paid to all current workers, given that plan provisions are not changed. No provision is made for any offsetting adjustment in wages, so a young worker who had recently joined the firm would now possibly represent a substantial net liability.

Second, if wages in the economy were growing at the interest rate young workers should be equally pleased by an increase in (defined benefit) pension benefits as older workers, assuming all workers stay with the firm until retirement age. For example, assume that pension benefits paid to a newly retired employee were $30 per month per year of service and that pension benefits were historically linked with salary.[11] Then a 10% increase in pension benefits raises all workers' pensions by 10%, and the present value of every worker's pension is identical.

Finally, the mix of wages and benefits matters because the mix is correlated with future compensation costs. For example, assume that medical costs are rising relative to wages. In a model with rigid time-series wage structure a firm would be unwilling to allow its young workers to split compensation w_0 into benefits p_0 and salary s_0 in any manner they desired. The reason is that in this model the rations of p_1 to p_0 and s_1 to s_0 are individually fixed (the benefits because it is assumed the contract provision will be the same in period 1 as in period 0, the salary by the rigid wage structure). This is in contrast to the economic model contract where the overall ratio of w_1 to w_0 is fixed. Therefore, if medical costs are growing faster than wages, p_1/p_0 exceeds s_1/s_0, and total compensation in period 1 will be increased if the workers can bias the composition of w_0 toward benefits.

Accrued pension benefits, like health benefits, go mostly to older workers. Thus, the previous paragraph could be repeated with only the substitution of the "pension" for "medical."

In the time-series equity model an individual's wages may not be affected by the benefits he receives. An alternative model in which this is also true is the hierarchical model. In this model, as in the other noneconomic models, the firm has information about an individual's benefit cost but is somehow restricted in using the information. The information may be stored in one part of the firm's hierarchy but either not made accessible to or at least not used by the part of the firm that negotiates a worker's salary. For example, in a university a department head may set salaries while benefits are determined independently by a university office.

In this model any benefit information made available to the salary negotiator is used, but some information simply is not available. There is no room in this model, then, for systematic biases in compensation between generations other than those differences that would arise in an economic model. This model is a close substitute for the cross-sectional equity model. The only difference is in the description of why the firm does not use all the information at its disposal. In the equity model a conscious decision is made to discriminate between employees with different characteristics. One way to distinguish the models is to adopt the fiction that wages and benefits are determined sequentially. For example, in the equity model the wages of all graduate students might be set according to merit and seniority, with married students subsequently given preference for housing subsidies. That is, there is a conscious institutional policy that benefits certain well-identified individuals. In the hierarchical model the firm may set benefits before setting salary, but the officer who determines salary may not be able to get good information about who is receiving a married student housing subsidy. The officer could still use whatever information was at his disposal to set salaries (and, for example, offer all married students lower scholarships because on average they receive greater housing benefits) but could not identify the specific individuals who received a specific benefit.

In summary, the noneconomic models generally have much in common with the economic models with asymmetric information. The difference is that in the noneconomic models the firm does not use all available information. Furthermore, in the time-series equity model the firm's value (and the present value of future employee compensation) is affected by the allocation of current compensation between wages and benefits. Thus, in the time-series equity model a firm with a defined benefit pension plan (that causes older workers to accrue a higher fraction of salary as pension benefits than young workers accrue) may be worse off than a defined contribution firm that was providing its current young employees with identical total compensation.

13.4 Empirical Work

We have described a number of alternative models of the worker-firm relationship. It would be interesting to conduct an empirical test of which type of model best describes reality. On way we can hope to do this is by concentrating on the following pivotal implication of our models: In the "economic" models, bargaining is over total compensation only; therefore, if an individual or group were inclined to use more of the firm's offered nonwage benefits, the wages of the individual or group would be adjusted downward accordingly. In contrast, in the basic noneconomic models we have described, a tendency to use more benefits might not result in any adjustment of wages. Therefore, a test of the competing models might be based on a test of whether subgroups of workers in a firm who use more benefits receive less wages than other workers.

We have obtained a microdata set, on Stanford University faculty salaries and pension benefits, that permits just such a test. Stanford University
will contribute 10% of a faculty member's salary to a pension plan if the
faculty member contributes 5% or more of his salary. If the faculty member pays in less than 5% the university makes no contribution. It is interesting to note that not all faculty members sign up for the program, as is
clear from table 13.1. In principle, then, we might test to see if professors
who do not sign up receive compensating increases in salary.

We were able to obtain the following data on 993 faculty members: age,
year of appointment, year of degree, rank (assistant professor, associate
without tenure, associate with tenure, full professor, adjunct, other),
school (law, business, humanities and sciences, medicine-clinical, medicine-
Ph.D., engineering), salary, and whether the employee was enrolled in the
pension plan.[12] The sample has two virtues. First, there were clearly no
problems of asymmetric information. The university knows exactly the
cost of each employee in the plan. In fact, it would be possible for the university to negotiate a total compensation package directly and then allow
each worker to contribute as much as desired to the pension plan, up to
the legal limit.[13] Second, the benefit is one that represents a large fraction
of the salary of some employees and is not received by others.

Our priors were that the university followed either a cross-sectional equity model or a hierarchical model, so that we would find little or no effect
of the pension acceptance variable on salary. The reasons were that (1) the
benefits office has a separate budget from the various dean's offices that
determine salary, and the deans claim to know nothing about whether a
worker is in the pension program; and (2) assistant professors (the group
that represent virtually all the action in our sample) tend to consider relative *salaries* as informative signals.[14]

A simple approach would be to regress professors' salaries on the observable determinants of salary, plus a dummy which is equal to one when

Table 13.1   Faculty in the Pension Plan/Total Faculty (by School and Rank).

Rank	Business and Law	Engineering	Humanities and Science	Medical Clinic	Medical Ph.D.	Total
Assistant	8/9	5/22	27/63	33/57	10/10	83/161
Associate	8/11	7/10	2/4	7/8	1/1	25/34
Associate with tenure	4/4	13/17	57/64	40/41	11/13	125/139
Full	59/59	125/125	272/287	75/77	38/40	569/588
Adjunct	0/0	10/14	11/11	2/2	1/2	24/29
Other	0/0	0/0	3/4	30/34	3/4	36/42
Total	79/83	160/188	372/433	187/219	64/70	862/993

the faculty member has elected the pension plan. The major problem with this is that the employees' mandatory contribution meant that some workers who did not sign up for the plan could be liquidity constrained. The liquidity constrained workers on average have lower salaries. Therefore, direct estimates of salary as a function of whether a worker received pension benefits are subject to simultaneity bias.[15] To avoid the simultaneity problem, we adopted a two-stage procedure. First we estimated a probability of pension acceptance as a function of all variables other than salary. We also estimated a "fitted salary" variable, which was formed by regressing salary on all the variables other than pension acceptance. In the second stage we regressed all the other variables in our data set plus a 0/1 instrument for the probability of pension acceptance times "fitted salary." The idea was to make the regression coefficient on pension acceptance interpretable as a percentage of salary. Included in the regression were dummies for all the schools and ranks listed in table 13.1. We tried using the estimated probabilities for pension acceptance directly in our second stage. We also ran separate regressions for each of the different ranks. In our pooled regressions we found a significiant coefficient for the pension acceptance variable. However, in the individual regressions by rank we found the reduction in salary for a worker signing up for a pension to be statistically insignificant.

We ran our regressions using two different defintions of salary for people on the medical school faculty, who are paid on an 11-month rather than a nine-month basis. We suspected that this would make almost no difference in our results since there was a school dummy, so on noticing that there was a difference in the estimated effect of pension acceptance, depending on whether the medical salaries were adjusted for a nine-month year, we decided to rerun our regressions excluding the medical school.

When the medical school was excluded we no longer got significant coefficients on the pension acceptance variable. Representative of the results we are now getting is the regression reported below, which estimates the salaries only of people in the school of humanities and sciences.

Variable	Parameter Estimate	Standard Error	t-Ratio
INTERCEPT	31317.	3875.7	8.08
AGE	−17.26	47.770	−.72
PSAL	−.019	.0645	−.30
YEAR-APP	−501.8	47.801	−1.50
PROF	11616.	2836.6	4.10
ASSIST	−9463.	3178.5	−2.98
ASSOC	−4580.	3727.8	−1.23
ASSOT	−1146.	2760.8	−.42
ADJUNCT	3545.	3099.0	1.14
YEARDEG	902.9	66.173	13.64

In the above regression, PSAL is the 0/1 instrument for pension acceptance multiplied by fitted salary. The interpretation of its coefficient is that signing up for the pension plan reduces one's salary by about 1.9% with a standard error of about 6.5%. In our economic models, we would predict a value of −.10 for PSAL.[16] Other regressions yield essentially similar results. Therefore, our data seem to indicate that our employer does not subscribe to any economic model. (Most Stanford economists will claim they always knew this about our university.)

We made several efforts to uncover a significant coefficient on the pension acceptance variable. For example, instead of using a 0/1 pension acceptance variable we tried using the probability of pension acceptance. We ran regressions just looking at the assistant professor population as a whole and separate regressions for the assistant professors in three schools. However, the result that an individual's salary was not signficantly affected by his pension acceptance decision was confirmed.

13.5 Conclusion

We have presented several alternative models of labor contracting. In our economic models we argued that, absent asymmetric information, firms would allow workers to choose individually how they would like to have their compensation divided between wages and benefits. Whether firms that offer greater benefit packages, or which skew benefits toward older workers, also tend to give older workers a greater fraction of the quasi rents on their firm-specific human capital is strictly an empirical question.

That part of compensation is paid in pension benefits is irrelevant for valuing the labor contract. Because each worker selects his own benefit package, there is no reason to expect firms to cater to certain types of workers (unless there is asymmetric information, or some benefits are in the nature of a public good).

In our noneconomic models benefits and wages do not necessarily balance. For the cross-sectional equity model the firm negotiates a total compensation package with a generation of workers, and all workers receive the same wage rather than the same total compensation. In the case of, say, health benefits an individual worker's salary would not be reduced if it became apparent that his future health costs would be high. However, growth in the overall cost of health benefits would slow wage growth so that total compensation for the group would be unaffected.

In the hierarchichal model much the same results obtain, though for slightly different reasons. Again, individual levels of total compensation can be affected by a proclivity to take of advantage of various benefits offered, but the firm's aggregate compensation bill is unaffected by projected increases in the relative price of benefits.

In the time-series equity model, firms and workers implicity agree to a rigid rate of wage growth and perhaps a fixed package of benefits. It is only in this model that the firm is not indifferent to the composition of a young worker's compensation package.

We attempted a test meant to distinguish between the economic and noneconomic models. While the results were not fully conclusive, they appeared to lend support to the noneconomic models. However, we cannot devise a test to distinguish among the noneconomic models given our limited data.

Notes

1. Woodbury (1983), using Chamber of Commerce survey data, estimates that employer payments to pension, health and life insurance, and other agreed-on items represented 9.6% of compensation in 1965 and 16.1% in 1978. (Total compensation excluded legally required payments such as social security, workers' compensation, and unemployment insurance.) Woodbury also cites a BLS study which estimates that supplements rose from 4.9% to 9.2% of total compensation from 1966 to 1976. See also Kotlikoff and Smith (1983), table 5.1.4, for more detailed data.

2. We will assume for convenience that workers are measured along a continuum, so that it is sensible to talk about fractional workers within a firm.

3. The assumption that bargaining skills are not revealed until the second period plays no essential role in our analysis. We employ it because it provides a novel yet simple means of motivating a desire for risk sharing. It is essentially equivalent to allowing certainty in bargaining outcomes plus randomness in production.

4. If employees knew their bargaining abilities in advance but firms could not identify bargaining talent, then of course two-period contracts, if enforceable in at least one direction, would cover all workers. This adverse selection motivation does not depend on risk aversion.

5. Kaiser Steel and the New York News are two examples of firms that have been deterred from closing operations and firing workers because paying high wages was preferable to paying high severance. See *Wall Street Journal*, November 29, 1982, p. 23: "High Cost of Liquidation Keeping Some Money-losing Plants Open."

6. See, e.g., Freeman (1985) in this volume.

7. For an early effort in this area, see Kotlikoff and Wise (1985) in this volume.

8. Of course, this analysis does not consider benefits that are public goods, such as a company swimming pool.

9. A firm that had not provided a benefit in the past could begin providing the benefit at a much lower cost than a firm with an established program, simply because its experienced workers may be a group that would not be costly to service.

10. This is the type of model most often implicitly assumed by authors who use a projected benefits method to value pension liabilities.

11. It is irrelevant whether that link occurred through the type of provision found in most pension plans for salaried workers or through periodic benefit increases in line with salary increases of the sort typically negotiated by unions.

12. The data file was produced by merging a provost's office file, with salary data for the last half of August 1982, with a benefits office file containing other data on workers for the first half of September 1982. Since Stanford's fiscal year runs from September 1 to August 31, the merged file unfortunately does not include people who either were not on the faculty or were on leave for the 1981–82 or 1982–83 school year.

13. This strategy, followed by the University of Rochester, has no adverse tax consequences and gives workers much greater flexibility over the timing of their contributions and withdrawals from the plan.

14. But see Scott et al. (1982), p. 32: *"Recommendation 4: The University retirement payment of 10 percent of salary should not be conditional on the amount of the employee's payment.* This would presumably mean that eligible employees not now participants in the plan could choose to enter it, and the University would begin contributing 10 percent of their salary. Currently eligible non-participants should not mistake this recommendation as bestowing a form of sudden pay increase; a decision to take a certain amount of pay in deferred form will of course affect the determination of the salary component of total compensation."

15. Of course, we are also missing many other variables that influence salary—e.g., publications, citations, awards, and other university benefits received. To the extent that any of these variables is correlated with pension acceptance there is an errors-in-variables problem. For example, workers benefiting from housing subsidies for new faculty or from tuition benefits for their children may have worse liquidity problems than other workers of the same age and salary and may not be in the pension plan. These workers may be compensated for lower pension benefits with their higher benefits in other areas rather than with higher salary.

16. The last seven variables in the equation are years since appointment to the university and dummies for the ranks of professor, assistant professor, associate professor, associate with tenure, adjunct, and years since Ph.D. respectively.

Comment   Daniel Feenberg

At the last edition of this conference, Jeremy Bulow propounded the notion that a firm's pension liability was best summarized by the present value of vested benefits, discounted at the nominal interest rate. He argued that the apparent backloading of the typical defined benefit plan does not necessarily mean that total compensation is similarly backloaded. Rather, we would expect wages to adjust until total compensation equaled marginal product. At the time many members of this conference found the spot market view of wages extreme, but few would doubt the lesson that compensation policy is part of the financial policy of the firm and that an understanding of the mechanism that determined the path of compensation through time was essential to determine the value of the firm. The present paper extends that argument considerably by showing how an efficient labor policy may be maintained by a firm using almost any compensation policy ranging from spot market wage rates to implicit or explicit contracts but that each rule affects the financial structure of the firm differently.

In the table that accompanies this discussion (table 13.C.1) I have tried to summarize the algebra of Bulow and Landsman's paper. The five compensation rules considered are listed across the top of the chart, and under each rule are expressions for the wage rates that might by paid by a firm that subscribed to that rule, so each column shows the time path of com-

We thank Ben Bernanke for valuable help.
Daniel Feenberg is a research associate of the National Bureau of Economic Research.

Table 13.C.1   Time Path of Compensation with Firm-specific Learning

Type of Worker	Marginal Product	Spot Wage	Long-Term Contract	Contract Binds Employer	Group Negotiation
Inexperienced	a	$a + \dfrac{(1-b)(1-a)}{1+r}$	w_0	$\leq a$	$a + \dfrac{1-a}{1+r} - \dfrac{a}{1+r}$
Experienced	1	$a+(1-a)b$	$(1+r)(a-w_0)+1$	$(1+r)(a-w_0)+1$	$a + B\left(\dfrac{1}{a} - a\right)$
Water	$\dfrac{1-a}{a(1+r)}$	$\dfrac{1-a}{a(1+r)} + \dfrac{(1-b)(1-a)}{1+r}$	$\dfrac{(1-a)}{a(1+r)} + a - w_0$	$\dfrac{(1-a)}{a(1+r)}$	$\dfrac{a-1}{a(1+r)} + \dfrac{B-a}{a(1+r)} + \dfrac{a^2(1-B)}{a(1+r)}$

Note: The model is a follows: firm revenue $= n_0^a + \frac{1}{a}n_1^a$, firm costs $= F + n_0 w_0 + n_1 w_1$ where $n_0 =$ inexperienced workers, $n_1 =$ experienced workers, and $F = (1+r+1/a)(1-a)/(1+r)$. A zero-profit constraint is assumed, and workers go to firms that offer highest PV of total compensation. The entries in the table are mostly copied from Bulow and Landsman, but I have filled in a few.

pensation under the given rule. Each of the paths has the same cost to the firm, the same present value of wages to the workers, and each controls turnover sufficiently well to prevent the waste of any firm-specific human capital. Even so, any positive rate of wage growth is admissible under at least one rule, and several of the rules allow wide variation in the compensation path. Nor is there any need to introduce an explicit pension plan to achieve efficiency. Indeed, the most obvious pay scheme of all (which pays marginal product in each period) has the desired effect on turnover without any deferred compensation. This irrelevance of compensation path to efficiency is not an artifact of the particular model developed here; rather, it is a consequence of firms and workers optimizing over their respective lifetimes.

In the last row of the chart the difference between the market value of the firm and its book value is given for each compensation path. This difference is here given the old-fashioned name "water," but no pejorative connotation is intended here. Water, of course, results from the failure to carry human capital on the books of the firm and the failure to capitalize on the start-up loss of $(1 - a)/a(1 + r)$.

Two empirical possibilities are suggested by the chart. First, one could estimate a wage equation as a function of personal characteristics, the change in present value of vested pension benefits, and the change in the expected value of nonvested benefits, where the last term could be interpreted broadly to include the expectation of future wages in excess of marginal product. Second, one might regress the market value of the firm on capital, debt, the present value of vested pension liabilities, and the present value of expected nonvested liabilities, defined consistent with the wage regression. The implicit contract view of the labor market suggests all four of these benefit coefficients will be minus one while the spot market view suggests that the coefficients on expected benefits will be zero. Consistency requires that firms and workers value benefits similarly. If workers systematically value benefits more highly than firms, it might serve as the basis for some government intervention. Such straightforward regressions may not be possible; certainly none have yet been presented to this conference.

The equation reported by Bulow and Landsman is a wage equation with the addition of a vested benefit to the right-hand side. In spite of the large size of the benefit, it does not seem to affect the wage rate to any measurable extent. Bulow and Landsman attribute this irrationality to the employer; however, surely it is as easy to attribute to the employees who decline the benefit.

The open discussion centered on the possible motivations of those who declined Stanford's generous offer. Albert Rees brought up the case of a well-known econometrician, formerly of Princeton, who was refused permission to decline a similar benefit offered by Princeton University. This individual argued that by the assumption of additional risk he might do better with 5% of his salary than CREF could do with 15%. Professors Samuelson and Summers agreed that over 30 years only a modest additional risk would be required to accomplish this seemingly herculean task. A few moments' reflection will suffice to recognize the limited applicability of this result. Unless the person is liquidity constrained, it is clear that accepting the pension contributions does not in any way limit their ability to bear risk, and that the optimal procedure would be to accept the pension and increase the riskiness of the nonpension portfolio by, for example, purchasing stocks on margin. Nor can a liquidity constraint be a convincing explanation, for the sum of money involved is less that $2000. In any case, the liquidity constraint must be temporary if the person is accumulating assets.

References

Akerloff, G. A. 1982. Labor contracts as a partial gift exchange. *Quarterly Journal of Economics* 97:543–69.

Bulow, J. I. 1982. What are corporate pension liabilities? *Quarterly Journal of Economics* 97:435–52.

Bulow, J. I., and Scholes, M. S. 1984. Who owns the assets in a defined benefit pension plan? In *Financial aspects of the United States pension system*, edited by Z. Bodie and J. Shoven. Chicago: University of Chicago Press (for NBER).

Kotlikoff, L. J., and Smith, D. E. 1983. *Pensions in the American economy*. Chicago: University of Chicago Press (for NBER).

Lazear, E. P. 1979. Why is there mandatory retirement? *Journal of Political Economy* 87:1261–84.

O'Boyle, T. F. 1982. High cost of a liquidation keeping some money-losing plants open. *Wall Street Journal*, 29 November, p. 23.

Scott, K.; Thomas, J.; Van Horne, J.; and Walecka, D. 1982. Report to the president of Stanford University of the Ad Hoc Committee for TIAA/CREF Alternatives. Mimeographed. Stanford, Calif.: Stanford University, May 21.

Woodbury, S. A. 1983. Substitution between wage and nonwage benefits. *American Economic Review* 73:166–82.

14 The Federal Civil Service Retirement System: An Analysis of Its Financial Condition and Current Reform Proposals

Herman B. Leonard

When career civil servants discuss the pay differential between government and private employment, they frequently remind each other to allow for the effects of their rather generous pension program. What has been a commonplace for federal employees—that the nation has incurred substantial future obligations to them—has not, however, attracted much attention from the public at large or even from commentators on government spending until very recently. When "federal borrowing" is discussed, the term almost never includes the borrowing implicit in making promises to pay future pensions. Even when "off-budget" spending is discussed, the failure to note promises of future pension payments in current budget documents is rarely mentioned. And when commentators try to reconstruct the actual deficit of the federal government, correcting for the absence of a capital budget and for credit and off-budget programs, accrual of liabilities for federal pensions is virtually never proposed.

The commitments embodied in the Federal Civil Service Retirement System exceed the currently and prospectively available assets out of which they are supposed to be paid by over one-half trillion dollars. Comparable estimates for the net liabilities of the military pension systems are of the same order of magnitude, and those for the social security system indicate net liabilities of over a trillion dollars. Thus, the three major "re-

Herman B. Leonard is associate professor of public policy at the John F. Kennedy School of Government at Harvard University and a faculty research fellow at the National Bureau of Economic Research.

Financial support for this research was provided by the NBER Public Sector Payrolls Project. I would like to acknowledge the helpful comments of Richard Zeckhauser, Barry Nalebuff, Jeremy Bulow, Zvi Bodie, Larry Kotlikoff, and the members of the NBER Public Sector Payrolls Project. Susan Bender and Karen Handmaker provided excellent research assistance; Susan Bender, who does not like the semicolon in this sentence, also provided helpful editorial assistance. No matter what I say, I will be forced to accept responsibility for any errors, so I will do so without protest.

tirement" programs of the federal government have net liabilities of approximately twice the currently officially recognized national debt. If the annual "deficit" and the size of the "national debt" are major political issues, the "quasidebt" constituted by the net liabilities of federal retirement systems should be an issue as well. Yet, because they are shrouded in the mystical cloak of "actuarial estimates" and are not treated in the standard budget documents considered by the Congress, they generally have received little attention. Recently the social security system has come under closer scrutiny, largely because it threatened to run out of cash. Until the latest round of considerable attention and public study, only a few of the most educated commentators were aware of its long-term actuarial position. The Civil Service Pension System and its military counterpart are hardly noticed at all.

An interesting example of the lack of enthusiasm for these issues may be found in a recent compendium of papers from the American Economic Association annual meetings. The *Proceedings* volume of the *American Economic Review* in May of 1982 devoted considerable space to a variety of papers discussing various aspects of the economics of government. A wide range of on- and off-budget programs were treated. Federal wages, tax expenditures, credit programs, and entitlement programs were scrutinized in detail. There is almost no mention of the Civil Service Retirement System.

This paper considers the fiscal condition of the federal Civil Service Retirement System and analyzes a major proposed reform of that system embodied in the budget requests currently before the Congress. The central findings of the study are:

1. The "unfunded liability" of the current system is approximately $540 billion in 1982 dollars.
2. Labor expenses recognized in the direct expenditures budget considered by Congress should be about 22% higher than they currently are to account for full funding of pension obligations accrued in each year. In 1982, this would increase federal labor expenses by about $14 billion.
3. The existing system provides a strong financial incentive for federal employees to continue working up until they attain full retirement eligibility—usually between ages 55 to 60. It then provides a strong incentive for them to retire.
4. The reform proposal advanced by the Office of Personnel Management (OPM) would constitute a major overhaul of retirement benefits. It would close the current funding gap solely by cutting benefits received by and net wages paid to current federal employees. It would constitute a 50% cut in the net pension wealth of current employees. It is comparable financially to a 15%–30% cut in the annual compensation of federal employees over the remainder of their working lives.

5. The OPM reform proposal would reduce the cash outlays of the retirement system funded by taxpayers by about $4 billion per year for the remaining years of this decade and by larger amounts in later years. It would cut the unfunded liability of the system by one-quarter, to $400 billion. It would reduce the full funding rate from 36% to 20%.

6. The OPM reform proposal would substantially alter the retirement incentives of the current system, completely eliminating the existing incentive to retire as soon as full eligibility is attained. This could have a considerable impact on the age and experience composition of the federal work force.

14.1   The Existing System

The Office of Personnel Management annually presents a number of reports on the status, changes, and prospects of the Civil Service Retirement System. These views are not entirely consistent with one another. The differences among them reflect differences in statutory requirements for how the system is to be viewed and funded. None gives an adequate picture of the condition of the fund.

14.1.1   Basic Characteristics of the Retirement System

The only widely agreed-on characteristics of the fund are those having to do with the objective facts of its operation and status—anything involving projections of its future operations is almost by definition a matter of controversy. The system is a defined benefit pension plan providing retirement and disability insurance benefits for a covered enrollment of approximately 2.7 million employees, 1.3 million retired employees, and 430 thousand survivors of employees or annuitants. The plan has provided benefits that are generous compared to most private pensions. Employees can currently retire with full benefits at age 55 with 30 years of service, at age 60 with 20 years of service, and at age 62 with five years of service. The current annuity formula provides benefits of 1 1/2 % of average salary per year of service for the first five years of service; 1 3/4% of average salary per year of service for the next five years of service; and 2% of average salary per year of service for any remaining years of service, with a maximum of 80% of average salary. Full disability benefits are available to any employee with five years of service. Disability benefits are 40% of salary or the retirement formula projecting service to age 60, whichever is higher.

A critical feature of the current system is that benefit payments are indexed to the cost of living after retirement. Moreover, the "average salary" used in the benefit formula refers to the three highest years of earnings (generally the last three years of employment). Thus, the level of benefits with which the retiree starts is also indexed to inflation, provided that fed-

eral salaries are increased to keep pace with the cost of living. Both of
these features have very large impacts on the financial status of the pension system, and both are the subjects of considerable controversy. Indeed, the appropriate treatment of these two features of the system is perhaps the most important choice involved in the actuarial estimation of the
financial condition of the system.

The benefits of the retirement system have been increased and the coverage extended to additional employees in a number of major revisions of
the system since its inception in 1920. Thus, the system has accrued substantial unfunded prior service costs over the years. The last major alteration in the system was in 1969, when the basis for the average salary calculation was reduced from the highest five years of earnings to the highest
three.

In theory, the system is funded out of contributions of 14% of payroll—7% each from employees and their agencies. In fact these payments
are not adequate to cover the current cash obligations of the system, and
the federal treasury annually makes an additional contribution to the
fund. This contribution is computed on the basis of an analysis of the
"unfunded liability" of the system and is supposed to constitute a payment in lieu of the interest that would have been earned on assets in the
fund if it were fully funded. The actuarial estimation of the obligations of
the fund, and thus its unfunded liability, is therefore an issue of current
operating interest both to the fund and to the Congress. Indeed, the Congress's direct interest in the matter led it to specify its intentions concerning how the fund's obligations were to be valued.

In part because the issue is of such material importance to the fund and
in part because the Congress specified its preferred form of valuation, a
variety of different accountings of the fund are rendered each year. Under
any estimation procedure, the present value of the obligations of the system substantially exceed the present value of its prospective income plus
its current assets. All valuations thus agree that the system has a large "unfunded liability." But different valuation methods lead to quite disparate
estimates of what this liability is, and hence to controversy about the appropriate methods of valuation. (Appendix 14.A discusses alternative
methods of valuation of pension obligations and evaluation of pension
fund performance.)

14.1.2   "Economic" Assumptions and Fund Valuation

In the actuarial valuation of any retirement system, a series of interrelated
assumptions about future economic conditions are crucial. Among these
are assumptions about the future values of interest rates, rates of salary
increase, increases in retirement benefits, and so on. In addition, the estimates rely upon the future stability of existing patterns of career promotions, promotion-related salary increases, and retirement decisions.

There is, however, one aspect of future economic conditions that should not make much difference in valuing the pension system. If inflation in general prices is treated consistently in the actuarial valuation, its assumed rate will be of little consequence. This is because any consistent valuation method will present the estimated values in real terms—that is, in terms relative to the rate of general price increases. So long as values are consistently expressed in real terms and the assumed rates of increase (or decrease) of specific values—like salaries or benefits after retirement—are expressed as real rates, the rate of inflation by itself is an unimportant assumption.[1]

What is crucial, then, is the assumed real rate of return on fund assets and the real rate of increase (or decrease) in salaries and benefits after retirement. There has been little controversy concerning the appropriate real rate of return to assume for fund assets. In contrast to a rather odd valuation in the 1980 annual report in which the Board of Actuaries for the fund assumed a 5% real rate of return on assets for the indefinite future, recent official reports of the fund's condition have presumed modest real rates of return in the range of 0.5%–2%. (In some cases real rates as high as 3%–5% have been assumed for the next one or two years.) Given the historical performance of the fund—invested by law in fixed interest special securities of the United States Treasury—it may be optimistic to presume that the real rate of return on fund assets will exceed zero—that is, that the fund will do any better than just keep even with inflation. If, however, the fund were somewhat more aggressively managed—not an inconceivable outcome of current criticism of its operations—it might well be able to achieve a modest positive real return.

The rate of return on fund assets is a crucial parameter because it provides the rate-of-time discount that allows us to compare the values of obligations in future periods with currently and prospectively available fund assets. It is, therefore, most appropriately interpreted as the rate at which we should discount the pension obligations of the government. Since we are trying to discern the value of these obligations on the theory that they constitute real governmental debts, there are powerful arguments for using the real risk-free rate of return in the economy—perhaps 1%–2%—as the appropriate discount rate. This choice is independent of the actual financial performance of the fund, as it should be since any eventual deficit in the fund will have to be paid by the Treasury. In the work presented here, all obligations have been discounted at an assumed risk-free rate of 1.5% in real terms.[2]

Different official reports of the fund are of different minds about how to treat future inflation. Table 14.1 shows three official estimates of the unfunded liability of the system. The first estimate is from *Fringe Benefit Facts 1980*, a publication of the Office of Personnel Management that provides an official overview of the fringe benefits received by federal em-

Table 14.1   **Official Estimates of the Unfunded Liabilities of the Civil Service Retirement System, September 1980 (1980 Dollars)**

	Total Unfunded Liability ($)	Unfunded Liability per Employee ($)
No future increases in salaries or benefits	166.4 billion	62,000
Future increases in benefits but not in salaries	357.3 billion	132,000
Future increases in both salaries and benefits	469.5 billion	174,000

Sources: Line 1: Office of Personnel Management, *Fringe Benefit* (1981a) p. 11. U.S. Government Printing Office.
Line 2: Office of Personnel Management (1982), table 1. Assumes no future general schedule increases in salaries; benefits after retirement are assumed to be constant in real terms.
Line 3: OPM (1982), table 4. Assumes salaries grow in real terms at ½% per year; benefits after retirement are assumed to be constant in real terms.

ployees and presents financial information associated with each plan. It assumes that there will be no future increases in either salaries or benefits other than those currently mandated. For purposes of this valuation, OPM interprets this to mean that there would be no future increases, even though benefits after retirement are indexed by law to the cost of living. Even with these highly restrictive assumptions, the unfunded liability of the system is over $160 billion, about $62 thousand for each current employee.

The "normal cost" of the system under these assumptions is worth noting. Normal cost is the percentage of an average employee's salary that must be put aside in each year of service in order to fund the pension over the employee's career. According to the fund's actuaries, if there is no future inflation in salaries or benefits, combined annual contributions from the employee and employer of about 14% of salary would be adequate to prevent deterioration in the financial integrity of the system. The current funding rate is consistent with the continued financial health of the system only in the absence of future inflation.

In its 1982 annual report, the Board of Actuaries of the fund presented an alternative set of estimates of the financial status of the system based on the assumption that retirement benefits would continue to be indexed to the cost of living and that inflation would continue at the (Office of Management and Budget estimated) rate of 5% per annum. They chose, however, to treat future increases in salaries as a matter of choice for the Congress, and therefore did not project any "general schedule" increases in future salaries. The result is shown in line 2 of table 14.1; the unfunded liabilities of the system are approximately $360 billion, about $130 thousand per current federal employee. At current average wages, this amounts to nearly six years of salary for each employee.

This is still not an accurate measure of the condition of the fund, because it ignores the effects of future salary increases. Such increases will have two effects. First, they will provide a larger source of incoming contributions. Second, and more powerfully, they will raise the retirement benefits of future retirees. The Board of Actuaries recognizes that ignoring these effects constitutes a potentially serious misrepresentation of the condition of the fund. Accordingly, they present an additional alternative set of calculations of the obligations of the fund based on the assumption that both benefits and salaries are likely to keep pace with future inflation. Specifically, the board assumed that salaries will rise in real terms by 0.5% per year and that benefits after retirement will stay constant in real terms. The results are shown in line 3 of table 14.1, taken from the 1982 annual report of the retirement system.

The substantive difference between the results in lines 2 and 3 of table 14.1 is in the estimated cost of future payments to those who have not yet retired. If salaries continue to keep pace with inflation (as is assumed in the calculations for line 3), benefit levels for employees who have not yet retired will be considerably higher. The projections for those who have retired already are unaffected, since in both valuations their benefits were presumed to be constant in real terms. The change is substantial; the unfunded liability rises by over $100 billion, to $469 billion, about 7.5 years of salary for the average federal employee.

Under these assumptions, the current funding structure of the retirement system is far from adequate. The normal cost computed by the Board of Actuaries allowing for inflation in both salaries and benefits after retirement amounts to 36% of payroll. Since the employees' contribution is 7% this would leave 29% to be paid by the government—four times current agency contributions. Recognizing the inadequacy of the current funding structure, Congress has moved to address the issue of the unfunded liability, albeit through rather an indirect method. As we shall see, even the device chosen by Congress will not long provide adequate coverage.

14.1.3   Current Treatment of the Unfunded Liability

The inadequacy of the funding of the retirement system has been a matter of more than academic interest for several years. The Congress moved during the 1970s to address the problem as a consequence of projections indicating that the fund would not only have a substantial and increasing unfunded liability but would also quickly run out of cash. The operating revenues of the system—the direct employer and employee contributions from payroll—were substantially less than fund disbursements in 1980. Table 14.2 shows the 1980 operating flows, the effect on available funds in

Table 14.2   **Operating Flows of the Civil Service Retirement System, 1980 (in Billions of Dollars)**

Assets available at year start			63.9
Investment income			
Net capital gains	(.3)		
Interest	5.1		
Contributions			
Employer	3.6		
Employee	3.7		
Total Additions		12.1	
Benefits paid	14.9		
Administrative expense	.1		
Total deductions		15.0	
Net flow from operations		(2.8)	
Prospective assets at year end			61.0
Supplemental Treasury payment			11.9
Actual assets at year end			73.0

Source: Office of Personnel Management (1982). Computed from figures in table 2.

the absence of congressional action, and the supplemental payment appropriated by Congress to maintain the cash basis integrity of the system.

If Congress had not supplemented the funding of the retirement system, the fund would have decreased by nearly $3 billion in 1980. This would have eroded the fund's earning potential and would have started a downward spiral leading quickly to bankruptcy. This prospect motivated the Congress to provide additional funding for the system during the 1970s. The action Congress took does not, however, guarantee the integrity of the fund. Congress chose a modestly rational and relatively inexpensive expedient that ensures only that the cash position of the fund will not deteriorate precipitously in the near future.

A standard solution to the problem that the retirement system faced—indeed, the solution that the Congress legislated for private pension funds in the Employee Retirement Income Security Act of 1974—consists of two parts: (1) Raise the contribution rate to the fund to the "full funding" level. Based on the "entry age normal" cost concept, this would mean raising the level of contributions from the current 14% rate to about 36% of payroll;[3] and (2) adopt a funding schedule to pay off the principal and accumulating interest of the "unfunded liability" of the system. In its 1980 annual report, the appointed Board of Actuaries of the system argued at length for these reforms. Congress had already chosen, however, to adopt a variant of the "interest" portion of part 2 of this program and not to adopt part 1 at all. Congress chose to pay only the interest on the unfunded liability, leaving the principal unamortized. The reason its method is a variant of this portion is that it chose to define the interest and the unfunded liability without reference to current or future inflation. The resulting construct is a strange animal indeed.

Why would the Congress choose not to amortize the principal of the indebtedness? Obviously, it is less expensive—currently—to ignore it. One rationale for ignoring it is that the current unfunded liability represents underfunded past service costs incurred on behalf of past taxpayers for services they received. These costs should have been borne at the time the services were rendered to the taxpayers who received them, but they were not. There is no obvious reason why current and future taxpayers should make back payments against this debt. According to this argument, there is no reason to retire the accumulated unfunded debt as long as the fund remains solvent on a cash basis.

This would make a good deal more sense if it were combined with a commitment to end the practice of underfunding from now on. The Congress chose, however, to continue adding to the unfunded liability in addition to ignoring its current size. It did, however, realize that the fund was losing interest because it was not fully funded. The interest income from the investments the system would make if it were fully funded would be an important source of additional cash for current payments. The Congress decided to "simulate" full funding: an annual payment is made to the fund representing the additional interest payments it would have received if it had been fully funded.

This left the problem of determining the rate of interest to be paid and the amount of the hypothetical funding on which to pay it. The rate was relatively simple: the interest is paid at the rate of other special issues of the Treasury, approximately—but typically a little below—the current long-term Treasury bond rate. As we have seen, however, the amount of the unfunded liability is a matter of some controversy. The legislation passed by the Congress establishing the "in lieu of interest" payments has been interpreted to mean that the unfunded liability of the system is to be evaluated under the assumption that there will be no inflation either in salaries or in benefits after retirement. This leads to a valuation like that shown in line 1 of table 14.1, which, as indicated above, gives far too favorable a view of the financial condition of the system.

There are three major conceptual flaws in the solution adopted by the Congress. First, the financial integrity of the system cannot be insured by any means that does not eventually bring the current funding into line with the current accrual of liabilities. Second, while payment of interest on the "unfunded liability" will keep the debt from growing any larger (if the current practice of underfunding is discontinued), it will not do so if the principal amount on which this interest is figured is grossly underestimated. Finally, if the purpose is to keep the unfunded liability from growing, this should probably be interpreted in real rather than nominal terms. Thus, the in lieu interest payment that the Congress should make should be figured on the basis of the real liability and should be figured at the real interest rate. By contrast, the Congress has chosen to pay interest on what might be termed the "nominal" liability—which ignores inflation and is far too small—and at the "nominal" interest rate, which includes a charge for the inflation erosion of principal.

As it turns out, the current high nominal interest rates, in conjunction with a substantially underestimated "debt" on which to pay them, led the Congress to pay, by accident and not by design, approximately the "right" amount of interest last year—about $10 billion—and perhaps even a bit more than would be required to pay the real interest rate on a more accurately estimated liability. The current economic setting might, therefore, provide a natural time to switch from the rather awkward method that has been employed to date toward one that has a better conceptual and practical basis.

14.1.4   The Financial Condition of the Civil Service Retirement System: The Baseline Simulation for 1981

To provide a baseline for comparison of the major reform proposal for the retirement system, an analysis of the Civil Service Retirement System for 1981 was prepared using a computer simulation model that represented 1700 age-experience categories of employees for each sex. Simulations were run for 120 years. All computations were carried out in real terms, and all economic assumptions were specified in terms of real rates. The rates of promotional salary increases; voluntary, involuntary, and disability retirement; and separation of employment due to withdrawal or death were projected from recent experience of the system, published in its annual reports.

Critical Economic Assumptions

The baseline simulation assumes that the fund will earn a risk-free real return of 1.5% on its assets. As indicated earlier, the fund could conceivably be managed so as to earn a higher expected rate of interest, but probably only by investment in higher-risk assets. On a risk-adjusted basis, this rate would appear to be reasonable. It simply assumes that there are no "bargains"—securities with higher than average risk-adjusted returns— available in the capital markets. A lower rate would be defensible, but in the spirit of erring on the side of conservatism in estimating the unfunded liability, this rate was chosen for the base case.[4]

General schedule increases in federal salaries are assumed to proceed at the rate of 1% annually in real terms. This presumption is based on the notion that long-term real national economic growth will be sustained in excess of 1% per annum, and the real wages of federal employees will not decline permanently relative to the real wages of private sector employees.

Under existing law, benefits paid to retired employees are indexed to the cost of living. In the past, the form of indexing guaranteed growth of these benefits in real terms. Recently, however, the indexing has been modified so that increases are granted only once each year and are related to the increase in the consumer price index over the preceding 12 months. Accordingly, the baseline simulation assumes that benefits after retirement will be constant in real terms.

Estimates of real values for the current retirement system are nearly neutral with respect to the assumed rate of inflation. The only aspect of the system that is defined in nominal terms is the computation of "average" salary, which is used to establish the annuity payment in the first year of retirement. This average, which is taken over the highest three years of salary, is lower relative to salary in the final year if inflation is high than if it is low. Even this effect, however, is relatively minor. The baseline simulation assumes continuing annual inflation at the rate of 5%.

Table 14.3 summarizes the fundamental assumptions of the baseline simulation.

Baseline Simulation Results

A summary of the results of the baseline simulation is shown in table 14.4. The unfunded liability of the retirement system as of October 1981 was about $540 billion. This net liability results from a current present value of projected benefit payments of $894 billion, with projected future collections (at a full funding rate) of $281 billion and current assets of $73 billion. The estimated present value of future benefit payments to employees now working or on the annuity rolls exceeds the present value of projected total future salary payments to current employees. Even if we used all of the current funds and contributed an amount equal to all future salary payments to existing employees, we would be unable to pay the benefits to these employees and those currently on the rolls. Cash solvency will only be maintained through supplemental appropriations and the contributions made by and on behalf of employees not yet employed.

The actuarial unfunded liability effectively assumes that future funding of the system will be at the full normal cost rate. As table 14.4 indicates,

Table 14.3   Baseline Simulation Assumptions

	Annual Rate (%)
Real rate of return on fund assets	1.5
Real rate of salary growth	1.0
Real rate of benefits growth (after retirement)	0
Rate of general price increase	5.0

Note: Retirement, disability, death, separation rates as reported in Office of Personnel Management (1981*b*).

Table 14.4   Baseline Simulation Results for the Civil Service Retirement System, October 1981

Present value of projected benefit payments:		
Current annuitants	$269 billion	
Future annuitants	$625 billion	
Total		$894 billion
Present value of projected future salaries:		
Current employees	$776 billion	
Present value of future contributions:		
Employees	$ 54 billion	
Employer (current funding rate)	$ 54 billion	
Total contributions		($108 billion)
Current assets		($ 73 billion)
Excess of liabilities over assets		$713 billion
(current funding rate)		
Additional employer contributions		($172 billion)
(full funding rate)		
Actuarial unfunded liability		$540 billion
Normal cost as percentage of salaries		36.2
Unfunded liability per employee		$200,000

Source: Simulation. See table 14.3 and text for assumptions.

this amounts to an additional contribution over the remaining working lives of current employees of about $172 billion (in present value) more than is currently contemplated under existing official employer contributions. Thus, an alternative way to read the results of the baseline simulation is to observe that if we make additional contributions over and above the official 7% of salaries in amounts equal to a present value of $172 billion, then we will only be behind in funding the retirement of current employees by $540 billion (in present value) when they retire. If we continue current underfunding, our net liability to these workers will be over $700 billion.

The full finding rate associated with the current employee, benefit, and economic structure of the retirement system is about 36% of payroll, roughly the same as that projected by the board of Actuaries on the basis of similar assumptions for the preceding year. Since the contribution rate (exempting the supplemental payment from the Treasury) is only 14% the annual underfunding of the current obligations of the system is approximately 22% of payroll, or about $14 billion this year. In addition to this underfunding, the fund is depleted by virtue of not receiving interest income on the investments it would have made with the extra funds it would have if it were fully funded. In 1981, with an unfunded liability of $540 billion and a presumed real rate of return of 1 1/2% this was an additional $8 billion loss.

The condition of the retirement system would have deteriorated by about $22 billion in real terms last year if the Treasury had made no supplemental contribution to it. As it was, with a supplemental contribution of about $14 billion, the financial condition of the fund deteriorated by about $8 billion. Thus, presuming 5% inflation, the current unfunded liability can be expected to be about $575 billion in 1982 dollars.

Under the baseline assumptions, the projected cash position of the retirement system is not critical for the moment, due to the projected continuing supplemental appropriations from the Treasury. In the early years of the next century, however, the situation can be expected to deteriorate. Following a decade of relative stability in the level of fund assets, funds will begin to flow out at the rate of about $3 billion per year. This trend will be exacerbated by the reduction in interest income received as the invested funds decrease and will not be offset under current projections of the Treasury's supplemental payment. The baseline simulation projects approximately $40 billion in available funds in the year 2000—roughly half today's assets—and a zero cash balance in 2008.

The financial condition of the current retirement system is precarious. The system has an enormous net liability—roughly half the size of the currently recognized national debt. In nominal terms, the unfunded liability of the civil service retirement system appears to be growing at roughly the same rate as the national debt, and so is staying about half as large. The nominal change in the national debt from year to year is referred to as the "budget deficit," and it attracts widespread attention in the Congress and in the media. The corresponding nominal "deficit" of the federal pension system this year is approximately $35 billion.

As with the explicit national debt, great care must be exercised in interpreting the quasi debt represented by the nation's civil service pension obligations. First, just as some of the costs are passed along to future taxpayers, some of the benefits may be also. If, for example, the pension obligations were incurred as federal workers built physical assets to be used in the future, some of the benefits will be received by future taxpayers. Second, while their liability is a real one, taxpayers presumably obtained some benefits in the form of reduced wages paid to federal workers as a consequence of the pension "compensation" those workers received. Indeed, there is evidence that, excluding pension compensation, federal employees receive lower pay than comparable workers in the private sector. If part of the (political) purpose of having a federal pension system is to move some of federal workers' compensation off budget, the political goal of reducing the apparent cost of government services to taxpayers is only met if the on-budget portion of compensation (wages) is in fact reduced. We would thus expect that pension obligations were incurred in exchange for some reduction in wages. However, this exchange is likely to be inefficient, because both workers and taxpayers appear to view $1 of present value of pension benefits as less valuable than $1 of current wages. If, for example, workers value $1 of pension benefits at 50 cents, then total compensation must be increased as wage reductions are achieved by granting pension benefits.

Moreover, many would argue that public debts should be a source of alarm only when they grow as a fraction of gross national product—that is, when the burden of taxes they represent grows as a fraction of taxpayers' incomes. Even on this standard, however, the nation's civil service pension obligations are growing, albeit rather slowly. Unlike the explicit national debt, which consists of nominal governmental obligations whose real burden is eroded by inflation, federal pensions are fully indexed, so that inflation does not materially alter the real size of the taxpayers' debt. In addition, continuing underfunding adds to the real unfunded liability each year. In 1982, a contribution of about $19 billion more than the official employee and employer funding would have been required to keep the pension obligation constant as a fraction of GNP (at about 20%). Even after the Treasury's supplement payment of $14 billion, an additional $5 billion would have been required. Thus, even viewed against the rather weak standard that public debts should not be permitted to rise faster than the economy is expanding, federal pension obligations constitute a material problem.

The magnitude of the pension debt might best be viewed in the context of the fact that while the national debt is ostensibly on behalf of and for the benefit of 230 million taxpayers, the pension fund is mainly for the benefit of 2.7 million current employees and 1.7 million annuitants. (The benefits to the taxpayer of accruing the fund—the services of the employees as they earned these pensions—have already been received.) This net liability is increasing at the rate of roughly $10 billion per year in real terms. Including the inflation adjustment in the outstanding principal, this year's increase is about $35 billion in nominal terms—$13 thousand for every current employee.

Some observers regard the public's pension obligations as less binding than the explicit national debt. There is no contractual obligation, they argue, and the rules are subject to change at any time. Thus, this argument concludes, we should be less concerned about pension obligations than about other federal commitments. There is clearly some force to this logic; as we will discuss in the next section, there is currently before Congress a proposal that would substantially alter the existing system. This should not, however, persuade us too easily to ignore the scope of the existing commitments. Precisely because they are a less visible and less directly costly form of compensation, it seems unlikely that they will disappear as a feature of the federal employment landscape.

14.2 The Current Reform Proposal

The financial condition of the Civil Service Pension System has finally begun to attract significant policy notice in Washington. The marked increase in attention is due in part to a spreading recognition and understanding of estimates like those presented in the last section and in part to the more intense scrutiny given to all government retirement programs in connection with studies of social security reform. The Office of Personnel Management is currently drawing up proposals for substantial reform. While they have not yet been formally presented to the Congress, their general outline is beginning to emerge. Administration budget requests for the new fiscal year base estimates for receipts and disbursements of the retirement fund on a system of benefits considerably different from that currently in place.

This section provides an analysis of the proposed new retirement system embodied in the president's proposed FY 1984 budget. While this may not be the final form of the reform proposal eventually presented to the Congress, it does represent one seriously contemplated revision of the current system. It provides an intriguing counterpoint to the existing structure.

14.2.1 The Perceived Problem

Why should the present system be reformed? A simple answer would be that it eventually will not be able to meet its obligations. As we saw in the last section, however, this is not an immediate problem. The current system can continue to meet its cash obligations until at least the turn of the century. Why, then, go to the trouble of reforming the system?

Officials involved in the reform process give two answers to this question. First, they observe that the system must be reformed at some point and that now is as good a time as any to begin dealing with the fund's long-term problems. Second, they observe that the system simply appears too costly, too generous, and too easy to abuse. It is costly in the sense that its normal funding cost is approximately twice that of a typical high-quality private sector pension plan. It is generous in that it provides a relatively high level of benefits to many employees who retire at an early age—some can retire as early as age 55 and qualify for pensions replacing nearly 60% of their preretirement incomes. Over half of federal employees retire before the age of 60; the comparable figure for the private sector is only 7%. The average replacement rate of pensions for preretirement income for federal retirees is over 55%, considerably higher than for their private sector counterparts. Finally, the system is easy to "abuse," in the view of some, because after retiring on an already generous federal pension at a young age, many former federal employees will take private sector jobs that will qualify them for at least the minimum benefit under social security. Indeed, about 75% of federal retirees receive social security benefits. This so-called double-dipping appears to many to be an excessively generous feature of the combined civil service retirement and social security systems.

One way to characterize this perceived problem is to examine the value of pension benefits received at different retirement ages. While this will differ for each employee, depending on when employment began, how long he or she will live after retirement, and so on, the general pattern will be similar across employees. As an illustration, we can look at the pension "entitlements" of a typical employee.

Figure 14.1 shows the capitalized value of the pension received under the current system by an employee who joins the system at age 25 and who receives "typical" longevity salary increases over his or her lifetime. General schedule increases compensate for a 5% annual rate of inflation and provide for a 1% real growth in salary. The figures are presented for an employee who would attain a nominal salary of $25,000 at the age of 58. In order to make the figures for the value of pension benefits to employees retiring at different ages comparable, the values are shown in terms of their equivalent capital values at age 65. For example, an employee retiring at age 40 would receive pension benefits equal in value to a $21,000 check received at age 65; if the employee retired at age 62, the benefits re-

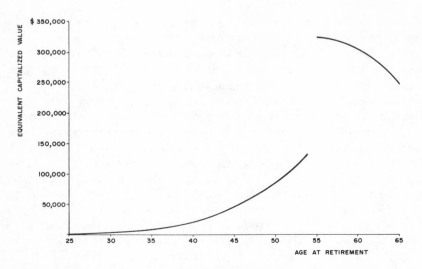

Fig. 14.1   Equivalent capitalized value of pension benefits at age 65 (computed for an illustrative federal employee). Taken from calculations. See text for assumptions.

ceived would be equal in value to a $290,000 check received at age 65. Both the government and the employee are assumed to value assets and obligations at 1 1/2% real rate of discount, and the employee is assumed to live until age 74.

As figure 14.1 shows, there is a substantial discontinuity in the value of pension entitlements when the employee becomes eligible for an immediate pension. Up to this point, the system provides for a deferred pension that starts at age 62. Deferred pension benefits are defined in nominal terms. Their present value is reduced by deferral and is also eroded by inflation between the time of retirement and the start of the annuity. By contrast, once the pension benefits start they are indexed to inflation, so that they stay constant in real terms. The twin effects of deferral and inflation erosion of the deferred pension benefits keep the value of the pension entitlement small until the employee becomes elegible for full retirement and an immediate pension.

The discontinuity in the entitlement system comes from the shift in the entitlement's value as the employee crosses this combination of age and experience boundary. As figure 14.1 shows, the value of pension entitlements for our illustrative employee accumulates slowly across his or her working life, reaching by age 54 an amount equivalent to about $130,000 given on his or her sixty-fifth birthday. The next year, when the employee qualifies for full retirement, the value suddenly jumps to the equivalent of $323,000. It stays at this level for approximately three years and then begins to fall, reaching $248,000 if the employee retires at age 65.

It is clear from figure 14.1 that federal employees have a substantial, increasing incentive to work until they reach eligibility for full retirement. At that point, the equivalent value of their entitlement peaks; if they continue working, it starts to fall. This is because the period of retirement gets shorter, an effect which outweighs the increase in pension benefits resulting from higher average salary at retirement and credits for additional service years. If the system is in fact too costly, it almost certainly has something to do with the level of entitlements attained at the ages of 55–60, and less to do with the entitlements thereafter.

To see this last point more clearly, we can examine the relationship between the age at retirement and the funding rate that would be required to set aside sufficient assets over the employee's working life to cover these pension benefits. Figure 14.2 shows that fraction of salary that would have to be set aside in order to fund the retirement obligations of the illustrative employee discussed above. The required funding rate rises slowly across the employee's working life; if he or she retires before age 54, the funding rate is below 15%. At the age of eligibility for full retirement, however, the required rate jumps sharply to about 36%. If the employee retires later, the rate drops steadily, reaching about 19% at age 65. If the cost of the pension system—in the sense of its normal cost funding rate—

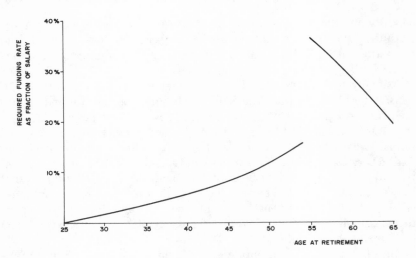

Fig. 14.2   Funding rates required for retirement for illustrative employee. Taken from calculations. See text for assumptions.

is regarded as too high, it is likely to have more to do with the problem of providing benefits for employees who retire in the early years after they become entitled to a full pension rather than with those who retire before age 55 or at the "normal" retirement age of 65.

14.2.2   The Proposed Reform Package

The reforms embodied in the president's FY84 budget request include four basic revisions in the pension benefits provided by the retirement system:

- *A change in the definition of "average salary" on which the pension is based.* Currently, the average is based on the highest three years of earnings; the new system would base it on the highest five years. This would be a return to the definition used up until 1969.
- *A modification of the credits for service years.* Currently, the system gives credits totaling 16.25% for the first 10 years of service and 2% for each year of service thereafter; the new system would give credits of 1.5% for every service year. This provision will only be invoked in FY89 and after, and then only if the calculated normal cost of the system continues to exceed 22%.
- *A reduction in the adjustment of pension benefits for inflation for those who are under 62 years of age.* Currently, all pension benefits are fully indexed. Under the new system, those under age 62 would receive cost of living adjustments equal to one-half of the increase in the general price level.
- *A penalty for early retirement.* Pension benefits would be reduced by 5% for each year of age at retirement under 65. Thus, an employee re-

tiring at age 58 would have benefits reduced by 7 times 5%. This penalty would be phased in by age cohort over a 10-year period. Thus, an employee who is 54 when the system is instituted would have benefits reduced by 1/2% for each year he or she retires before age 65; an employee who is 53 would have benefits reduced by 1% per year, and so on. Employees under the age of 45 would retire under a system with the full early retirement penalty.

In addition to these alterations in the benefits formulas and cost-of-living adjustments, the proposed package would alter both employee and employer contributions. In the first year, contributions for both employees and the Treasury would be raised from the current 7% of salary to 9%; in the following year and thereafter both would be set at 11%.

These adjustments in the benefit package are quite substantial, both individually and in combination. Table 14.5 shows the effect of shifting the definition of average salary from a three-year to a five-year basis. Since the average salary calculation is defined in nominal terms, this effect is a function of the underlying rate of inflation. As table 14.5 indicates, the adjustment will reduce pension entitlements for all employees by roughly 4%–9%, depending on the rate of inflation.

For those retiring after more than 10 years of service, changing the credit for service years also represents a substantial reduction in pension benefits. Table 14.6 shows the current and new annual pension entitlements as fractions of "average" salary and the resulting percentage reduction in benefits. As table 14.6 shows, those who retire with more than 20 years of service face reductions of roughly 20% in their pension benefits relative to those received under the current system.

The benefit reductions from the proposed change in the cost-of-living indexing for pensioners under age 62 and the early retirement penalty affect only those who retire between the age of 55 and 65. Lowering the cost-

Table 14.5   **Reductions in Pension Entitlements from Change in Definition of Average Salary**

	Inflation Rate		
	2%	5%	8%
Three-year average (final salary)	.957	.931	.906
Five-year average (final salary)	.916	.868	.824
Reduction from using five-year instead of three-year average	4.3%	6.8%	9.1%

Source: Calculations based on average rates of salary increase due to seniority plus an assumed real growth of 1% per year in federal wages.

Table 14.6   Reductions in Pension Entitlements from Change in the Credit for Years of Service

Service Years at Retirement	Pension as a Percentage of "Average" Salary		Reduction
	Current	Proposed	%
5	7.5	7.5	0
10	16.3	15.0	7.7
15	26.3	22.5	14.3
20	36.3	30.0	17.2
25	46.3	37.5	18.9
30	56.3	45.0	20.0
35	66.3	52.5	20.8
40	76.3	60.0	21.3

Source: Calculations based on current and proposed pension benefit formulas.

of-living adjustment for early retirees reduces the value of the benefits that will be received for the rest of the employee's life. The net reduction in benefits therefore depends on pensioner longevity. If the employee were to die shortly after age 62, the reduction would be a smaller percentage of the total value of the pension than if the reduced pension is received for a long period. An illustration using our illustrative employee may be helpful. Table 14.7 shows the reduction in the present value of pension entitlements from adopting the proposed change in the cost-of-living adjustment for a retiree under the age of 62. The employee is assumed to live to the age of 74 and to discount at a rate of 1.5% in real terms. As table 14.7 indicates, early retirees may face an overall loss of over 10% of the present value of their pension entitlements even if the rate of inflation is only 5% per year.

The effect of the early retirement penalty is, of course, the easiest to describe; it simply amounts to a 5% penalty for each year of early retirement, where "early" is defined as under age 65. Once this feature is fully phased in, it amounts to a loss of one-half of the pension entitlements (relative to the old system) for anyone retiring at age 55.

Taken together, the proposed reforms amount to a considerable overhaul of the pension entitlements embodied in the Civil Service Retirement system, particularly for those who retire between the ages of 55 to 60. Table 14.8 shows the percentage reduction for various retirement ages from each of the changes separately and for the package as a whole for the illustrative employee discussed above. These calculations assume a rate of inflation of 5%. As table 14.8 indicates, even for the least affected group retiring at age 65, the package of reforms amounts to a reduction in benefits of more than one-quarter. For those who choose to retire as early as age 55, the entitlement is reduced almost 70%.

Table 14.7   **Percentage Reduction in Present Value of Pension Entitlements from One-Half Instead of Full Cost-of-Living Indexing to Age 62**

Age at Retirement	Inflation Rate		
	2%	5%	8%
55	5.6	13.3	20.2
56	5.0	11.8	18.0
57	4.3	10.2	15.7
58	3.5	8.5	13.1
59	2.7	6.7	10.4
60	1.9	4.6	7.3
61	1.0	2.4	3.8
62	—	—	—

Source: Calculations based on typical longevity salary increases and assuming real salaries increase at 1% per year in real terms. Based on an employee who will live to age 74 and who discounts at 1.5% in real terms.

Table 14.8   **Reductions in the Present Value of Pension Entitlements from Proposed Reforms for Illustrative Employee**

Age at Retirement	Percentage Reduction in Present Value of Pension Benefits from Change in				
	Definition of "Average" Salary	Service Year Credits	1/2 COLA <62	Early Retirement Penalty	Entire Package*
30	8	0			8
40	7	14			20
50	7	19			25
55	7	20	13	50	68
56	7	20	12	45	64
57	7	20	10	40	60
58	7	21	9	35	56
59	7	21	7	30	52
60	7	21	5	25	47
61	7	21	2	20	42
62	7	21		15	37
63	7	21		10	34
64	7	21		5	30
65	7	21			27

Source: Calculations. See text for assumptions.

*Individual reductions do not add to combined reduction because effects are multiplicative, not additive.

Figure 14.3 shows the effect of these reductions on the rate of funding (as a fraction of salary) that would be required to support the resulting pension benefits for our illustrative employee. The most dramatic reductions are from the changes in the service years credits and from the early

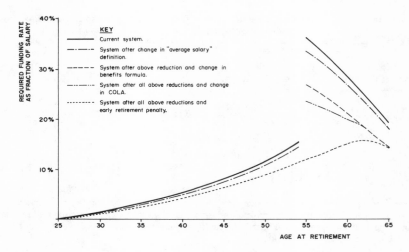

Fig. 14.3   Funding rates required for retirement benefits for illustrative
employee, before and after benefit reductions. Taken from
calculations. See text for assumptions.

retirement penalty. The combined effect of the reductions is heavily concentrated on ages 55–60, as table 14.8 indicated. Figure 14.3 shows that
the combination of the proposed reductions results in the virtual removal
of the anomalous discontinuity under the current system that occurs when
the employee attains eligibility for full retirement. Reducing the anomaly
of the old system is achieved through a series of changes that decrease the
level of benefits at every age, selectively targeted so that the reduction is
greatest where the anomaly of the current system is largest.

14.2.3   Effects of the Proposed Reductions in Benefits

The proposed changes would substantially reduce the costs associated
with the federal pension system under any but the most perverse assumptions about the effects of the reductions on retirement behavior. The funding rate associated with full retirement under the proposed system is less
than that under the current system at practically any age. Almost irrespective of retirement behavior under the two systems, the new system will be
less expensive than the old.

Examination of the detailed simulation results for the proposed system
confirms this impression. Table 14.9 presents results for the new system
under the (rather strong) assumption that retirement and other experience
rates in the system are invariant to the regime of benefit formulas. The
proposed benefit cuts would reduce the unfunded liability of the system
by about $140 billion, to about $400 billion, and would reduce the full
funding rate from about 36% to about 20% of salaries. Given the changes
in the contribution rates embodied in the reform proposal, contributions

Table 14.9   **Simulation Results for the Civil Service Retirement System with Proposed Benefit Reductions, October 1981**

Present value of projected benefit payments:		
Current annuitants	$256 billion	
Future annuitants	$366 billion	
Total		$622 billion
Present value of projected future salaries:		
Current employees	$776 billion	
Present value of future contributions:		
Employees	$ 84 billion	
Employer	$ 66 billion	
Total contributions		($151 billion)
Current assets		($ 73 billion)
Actuarial unfunded liability		$398 billion
Normal cost as percentage of salaries		19.5
Unfunded liability per employee		$147,000

Source: Simulation. See text for assumptions. Assumes no change in disability and retirement rates from baseline case.

would be approximately at the level of normal service costs, effectively putting the system on a full funding basis. By any standard, this would be regarded as a significant alteration in the long-term position of the fund. What is perhaps surprising, however, is that, sizable and significant as these proposed cuts are, the system still has an unfunded liability of about $400 billion. These alterations will not come close to eliminating the long-term net liabilities of the pension system.

If these reductions are not sufficient to eliminate the unfunded liability of the system, just what do they do? One answer comes from comparing the current and proposed systems in terms of the overall entitlements of current participants. Table 14.10 shows the net pension wealth of current federal employees under the two systems. The effect of the benefit reductions on the entitlements of current participants is dramatic, even if the impact on the unfunded liability is not. Under today's system, existing federal employees will receive benefits whose present value exceeds their future contributions by about $570 billion, or about $211 thousand per current employee. Under the proposed modifications to the system, this would be reduced to about $280 billion, or by almost $107 thousand per current employee. This is a reduction of over one-half in the net entitlements of current federal employees. If the federal government had been putting aside funds to cover its pension obligations on a full funding basis in bank accounts with its employees' names on them, then the proposed modifications of the system would remove half of the amounts in those

Table 14.10   **Net Pension Wealth of Current Federal Employees under Current and Proposed Retirement Systems (1981 Dollars)**

	Current System	Proposed System	Change
Present value of pension benefits to future annuitants	$625 B	$366 B	($259 B)
Present value of future contributions by current employees	($ 54 B)	($ 84 B)	($ 30 B)
Net pension wealth	$571 B	$282 B	($289 B)
Per employee pension wealth	$211 K	$105 K	($107 K)

Source: Simulations. See text for assumptions.

accounts. For the advantage of a $53,000 per employee reduction in unfunded liability and reduced requirements for taxpayer contributions, existing employees lose $107 each in net pension entitlements.

What cut in annual pay would be financially comparable to these benefit reductions? The answer for any particular employee depends on his or her current age, the age at which he or she joined the system, current salary, and the age at retirement. We can, however, easily compute the average for new employees entering the system. Over the course of their working lives, employees within the current system receive pension benefits equal in value to 36.2% of the value of their salaries; they make a contribution of 7% of their salaries toward these benefits, so the current retirement system constitutes, on average, a 29.2% supplement to wage income. The proposed system has a funding rate of 19.5%, and employees would contribute 11% of this; it thus constitutes an 8.5% supplement to wage income. Stated in terms of its impact on total compensation by employees over the course of their working lives, then, the proposed system represents a reduction from 129.2% to 108.5% of current wage income. This is equivalent to a 16% reduction in total compensation for employees with the bulk of their working lives ahead of them.

For employees who have already been in the system for a number of years, the annual pay cut equivalent to these pension entitlement reductions is substantially larger. The size of the pension entitlement cut is similar, but there are fewer working years remaining over which to amortize it. Consider, once again, the employee discussed above, and assume that he or she is currently 40 years old and has 15 years of service. In working from age 40 until retirement, the employee will be "paid" in two ways: the receipt of an annual salary, and an increase in the value of pension benefits. Column 1 of table 14.11 shows the percentage of such an employee's total compensation that would be expected to come in the form of increases in the value of pension benefit entitlements from the age of 40 up

Table 14.11   Pension Reductions as an Equivalent Percentage Reduction in Total Compensation for the Remainder of the Illustrative Employee's Working Life (to Nearest %)

Age at Retirement	Pension Compensation Total Compensation (1)	Pension Cut Pension Compensation (2)	Pension Cut Total Compensation (3 = 1*2)	Wage Cut Total Compensation (4)	Total Cut Total Compensation (5)
55	37	73	27	2	29
56	35	68	24	2	27
57	34	64	22	2	24
58	32	60	19	2	22
59	31	55	17	2	20
60	28	51	14	2	17
61	27	46	12	2	15
62	25	40	10	2	13
63	24	37	9	3	12
64	22	32	7	3	10
65	20	29	6	3	9

Col. 1:   Pension compensation as a percentage of total compensation, age 40 to retirement, current system.
Col. 2:   Percentage reduction in pension compensation, age 40 to retirement, from proposed changes in pension entitlements.
Col. 3:   Percentage reduction in total compensation, age 40 to retirement, from proposed reduction in pension benefits (col. 1 * col. 2).
Col. 4:   Percentage reduction in total compensation, age 40 to retirement, from 4% decrease in net wages due to increase in employee contribution.
Col. 5:   Total percentage reduction in total compensation (does not equal col. 3 + col. 4 because effects are multiplicative).

Source: Calculations. See text for assumptions.

to various retirement ages. Column 2 shows the percentage reduction in the value of these entitlements. Column 3 shows the resulting percentage reduction in total compensation stemming from entitlement cuts; it is the product of columns 1 and 2. Column 4 shows the percentage reduction in total compensation stemming from the increased employee contribution to the retirement system. This represents a 4% cut in net wages; it is a smaller fraction of total compensation. Column 5 shows the combined effect of the reduction in pension benefits and the reduction in net wages as a percentage of compensation that would have been received under the current system. This gives the impact of the pension reductions, measured as a pay cut. As table 14.11 indicates, the proposed reforms reduce annual compensation by nearly 30% for a 40-year-old employee who planned to retire at 55. Even if the employee does not plan to retire for another 25 years, the proposed pension adjustments reduce annual pay by about 10% over his or her remaining working life. Viewed in terms of its equivalent in the form of a general salary reduction, the proposed reform package clearly constitutes a sizable alteration from current policies.

The proposed modifications close the gap that currently exists between the contributions to the fund and the normal service costs of the system. Resources to close the gap must have come from somewhere. How much was involved, and where did it come from? A simple way to examine this issue is to compare the hypothetical "balance sheets" of the current and proposed systems through a "sources and uses" analysis. Table 14.12 presents the balance sheets, and table 14.13 shows the "sources" of funds in-

Table 14.12   **Comparative Actuarial Balance Sheets, Current and Proposed Retirement Systems (in Billions of 1981 Dollars)**

	Current System	Proposed System
Assets		
Current assets	73	73
Present value of future contributions		
Current employees	54	84
Employer (at full funding rate)	227	67
Total assets	354	224
Liabilities		
Present value of future benefits		
Current annuitants	269	256
Current employees	625	366
Total	894	622
Fund balance (unfunded liability)	(540)	(398)
Total liabilities and fund balance	354	224

Source: Simulations. See text for assumptions.

Table 14.13   **Sources and Uses Analysis of Proposed Pension System Modifications (All Figures in Present Value, Billions of 1981 Dollars)**

Sources of funds:	
Increases in future contributions by current employees	30
Reductions in benefits to current annuitants	13
Reductions in benefits to current employees	259
Total sources of funds	302
Uses of funds:	
Reduction in future contributions by employer (at full funding rate)	160
Reduction in unfunded liability	142
Total uses of funds	$302

Source: Calculations based on table 14.11.

volved in the change from the current to the proposed system and the "uses" to which these funds have effectively been put.

Table 14.13 indicates that all of the sources are effectively from current or former employees, while all of the uses of funds are to reduce obligations or payments of taxpayers. Employees pay more and receive less. Taxpayers are projected to pay less and are responsible for a smaller unfunded liability. The proposed package of plan revisions amounts to a very considerable reduction of taxpayer obligations. Faced with a gap between obligations and income, the Office of Personnel Management proposal balances the system solely by cutting taxpayer obligations. As table 14.13 shows, this would constitute a $300 billion shift from current federal employees and annuitants to taxpayers.

14.2.4   The Cash Implications of the Proposed Reforms

Though they would reduce the net pension wealth of current employees by over one-half, the proposed reforms have a relatively small effect on the cash outflow from the retirement system over the next few years. Table 14.14 shows estimates of the excess of benefit payments over employee contributions under the current and proposed systems for 1983–2050. This represents the annual cash deficiency of the fund, before employer contributions, interest on fund assets, and supplemental payments from the Treasury. It is the amount that must be made up out of some combination of payments from the Treasury and reductions in fund assets. As table 14.14 indicates, the cash deficiency of the fund under the current system is approximately $20 billion per year (in 1981 dollars) over the next seven years. Under the proposed system, this would be reduced to about $16 billion per year, or by about 20%. Thus, the net cash outflow from the Treasury (including the employer contribution, interest on the fund, supplemental payments, and so on) is reduced by about $4 billion per year in the early years of the reform. For the years from 2000 to 2050, the annual

Table 14.14   Estimated Annual Cash Deficiencies of the Current and Proposed Retirement Systems, 1983 to 2050 (All Figures in Billions of 1981 Dollars)

Year	Current System	Proposed System	Change
1983	18.2	14.8	3.4
1984	19.4	15.9	3.5
1985	20.4	16.8	3.8
1986	21.4	17.1	4.3
1987	22.2	17.4	4.8
1988	22.9	17.6	5.3
1989	23.5	17.6	5.9
1990	23.9	17.7	6.2
2000	26.3	15.7	10.6
2010	27.4	13.5	13.9
2020	22.8	9.7	13.1
2050	12.8	4.0	8.8

Source: Simulations. See text for assumptions.

cash deficiency will have been reduced by $10–$15 billion per year. Thus, the major gains of the proposed reforms—viewed from the Treasury's perspective on a cash basis—are not realized for many years.

14.2.5   Incentive Effects of the Proposed Reforms

In addition to changing the level of pension benefits that will be received by federal workers, the proposed reforms dramatically change the time pattern of benefit accruals. Since the annual increments in pension entitlements are a considerable fraction of total compensation under the current system, the proposed system will have a strikingly different set of incentives for retirement behavior. The incentives for any given worker depend on personal salary history, years of experience, age, and prospective life span. For purposes of illustration, we can examine the incentives implicit in the current and proposed systems for the employee used in the examples discussed above. Table 14.15 shows the annual salary and annual increments to pension entitlements (both in real terms) under the current and proposed systems for an employee who enters the system at age 25 and who receives the average annual longevity salary increases as well as general schedule increases averaging 1% in real terms. In assessing the value of pension benefits, I assume that the employee uses a discount rate of 1.5% in real terms and that he or she will live to age 74. To make it comparable to an annual salary figure, the annual increase in pension entitlements is measured as the change in the present value of future pension benefits above a 1.5% real return on the existing entitlement. It can be interpreted as the amount that was added in a given year to the pension enti-

Table 14.15   **Annual Salaries and Increments to Pension Entitlements (in Excess of Normal Return to Accrued Entitlement), Illustrative Employee (All Dollar Figures in Thousands)**

Age	Real Salary (1)	Current System Increase in Real Pension Entitlement (2)	Current System Total Annual Compensation (3 = 1 + 2)	Proposed System Increase in Real Pension Entitlement (4)	Proposed System Total Annual Compensation (5 = 1 + 4)
45	$17.1	$ 3.0	$ 20.2	$2.3	$19.4
50	20.1	5.5	25.6	4.0	24.1
51	20.7	6.1	26.7	4.5	25.2
52	21.3	6.8	28.1	5.0	26.3
53	21.8	7.7	29.5	5.6	27.4
54	22.5	8.6	31.1	6.3	28.8
55	23.0	117.0	140.1	3.6	26.6
56	23.7	.0	23.7	7.6	31.3
57	24.4	− .8	23.5	7.7	32.0
58	25.0	− 1.8	23.2	7.6	32.6
59	25.6	− 3.0	22.7	7.3	33.0
60	26.3	− 4.1	22.2	7.3	33.6
61	27.0	− 5.5	21.4	6.7	33.6
62	27.6	− 6.9	20.7	6.1	33.7
63	28.3	− 8.4	19.9	1.7	30.0
64	29.0	− 9.9	19.1	.2	29.1
65	29.6	− 11.6	18.1	− 1.7	27.9

Source: Calculations. See text for assumptions.

tlements in addition to crediting an annual interest payment of 1.5% in real terms.[5]

There is a sharp contrast in retirement incentives between the current and proposed systems. Under the current system, annual increments in the pension (in excess of the normal rate of return on what had already been accrued) are roughly 30%–35% of salary in the years from age 50 to age 54. As the employee works from age 54 to age 55, the pension entitlement jumps markedly, as we saw in figure 14.1; in this year the increment to pension wealth is over five times the salary. After age 56, however, the pension wealth falls with additional years of work; the pension system actually constitutes a negative component in total compensation after employees become eligible for full retirement. By the time our illustrative employee reaches age 60, the pension system is acting as a 15% cut in salary; by age 62 it has become a 25% cut. The net effect of this pattern of pension entitlement increases together with longevity and general schedule increases in wages is to make total annual compensation climb steeply in real terms in the years before full eligibility and to make it drop dramatically when full eligibility is reached. Thus, under the current system federal workers have a strong incentive to continue working in the last few years before they become eligible for full retirement; in the years thereafter, they have as strong an incentive to retire.

In contrast, the pension entitlements in the proposed retirement system provide a relatively large supplement to salaries for continued work through age 62. As our illustrative employee works from age 52 through age 61, the increment to pension entitlements (in excess of the real return on the portion already accrued) represents the equivalent of a 20%–30% salary supplement. The only anomaly is at age 55, when the early retirement penalty of the new system has a particularly strong effect. Under the proposed system, total compensation for a year's work rises in real terms relatively smoothly up to about age 62. No sudden jumps in effective annual compensation would give the employee a strong incentive to retire early. Moreover, the reduction in the level of pension benefits may provide an additional incentive to keep working; many employees may not feel they can afford to retire.

As a consequence of these alterations in the retirement incentives, the adjustment in retirement behavior and in the age structure of federal employment could be dramatic if the proposed system were adopted. This may well be desirable, if, for example, too many highly experienced workers are retiring too early under the current system. On the other hand, its implications for the flexibility of the system and the opportunities for advancement for younger workers are obvious. Since this change may have a material effect on the workings of the entire federal employment system, its implications should be carefully reviewed.

14.3 Reforming the Funding of the Retirement System

The Civil Service Retirement System is in need of reform. The current funding system is not fully coherent and is far from adequate. It represents neither full funding of current obligations nor a conceptually sound means of coping with past underfunding. There is a large and growing gap between the assets and obligations of the fund. It can be closed only by putting more money in or by taking less money out.

The reform proposal embodied in the president's FY84 budget request goes a long way toward closing the existing gap through a series of benefit reductions. The unfunded liability would be cut by some $140 billion to about $400 billion, and the funding rate would fall from 36.2% to 19.5%. The government's required cash payments would be reduced by about $4 billion per year for the rest of this decade and by larger annual amounts thereafter.

Reducing the government's liabilities—which ultimately reduces funds taken in one form or another from taxpayers—is one side of the story. The other side consists of a series of substantial benefit reductions for current federal employees. The present value of their pension entitlements (net of the value of their future contributions) would be cut by approximately one-half, or by about $105 thousand for each current federal employee. This is equivalent to a general schedule decrease of about 15% on average for employees who have joined recently; the effective reduction in annual compensation for some employees who have been in the system for more than 15 years is over 30%.

Whether such a substantial reconfiguration of the compensation of federal workers is wise or fair is eminently debatable. The issue cannot be settled with reference to the retirement system alone; pension benefits are one component of a total compensation package that includes wages and other fringe benefits. A full review of the level of total federal compensation is well beyond the scope of this paper; it should be obvious that no conclusions about "fairness" can be reached in the absence of such an analysis.

Some observers have argued that the level of federal pension compensation is simply too high on an absolute scale. Such arguments are often raised on the basis of comparisons with private sector pension plans. Most private plans provide benefits substantially less than those of federal retirees and have full funding rates that are correspondingly lower than that of the federal system. Without a similar comparison of the wage compensation received by federal and private workers, it is impossible to draw any inference from such observations.

There is another reason to believe that such a comparison may be misleading. It is by no means obvious that private workers are appropriately providing for their retirement through their pension plans or through personal saving, even allowing for their access to social security. Most private pensions and other personal savings plans may not provide adequately for increasingly long retirements.

Consider, for example, an employee whose income rises by 2%–3% in real terms across a working life of 40 years. Suppose that employee will live for 18 years after retiring and desires a retirement income that is constant in real terms at a level of 70% of income before retirement. If the rate of return on assets put aside to provide this retirement income is 1.5% in real terms, then the employee should be saving about one-third of income during the working years. Because of our increasingly long life spans and the low real rates of return on invested assets (particularly on low-risk investments, after allowing for taxes), retirement is an extremely expensive consumption item.

Rather than criticizing the federal system for providing more than private plans, one might instead ask whether the retirement benefits those plans provide are adequate. It is commonly alleged that the provision of benefits fully indexed to inflation is bankrupting the federal pension system. But who among us would care to retire on a pension that provided a fixed annuity in a world where we might live as long as 25 years in retirement and where we have recently witnessed periods of unexpected inflation that in five years cut the purchasing power of fixed annuities in half?

If, instead of criticizing the federal system for its relative expense, we focus instead on the fact that it is nearly alone in providing well for what is a demonstrably—and surprisingly—expensive part of life, then we may be led to diagnose a very different set of "problems" of the federal compensation system. First, it may shift our attention to federal wages rather than pension benefits. If retirement is expensive and federal employees want to provide for it through an (appropriately) expensive pension system, then they should not also expect their wages to be comparable to those in the private sector. Private sector workers have less generous pension plans and are—we hope—using their higher current incomes to set aside personal assets to supplement their inadequate pensions. Arguably, if the total compensation of federal workers is too high, it is perhaps their wages, rather than their pension benefits, that are out of line.

This suggests that we may want to look beyond benefit reductions as a means of closing the existing gap in the retirement system. Congress may eventually decide that the pension system is configured about right—that is, that fully indexed pensions are the right form and that the current level of benefits is appropriate. In that case, the gap would have to be closed from the other side, by finding additional funding either from the employees—that is, from reductions in the net wages of federal workers—or from taxpayers, in one form or another.

If we believe that the pension benefit adequacy of the federal system should be viewed as a strength rather than as a weakness, a second problem that emerges is the retirement behavior of federal workers. If the level of benefits granted is roughly right, but the system is too expensive, then perhaps the average employee works for too short and retires for too long a period. This view is entirely consistent with the existing structure of pay incentives, which provide substantially lower effective annual compensation for work after attainment of full retirement eligibility. It is also consistent with the evidence that half of federal workers retire before age 60. If we take this view, then, a crucial problem of the existing system lies not in its level of benefits but in the fact that they are accrued too early.

This view suggests that one approach to reforming the retirement system would include a combination of benefit adjustments to reconfigure retirement incentives and additional funding to permit maintenance of pension adequacy. In this case, the following options may be in the right direction.

14.3.1   Improvements in Disclosure

The public is almost completely unaware of the magnitude of the future burden represented by the net liabilities of the retirement system. Even knowledgeable commentators on federal budget issues are largely ignorant of the size of the system's quasi debt. Substantially improved disclosure—more frequent, less arcane, more accurate, and better presented reports on system status—is a prerequisite to serious attention. As with most off-budget expenditures, a strong dose of public scrutiny might have a salutary effect.

Disclosure may also help make federal decision makers aware of the full cost of federal employees. Current guidelines for costing employee time take account of "fringe benefits" but substantially underestimate the expense associated with the retirement system. Making this correction could bring decisions on labor expense and, for example, the advisability of substituting capital for labor in the federal government more into line with reality.

14.3.2   Increasing Officially Mandated Contributions

The fund can continue to operate on a cash basis with little or no change in its funding for at least another 20 years, given current estimates of supplemental Treasury payments. Continuing the practice of underfunding, the pension system will add to the burden future taxpayers bear for benefits presumably received by current taxpayers. Currently, roughly half of the system's obligations are being funded by "debt"—increases in the unfunded liability. We may wish to continue funding some of the obligations of the retirement system through debt, but if we choose to do so our choice should be deliberate and considered. To make it explicit, we could first make contributions to the pension system at the fully funded rate, and then, as a separate action, decide how much of the current funding should be raised from a debt issue and how much should come from current funds.

Putting the system on a fully funded current basis calls for contributing about 36% of payroll annually, or about $14 billion more than the current official contribution rate provides. This year the Treasury made a supplemental payment of about this amount to the fund. Rather than simulating interest payments on nonexistent assets, supplemental payments could be calculated based on the full funding rate. This would shift the basis of accounting for this transaction to a more consistent and conceptually sound foundation without increasing the funds transferred by the Treasury. Now seems to be an opportune time to change the basis of accounting for this transaction.

14.3.3   Making the Unfunded Liability More Explicit

The principal and accumulated (and accumulating) interest on the existing unfunded liability is properly a responsibility of former taxpayers. There is no longer any practical way to make them responsible for it. How, if at all, should this accumulated "debt" be "funded"?

One possible approach would be to convert the unfunded liability to an explicit debt. Suppose, for example, that the government funded the system by issuing debt securities. The cash raised would be transferred to the retirement system, which is allowed to invest only in Treasury securities. Thus it would wind up taking the money and buying back the securities issued to fund it. The net transaction is simply that the Treasury printed additional special obligations and gave them to the retirement fund to hold in its portfolio. No net funds would be exchanged.[6] The liability of the fund would now be backed by an explicit Treasury promise in the form of the securities held in the retirement system vault. What really backs the pensions is unchanged—it is still a promise that the federal government will make the necessary funds available when the time comes. The obligation would simply be a little more explicit.

This more explicit recognition has a number of potential advantages. For one thing, the fund—and the obligation—might be taken more seriously by the public. The obligation might be easier to understand, and changes in the annual performance and experience of the fund might be easier to observe. These subtle changes of recognition are the stuff of which real scrutiny and eventual policy may be made.

Moreover, the Treasury would owe interest on the obligations, and the fund would receive these payments annually. In a sense, it is exactly this transaction that the annual supplemental payment appropriated by the Congress is simulating. Thus, the current funding arrangement is equivalent to what would obtain if the Congress ordered the Treasury to borrow funds equal to the unfunded liability and put them on deposit in the retirement system account. The rest of the transaction—printing these securities and handing them to the retirement system—is merely a paper transaction. We might say that the Congress, recognizing this, has merely decided not to carry out the paper shuffle but has carried out the real part of the transaction—the actual payment of interest.

The "simulation" approach adopted by the Congress thus misses a potentially important opportunity to provide a more explicit and understandable method for scrutinizing the fund's status and performance. If the fund held the securities, it would be much easier for the public and commentators to understand the whole system. Making the obligation explicit avoids the arcane notions of "unfunded liabilities" and payments of pseudointerest on hypothetical securities. The change would relieve the fund of its mysterious cloak of subtlety, which currently masks what is in fact a relatively simple set of transactions and relationships.

Another possibility would be to raise the funds to cover the unfunded liability through additional taxes or through expenditure reductions. Virtually no one would seriously propose such a drastic action. Actually raising the funds would explicitly back the government's obligations but would be accompanied by extensive dislocations. The net impact on the economy will be difficult to judge, even if we know whether the funds came from net borrowing, taxes, or expenditures. Explicit federal borrowing may displace other borrowing or may call forth more lending. If the former, what projects were displaced? If the latter, what would those funds now lent have been spent on otherwise? If the funds came from taxes or expenditures, what are the ultimate sources? What other spending was not done? Speculation about the ultimate source of the funds will quickly become ethereal. This is perhaps the most powerful conceptual reason for arguing that the unfunded liability of the system should be explicitly recognized, and prevented from growing, but not necessarily reduced through direct funding. Instead, the most sensible policy goal may be to move toward a system that (1) is fully funded on a current basis and (2) has explicitly recognized obligations.

14.4 Conclusion

The Federal Civil Service Retirement System constitutes a very large component of the federal government's future promises to pay. Its current size—approximately $540 billion—is roughly half that of the explicitly recognized national debt. It is also about one-half the size of the social security quasi debt, which is a net liability on behalf of a considerably greater number of beneficiaries.

The retirement system can, in all likelihood, live out this century under the current arrangement without running out of cash, but it cannot live 10 years into the next century without additional funding. By any standard, it represents a very large obligation of which the public is at best only dimly aware.

What should be done to reform its benefit structure is sure to be debated vigorously. Some will argue that the current system is far too generous and that it amounts to considerably overpaying federal workers. Others will argue that changing the system now amounts to repudiating solemn promises of the government. Ultimately, the Congress will have to decide.

What, if anything, might or should be done to reform its funding is also a complicated issue. Does it make any difference if the Congress recognizes the obligations to pensioners in the form of explicit Treasury securities held in a retirement system vault? If so, why not fund it fully? If not, why fund it at all, since all of its investible funds are held in the form of Treasury securities?

At the present time, it could be placed on a more solid long-term funding basis with little change in the current net flows from the Treasury. Funding crises do not lead to conceptually sound reforms; there is little reason to await the next crisis in the hope that it will generate fundamental improvement. This would seem to be an opportune time to improve the conceptual basis of the funding foundation on which the federal retirement system rests.

Appendix 14.A
Evaluation of Pension Fund Obligations and Financial Condition

A number of measures of the soundness of pension systems have been articulated by actuaries, accountants, economists, budget analysts, and others. Many of the proposed measures—like those adopted by the Congress—are internally inconsistent. The proliferation of such measures reflects the fact that there are several dimensions to the financial condition of a pension fund, and no one measure will appropriately summarize all of them.

Accountants argue persuasively that the only appropriate basis on which to evaluate the condition of any institution is the accrual basis. The future obligations that the organization has already contracted to meet are treated as liabilities, and the future contractual obligations of others to it are treated as assets. This perspective allows two interrelated portraits of the organization's solvency. First, one can present a snapshot of the condition at a given instant consisting of a summary of the existing liabilities and assets, and thus of the net liabilities (called the "unfunded liability") of the system. Second, the annual changes in the unfunded liability can be examined as a measure of the performance of the fund in a particular year.

The Unfunded Liability

The essence of the "unfunded liability" measure is that it represents only the existing accrued deficit. If the system has made more promises than it has collected funds to back, it has an unfunded liability. But this liability should reflect only promises already made. This means that, in computing the current unfunded liability, one must presume (for the sake of the computation only) that future contributions to the fund will be on a full funding basis. If the fund has been collecting 10% of payroll when 20% would be required for full funding, the computation of the current unfunded liability assumes that all future payroll contributions will be at the full funding rate of 20%. This counterfactual presumption is made so that the resulting deficit reflects only the failure to fully fund the system to date, not the possibility of future underfunding.

There is a further complication in choosing the funding method under which the system is to be evaluated. In the view of some, current funding of the system should be strictly construed. For example, if a given worker is currently entitled to no pension because he or she has not yet worked for enough years to qualify, a strict construction of the fund's existing obligation to that worker would deny any liability. This approach is known as the "vested benefits" valuation method. This method recognizes only current contractual obligations independent of the future career of the worker.

The fundamental principle underlying this notion is that pension obligations are merely a part of an employee's compensation package; since we do not accrue liabilities for future salary payments, why should we for pensions?

To many, this is an unduly conservative estimation procedure. If, for example, half of the workers in the same age and experience category as the worker in question will, on a statistical basis, go on to collect pension benefits, it seems imprudent not to recognize that the system has accrued some (albeit statistical) obligation to them. This would appear to be particularly relevant to the federal system, in which both employees and the employer frequently treat prospective pension benefits as "entitlements."[7]

The central question concerns the appropriate time pattern for this recognition. Using a statistical view of the cohort of employees rather than the micro view of each individual employee suggests that there should be an annual allowance for pension obligation buildup over the worker's lifetime. There are many ways in which this statistical obligation could be amortized across the years of the employee's career. A common approach is to amortize the projected expenses through a contribution stream that is a level fraction of the employee's salary over his or her career. This is easy to understand and to administer. It leads to more funding later in the career than would a level payment in nominal terms, preventing any substantial changes in the "effective rate" of the contribution as a fraction of income. This method is referred to as the "normal cost" approach to pension funding.

There is one further ambiguity within this approach. The fraction of salary required to fund a pension for a worker who enters the system at age 40 may be different from that required for a worker who enters at age 25. Depending on the benefit structure and projected salary trajectories, the appropriate funding rate may be either higher or lower for the worker who enters later in life. Rather than recognize a different funding rate for each entry-age cohort of workers, most systems compute an average funding rate appropriate for the mix of entry ages they experience. This is known as the "entry age normal" funding method. It is used as the basis for estimating the unfunded liabilities discussed in this paper.

Changes in the Unfunded Liability

While the unfunded liability provides a useful snapshot of the condition of a retirement system at a given instant, its effect is to show only the accrued excess of obligations the system has accepted over its current and prospective available funds. This measure shows only status; it cannot show direction. We can, however, get a measure of the current performance of a system by focusing on changes in the unfunded liabilities from year to year. The unfunded liability shows the accumulated history from the start of the fund to the present; the change in the unfunded liability focuses on the current performance of the fund—whether its funds are well invested, whether it continues to extend more promises than it is collecting funds to back, and so on.

The Current and Prospective Cash Balance of the Fund

The accrual basis for evaluating a retirement system is designed to match the future income and obligations of the fund to give a coherent picture of its current status. It cannot, however, provide a summary of the current and prospective cash position of the fund, which is an equally vital aspect of its financial condition. Thus, in addition to examining appropriate estimates of the unfunded liability of the fund and of the year-to-year changes in the unfunded debt, it is important to develop projections of the cash balances of the fund. This effort is complicated by the fact that it depends on the number and average salary of employees who have not yet entered the employment system. (The measures that concentrate on unfunded liabilities can be computed with reference only to current employees and annuitants.) Thus, an evaluation of the fund's cash position involves projections of the size of the federal civil service over a considerable time period and must be viewed as uncertain. However, given the importance of the cash basis integrity of the fund—and particularly noting Congress's efforts to prevent, or at least delay, cash insolvency in the retirement system—we cannot completely avoid making cash projections.

Appendix 14.B
Sensitivity of the Estimates

The estimates presented here are, in a qualitative sense, relatively insensitive to the parametric assumptions of the model. Because civil service retirement benefits are indexed, the assumed rate of inflation is practically immaterial. Perhaps surprisingly, the unfunded liability is also insensitive to changes in the assumed rate of real salary growth. Briefly, this results from the rough balance between two offsetting effects: while more rapid growth of salaries would increase future pension costs, it also increases future contributions (at the full funding rate used in calculating the current unfunded liability). Changing the assumed annual rate of real salary increase from 1% (used in the estimates reported in the text) to 0% or 2% generally changes the estimated unfunded liability by only $20–$30 billion (depending on the other assumptions made), or by about 4%–5%.

The one major assumption that does have a considerable impact on the estimated unfunded liability is the rate at which future flows are discounted.

Because the bulk of both revenues and benefit payments lies well in the future, the rate at which they are discounted has a notable effect. Moreover, since we know that benefit payments exceed anticipated contributions but on average occur later, it is clear that the unfunded liability will be lower the higher is the assumed rate of discount. Table 14.A.1 shows the estimated unfunded liability under the baseline assumptions for other parameters and a range of discount rates. It is clear that any tenable assumption about the long-term real discount rate results in a very large unfunded liability. Even if we discount at 3% in real terms—whch seems very generous—the unfunded liability remains over $400 billion. Perhaps the most optimistic way to read the results in table 14.A.1 is to note that even if we should be using a lower rate of discount—1% instead of 1.5% for example—the unfunded liability remains below $600 billion.

What rate of discount should we use? The discount rate should be the long-term risk-free rate of return in the economy. A number of researchers (see, e.g., Carlson 1977; Garbade and Wachtel 1978; Bodie 1980) have presented evidence that one proxy for this rate, the real rate of return on short-term Treasury debt, ranged from approximately zero to about 3% over the period 1950–75, with most values between 1% and 2%. Since the Federal Reserve Bank changed its monetary management policies in October of 1979, real returns have been considerably higher, at times as high as 6%–8%. On the theory that financial effects are likely to be more volatile than real effects, and that the real discount rate should ultimately reflect the real rate of sustainable long-term economic growth, a moderate rate of 1.5% has been used here. To some this will seem very high when compared to the long-term rates of return achieved in the last 30 years. To others it will seem too low as an estimate of what well-managed economic growth might produce. We can take some solace in the fact that the comparisons among alternative policies—the main focus of this paper—are likely to be little affected by changes in the discount rate.

Table 14.A.1   **Sensitivity of Unfunded Liability Estimates to Changes in the Assumed Discount Rate**

Assumed Discount Rate (%)	Unfunded Liability ($ Billion)
.8	605
1.0	586
1.5	549
2.0	499
2.5	462
3.0	428

Source: Simulation. Parameters are as in baseline case except for discount rate.

Notes

1. It is not completely immaterial in the Civil Service Retirement System because of an anomaly in the calculation of benefits. Since the salary history used to compute the retirement benefit is an average of three years' salary—expressed in nominal terms—the nominal rate of salary increases has a slight impact on the relation between the salaries paid and the retirement benefits, when both are converted into real terms. In addition, some reform proposals cut the rate of increase in pension benefits after retirement to something less than the full cost of living increase. If such a system were adopted, the real value of benefits received would depend on the rate of inflation. In every other respect, holding all real rates constant, changing the assumed rate of inflation has no impact.

2. Taking this view raises an interesting point of controversy. I assume that assets in the fund are worth their current market value. In fact, however, they may be worth less than this, because there appears to be a consistent fund policy of investing them in below-market rate of return "special" federal securities.

3. The appendix discusses the determination of "normal cost" and other technical aspects of the valuation of pension fund assets and liabilities.

4. This rate was used throughout the analyses presented here; comparisons of different scenarios should be little affected by this choice. The basis for this choice, and the sensitivity of the resulting estimates of the unfunded liability, is discussed in appendix 14.B.

5. This effectively assumes that a 1.5% real return to the entitlements already accrued should not be viewed as a part of annual compensation because it is not a return received for working. Rather, it is an interest payment on amounts credited for earlier work.

6. Because no funds actually need to be borrowed from private lenders, this transaction should have no direct impact on securities markets.

7. The Office of Management and Budget classifies the Civil Service Retirement System as an "entitlement" program. It does not, however, classify the wages of federal employees as an entitlement. This is a puzzling distinction, since both are part of compensation for federal employment.

Comment   Paul A. Samuelson

Herman Leonard has done a good job in reckoning numerically the intricate actuarial costs that are involved in the federal government's pension arrangements. The final number is large, surprisingly large even to those who had a vague presentiment concerning the size of the unfunded liability.

There are various levels at which the economic analysis of unfunded pension liabilities can be pitched. There is the narrow private view. I am about to take over a company such as Western Union: what is the cash value of the pension liabilities I am taking on? Leonard has stuck to this aspect of the question.

There is also a broader economic view. Pensions are an important part of life-cycle saving, and how they are handled raises all the questions that go into an overlapping generations macro model. Thus, suppose our mixed economy became a thoroughgoing socialism. Then we should all be government employees. It is a problem for intricate economic analysis to

Paul A. Samuelson is institute professor, Massachusetts Institute of Technology.

investigate what differences it might make if *all* employers did fully fund their pension liabilities or if, in the manner of Leonard's federal government, all employers left much of the liability unfunded. Less intricate are the issues that would be raised if employers generally introduced age and years-of-service profiles in their pension options that were as eccentric as those of the federal government.

First, stick to the narrow view. Leonard estimates the federal unfunded pension liability at almost $600 billion (in 1982 dollars), which is fully half of the well-publicized total public debt. That does not include the pension liabilities of the armed services: when Leonard proceeds to make the similar calculation for it, he expects to come out with a number that also exceeds half the conventional public debt. So, many people who think that the public debt for which there will have to be taxes in the future is only about four months of current GNP ought to more than double that number. When the pension liabilities of the Post Office are added in, and the open-ended commitment of the government to give medical care gratis to veterans who reach a certain age, we might be talking about a debt obligation of almost a year of GNP.

Robert Hall and Robert Barro have formulated models of life-cycle and bequest spending in which any future tax collections to handle the public debt are already factored into people's current spending and saving behavior. The plausibility of this polar case and the support it receives from fragmentary empirical evidence I do not find to be impressive. But to the extent that it is valid, and to the extent that Leonard has brought new information to us people who are supposed to be acting in the Hall-Barro way, one would have to expect that these revelations would cause us to be spending less than would otherwise be the case, as we try to perform private thrift to offset our public thriftlessness. (I offer myself as a guinea pig, as one more likely than most to keep bequest motives in mind and to keep an eye on future tax loads. What I want for my immediate progeny is a place a little more favorable in the relative income distribution; so long as I know that Leonard's burden will be on all my heirs' neighbors as well as on them, I won't cut out my planned trip to Europe because of Leonard's news.)

Idiosyncratic Retirement Options

How this all came about is no mystery. Congress legislated it, and did so in a fairly unconscious manner—the more so because many of the costs did not have to be faced up to in the immediate future. Civil servants with 30 years' service were given the right to retire with full benefits at 55; those with 20 years of service could retire at 60; those with 5 years of service at 62. And the scale of benefits was to be set by the highest three years of earnings, as applied to a convex function that depends on the number of years of service.

As Leonard's charts show, this is indeed an idiosyncratic schedule of lifetime payments. Many people are practically bribed to retire at early ages; staying on will earn them little or even cost them money.

Some people see Pareto optimality everywhere. To them it may be rational for the government to have a need for the kinds of employees who treasure job security and who are anxious to retire earlier than the median person. There may even be a gain in efficiency if people who have grown stale on the job are encouraged to make way for fresher people; and as the retired civil servants find new careers in the private sector their torpid faculties are encouraged to come to life again. Even in the absence of induced changes in efficiency, an employer (like the federal government) that trades off high wages now for higher retirement benefits can expect to attract the subset of the labor force that has least Bohm-Bawerkian time preference.

I go along with this analysis in some measure. But the sharp corners and kinks that got put into the federal system suggest to me not conscious adaptation and selection but rather absent-mindedness and inefficiency. There is a presumption in favor of legislative reforms.

On the other hand, the proposed reforms that Leonard carefully describes are extreme to the point of being draconian. As he indicates, a sizable capital levy is to be imposed without much public discussion or debate on various subgenerations of federal employees, many of whom entered the system in good faith and not a few of whom did so only because of the bait of retirement options better than those in private industry. Perhaps the greatest surprise in Leonard's calculations is the demonstration that even the proposed draconian reforms will reduce his liability of $540 billion (1982 dollars) only to $400 billion. One supposes that this limited change must be due to the gradual easing in of the new system; and if that is a correct supposition, we probably have to temper our designation of the reforms as draconian.

Broad Issues of Public Thriftiness

The numbers we have been talking about are seen to be large enough to be comparable with the numbers representing official deficits. At least until recently macromodels typically assumed that the size and composition of fiscal spending and taxing had effects on the total of production, employment, and unemployment. To the degree this is so, we cannot simply assume that if the federal government had been more provident in meeting currently its accruing pension liabilities, economic history would have been pretty much the same as it actually turned out to be.

Consider the 1930s. On a simple Keynesian view, real income was stuck in a low-employment equilibrium. (With short-term interest rates virtually zero, open-market purchases would simply substitute idle money for low-interest bonds that people and banks would hold. Or, in less extreme versions, it might be deemed simply unfeasible to get the Federal Reserve to expand the money supply in a way that would get rid of idle economic resources.) Now, suppose Congress then hired many civil servants and let the pension liability on their account go unfunded. The effects of this heterodox decision would be to raise American GNP, raise employment, lower unemployment, raise current consumption and profits, and perhaps even induce more private capital formation than would otherwise have taken place. All these effects are in comparison with raising taxes contemporaneously to fund the future pension liabilities. For, on the simple Keynesian view of depression economics, such tax collections would depress disposable incomes and thereby depress consumption spending (there being no realistic Hall-Barro offset). With short interest rates already at rock bottom and long rates hard to nudge faster downward, and with the marginal efficiency schedule of investment perhaps inelastic, it would be unrealistic to think that corresponding to the government's increment of pension assets there has been any appreciable deepening of capital.

You will recognize that in terms of such a depression mode, it was indeed the case that the naval battleships built during the early 1930s cost the economy nothing—indeed, they involved a negative real cost. Similarly, in such a model it would have been a mistake to try to fund social security on an actuarial basis. If pay-as-you-go social security lowered the schedule of effective thriftiness for the nation, then that would end up raising the amount of real capital that later generations are endowed with, in accordance with the paradox of thrift.

I don't have to remind you that things are quite otherwise in a model based on rational expectations. If all markets clear, the Great Depression never happened. If it didn't happen, then a reduction in public thriftiness that is not recognized and offset by an increase in private thriftiness will result in a higher consumption mix of the perpetual full-employment equilibrium. So, even if it is efficient to have government workers labor for so brief a period in their life, and consume so much in retirement at the expense of what they consume in their working years, the failure to fully fund federal pensions will have created no increment of productive capital that can be tapped when the load of federal pensioners rises relative to the working population.

The real world, I have to believe, is somewhere in between that of the depression economics model and the rational expectations version—perhaps these days nearer to the latter than the former. Particularly in the age of Reaganomics, which suffers from a bad dose of Laffer-Kemp supply side economics, America is an undertaxed nation. I am not referring to the recession deficit but rather to the structural deficit that looms ahead at high employment levels. I must confess that it was my expectation that conservative Republicans would long since have tried to sell the country broadbased sales and value-added taxes—at least to the extent that they are unable to force down civilian federal expenditures. Leonard's calculations show us that things are even worse in this regard than one had thought.

Let me conclude with some reflections that make it plausible that populist democracy will tend to go down the primrose path of unfunded employee pensions and inadequately funded social security programs. This is almost a theorem in demographic mathematics.

1. At the beginning of a new system it needs little cash because retirements are few relative to contributors. The temptation is to vote generous benefits for the few and to vote much less than steady-state actuarial rates on the many.

2. If the Ponzi game grows at a fast enough exponential rate, the primrose path can look good forever. The unfunded liability goes toward infinity but the revenues collected currently at below-actuarial rates are enough to finance the benefits of the pensioners (whose numbers stay at an abnormally low ratio to workers).

3. When population growth slows down, so that we no longer have the comfortable Ponzi rate of growth or we even begin to register a decline in total numbers, then the thorns along the primrose path reveal themselves with a vengeance.

As Leonard shows, what has come to pass in the field of social security has also begun to come to pass in the field of federal pension provision.

References

Bodie, Z. 1980. An innovation for stable real retirement income. *Journal of Portfolio Management* 7:5–13.

Carlson, J. A. 1977. Short-term interest rates as predictors of inflation: Comment. *American Economic Review* 67:469–75.

Garbade, K., and Wachtel, P. 1978. Time variation in the relationship between inflation and interest rates. *Journal of Monetary Economics* 4:755–65.

Hartman, R. W. 1983. *Pay and pensions for federal workers*. Washington, D.C.: Brookings Institution.

Jump, B., Jr. 1976. Compensating government employees: Pension benefit objectives, cost measurement, and financing. *National Tax Journal* 29:240–56.

Munnell, A. H., and Connolly, A. M. 1976. Funding government pensions: State-local, civil service, and military. *Federal Reserve Bank of Boston Conference Proceedings*, pp. 72–133.

Office of Personnel Management. 1980. *Board of Actuaries of the Civil Service Retirement System fifty-seventh annual report*. Washington, D.C.: Government Printing Office.

———. 1981*a*. *Fringe benefit facts 1980.* Washington, D.C.: Government Printing Office.

———. 1981*b*. *Annual report of the Civil Service Pension System, 1980.* Washington, D.C.: Government Printing Office.

———. 1982. Statement of general information for the Civil Service Retirement System Plan year ending September 20, 1980. Mimeographed. Washington, D.C.: Office of Personnel Management.

Quinn, J. F. 1982. Pension wealth of government and private sector workers. *American Economic Review Papers and Proceedings* 72:283–87.

Smith, Sharon P. 1982. Prospects for reforming federal pay. *American Economic Review Papers and Proceedings* 72:273–77.

Contributors

Henry J. Aaron
The Brookings Institution
1775 Massachusetts Avenue, NW
Washington, DC 20036

Alan J. Auerbach
Department of Economics
University of Pennsylvania
160 McNeil Building/CR
Philadelphia, PA 19104

Zvi Bodie
School of Management
Boston University
704 Commonwealth Avenue
Boston, MA 02215

Jeremy Bulow
Graduate School of Business
Stanford University
Stanford, CA 94305

Gary Burtless
The Brookings Institution
1775 Massachusetts Avenue, NW
Washington, DC 20036

Peter A. Diamond
Massachusetts Institute of Technology
Cambridge, MA 02139

David T. Ellwood
John F. Kennedy School of
  Government
Harvard University
79 JFK Street
Cambridge, MA 02138

Daniel Feenberg
National Bureau of Economic
  Research
1050 Massachusetts Avenue
Cambridge, MA 02138

Richard B. Freeman
Department of Economics
Littauer Center
Harvard University
Cambridge, MA 02138

Victor R. Fuchs
National Bureau of Economic
  Research
204 Junipero Serra Boulevard
Stanford, CA 94305

Roger H. Gordon
Department of Economics
University of Michigan
Ann Arbor, MI 48109

Jerry R. Green
Department of Economics
Littauer Center
Harvard University
Cambridge, MA 02138

Jerry A. Hausman
Department of Economics
Massachusetts Institute of Technology
E52-271A
Cambridge, MA 02139

Michael D. Hurd
Department of Economics
State University of New York,
Stony Brook
Stony Brook, NY 11794

Laurence J. Kotlikoff
Department of Economics
Boston University
Boston, MA 02115

Wayne Landsman
Graduate School of Business
Stanford University
Stanford, CA 94305

Edward P. Lazear
Graduate School of Business
University of Chicago
1101 East 58th Street
Chicago, IL 60637

Herman B. Leonard
John F. Kennedy School of
  Government
Harvard University
79 JFK Street
Cambridge, MA 02138

Robert C. Merton
Sloan School of Management
Massachusetts Institute of Technology
Cambridge, MA 02139

James A. Mirrlees
Nuffield College
Oxford University
Oxford, OX1 1NF
England

Barry Nalebuff
John F. Kennedy School of
  Government
Harvard University
79 JFK Street
Cambridge, MA 02138

Albert Rees
Alfred P. Sloan Foundation
630 Fifth Avenue
New York, NY 10111

Sherwin Rosen
Department of Economics
University of Chicago
1126 East 59th Street
Chicago, IL 60637

Paul A. Samuelson
Department of Economics
Massachusetts Institute of Technology
Cambridge, MA 02139

John B. Shoven
Department of Economics
Stanford University
Stanford, CA 94305

Paul Taubman
Department of Economics
University of Pennsylvania
3718 Locust Walk/CR
Philadelphia, PA 19104

W. Kip Viscusi
Center for the Study of Business
  Regulation
Fuqua School of Business
Duke University
Durham, NC 27706

David A. Wise
John F. Kennedy School of
  Government
Harvard University
79 JFK Street
Cambridge, MA 02138

Richard J. Zeckhauser
John F. Kennedy School of
  Government
Harvard University
79 JFK Street
Cambridge, MA 02138

Author Index

Subject Index